D1067539

WITHDRAWN

262.13 R476v
RHODES
THE VATICAN IN THE AGE OF   FV
THE DICTATORS
                    7.95

JUNIOR COLLEGE DISTRICT
of St. Louis - St. Louis County
LIBRARY
5801 Wilson Ave.
St. Louis, Missouri 63110

BRO
DART   PRINTED IN U.S.A.

THE VATICAN IN THE AGE OF THE DICTATORS
1922–1945

By the same author

Fiction
THE UNIFORM
A BALL IN VENICE
THE GENERAL'S SUMMER-HOUSE
THE PROPHET'S CARPET

War Memoirs
SWORD OF BONE (THE DUNKIRK CAMPAIGN)
JOURNEY TO BUDAPEST 1956 (TEN YEARS AFTER)

Biography
THE POET AS SUPERMAN—A LIFE OF D'ANNUNZIO
THE RISE AND FALL OF LOUIS RENAULT

Travel
A SABINE JOURNEY
THE DALMATIAN COAST
WHERE THE TURK TROD
ART TREASURES OF EASTERN EUROPE

ANTHONY RHODES

The Vatican in the Age of the Dictators 1922–1945

HOLT, RINEHART AND WINSTON
NEW YORK CHICAGO SAN FRANCISCO

8/29/74

Copyright © 1973 by Anthony Rhodes. All rights reserved,
including the right to reproduce this book or
portions thereof in any form.

Library of Congress Cataloging in Publication Data

Rhodes, Anthony Richard Ewart.
The Vatican in the age of the dictators, 1922–1945.

Bibliography: p.
1. Papacy—History—20th century. 2. Church and
state in Europe. 3. World War, 1939–1945—Catholic
Church. 4. Pius XI, Pope 1857–1939. 5. Pius
XII, Pope, 1876–1958, I. Title.
BX1389.R48 1974   262'.13   72–91593
ISBN: 0-03-007736-2

First published in the United States in 1974
Printed in the United States of America

Sources and Acknowledgments

Of the new sources consulted the German Foreign Office documents in Bonn are the most important (*Auswärtiges Amt* here referred to as *A.A.*). They were captured intact by the Allies in 1945 and have been available in their present classified form for the last six years, thanks to the work of a group of eminent British and American historians. The British Foreign Office documents (1922–45) have also become available in the last four years, since the British government changed the fifty-year rule to the thirty-year rule (here referred to as F.O.). The third principal source of new information is the Vatican publication, *Actes et Documents du Saint Siège relatifs à la Seconde Guerre Mondiale*, which began coming out in 1967. The most important personal documents consulted were of Baron Diego von Bergen in the *A.A.* files. He was German Ambassador to the Holy See for the unprecedented period of twenty-two years, spanning almost exactly the period covered by this book.

I wish to thank two friends who were kind enough to read the MS. and give me valuable advice: Père Jean Charles-Roux and Sir Alec Randall, K.C.M.G. For further help or advice I am also indebted to: Mr. Noel Blakiston (Keeper of the Public Records Office), Sir James Bowker, K.C.M.G., Father C. Burns (Vatican Secret Archives), Mr. Maurice Edelman, M.P., Father Robert A. Graham, S.J., Sir Douglas Howard, K.C.M.G. (British Minister to the Vatican), Principe Francesco Lancillotti, Professor F. Leoni, Padre A. Martini, S.J., Comte Vladimir d'Ormesson (French Ambassador to the Vatican), M. Casimir Papée (Polish Ambassador to the Vatican), Sir Frank Roberts, Herr F. Sasse (Director of the Politisches Archiv, Auswärtiges Amt, Bonn), Father B. Scheider, S.J., Conte A. Secco-Suardi, H. E. Cardinal Tisserant, Sir Philip de Zulueta, the Phoenix Trust for its generous grant; and lastly to Rosaleen Rhodes for her great help in research, and for reading the manuscript.

Although the distinction between the terms "Holy See" and "Vatican" is well enough known, I have preferred for simplicity throughout this book to refer to the "Vatican".

"We Communists," said Chicherin, the Soviet Foreign Minister, in 1925 to Mgr. d'Herbigny, "feel pretty sure we can triumph over London capitalism [sic]. But Rome will prove a harder nut to crack. If Rome did not exist, we would be able to deal with all the various brands of Christianity. They would all capitulate before us. Without Rome, religion would die. But Rome sends out for the service of her religion propagandists of every nationality. They are more effective than guns or armies . . . The result of the struggle, my friend, is uncertain. What *is* certain is that it will be long."

German Foreign Office report in
Beziehungen des Vatikans zu Russland,
Vol. 1, 1925

Contents

8   *Contents*

Illustrations

———

---

[1] Radio Times Hulton Picture Library
[2] Camera Press Ltd
[3] *The Times*
[4] Associated Press

Preface

In a speech on his appointment as Moderator of the Council of Free Churches in 1944, a certain Dr. Henry Townsend delivered a philippic against the Vatican. There was nothing particularly original in that. Many, more violent, attacks on Rome have been made since the foundation of the Church. Nor was his speech notable for its oratory. What marked it as important for students of Papal foreign policy between the two world wars was that it listed shortly and succinctly the principal criticisms which have been levelled against the Vatican in that period. Dr. Townsend said that since 1919 "the policy of the Vatican in four European countries has given one severe blow after another to the Christian religion". The Vatican, he said, had supported Fascism; it had "given its blessing to the Italian campaign in Abyssinia, sprinkling Mussolini with Holy Water, and calling him 'God's Man' ". Then came the Spanish civil war, "a large part of which was provoked by the Church". Neither the use of poison gas in Abyssinia, nor "the blood bath of Guernica caused by German air attacks", had been condemned. Nor had the Vatican denounced the German invasion in 1940 of five neutral countries. Dr. Townsend referred to the brutality of Fascism in Italy, its "island prisons", the Nazis' murder of political prisoners and, in the Second World War, their diabolical extermination of the Jews. Against none of these monstrous crimes had the Vatican taken any definite stand.

His views were echoed on the 22nd February, 1945 by Mr. Kenneth Leslie, editor of the American magazine *Protestant*, who sent a long cable to Winston Churchill on behalf of 1600 ordained Christian ministers in the U.S.A. "The Vatican," he wrote, "has thrown its weight into the scales of the present human struggle on the side of Democracy's enemies". Certain other religious journals such as *Christians and Crisis* and *Christian Century* took up the cry, with fiery articles attacking the war-time record of the Vatican.

Since those immediate post-war days a number of more pondered works by such writers as Gunter Levy, Saul Friedlander and Gordon Zahn, to name only a few, have taken up the theme, and at greater length. Best known of all is Herr Rolf Hochhuth's play *The Representative* in which the war-time Pope, Pius XII, is depicted most unfavourably, as cynical, money-minded and callous, particularly in regard to the Nazi persecution of the Jews. As a dramatist, Herr Hochhuth avails himself freely, and perfectly legitimately, of "poetic licence"; and he is an excellent dramatist. But is his play accurate historically? As will be seen, examination of the German diplomatic documents reveals that he has often confounded fact and fiction.

All these writers examine the relations of the Vatican with Nazi Germany, without referring to other aspects of Vatican diplomacy in the inter-war years. In this book, an attempt has been made not only to assess the validity of these accusations against the Vatican, but also to show that its attitude towards Nazi Germany was the logical sequence of the new foreign policy inaugurated by Pius XI immediately after the First World War, and applied in his dealings with a number of other European States.

In 1918 a new Europe had arisen, three great monarchies had foundered, and a crop of small hybrid States had sprung up on the ruins. The monarchies and aristocracies with which the Vatican had been accustomed to deal had been replaced as rulers by the "common man", generally in the shape of a Dictator, often arrogantly proclaiming his atheism.[1] These men demanded a special type of treatment. In the preceding three centuries, the Kings and Princes with whom the Vatican

---

[1] Between 1922 and 1945 Europe was ruled by the following Dictators (in chronological order): Lenin, Mussolini, Pilsudski, Primo de Rivera, Horthy, Salazar, Valdemaras, Hitler, Dollfus, King Alexander, Franco, Antonescu, Pavelitch, Tito, Tiso. There had never been so many in Europe before or since. Most of them were irreligious (except Dollfus and Salazar who were devout Catholics).

had to deal based their rule on tradition and at least overt acceptance of Christian morality. Even then, the Papacy had had its scourges, Louis XIV with his Gallicanism, Joseph II with Josephismus. But these Princes presented a simpler problem for the Papacy than the modern Dictators who rejected all transcendental beliefs, recognised no laws save their own immanent morality, and preached a doctrine of open revolt against established values. Dealing with these upstart, cynical and powerful men demanded unusual patience, tenacity and diplomatic skill.

Papal diplomatic policy was from early times founded on the notion of dual allegiance of Christian populations, that peculiar doctrine which the Catholic Church introduced into the Greco-Roman world of antiquity, and imposed with varying degrees of success until the Reformation. The conception is of men owing allegiance in civic matters to their temporal rulers, and in spiritual matters to the Pope. The Popes argue that this dual allegiance, although often accompanied by stresses and strains, is the surest guarantee of European civilisation, and of the human liberty and vigour which have distinguished that civilisation from others.

With the breakdown of this dual allegiance after the Reformation, and the emergence of the omnicompetent secular State, the Popes maintained that disastrous results ensued. The secularisation of European society and its indifference to Christian moral law or Papal precept in the nineteenth century led to laissez-faire economy, particularly in England and the U.S.A., "the Tyranny of the Astute"; and that in turn to the collective Democracy, "the Tyranny of the supposed will of the majority". This was followed in the twentieth century by wars conducted between entire nations, by economic anarchy (1929), which in turn produced the Dictator state, "the Tyranny of unscrupulous armed groups". It was a far cry from the great days of Hildebrand, that apogee of the Papacy, when the Church possessed power over men's minds greater than armies. Then if the Pope pronounced or threatened excommunication, spirits were troubled, loyalties loosened, a great body of opinion was swung from its moorings. But what effect would a Papal anathema have on men like Hitler or Stalin? The Pope who ascended the throne of St. Peter in 1922 was faced with one of the most turbulent periods in the history of the Church since the Reformation.

It is often supposed that there are, broadly, two kinds of Popes, those who are "political" and those who are "spiritual" the implication being that the latter is the true form for the Vicar of Christ, and that there is something vaguely improper about a "political" Pope. Nevertheless, the

Pope's power over the Church and its 300 million faithful is such that, whether he likes it or not, his actions and pronouncements must inevitably produce political consequences. When Pius X was elected Pope in 1904 Delcassé, the French Foreign Minister, was informed that he was very "spiritual" and unworldly. The Frenchman pointed out that for a Church such as the Catholic, world-wide in its responsibilities and in the scope of its activities, *all* acts of its leader are political acts — and that a purely "spiritual" Pope, acting only according to the dictates of his conscience as a priest, without considering their possible political effect, would be acting very dangerously both for the Church and the world.

In the late nineteenth and early twentieth centuries the Popes had been "political", in the sense that they had supported Catholic political parties, such as the Centre Party in Germany, which represented Catholic interests in the Reichstag, and the Popular Party in Italy led by the priest Don Sturzo. These parties had been necessary during the period after 1870, if only to defend Catholics against the violently anti-clerical governments which then dominated Prussia, France and Italy. And they had been remarkably successful. The Centre Party in Germany had successfully opposed Bismarck's *Kulturkampf* against the Catholic Church, and later had been prominent in all the Weimar governments. The Action Française in France had championed the Church against a succession of anti-clerical Third Republic governments. In Italy, the Popular Party had by 1921 effectively opposed the Communists and become the second largest party in the land, with 110 Deputies.

Yet the new Pope, Pius XI, who ascended the throne of St. Peter in 1922, decided not to follow the policy of his predecessors in regard to these Catholic political parties. He believed that, in the greatly changed social conditions after the First World War, they had served their purpose, and that the participation of priests in politics (many of them were Deputies in the Parliaments of these countries) could only detract from the Church's essential spiritual function. Political parties the world over were, he believed, in a transitional stage, and he did not wish to compromise the Church by identifying it with any of them. He preferred a position in which what he regarded as *permanent* Catholic interests could be made secure from the whims of transient political systems. In face of twentieth-century technical advance which seemed to be absorbing all man's energy, he wished to encourage a return to spiritual values and Christian living. In the words of Sir O. Russell, the

British Minister to the Vatican, "Pius XI wishes to withdraw the Church as far as possible from politics, so that Catholics may unite on a religious and moral basis."[2] Instead of political parties, he put his faith in a lay organisation which he founded, Catholic Action, which was to eschew politics entirely. In a letter to Cardinal Bertram of Breslau he described it as "an organisation of lay Catholics which, on no other basis than that of their religion and loyalty to their bishops and the Pope, shall co-ordinate and amplify such Catholic charitable, social, moral, educational and religious societies as already exist, with the object of applying the principles of Christianity as interpreted by the Catholic Church to penetrate the life of the community". It was, he contended, the only weapon capable of combating what he called "the dizzy swirl of modern life". He accordingly discouraged priests from belonging to political parties, from supporting candidates at elections or contributing political articles to newspapers; and he ordered a complete separation of Catholic Action, together with its charitable, social and youth organisations from the Popular Party. The priest Don Sturzo who led this party was more or less disowned by the Vatican and went into exile. The same could be said in the case of Mgr. Kaas, leader of the Centre Party in Germany. In Poland the Pope forced the Prince Bishop of Cracow and the Archbishop of Lwov to resign their seats in the Senate to which they had just been elected. With his withdrawal of support for the Popular Party in Italy and the Centre Party in Germany, and his actual condemnation of the Action Française in France, these parties gradually collapsed, and a new era of Papal politics began.

[2] F.O. Annual Report for 1927.

I

The New Pope, Pius XI

———

PIUS XI WAS BORN ACHILLE RATTI AT DEZIO, A VILLAGE IN the sub-alpine landscape of Como, the lake and scenery immortalised by Manzoni. Of peasant stock, he was the fourth of five sons. Already in his childhood, we are told, he revealed a gravity and practical judgment beyond his years, patient, reflective, resolute, qualities which may explain his early decision to become a priest. The courage which he showed later, both physical and moral, may also be related to his hobby as a youth of mountaineering, scaling a number of formidable peaks in the Alps. He took his doctorate in theology in 1882 with such distinction that he came to the notice of Leo XIII, who congratulated him personally. In this way the Pope of the old world unknowingly met the Pope of the new; the Pope formed in the Europe of Chateaubriand and de Maistre met the man whose business was to be with Hitler, Mussolini and Stalin.

The first forty-five years of his career were spent almost entirely in libraries, and in teaching theology. Most of his writings appeared in learned reviews, with such titles as, "Did the poet Bonvesin de la Riva belong to the Third Order of the Humiliation, or to that of St. Francis?" His principal work at the Vatican consisted in compiling the Codices Vaticana. F. Charles-Roux, the French Ambassador at the Vatican, says that what struck him at his first private audience with the Pope were the books piled on all the tables, even on the floor.[1] The Pope's conversation was literary, and when Charles-Roux once apologised for coming to an audience in an ordinary suit, and not in diplomatic uniform, the Pope laughed, "Ah yes, you normally visit me in a leather-bound edition, don't you? Today you've come in a paperback." Like a true literary man, he thought little of newspapers and told Charles-Roux, "We don't even read our own" (the *Osservatore Romano*). At the beginning of the First World War, he was still working in the libraries, destined it appeared to stay with his beloved books for ever. But within seven years the paleographer had become a diplomat, the diplomat an Archbishop, the Archbishop a Cardinal: and within six more months Achille Ratti was Pope.

During his years in the Vatican library, he had become well known to Benedict XV, who appreciated his learning and knowledge of diocesan affairs. When in 1918 the Polish Catholic Church asked for an Apostolic Visitor to consult with over the diocesan boundaries of the new State, Benedict therefore selected Mgr. Ratti. The Pope was very much concerned about the fate of 125,000 Catholics, mostly Polish or Lithuanian, who had been deported by the Russian Communists to Siberia. Mgr. Ratti played an important part in the next two years in obtaining information about these unfortunate people, and in the consolidation of the new Polish State, revealing an unsuspected diplomatic skill. In the face of Communist opposition, he restored a number of episcopal sees. He courageously remained in Warsaw when the Soviet armies were besieging it in 1920, and most of the other diplomatic missions had fled. This Polish experience was to determine his attitude to Communism for the rest of his life. Here he learned from the refugees of the "Anti-God Museums" in Russia, of the twenty-six bishops and thousands of priests who had been executed. Having seen the Bolshevik armies besieging Warsaw he knew that, had they not been repelled, they could have flooded into Germany, not stopping till they reached the Rhine. Later when he was Pope, the British Minister at the Vatican, Count de Salis, wrote: "Everything in the Vatican is dominated by the Pope's fear of Russian Communism, that the Soviets may reach Western Europe."[2] Von Bergen, the German Ambassador to the Vatican,

[1] F. Charles-Roux, *Huit ans au Vatican* (Flammarion, 1949).

[2] F.O. Vatican relations with Italy, Annual Report, 25th October, 1922.

confirms this. He was always being asked at the Vatican, he says, what Germany would do if Russia occupied all Poland and reached the German frontier.[3]

In 1920 Mgr. Ratti was recalled to Italy and given the most important Italian bishopric, Milan. A year later he received the biretta. He had also been in Milan only a year when Benedict XV died (January 1922), and he went to Rome for the election of the new Pope. Two main groups were confronted in the Consistory, one supporting Cardinal Gasparri, the Secretary of State, the other Cardinal Merry del Val. After several ballots, neither could obtain the two-thirds majority, and on the third day a name that had received only five votes emerged, Cardinal Ratti. During that day he received in consecutive ballots eleven, twelve, twenty-four and twenty-seven votes. On the fourth day he received forty-two, which made him Pope with six votes to spare. At some stage the Cardinals had evidently opted for a less prominent candidate, or they had elected Ratti as the Cardinal best qualified after his Polish experience to deal with the greatest danger the Church had known since the Reformation, Atheistic Communism.

The new Pope was sixty-five, portly and bullet-headed; behind gold-rimmed spectacles gleamed small, penetrating eyes. The British Chargé d'Affaires at the Vatican, Mr. Ogilvy-Forbes, writes:

He leaves on one the impression of being a man of the school-master type. Change his skull-cap and soutane for the M.A.'s mortar-board and gown — and there is your Headmaster as depicted in Victorian schoolboy stories. On ascending from the Secretary of State's rooms to the Papal apartments, one passes all the guards, Swiss, Palatine and Noble in uniforms reminiscent of Waterloo, to find oneself in an entirely different atmosphere, that of the headmaster's study. Kindly and considerate he is, it is true, but one who regards laymen as a master would his pupils, with whom it is not fitting to discuss matters concerning the running of the school or the conduct of the assistant masters.[4]

It soon appeared that this apparently mild school-master was a martinet. The diplomat Baron Beyens writes: "After he became Pope there was only one word on every tongue, *obbedire*, obey. For thirty years as an

[3] *A.A. Beziehungen des päpstlichen Stuhls zu fremden Staaten*, Vol. 1, 8th August, 1920.

[4] F.O. Vatican relations with Italy, 12th August, 1930.

ordinary priest Achille Ratti had obeyed with an apparent unawareness that any other course was possible. Like all those who have obeyed, he instinctively commanded with equal unawareness when authority came to him."[5] That he soon learned how to confront Mussolini is revealed in a report by the German Ambassador, von Bergen: "the real danger of a sudden eruption lies not so much in the inflammable material as in the temperament of the two men, in their ever-increasing totalitarian and absolutist pretensions, and in their tendency not to listen to the advice of subordinates".[6] He brought the obstinate and over-bearing Lord Strickland, the Prime Minister of Malta, to a new Canossa; and he destroyed the powerful *Action Française* party in France almost single-handed. Lastly, just before his death, he flayed the Nazis in his encyclical *Mit brennender Sorge*, which they unsuccessfully tried to prevent from being read in the pulpits of Germany. On hearing of his death in 1939, Mussolini exclaimed, "Thank God the stubborn old man has gone!"[7]

Pius XI had few counsellors, which was resented by some of the Curial Cardinals. The decisions taken by the Vatican during his reign were his own, often at the last moment, and sometimes conflicting with the views of his Secretary of State. Negotiations for the Italian Concordat in 1929 were carried out in complete secrecy, without even the knowledge of the Curia. Mr. Hugh Montgomery, sometime British Chargé d'Affaires at the Vatican, says of him, "a ruler at once so despotic and so averse from back-stair influences that when a Cardinal once told him he thought it his duty to offer advice, the Pope replied sharply, 'Yes, when you're asked for it' ".[8]

A minor but likeable quality was Pius XI's attitude towards money. Sir Odo Russell, the British Minister to the Vatican, writes, "From one's personal observations it would be easy to deduce that His Holiness conducts his finances in a manner pleasantly reminiscent of St. Francis of Assisi, receiving gifts and handing them out again whenever there is a need, with no thought of the future."[9] Others relate that the Pope kept in a drawer in his desk a most heterogeneous collection of coins and notes from currencies all over the world, which he would dole out personally to deserving cases. A large part of the gift to the victims of the Palestine earthquake, for instance, were sent out in this fashion, lire notes, French

[5] In his book, *Quatre ans à Rome*.
[6] *A.A. Beziehungen des päpstlichen Stuhls zu Italien*, Vol. 2, 12th June, 1931.
[7] Bernard Wall, *Report on the Vatican* (Weidenfeld, 1956).
[8] F.O. 371/17759, despatch from Mr. Montgomery, 10th August, 1934.
[9] F.O. 371/12199, Sir O. Russell to Sir A. Chamberlain, 18th October, 1927.

billets de banque, dollar bills and English cheques, all stuffed into an envelope and given personally by the Pope to his emissary, without the intervention of any bank.[10]

Pius XI's rule will be found in the next seventeen years to demonstrate all the traditional tenacity of purpose of the Vatican, resisting on the one hand the disruptive influence of Bolshevism, and on the other attempting to moderate the fanatical new nationalism in Germany and Italy.

[10] Sir Alec Randall comments on this: "I said to the emissary, Mgr. Pascale Robinson, that it seemed rather unwise to go with such a large amount merely in a handbag; and Mgr. Robinson came with me to a bank which took the cash and arranged to transfer it to him through their Jerusalem branch."

2

The Arrival of Fascism

WHEN PIUS XI WAS CROWNED, THE POPES HAD BEEN LIVING for fifty-two years, since the 20th September, 1870, in self-imposed incarceration in the Vatican. On that day, Royalist troops had occupied the Papal city of Rome, leaving the Pope only the Vatican buildings. The Vatican had refused to recognise this act of force, and all suggestions since then for a peace treaty had been met with Pius IX's famous *Non possumus*. The Vatican based its claim to Rome and the Papal States on the *Patrimonium Petri*, the gift of the French King Pepin in 754. For over a thousand years, the Popes had ruled over Rome and the territory extending to the Exarchate of Ravenna and the five Adriatic towns, Rimini, Pesaro, Fano, Sinigaglia and Ancona. The first occasion since Napoleon when the Papal States had seemed in danger was in 1849, during Garibaldi's first campaign. The Pope had summoned the help of France, Austria and Spain against the usurper, justifying his summons: "A temporal Princedom is necessary to the Papacy, so that it may in freedom exercise its holy power for the benefit of religion." On that occasion their help was effective. But twenty-one years later, in 1870, they could do nothing, and the Papal territory was seized by the new Italian State. In compensation, the State offered the Guarantee Laws, guaranteeing the Pope residence in the Vatican and a large sum of money. The Pope, Pius IX, refused the offer, because acceptance would mean he recognised that the Papal States were lost, and that he was henceforth living in the Vatican on State charity, not in his own right; for Article 5 of the proposed Guarantee Laws said, "The Pope will continue to enjoy (*godere*) the habitation of the Vatican and the Apostolic palaces". The word "enjoy", the Pope contended, implied that these buildings did not belong to him. A new Italian government could, if it wished, always repeal the Guarantee Laws and eject him, as a landlord ejects a tenant. The *Osservatore Romano* said that if he accepted, his position would be reduced to that of "a chaplain in the service of a Prince on whose grace he would be dependent".[1] Moreover, other countries might well consider that he was a creature in the service of Italy. The result would be more national Churches and schisms. Hence, the "Roman Question" as it was called, could be solved only "with complete independence of the Pope in the eyes of all believers". He must be recognised as a sovereign in virtue of his office, and not in virtue of a law which could be repealed.

The Pope therefore not only rejected the Guarantee Laws, but refused to set foot on the soil which he regarded as having been illegally taken from him, preferring to remain "a prisoner in the Vatican". In retaliation, he used about the only weapon which still remained to him. He forbade all Catholics, on pain of excommunication, to vote at Italian parliamentary elections, or to stand as candidates — the *Non Expedit*. In reply to this, the Italian State suspended a number of religious Orders in the old Papal States and confiscated their property; it secularised monasteries and extended military conscription to ecclesiastics. By the Siccardi Laws which were directed against the Church and the religious Orders the Archbishop of Turin was imprisoned and the entire episcopate of Piedmont prevented from communicating freely with the Pope. The funds of the Church's department for foreign missions were seized and Catholic social societies dissolved. In 1887 Crispi said in a famous speech, "We will bring the Pope to his knees." Tacit permission was given to everyone to insult the Pope. When Pius IX's body was being transported from St. Peter's to the basilica of St. Lorenzo, a mob surrounded it, singing obscene and blasphemous songs, and tried to tip it into the Tiber. The police, like the carabinieri of Offenbach, conveniently arrived on the scene when all was over.

The period from 1870 to 1922 in Italy is known by the Church as that of the "anti-clerical, Liberal governments". The terms "anti-clerical" and "Liberal" require a word of explanation. The Englishman or American

[1] 14th October, 1927.

imagines an anti-clerical as a reasonable enough person, who merely wishes to prevent the clergy from interfering in his private life, to avoid them as he might the doctor or the lawyer. In the Latin countries, however, the anti-clerical is more fanatical than reasonable, a dedicated iconoclast and often an atheist. By the word "Liberal", too, the Anglo-Saxons understand something favourable, a kind of Mr. Gladstone, upright if somewhat sanctimonious. But the "Liberal" to the Vatican is quite different, being virtually synonymous with "Socialist", "atheist" and "Communist"; to the Vatican there is only a small difference of degree between these four types of man. Pius XI's interpretation of the word was clear in a speech he made, when referring to Mussolini, "a man free of the prejudices of the *'Liberal'* school, a man in whose eyes their laws and orders, or rather disorders, are monstrous and misshapen".[2]

Other Catholic nations, France, Spain and Austria, had stated since the middle of the nineteenth century that they wished to be consulted about the Roman Question. But when in 1870 they were faced with the *fait accompli* by Royalist Italy, the only country which spoke up on behalf of the Pope was the diminutive Ecuador. In view of such indifference, the Roman Question soon lost its importance, and the Italian State was quick to make it a purely "Italian Question". By offering the Guarantee Laws, Italy was anxious to avoid any international settlement of the problem. In the Italian State documents between 1875 and 1916 is this entry, "Over the Roman Question, Italy must allow no interference by other states. Further, we must refuse to take any part in diplomatic discussions implying that the Holy See has any temporal power." Consecutive Liberal Italian governments therefore prevented the Vatican from being invited to the Hague Conferences of 1899 and 1907. In 1915, one of the Italian conditions in the secret treaty of London, which was to bring Italy into the war, was that the victorious Allies should not invite the Vatican to the Peace Conference.

A legal problem illustrates the anomalous situation which lasted all these years. While the Pope was entering St. Peter's one Sunday in 1926 a clerk from the State Finance Ministry got up and began shrieking insults and blasphemies. He was arrested by the Vatican police; but no one knew what to do with him. Article 2 of the Guarantee Laws provided punishment for those "who insult the person of the Pope". The Pope had not accepted the Guarantee Laws, but the State considered they were in force. St. Peter's was regarded by the State not as the possession of the

[2] F.O. Vatican relations with Italy, despatch of Sir R. Graham, 13th February, 1929.

Vatican, but as "a national monument inhabited by the Pope": and so in the eyes of the State the offender should have been handed over to the carabinieri. The latter however could not enter the precincts, because Article 7 of the Guarantee Laws states, "No Italian State official in pursuance of his duties may enter St. Peter's without Papal permission". According also to the Guarantee Laws, a man could not be punished, as of old, by a Papal court because "the Pope possesses no right of punishment over Italian State citizens". Nothing, it appeared, could be brought against the offender. After much delay and discussion he was handed over to the State police at the bronze doors and he received a short term of imprisonment. That the Vatican transferred him implied, however, tacit recognition of the Italian State by the Papacy.[3]

In the first decades of the twentieth century, this kind of tacit recognition increased. The prohibition on Catholics voting in State parliamentary elections, the *Non Expedit*, was gradually relaxed. In practice, this prohibition had merely meant that Catholics could have no influence on the political life of the country, while the socialists, atheists and free-thinkers dominated the polls. Pius X accordingly left this to the local bishops who could suspend the *Non Expedit* whenever participation of Catholics might be beneficial to religion. Such was the situation when the new Fascist State assumed power on 22nd October, 1922, nine months after Pius XI had been elected.

One of Mussolini's first acts was to suppress the Communists who had in the last four years threatened both Church and State. They had incited the series of great strikes and invasions of private property for which the years 1919 and 1920 have never been forgotten in Italy. Their Peasant League, operating on the Ferrara-Bologna plain, had instituted a sort of agrarian terror. Workers' syndicates took possession of villages and municipalities, ejecting the mayor and his officials. They were confident that it was only a matter of months before the whole of Europe had imitated the Bolshevists, that the Soviets themselves would soon arrive. Confident of this, they occupied the big factories, using methods copied entirely from the Russian model. Mussolini put an end to all this, and the British Minister to the Vatican, Sir Odo Russell, reported: "The Vatican realises that Mussolini is the only man who can steer the ship of state into smoother waters, and give Italy the strong hand she needs."[4]

Before attaining power Mussolini had been a noisy anti-clerical, the

[3] *A.A. Beziehungen des päpstlichen Stuhls zu Italien*, Vol. 2, 11th June, 1926.

[4] F.O. Vatican relations with Italy, Annual Report for 1924, 25th February, 1925.

author of a novel, *The Cardinal's Daughter*, in which he described priests as "black microbes as fatal to mankind as tuberculosis germs". As late as 1919 he was writing in his newspaper the *Popolo d'Italia* (12th December, 1919), "Detesting as we do all forms of Christianity, that of Jesus as of Marx, we feel an immense sympathy with the modern revival of the pagan worship of strength and courage." In the same paper he wrote, "Our party demands the separation of Church and State; the abolition of all privileges for the Catholic religion and the confiscation of Church property. The State must regard the Church as a purely private society subordinate to Common Law. Religious education must be limited to the nave of the Church."[5] Benedict XV had even protested publicly against "the terrible blasphemies uttered against the person of our Divine Redeemer by a man who unjustly proclaims himself to be a representative of the Italian people".

Since then, however, Mussolini had learned more about the Church, its influence at home and abroad, and he no longer wanted it as an enemy. His rapidly changing attitude as he approached power was revealed in a speech on the 21st April, 1921: "I am perturbed when I see national Churches forming in other nations, because this will mean that millions of human beings will no longer look to Rome." In his first speech as Prime Minister, he even evoked the help of religion, claiming that he had been summoned to govern "by divine decree", finishing with the words, "May God help me to bring my heavy and difficult task to a successful conclusion." He also spoke of freedom for all religions in Italy, but "with particular regard to the dominant position of Catholicism". For a new and revolutionary regime striving for recognition in the world, he now realised the advantages of an alliance with an organisation as ancient and honoured as the Catholic Church.

One of his first acts was to restore the Cross in the Coliseum, where the blood of the first martyrs had been shed. It had been erected in 675; but in 1874 a Freemason politician had replaced it by a statue of *Roma Triumfans*, in whose hand was a lance instead of a cross. A few months later, his Fascist government announced that the Crucifix was to hang again in the Law Courts "as a sign of Divine Justice"; it would also be replaced in the schools beside the picture of the King of Italy. The government also announced that blasphemy, which had not been punished under the old Liberal governments, was to be a penal offence again.

To these advances the Vatican responded warily. Although it could

5 11th May, 1919.

only applaud Mussolini's overthrow of the Communists, Socialists and Liberals, it at first revealed a certain nervousness about the new regime and its extreme nationalism. The almost indecent haste with which Mussolini sought to please seemed a little suspicious; and the Church, which thinks in terms of centuries, did not forget that he was mortal. The aged and cautious counsellors at the Vatican would wait until he was more firmly in the saddle. Moreover, the Vatican did not wish to antagonise France and Spain by sudden friendship with a chauvinist Italy; nor America, by approving a regime which openly reviled all the principles of Western democracy. In his first encyclical, *Ubi arcano Dei consilio* (January 1923), the Pope still complained of the Italian State which had dispossessed him of his patrimony — but in a milder way; and he insisted on his Italian ancestry, speaking of his "Mother country", a word that none of his immediate predecessors would have dreamt of using.

But the regime seemed determined to ingratiate itself, and continued the good works. Since 1870 it had not participated in the great Church festivals, such as centenaries of saints, Holy Years and so on. As far as the State was concerned they did not exist. Now at the seventh centenary of St. Francis of Assisi, at which the Pope was represented by his legate, Cardinal Merry del Val, the State put a special train at his disposal. At stations on the way, Orte, Terni and Spoleto, a band on the platform played the Italian national anthem. On reaching Assisi, the Cardinal was greeted with a twenty-one-gun salute. The next day the festivities were bright with carabinieri in gala dress; and over the sacred Portiuncola, centre of the ceremony in Santa degli Angeli, hung the Papal flag beside the red, white and green of Italy. In his speech Cardinal Merry del Val spoke of Mussolini as "the man who has raised Italy's reputation in the world, and is visibly protected by God".

This last was a reference to a recent attempt on the Dictator's life by a demented English spinster. Later, the *Osservatore Romano* also referred to it, indicating that the Church feared that the disappearance of Mussolini would be followed by anti-clerical activity. It wrote favourably of "the new currents, new forces, the new attitude of the government whose sense of historical reality and political influence stand out prominently and undeniably above all the old petty party notions".[6] The Fascists were so pleased with this article that they printed it in its entirety in their press. Other, lesser instances of the government's desire to be conciliatory were: at Easter the great bell on the Capitol, which belonged to the

[6] 4th November, 1925.

Roman municipality, was rung for the first time since 1870 in the Easter jubilation; the Church of the Sapienza of Rome University, which had not been used for services since the Savoyard occupation of Rome in 1870, was newly consecrated, and the Rector Manificus invited all professors for the inaugural ceremony. A Jewish *Dozent* who deliberately absented himself was publicly reprimanded.

One less important, if more picturesque, form of Fascist blandishment may be finally mentioned. In 1923, a number of rich American Methodists had settled in Rome and began pronouncing against "the Whore of Babylon". Such impertinence in the city of the Pope was unheard of; but although numerically weak they were rich, which enabled them to buy a large tract of land on Monte Mario near the Vatican. Here they announced they would build a Methodist university, chapel and school. The European edition of the *Chicago Tribune* wrote, "it will be a Mecca for Protestants, to which people will come from all over the world, as on a pilgrimage".[7] The Vatican immediately complained to the Fascist government, who lost no time in announcing that "such a profanation of Rome could not be tolerated". Municipal building permission was refused, and the government announced that the land would either be bought back from the Methodists or, if they refused to sell, it would be expropriated for the erection of a Dante monument. The costs would be met by public subscription aided by contributions from the Italian press.[8]

In making these overtures Mussolini had of course political motives, but, in his capacity as the new Roman Dux, emotional ones played a part too. The conception *Roma caput mundi* could be shared by both Dictator and Pontiff; for the whole nomenclature of Fascism was Roman, and the surviving imperial tradition of the Vatican made a strong appeal to him. His conception of a modernised version of the Holy Roman Empire was mentioned or implied in every speech he made. To a Spanish journalist he said, "The Italians venerate the Sovereign Pontiff as the head of their religion; but in him they also venerate the symbol of that church of Rome without which, since the Middle Ages, our history would be incomprehensible. Many political phenomena in Italy today which are not altogether understood are phenomena of a spiritual revival. The

[7] 17th April, 1923.

[8] *A.A. Beziehungen des päpstlichen Stuhls zu fremden Staaten*, Vol. 2, 6th June, 1923.

religious policy of the Italian State has to be reconstructed on a completely new basis."

Mussolini now introduced a scheme for the reform of ecclesiastical legislation and improving conditions for the clergy. A Commission selected by himself, containing three churchmen and headed by a government minister, Gentile, was appointed. The British Minister at the Vatican reported that, "the Catholic ecclesiastics expressed themselves very warmly regarding the readiness of the Commission to meet their views".[9] The Commission proposed the legal recognition of all public churches and religious houses; state pensions for the clergy; the suppression of the *placet* necessary for the appointment of bishops, and its substitution by a system of previous consultation between the civil and religious authorities.

The favourable character of these proposals suggested that there may have been some earlier consultation between the Commission and the Vatican. This was denied by the *Osservatore Romano*,[10] which stated that the government alone was responsible, that the three ecclesiastics on the Commission had not been appointed by the Vatican, but were there at their own wish. It added that if this legislation presented a marked improvement on the previous laws, it was far from representing all that was necessary for complete reparation of the wrongs done to the Papacy by the Italian State. The Cardinal Secretary of State Gasparri also told Sir Odo Russell, the British Minister, that the whole Catholic world should be made clearly aware that, whatever the favourable tendency of this Italian legislation, the fundamental issue had not been touched. Restitution had not been made for the wrong done in 1870."[11]

The Vatican had, of course, much more in common with the Fascist State than with the earlier Liberal regimes. Both Catholicism and Fascism were autocratic, ruled by one man; both were absolutist, admitting no question of their creeds; both insisted on the submission of the individual to the system, both attached importance to external ceremonies and mass psychology; both encouraged large families. A Jesuit magazine wrote:

The earlier Liberal State professed to ignore religion; more than that, it actually persecuted it. Fascism, on the contrary, recognises

---

[9] F.O. Vatican relations with Italy, 15th February, 1926.
[10] 12th January, 1926.
[11] A.A. Beziehungen des päpstlichen Stuhls zu Italien, Vol. 2, 15th January, 1926.

the social importance of religion, and of the Church as a force useful to the government, with some of the same ideals. Its ecclesiastical policy is a recognition and a restitution of the rights of the Catholic conscience and the clergy which have been violated during fifty years of liberal-democratic government.

It was here, in connection with the Catholic political party, the Popular Party, that the Church made its first great concession to Mussolini, and the path towards reconciliation and the Concordat was opened.

Catholic political parties were a late nineteenth-century innovation, for the Church objected on principle to parliamentary democracy. But Leo XIII had recognised in his famous social encyclical *Rerum Novarum* (1891), that in the new industrial society Catholic associations of working men were necessary, to combat the Socialists. He saw that, faced with evangelical Marxism in the growing cities, the Church must attract the new industrial proletariat, or lose believers. In November 1919 therefore the Vatican supported the Popular Party which had been founded by a Sicilian priest, Don Luigi Sturzo, on the ideals embodied in his encyclical, with a Liberal programme of social and agricultural reform. By 1921, it had 110 Deputies in the Chamber where it was, after the Socialists, the largest party.

In the words of Mr. Colin Coote, "Don Sturzo combined into one organisation all the Catholic political fragments which had arisen since the removal of the *non-expedit*; and in two years the Popular Party became the arbiter of Italian politics, so that no government could survive without its sanction. During the so-called "Red Years", 1919–22, it was a formidable competitor of Socialism, and divided with that movement the mass of the active political vote."[12]

After Mussolini had eliminated the Socialists, the Popular Party provided the only real opposition in the land to Fascism; but Mussolini had no intention of allowing any opposition in his new totalitarian State. When in the 1924 elections the Popular Party polled 24,000 votes in Brianza, and the Fascists only 12,000, matters came to a head. The Fascist storm-troops attacked members of the Catholic Boy Scouts (a department of Catholic Action) and tore off their badges and insignia. Farinacci, one of Mussolini's most fanatical lieutenants, accused the Vatican of being too much identified with the Popular Party. He and Mussolini knew perfectly well that Pius XI had little sympathy with Catholic political parties,

[12] In *Italian Town and Country Life* by Colin R. Coote (now Sir Colin Coote), who was *The Times* representative in Italy at the time.

particularly those led by priests, and would prefer the country to be ruled by a party with which the Vatican had no links, but which was pro-Vatican in that it enabled the Church to carry out its apostolic mission in peace and security. This, they were determined, should be the Fascist party. Mussolini played his hand skilfully because, after this and similar incidents, it seemed to the Vatican that as long as the Popular Party existed, claiming to represent all Catholic and Church interests in public matters, including those of Catholic Action, and being resolutely anti-Fascist, incidents of this kind were bound to recur. The Pope therefore decided to withdraw his support from the Popular Party. He was by now convinced that the Church could obtain greater religious influence in public life from a stable government under an energetic, all-powerful ruler than it could through democratic party political strife. On the 1st February, 1924, he accordingly forbade priests, both secular and regular, from belonging to political parties. He also ordered complete separation of the Catholic Action, together with its charitable, social and youth organisations, from the Popular Party. Whereupon, Don Sturzo resigned as secretary of that party, in July 1924, and went into exile abroad. In this way the Pope abandoned the one mass political movement of Italian Catholics, in return for what he hoped would be the settlement of the Roman Question, and recognition by the Fascist State of the apolitical Catholic Action and its affiliated organisations. In the words of Mr. Colin Coote, writing at the time, "These orders constitute a terrible blow to the Popular Party, because hitherto the local priests have been the best election agents."

In the new legislation introduced by the Fascist regime were a number of measures which the Church could only approve, in particular those for protecting public morality and the family.[13] But whenever Fascist ideology or practice conflicted with Catholic principles, as in its over-weening chauvinism, the Church did not hesitate to protest, either in Papal addresses or through the semi-official Vatican newspaper, the *Osservatore Romano*, or in the Jesuit review *Civiltà Cattolica*. It objected strongly, for instance, to the speech made by the Minister of Education, Signor Rocco, in March 1926 at Bari in which he expressed the party's new imperialism, associating it with the Catholic Church: "Italy cannot exist as a state without a world mission—and this mission cannot be anything but

[13] One of these was Mussolini's prohibition on Italians taking another nationality to obtain a civil divorce and then returning to take up Italian nationality again. Under the Liberal regimes this had been going on for years.

Roman and Catholic. Signor Mussolini is the greatest instrument in the hand of God since Charlemagne." These speeches were repugnant to a Church which saw in them a rebirth of the old Caesaro-Papism, of the desire to use the Church purely as a means to Italian imperial expansion.

These differences began to emerge after the first brief honeymoon between Church and State. Most irreconcilable of all was the question of the education of youth, which was to dominate relations between Church and State in the Dictator countries for the next two decades. In his encyclical *Non Abbiamo Bisogno*, the Pope showed he was fully aware of the danger: "The undoubted resolve to monopolise completely the young, from their tenderest years up to manhood and womanhood, for the full and exclusive advantages of a party or regime is no less in full conflict with the natural rights of the family as with the supernatural rights of the Church." In the view of the Catholic Church youth should be educated by three "societies", the family, the Church, and, lastly, the State. First comes the family which has a natural God-given right to bring up its offspring, to nourish it, love it and teach it the elements of civic behaviour. Should the family not have the financial means to do this, the State must step in—but only to help. The Church possesses all the means for the eternal salvation of the human being; and the education, therefore, of that human being, which means the inculcation of moral as well as intellectual values, is the responsibility of the Church.

In view of Mussolini's reconciliatory attitude in the early days and his need for Catholic support, it was some time before the education issue was joined. The first incidents occurred over the youth groups of the Catholic Action. The Fascist youth, the Balilla,[14] contended that physical or sporting education was its exclusive right, and that the Catholic Action youth group should confine itself strictly to spiritual matters. The Fascists were well aware of the attraction of sport to the young; football, hiking, scouting, miniature range shooting, were to be their preserve. Also reserved for them was the wearing of uniforms, the carrying of flags and banners, the wearing of shoulder-straps and other insignia by which the adolescent sets such store. In this way they effectively diminished the attractions of the Catholic Boy Scouts who were a part of Catholic Action, and many children transferred to the Balilla. When the Vatican objected, the extreme Fascist paper, *Il Tevere*, took the Church to task for supporting a youth movement "which was founded by a Protestant, Baden-Powell, the follower of the theosophist,

[14] Balilla was the surname of an Italian youth who had courageously attacked the Habsburg forces during their domination of northern Italy.

Annie Besant, who believed that the Messiah would shortly appear at a second coming in the form of a beautiful young Indian".

On the 4th May, 1928, one of those enormous demonstrations so dear to totalitarian states took place in the Stadium, where thousands of Balilla girls clad in gym clothes gave a physical-training display, and hurled javelins. They then marched in ranks through Rome with rifles raised at arm's-length, chanting Fascist catch-words. On the 11th May, the *Osservatore Romano* expressed the Vatican's disapproval at "these groups of Fascist womanhood departing from the principle of modesty and reserve which should govern the education of girls and young women". It was not in keeping with Christian ideals of feminine education for girls to be taught violent physical exercises and to carry fire-arms; nor for scantily dressed young women to disport themselves in front of pre-dominantly male audiences. It was as indecorous for girls to "raise their rifles to heaven", as for the boys to be told "to carry their daggers between the teeth". "When female hands are raised to heaven," said the Pope in an allocution, "they should be in prayer, not holding rifles."

To this the secretary of the Fascist party, Turati, replied in *Il Tevere* that physical exercise had a beneficial effect on the mind. It was better for young girls to take part in such displays than to spend the day covering their faces with make-up. As for rifles, the regime had no intention of turning the girls into auxiliary troops; it merely wanted to train them not to faint at the sight of a loaded weapon, or when they heard a shot fired in war. To this the *Osservatore Romano* replied that the girls could perfectly well undergo physical training in the privacy of their school. The paper recalled a speech by Mussolini on the 18th May, 1927, in which he said he wanted the modern female youth of Italy to remain essentially "Latin", and not to allow themselves, "under the influence of the cinema and other forms of modernism, to become Americanised". Well, said the *Osservatore Romano*, that was precisely what the govern-ment was doing with these immodest public displays. The notion of females taking part in sporting competitions was exclusively Anglo-Saxon. The Balilla refused to cancel these displays, but finally agreed, as a concession to the Church susceptibilities, that the girls should henceforth carry not rifles but bows and arrows.

Religious education had been reinstated by the Fascists in the State schools, making it obligatory in elementary schools, but optional in high schools, in which "free thought and criticism were to be allowed and were to be open to the philosophy of Kant and Hegel". In a speech in Naples, Signor Gentile, the party theoretician, said that Catholicism was certainly a part of Italian life and tradition, and that everyone was dissatisfied with the exclusively lay education introduced by the old Liberal governments; but that the Church was too dogmatic in its educational methods, thereby hindering "the process of scientific education".

The *Osservatore Romano* took this up,[15] pointing out that dogma was an essential part of the Catholic faith, and that Gentile was contradicting himself if he said that education must be simultaneously Catholic and undogmatic. To assert that religion and truth, belief and knowledge, were antitheses, was as erroneous as to maintain that the religious problem had been solved in Italy. The paper objected to the way in which Gentile claimed that Fascism had "given Catholicism back to Italy". The Catholic Church was not a beggar who picked up crumbs fallen from the national table. The Church had a divine right to educate the young and the government was only restoring something inalienable which should never have been removed. A State which recognised the Catholic faith must, logically, also follow the social lessons of the Catholic religion. The *Osservatore Romano* objected that although the catechism was taught in the elementary schools, in the higher ones "free rationalism" was permitted.[16]

The arguments about education went on for years in the Vatican and Fascist press. Neither side would retract, and it became clear that nothing more could be achieved until an official agreement perhaps in the form of a concordat was reached between Church and State.

[15] The polemic described here is taken from the report of the German Chargé d'Affaires at the Vatican, Brentano, in *A.A. Beziehungen des päpstlichen Stuhls zu Italien*, Vol. 4, February 1928.

[16] 25th March, 1928.

3

The Italian Concordat, 1929

———

THE POPES HAD ALWAYS MAINTAINED THAT THEY MUST HAVE A temporal state. Pius IX told Sir Odo Russell in 1862, "My Son, the Temporal Domination was given by God to His Vicar on Earth. God alone can take it from Him. The Lord's will be done."[1] Certain foreign statesmen also thought a temporal state was necessary, although for different reasons. To the English envoy at the Vatican, Palmerston wrote on the 5th January, 1849, "It is clearly desirable that a personality who in his spiritual quality possesses such influence over most European countries should be in such an independent position that he cannot be used by any one European power as a political tool to the disadvantage of other powers. From this point of view alone it is desirable that the Pope should remain sovereign in his own state." The same feelings were expressed by a commission from all French parties convoked to study the question of the Pope's worldly status in October 1849, when he had been ejected from the Vatican and had taken refuge in Gaeta. It agreed unanimously that for the benefit of all his independence was essential and "that there is no other form of independence but sovereignty".[2] He must be reinstated in the

[1] Noel Blakiston, *The Roman Question* (Chapman and Hall, 1962), p. 236.
[2] *A.A. Beziehungen des päpstlichen Stuhls zu Italien*, Vol. 5, von Bergen's report to von Bulow.

Vatican. Moreover, should a Pope wish to abandon this claim to sovereignty, he would be breaking the oath which he, in common with all the Cardinals, takes at a Papal election that no one of them, should he be elected, will renounce the claim.

As long as Italy had remained "a geographical expression", that is up till 1870, the fact that the Pope and members of the Curia were Italians was a guarantee that the Papacy would remain outside major European rivalries. Hence the Catholic Great Powers had always been prepared to accept an Italian Papacy. The Vatican policy in those long centuries was comparatively simple — to prevent any of these Great Powers which had a stake in the peninsula, Spain, France and Austria, from acquiring a dominant position there and over-shadowing the Vatican. To secure this aim, the Papal State had only to play off one Power against the other by exploiting their rivalries and, if necessary, combining with one or two of them against the most threatening rival of the moment. But in the nineteenth century the growth of Italian nationalism, which culminated in the unification of Italy, presented the Papacy with a much more difficult problem. The establishment of the capital of the new kingdom in Rome not merely meant the end of the former States of the Church, but the new Italy tended to eclipse the Papacy and, even worse, it awoke the suspicion among other nations that the Vatican was now under the influence of the Italian government. In this way the unification of Italy was a serious blow to Papal policy. The policy of "non-recognition" and hostility towards Italy pursued at first meant that the Vatican territorial basis remained insecure for, if an Italian government emerged which wished to carry the dispute to its logical conclusion, it could expel the Papacy from Rome. A settlement was therefore necessary both in the interests of the local Italian Church, and also in order to place the international status of the Papacy beyond doubt, by giving it once more a territorial basis.

Negotiations for a concordat with the Italian State to achieve this sovereignty were not begun formally until 1927 although contacts and feelers, principally from the Italian side, had been already made. The Vatican had no intention of taking the initiative. Its view was that the Italian State had been the aggressor in 1870, and that the first conciliatory steps must come from the Italian side.

In 1927 the British Ambassador at the Quirinal, Sir Ronald Graham, had an audience with Mussolini at which he asked if recent articles in the *Osservatore Romano* which were said to have been written by the Secretary of State at the Vatican, Cardinal Gasparri, could be considered a step forward in the relations between the Vatican and the Italian government.[3] Mussolini said this was so, adding that what he particularly approved in these articles was that they recommended a direct settlement with the Italian government, and deprecated foreign intervention. He then made the important point that if any suggestions included a provision for a territorial increase to the Vatican, then no further progress could be made. What he altogether excluded was a corridor to the sea. The very name, "corridor" (in connection with Danzig), was sinister, and he was sure it would cause even more trouble in the future than it had in the past. It was obvious therefore, says the British Ambassador, that Mussolini was not going to allow the Papacy direct access to foreign states. The boat of St. Peter would not be allowed to anchor at the mouth of the Tiber. Graham adds that he put much the same question to the Italian Foreign Minister, Conte Grandi, who replied that the Italian government should "always follow a concordat policy, but never make a concordat". "I would find it hard," concludes Sir Ronald Graham, "to improve upon this definition of Italian policy towards the Vatican."

A concordat is, in the definition of Father R. A. Graham in his standard work on *Vatican Diplomacy*, "a formal treaty or agreement entered into by the Holy See and individual States for defining the respective roles of the two parties in *fields where conflict tends to arise*". The last words are important for the word has generally had unpleasant associations for the Vatican. *Historia concordatorium historia dolorum*. A treaty is signed between lay States either when a period of warfare is ended, or so that the citizens of one State may obtain concessions on the territory of the other. The concordats made by the Vatican with lay States however do not aim at obtaining concessions for the Vatican itself, but for the Catholic citizens of the lay State in question. For as well as allegiance to the State, these citizens also have an allegiance to the Catholic Church. Disputes over this allegiance have often arisen between the two powers; and they are settled by concordats which define their limits of responsibility. Concordats generally result in a surrender of Church privileges in return for permission to carry out its evangelical mission and educate the young in Christian principles. For this no sacrifice is too great, and Pius XI said he would negotiate with the Devil

[3] F.O. 371/12204, interview reported by Sir R. Graham to Sir A. Chamberlain, 21st October, 1927.

if the good of souls required it.[4] Concordats lapse if either party undergoes a substantial change. This means in effect a change in the State, for the Church changes hardly at all.

The negotiations on the Vatican side were conducted by Cardinal Gasparri, who had been Secretary of State since 1914 and probably had as much experience of diplomacy as anyone in Europe. This squat, ill-favoured Tuscan peasant was a cynic, unlikely to be dazzled by Fascist promises and blandishments, and he had the reputation of being double-faced. "Gasparri", wrote Sir Charles Wingfield, the British Minister to the Vatican, "is far from candid with diplomats accredited here — or put more bluntly he can lie well." The French Ambassador, the Vicomte de Fontenoy, once accused Cardinal Gasparri of lying, to which the Cardinal coolly replied that he was merely doing what all diplomats did, and that in any case the Pope would give him absolution if necessary.

Although Gasparri was in favour of a concordat, he believed that its advantages to the State would outweigh those to the Vatican, and he bargained stubbornly. By becoming sovereign of a temporal state, and having good relations with the Italian government, the Pope would no longer be regarded with sympathy throughout the world as "the prisoner in the Vatican". He would lose a good grievance. A minor sovereign living in the shadow of the Quirinal, he would also come to be regarded abroad as a political appendage of the Italian government. On the other hand for the State, a concordat would enhance its prestige and make the upstart regime more respectable. The Fascists' desire that Italy should replace Austria-Hungary or Spain as the principal patron of the Church would also be partially satisfied. Best of all, by a Reconciliation with the Papacy, the Italian State might profit from the recent Vatican troubles with France over anti-clericalism in Syria, and advance the case for an eventual Italian mandate in the Middle East. Mussolini hoped too to be able to intervene in the disagreement between the Vatican and Yugoslavia over the question of the Slav liturgy for the Roman Catholic Church in the Triune kingdom, and perhaps obtain concessions on the Adriatic coast. The Vatican was also deeply involved in controversy with England at the moment, over the religious problem in Malta, and he hoped here again to obtain advantages. Fascist maps of the Mediterranean showed Malta as an Italian island.

Gasparri did not believe that the Fascist State would last, and he made

[4] When he said this to the College of the Mandragone on the 14th May, 1929, he could hardly have foreseen that in less than ten years' time he would be doing this almost literally with the diabolical ruler of Germany.

a remarkably accurate forecast of its duration. Charles-Roux, the French Ambassador, says that to an inquisitive visitor who asked Gasparri how long he thought Fascism would last, Gasparri replied: "About twenty years."

"And what will come after that?"

"Why, Giolitti, of course!" (Giolitti was the Grand Old Man of the past thirty years of Liberal coalitions, who had been in and out of office a score of times.)[5]

This was perhaps the principal reason why Gasparri thought that negotiations with the Fascist government were worth undertaking. With a democratic or parliamentary government there could never be a concordat; and if Gasparri was suspicious of Fascism, he, like his master, loathed parliamentary parties. He told the French Ambassador of a conversation he had with Mussolini before the Dictator came to power, when Italy was ruled by the old parliamentary parties. Mussolini had suggested that the Roman Question might be solved by the State granting the Pope sovereignty over the Vatican buildings and gardens.

"But you won't get the votes in the Chamber," Gasparri replied.

"Well then, we'll change the Chamber," said Mussolini.

"But if you change the Chamber without changing the electoral law, the public will vote back exactly the same Chamber, with the same deputies."

"All right," said Mussolini, "then we'll change the electoral law."

"With such a man," said Gasparri, "I knew we could do business."[6]

One of the stumbling-blocks was the attitude of the King, who was anti-clerical. Brought up in the Liberal spirit of the Risorgimento and true to the tradition of the House of Savoy, he had retained his suspicion of priests. He also feared that the Pope might replace him in popularity, not only in the capital but throughout Italy. He had been offended in 1926 when his mother died, and the Pope had refused to take part in any ceremony connected with her memory — simply because she was a Savoyard. The Queen Mother had been noted for her piety and good works; and von Bergen, the German Ambassador, reported that Conte della Torre, the editor of the *Osservatore Romano*, had prepared a favourable obituary, but he was instructed by the Pope not to print it.[7] Her death was merely mentioned briefly. On the other hand the Crown Prince, Umberto, was reported to take a different view from his father.

[5] F. Charles-Roux, op. cit.
[6] Ibid., p. 47.
[7] *A.A. Beziehungen des päpstlichen Stuhls zu Italien*, Vol. 2, 23rd January, 1926.

A devout Catholic, he had announced that he hoped his forthcoming marriage with a Belgian princess might be celebrated in Rome — for which the formal consent of the Bishop of Rome (the Pope) would be required.

At this point a Jesuit priest, Father Tacchi-Venturi, who knew Mussolini well, was employed as an intermediary between Church and State. The Fascists approved of him on account of his patriotic behaviour during the First World War and his advocacy of Italian unity. The Church approved of his announcement that the annual ceremonies on the 20th September (the day when the Royal forces had taken possession of the Papal city in 1870), should be abrogated, because they had been superseded by the "greater victory of Italian unity" at Vittorio Veneto in 1918. Tacchi-Venturi accordingly persuaded Mussolini to moderate the 20th September celebrations which had for sixty years caused such offence at the Vatican. Mussolini gave him a signed portrait with the inscription: "Affectionately to my friend, the loyal and sincere counsellor."[8]

The first intimations to the general public that negotiations were taking place appeared in *Germania*, the German Catholic paper on the 25th December, 1928. It reported that the Roman lawyer Francesco Pacelli[9] had represented the Vatican in negotiations with Commendatore Barone of the Italian government. We now know from Francesco Pacelli's own account in the *Popolo d'Italia* (14th February, 1929) how protracted they were.[10] Pacelli describes them:

I was telephoned one evening by the head of the government [Mussolini] who wished to see me . . . the next morning I had my first meeting with him. He told me he now intended to take charge of the negotiations himself — and he gave me another appointment for that evening. Thereafter, I visited him frequently, mostly in the evening at his private house in via Rasella. The discussions began at 9 p.m. and lasted sometimes till one in the morning. I looked with boundless admiration at this man seated opposite me who, day and night, had no rest, but thought only of his unceasing dedicated service to the nation. Mussolini went over the entire treaty point by point, again and again.

[8] Ibid., 9th January, 1926.
[9] Brother of the then Papal Nuncio in Berlin, Eugenio Pacelli (later Pope Pius XII).
[10] See also *Diario della Conciliazione*, Francesco Pacelli's account of the negotiations (Lib. Ed. Vaticana, 1959), and Sir Alec Randall, "The Pacelli Diary", *Dublin Review*, Summer 1959.

The result was that the negotiations could proceed far more quickly. Since there was no intermediary, I was able to report every morning to the Holy Father what I had discussed with Signor Mussolini the night before . . .

An even more revealing account of Pacelli's activities, and of his friendship with the German Ambassador, von Bergen, is contained in a secret report on the negotiations to the Wilhelmstrasse.[11] Von Bergen says he had it all from a trustworthy "informant" at the Vatican. He does not mention Pacelli by name, always alluding to the informant as his *Vertrauensmann* or *Gewährsmann*, but his remark that this man always sees the Pope the next morning after evening discussions with Mussolini tallies exactly with Pacelli's last remark in his *Popolo d'Italia* article. The German Ambassador's informant must have been Francesco Pacelli. To summarise the German document:

It appears that the negotiations had almost been completed as early as 1927, but had then been suspended for a year because Mussolini believed that, faced with Cardinal Gasparri's intransigence, the State had made too many concessions. In particular he objected to the Vatican demand for a corridor to the sea, leading to near Ostia; this would give the Vatican direct access to foreign states by ship without crossing Italian territory.

This delay had annoyed the Pope (so the "informant", Pacelli, tells von Bergen), and he hinted at a number of measures the Vatican would take. They are important because they reveal how the Vatican, theoretically powerless, can apply pressure if it wishes. Rumours were allowed to circulate that an encyclical forbidding the bishops and clergy from taking part in Fascist demonstrations and celebrations was being prepared: they would henceforth not be allowed to bless the Fascist flags and standards. Permission was also to be retracted for mass to be said at the grave of the Unknown Soldier. The Vatican, so the word went round, would not make the army chaplain, Mgr. Panizzardi, an army bishop, although Mussolini had officially requested it. These examples reveal that, even if most of the leaders of the Fascist movement were irreligious, they dared not lose the rank and file of the party, to many of whom these rituals were hallowed. Not until the 3rd December, 1928, after more prolonged discussions between the Pope and Pacelli, alternating with those between Mussolini and Pacelli, was permission given that at least a Te Deum could be sung at the anniversary of the Unknown Soldier.

[11] *A.A. Beziehungen des päpstlichen Stuhls zu Italien*, Vol. 5, 4th February, 1929.

Von Bergen goes on to report Mussolini's complaints to Pacelli that while he always tried to be as obliging as possible to the Vatican, it invariably responded with threats of this kind which offended the "honour and dignity of Fascism, and of the government itself". He asked Pacelli to ascertain if this attitude was inspired by the Pope himself, or should it be attributed to "the arbitrary behaviour of his collaborators" (a reference to Gasparri, whom the Fascists loathed). Pacelli transmitted this message to the Pope who said he wanted no more discussions; the question should either be solved radically *now*, or there would be a complete break. For a year, said the Pope, Mussolini had had full details of a concordat which had been drawn up by responsible representatives of both sides. He should make up his mind now, particularly as he himself had suggested the negotiations. If a precise answer was not received, the Pope would act according to his conscience.

At this point two unexpected events precipitated matters. The French, who had been watching with apprehension these manoeuvres which would benefit Italy, were unwise enough to intervene. Briand, the French Foreign Minister, on hearing that a concordat was being mooted, told his Ambassador at the Vatican to inform Cardinal Gasparri that "France trusted the rights of France would not be altered adversely as a result of an Italian concordat". In diplomatic language, this meant that he was convinced that they *would* be altered adversely. In January 1929, the Archbishop of Paris, Cardinal Dubois, appeared in Rome in a last-minute attempt to dissuade the Pope from an agreement which, he said, would alienate all French Catholics. On hearing this Mussolini flew into a rage and informed the Vatican that he intended to place the treaty before Parliament immediately before France could interfere further. The second unforeseen event was that the Vatican banks, most of which had been founded in the Marche and Abruzzi for the savings of the peasantry, went bankrupt. Mussolini immediately offered a State guarantee for them.

There was now little that the Pope and Gasparri could do, although they would have preferred to continue the discussions. Pacelli told von Bergen that the Pope became almost hysterical, contending (in contradiction to what he had said about Mussolini) that he was being rushed into an agreement for which he would, according to normal Vatican negotiations, have preferred several more months, if not years. In front of Francesco Pacelli, he knelt down and prayed; then after a few moments he said: "The Lord has spoken, the Lord has heard Thy servant! So be it! It is the will of the Lord." Nevertheless just before the signing, he had further misgivings. He told Gasparri that it might be better to complete the negotiations, but leave the actual signing to his successor. But Gasparri had just heard that the objections of the King had also been overcome by Cardinal Maffi of Pisa, a personal friend of the Royal Family; and he believed the terms were as good as they would ever get. He therefore said to the Pope (again according to von Bergen's account of his conversation with Francesco Pacelli), "No, no, Your Holiness! Now or never!" The Pope agreed and on the 7th February, 1929, the Cardinal Secretary of State, Gasparri, summoned the heads of diplomatic missions at the Vatican and formally announced that the "Roman Question" had been solved.

By the Lateran Agreements the Italian State renounced all claim to Vatican Territory in Rome; and the Vatican City became an independent sovereign state with an area of 108.7 acres (a little bigger than St. James's Park). In return for a money payment, the Vatican for its part renounced all claim to the previous Papal States. In the bargaining, Gasparri had pressed for a single cash payment, so as to free the Vatican from the foreign suspicion that, if Italian shares were accepted, it would be bound up financially with the Italian State. But the Fascist government would not agree to this. It stipulated that the Vatican should receive 750 million lire in cash, and 1000 million lire in Italian five per cent consolidated stock. A proportion of the cash payment also must be invested in Italian funds. In this way the new Vatican State found itself with a heavy stake in the financial fortunes of a European great power.

Unlike the Guarantee Laws suggested in 1870, by which the Pope was to be regarded as an Italian subject to whom the State would grant certain rights and privileges, the Lateran Agreements regarded him as a foreigner, and a foreign *ruler*. They consisted of two documents. The first regulated the relations between the sovereign States, Italy and the Vatican, including the territorial arrangements by which the Vatican State came into being, and the economic ones. This was the Lateran Treaty proper. The second, the Concordat, defined the rights of the two States in the realm of education and spiritual matters. Catholicism was recognised as the State religion and — most important for the Vatican — the Pope's beloved Catholic Action was granted full recognition and autonomy. Church buildings were restored, and religious education in schools was made compulsory. The propaganda of Freemasons, Methodists and other heretics could in certain cases be a penal offence; as could dancing and other uproarious activities during Lent. A more stringent control over the theatre and cinema was envisaged.[12] Perhaps the most important concession to the Vatican was the ruling about marriage, which henceforth had to be canonical. Before the Concordat, bigamists in Italy had had a high old time, thanks to the existence of civil marriage. The Church did not recognise civil marriage, so they would marry in church; then, if they so wished, abandon their families and remarry civilly, without committing any offence in law.

The Lateran Agreements were signed on the 11th February, 1929, by Mussolini and Cardinal Gasparri in the famous Council Hall near the Triclinium where Charlemagne had been received by Leo III. In the square of St. Peter's a large crowd gathered in the pouring rain waiting for Pius XI to come out on the balcony. When he appeared, thousands knelt in the pools of water, crossing themselves, weeping, waving scarves and handkerchiefs. The Pope, now freed from his "imprisonment" in the Vatican, raised his hand again and again in silent apostolic benediction. He had, he said, "given Italy back to God, and God back to Italy".

Church and State in Italy now seemed in such harmony that their adversaries, chiefly in France, spoke of a "new Inquisition, by which the secular arm would again carry out the behest of the 'spiritual' ". They referred to the fulsome praise of Fascism in the sermons of certain Cardinals and bishops. In Naples on the 14th February, 1929, Cardinal Ascalesi spoke of Mussolini as "the renewer of the fatherland", who had "rescued Italy from the humiliations of Versailles". At the Eucharistic Conference in Sulmona, Cardinal Enrico Gasparri (a nephew of the Secretary of State) said: "Only one man in the present world chaos has a clear view — Mussolini." On the 17th February, 1929, in Trieste, Bishop Fogar said to a number of foreign consular officials, "Announce to your governments and peoples that henceforth Italy has become the protector of the Pope and Church."[13] The Pope himself in a speech to visiting Milanese professors referred to Mussolini as "the man sent by Providence".[14]

[12] F.O. Vatican relations with Italy, Sir F. Clive's report for 1927. Pius XI regarded the influence of the cinema as "almost wholly evil". At an audience given to the International Federation of the Film Press he referred to two films, *Ecstasy* and *Amok*. Eighty-seven million people a year, he told the surprised film-men, went to see this rubbish; the film-men ought to take as their motto Manzoni's "Never utter a word which applauds vice and derides virtue". Most of the film-men had never heard of Manzoni and he commended to them the Clean Film Crusade promoted by a group of American bishops.

[13] *A.A. Beziehungen des päpstlichen Stuhls zu Italien*, Vol. 12, 19th December, 1932.

[14] Ibid., Vol. 6. Von Bergen states that the Pope said this against the advice of his Secretary of State, Gasparri.

In Italy only among certain bourgeois intellectual circles were there doubts. Benedetto Croce and his friends in Naples regarded the Concordat as a blow to their Liberal hopes, a revocation of all the good done in Italy since the Risorgimento, a return to the Holy Alliance of Throne and Altar, to "the blackest times of clericalism". Such views could not be expressed publicly in Fascist Italy, but they could be abroad, particularly in France. In *L'Ere Nouvelle* (19th February, 1929) Edouard Herriot stigmatised the Concordat as "an alliance of the Papacy with a regime which has suppressed the liberties of a great nation". Léon Blum in *Le Populaire* (14th February, 1929) said that the Church had once again shown that it had no understanding of modern society; he reproached the Vatican for demanding nothing in the Concordat on behalf of the banished Popular Party.

Not a word [he said] for this party which has been so loyal to the Church in the past . . . this party of modest little people, all good Catholics, yet intent on justice and equality — and therefore suspect to the hierarchies, whether the great Church dignitaries or the privileged members of a social class . . . The Church eliminates every form of Christian Democracy or Christian Socialism. This has been its great error and undoing for over a century . . . it condemns or annuls any enterprise like the Popular Party likely to bring into contact the Christian faith and proletarian demands . . .

René Pinon in the *Revue des Deux Mondes* (February 1929) saw something even more sinister in the Lateran accords, quoting Proudhon: "The Italians are still nourished on their grandiose and glorious past, and they dream of making their country the sixth great World Power — they intend to do it after having subordinated the Papacy to the Throne, by conferring on the latter the protectorate of Catholicism. *L'Italie impériale et sacerdotale*! *That* is the danger!" *Le Temps* observed how curious it was that all the money of one sovereign state should be held in the banks of another (25th February, 1929).

One result of the Concordat, all these liberal Frenchmen contended, would be that good Catholics in France, Belgium, Spain, South America and other Latin countries would now regard Fascism favourably and, as *Le Temps* said, become "its active agents". Even England had a view on the matter. Stresemann reports that in conversation with Sir Austen Chamberlain, the British Foreign Secretary said that England saw in the

Concordat "a weakening of the spiritual influence of the Church".[15]

Objections to the Concordat were also made by Italian Jewry, which claimed that the sufferings of the Jews in medieval Italy ceased only when Church and State were separated. The Catholic Church had the privileged position of a State religion again. The State would now contribute to Catholic education in elementary schools, but would not give anything for Jewish education. "A moral pogrom", the Jewish senator Polacco called it.[16] Nor did the Orthodox Church look on the treaty with much favour, commenting that whereas in the Orthodox Church care was taken to see that all power was not concentrated in the hands of one man, the Italian State had recognised the Pope as the all-powerful priest. Hamilcar S. Alivisatos, a professor at Athens University asked (19th February, 1929), "Did not Christ say 'My realm is not of this world'? (John 18:36). And yet here is the Catholic Church recognised again as a temporal power with monarchical attributions."

The first fruits of the Concordat for the State appeared in the March 1929 elections, when most of the clergy instructed their flock to vote for the Fascist candidates. The Civiltà Cattolica said that everyone should vote, so that "foreign countries which criticise the Concordat will see that the Italian people approve of the moral and religious rebirth of our land". It was not long however before some of the objections raised by Croce and the foreigners appeared justified. The twentieth-century Dictators have since proved to be men who, if treated with deference, are scornful; but if opposed resolutely, are respectful. Now that the Church had, as Mussolini thought, yielded, he began to speak of it in a patronising tone. His long parliamentary speech of the 13th May, 1929[17] must have been addressed to his more fanatical followers, for in it he made sarcastic references to Church history, deriding the old Papal armies and Sixtus V. He said the Church had been founded, "quite by chance in Palestine and not in Rome, which would have been more suitable for it, and to which it later transferred". Had the Christian faith not found in Rome good nourishing soil and propagation possibilities, it would have remained no more than the faith of "an obscure Jewish sect in Palestine which would finally have ebbed away entirely".

The Vatican took great offence at this last suggestion. But worse was to come. Mussolini then implied that the present Pope was in such a weak

[15] Ibid., 7th March, 1929.

[16] Judische Telegrafen Agentur, 4th July, 1929.

[17] A.A. Beziehungen des päpstlichen Stuhls zu Italien, Vol. 8, reported by von Neurath, German Ambassador to the Italian State.

position that he had had to yield and adopt a friendly attitude towards Fascism. The Pope should not think that now, with the Concordat, he could return to the times when the Church ruled Italy and suppressed her free spiritual development. The statues of Giordano Bruno and Garibaldi would remain where they were.[18] To support these views Mussolini quoted from Duchesne's *Histoire de l'ancienne église*, a work which since 1912 had been on the Index. He said that the new Fascist State would be "independent of both Freemasons and clerics". Most significant of all, he said, "in the sphere of education we remain intractable. Youth shall be ours!"

Von Neurath, the German Ambassador at the Quirinal, in his report of this speech[19] expresses surprise that Mussolini should "so overrate himself and underrate his opponents". Indeed, the Italian Dictator was beginning to display that bravado by which he is principally remembered today. Not content with abusing the Church in this speech, he then insulted France, England and the League of Nations. "He spoke," wrote von Neurath, "for more than three and a half hours in his most energetic and boastful speech yet." (In view of what was to come in Germany, von Neurath's last observation about the new Italian Parliament has an unconscious irony, "whose mediocre members have apparently nothing better to do than express endless uncritical admiration for Fascism and its leader".)

To all this the Vatican was quick to reply. In an open letter to the Cardinal Secretary of State on the 15th May, 1929, the Pope described certain passages in Mussolini's speech as "heretical and worse than heretical". He emphatically refuted Mussolini's claim that the education of the young was solely the affair of the State. The Church would maintain its claim to education, "even if it has to fight with the Devil himself". He ended by regretting that "the genuine joy in the world which had greeted the Concordat should so soon have suffered such a blow". His letter was published in the *Osservatore Romano* and in the Catholic Youth magazine, *Azione Giovanile*. While the editor of *Civiltà Cattolica*, the Jesuit Father Rosa, compared these Papal warnings to Mussolini with those of Pius VI to Napoleon 120 years before.[20] The Frenchman, he pointed out, also made a concordat with the Vatican and re-established the Catholic faith in Europe — an act which was widely

---

[18] The Church had complained about these, the latter being an equestrian monument on the Gianicolo looking out defiantly towards the Vatican.

[19] *A.A. Beziehungen des päpstlichen Stuhls zu Italien*, Vol. 8

[20] *Civiltà Cattolica*, 20th June, 1929; the article entitled "Ratifiche e Rettifiche".

acclaimed, and which contributed greatly to Napoleon's success in the 1802 plebiscite. But Napoleon did not interpret the Concordat fairly; on the contrary, he distorted its provisions for his own purposes and persecuted the Church. On that occasion, too, the Pope replied with a strong protest, although he had no material power. He opposed this Colossus who had all Europe at his feet. And what happened? He was still Pope when the Colossus was on St. Helena.

A howl of fury from the Fascists greeted this article. The *Tribuna* found the parallel with St. Helena, "insulting and provocative", and demanded that the *Civiltà Cattolica*, "the newspaper of another country", should be banned in Italy, and Father Rosa dismissed. The number containing his article was confiscated. The Fascists also began to attack Catholic Action, the Pope's cherished lay organisation which had been recognised in the Concordat. It was divided in Italy into a number of sections: the Catholic Italian Youth; the Catholic University Federation; the Italian Federation of Catholic Men; the Italian Union of Catholic Women, etc., with a membership of about a million. In Article 43 of the Concordat these associations were recognised by the State, "as long as they developed their activity according to the instructions of the Holy See, and remained outside the influence of any political party". Their direction lay in the hands of diocesan committees, some of whom had formerly been connected with the Popular Party of Don Sturzo. Because Catholic Action was now the only non-Fascist organisation permitted, there was it is true a tendency for any elements hostile to the Fascist regime to gravitate towards it — Liberals, Socialists, old Popular Party members. In the last years of the twenties it attracted a number of professional men, lawyers, doctors, engineers, etc., who also preferred its insurance schemes to those sponsored by the State. Somewhat earlier than this Mr. Colin Coote had written, "The Fascists pour out the vials of their wrath upon those Catholic institutions of a semi-charitable nature (Catholic Action), but which labour under the suspicion of being connected with the Popular Party."

On the 8th July, 1931, the Fascist paper *Lavoro Fascista* published the sensational news that Mgr. Pizzardo, the Under-Secretary of State, and Conte della Torre, the editor of the *Osservatore Romano*, were in league with the exiled Don Sturzo in London who, with the help of the French Socialists, were planning to overthrow the Fascist government in Italy. Accusations of this kind in totalitarian states are generally the forerunner of some form of physical violence; and shortly after this, Fascist students in Rome publicly burnt a large painting of the Pope. In Priverno, the

Pope's portrait was taken from a church and later found hanging in a public urinal accompanied by an obscene text.[21] The Fascist youth leader, Scorza, made a series of speeches accusing the Catholic priests of immorality. The Fascists also maintained that the "anti-patriotic attitude of the Vatican" was proved by documents confiscated in a raid on the Catholic Action headquarters.

These continuous attacks on the Vatican at last began to have an effect. The first sign that the Vatican was yielding was seen in the replacement of the Jesuit Father Rosa, the editor of *Civiltà Cattolica*. He was down-graded to *scriptor*, and sent off on a long holiday to Spain. The Vatican also agreed to certain modifications in the statutes of Catholic Action. The lay committees which controlled it were, the Fascists contended, staffed with ex-members of the Popular Party. True or not, these committees were now disbanded and Catholic Action came henceforth directly under the control of the local bishop, who nominated its officials, none of whom might have been a member of the Popular Party. The Fascist suspicion therefore that Don Sturzo and his followers might direct or influence Catholic Action from abroad was now completely eliminated.

In return, the Vatican received certain small face-saving concessions. For example, the Church had long regarded the date, the 20th September, which was celebrated annually as the anniversary of the Savoyard occupation of Rome, as an open insult. The Fascist government now suspended these celebrations, replacing them with those of the 11th February, the date of the Concordat. Similar concessions concerned the replacement of the fiery anti-clerical youth leader Scorza by the less militant Giurati. In the matter of girls' athletics, there was to be no more musket-carrying or unseemly high jinks in front of male audiences; and the girls were to be decently clad. Lastly, at the ceremonies for the anniversary of the death of Garibaldi, his grandson, Enzio, was forbidden from delivering his customary tirade against religion.

Peace of some sort was now established between Church and State, and Mussolini was received by the Pope on the 11th February, 1932, exactly three years after the Concordat. The audience lasted an hour, and appears to have been formally polite — at least if the deluge of decorations which were then showered on those who had taken part in the Concordat negotiations is any indication. The head of the Italian State, King Victor Emmanuel II, probably the most anti-clerical monarch in Europe, received the highest Vatican award, the collar of the Supreme

[21] *Osservatore Romano*, 10th June, 1931.

Order of Christ;[22] while Mussolini was given the Papal Order of the Golden Spur. On the Church side Francesco Pacelli, the Consistorial lawyer who had negotiated the Concordat, received the Order of the Annunziata, the highest decoration in the Italian State. It was also conferred on Gasparri and the Jesuit, Tacchi-Venturi, the intermediary in the negotiations.

By the mid-thirties relations between Church and State had become almost cordial. The Fascists even began to use hagiographical language when commemorating their paladins and heroes. Their newspaper described an exhibition of the "Fascist Revolution" as "Fascism's Holy Year", and referred to "the blood of our martyrs which will one day liquefy as does that of Saint Januarius in Naples". Another Fascist paper wrote of the Italian Trient irredentists, Battisti and Sanro, who had been executed by the Austrians — "There is a halo round the brow of Battisti, whose journey through Trient on the hangman's waggon recalls the journey to Golgotha of the flagellated Christ"; while Sanro's mother "wept before her son's body as did Mary under the Cross". The fertile imagination of one Neapolitan journalist became lyrical over a Fascist who had been killed by the Communists — "His martyrdom was perhaps greater than that of the blond Nazarene [sic], for the Nazarene was accompanied to his execution by his mother and Mary Magdalene; but our man had no one to support him." The *Osservatore Romano* commented tartly on all this that such attempts to glorify earthly things had in fact the reverse effect. To bring godly and human things together in this way did not of course damage the godly; it only rendered the worldly ridiculous.

[22] This decoration had been conferred some fifty years before on Bismarck, the "hammer of the Church". Uncharitable comment was, "The harder you hit the Church, the more it gives you."

4

Exploiting the Concordat in Malta and the Holy Places

AFTER THE SIGNATURE OF THE LATERAN AGREEMENTS IN 1929, rumours of secret clauses quickly circulated. The Fascist press did nothing to allay them, claiming that the solution of the Roman Question had put into the hands of Mussolini a matchless instrument for furthering his designs, and fostering the spread of *Italianità* throughout the world. The phrase *Mare Nostrum* was being used for the Mediterranean, and Mussolini was already thinking in terms of expansion east, towards Egypt and Abyssinia. For and against such plans, the island of Malta, strategically placed between Sicily and Africa, was to play an important part.

The Italians have always regarded it as an Italian island, and not without reason. For nearly 700 years, since Count Roger of Sicily conquered it from the Arabs, it was connected with Naples and Sicily; and the British did not gain possession until the beginning of the nineteenth century. This accounts for the strong hold which the Italian language and culture have on the educated portion of the population, a hold which the deeply religious nature of the Maltese people, who are accustomed to the Italian of the Catholic Church, has strengthened. There are in Malta a greater number of ecclesiastics and members of religious Orders than anywhere else in Christendom, in proportion to the population. Moreover, by long tradition, the clergy have always taken part in politics. The Bishop of Malta can nominate senators, and the habit of distributing political pamphlets in church is old and well established. However much the Vatican, following Pius XI's new directives not to interfere in politics, might deplore these practices, they were very difficult to eradicate. In the words of the English Catholic journal, *The Tablet,* "In Malta the Church and churchmen bulk much bigger in the island's life than do churches and clergymen in England. Therefore, religious questions get into Maltese politics, just as the revised Prayer Book got into British politics."[1]

A letter to the British Home Secretary, Mr. Clynes, in 1930 from an inhabitant of Malta, Mr. P. Boffa, warned Britain about the Concordat just concluded between Italy and the Vatican. "Two Bishops are now dominating Malta," he writes. "One of the secret clauses of the Lateran treaties is political help to Mussolini in Malta and Tunis . . . It is essential that self-government in Malta be amended until such time as Mussolini no longer controls the Church in Malta."[2] Somewhat before this Mr. Harold Nicolson, then a junior official at the Foreign Office, commented on a minute, "There is no doubt that the Italians and the Vatican are indulging in very intensive propaganda in Malta."[3] While Lord Strickland, the Prime Minister of the island, contended that "the Italian Fascists, aided by the Jesuits, are indulging in a violent pro-Italian propaganda in Malta, aimed at establishing the Italian language and culture, and ousting English and the vernacular Maltese".[4] He said that the Vatican was now appointing Italians, not Maltese, as heads of religious Orders in Malta, with the intention of restoring such Orders, and eventually the Maltese Church, to the position they occupied before the arrival of British rule — that is, of complete dependence on Italy and Sicily, where most of them had their headquarters.

A Foreign Office report of the 31st December, 1929 refers to a Mr. Charles Plowden, head of a family bank in Rome where he had lived much of his life and,

who knows pretty intimately a good many people in Italian society and politics, both "Black" and "White". He says an active intrigue is

[1] 31st August, 1929.

[2] F.O. 371/14409, P. Boffa to the Home Secretary, 10th May, 1930.

[3] F.O. 371/12949, memorandum of notes left with H.M.'s representative at the Vatican for communication to the Vatican, 17th November, 1928.

[4] F.O. 371/10789, note from Lord Strickland, 24th February, 1925.

afoot for promoting Italian influence in Malta; and in the first instance for making Italian the predominant or exclusive language of the island. The idea apparently is that Malta should be prepared for eventual reunion with Italy, and that in this scheme the Knights of Malta are to play a prominent part. Mr. Plowden wants us to realise that in these questions the Quirinal and the Vatican are working closely together. He hopes we realise that if we do not take a stand against the Vatican now, our troubles later will be greatly increased. He feels bound to say this, although he is himself a devout and practising Catholic.[5]

Suspicion in H.M.'s government had been aroused even earlier than this, in 1924, when a document in Bologna University was sent mysteriously to the British Ambassador in Rome revealing Italian intentions of installing, if they could, an Italian professor for Language and Literature in Malta University for "national reasons", in place of the usual Maltese professor. If this can be achieved, the document goes on to say, the Italian government would anonymously subsidise the Italian professor.[6] The British Ambassador to the Quirinal, Sir Ronald Graham, was instructed to ask Mussolini about this apparent interference in the affairs of a foreign country. Mussolini said he knew nothing about it, but would look into the matter. After that, no more was heard of it, and no Italian professor was engaged. But on the 2nd May, 1924, a group of Maltese students belonging to the Fondazione da Vinci (for "The Diffusion of Italian Culture Abroad") was received by the Pope, who referred in his allocution to "their racial, cultural and religious affinities with the glorious Italian empire", and also to the "Latinity" of Malta.[7]

That Mussolini might well covet Malta for his imperial plans is also mentioned in German diplomatic quarters. In the German Foreign Office files is an entry for the 8th May, 1930 emphasising the importance of the island to the British who can "thereby disturb the Italian Sicily–Tripoli communications".[8] The German adds that, although the Italians are using culture and the Vatican to further their claims, "what they are really after is the many marvellous harbours".

For over a hundred years of British rule, Malta had remained one of

---

[5] F.O. 371/13682, 31st December, 1929.
[6] F.O. 371/9948, despatch by Sir R. Graham, March 1924.
[7] Ibid., 2nd May, 1924.
[8] *A.A. Beziehungen des Vatikans zu Englischen Dominien*, Vol. 1, October 1927–August 1930.

the quietest and most contented countries in the Empire, undisturbed by political crises, its natives obtaining great commercial advantages from the British naval base in Valetta. Although the British gradually changed it from a theocracy ruled by a religious Order, the Jesuits, into a self-governing colony, they were careful not to offend the Catholic Church. Indeed, they recognised the Catholic as the established religion, even protecting it from the competition of other religions, restricting for instance the activities of such English Protestant groups as the Salvation Army and the Bible Society. Catholic precepts concerning education and marriage were upheld. Divorce and civil marriage were not permitted. The Archbishop of Malta was accorded high honours, and in order of precedence came second only to the Governor. Article 161 of the Criminal Code made it an offence to vilify in public the Catholic religion or its ministers. In any case, after 1870 any objection this very Catholic people may have had to British rule was greatly outweighed by their dislike of the new Italian monarchy which had despoiled the Pope of his territorial possessions and immured him in the Vatican. As long as the "Roman Question" existed, the cry of *Italia Irridenta* would find little echo in Malta. But now the Question had been settled.

After the Great War the island became imbued, like so many other communities, with the prevailing enthusiasm for a democratic constitution; and was duly furnished with one in 1921, embodying two Chambers on the British model, a government responsible to them, a wide franchise for the island's quarter of a million inhabitants. From then on, the long stagnation of its civic life was stirred. The natural bent of the islanders for political disputation now had all the apparatus with which to express itself. It was not long before a profound contrast became noticeable between the new political restlessness and the ancient habits of an island race steeped in the unchanging tenets of the Roman Catholic faith, in medieval customs and beliefs.

The two political parties which the British had permitted, and even encouraged, were the Nationalists and the Constitutionalists, the former being clerical and Italophile. The latter, which came to power under Lord Strickland in 1927, supported the British connection, and contended that the Italian language was being used in the island as a vehicle for Fascist propaganda. In principle Lord Strickland's party was not anti-clerical, for he and most of his Ministers were practising Catholics; but as a result of the attitude taken by the Vatican in defence of the

Italian language, he soon found himself being driven into the position of anti-clerical politician. Sir Alec Randall in his book *Vatican Assignment* points out that

> the privileged position of the Italian language in Malta was, in general, supported by the Church and the legal professions. To this the British government could afford to be indulgent *as long as Italy was our friend* ... But with the intensification of aggressive Italian nationalism under the Fascist regime, there was evidently a danger that Italian cultural expansion would be used to further Fascist political designs, with the scarcely disguised aim of challenging British security in the Mediterranean, of which Malta is the key.

On assuming office in 1927 Lord Strickland announced that education in Malta would henceforth be conducted exclusively in Maltese and English, and that the heads of religious educational establishments were to be English or Maltese. This attitude towards the Italian language brought him into sharp conflict with the religious Orders most of whose Superiors, sent from Rome or Sicily, were Italian; and also with Mussolinian Italy whose newspaper *La Tribuna* on the 17th August, 1927 referred to "the vulgar anti-Fascism of that renegade Strickland who is a Freemason and an anti-Catholic".

Lord Strickland was a powerful, self-willed and obstinate man, accustomed after his governorship in Australia to be instantly obeyed. He now had no compunction in openly criticising the Vatican, not hesitating to refer to the august person of the Holy Father himself, writing in a newspaper article that "if enough money were forthcoming, the Pope would make a horse a Papal Marquis"; on another occasion he described the Vatican as "a business concern". In Parliament he attacked the history of the Catholic Church in Malta for "keeping eighty per cent of the population in ignorance for centuries, and now the people will turn against the priests who are Italian politicians first and priests afterwards". Earlier, his newspaper, *Il Progresso*, offered a money prize to those readers who could suggest the best reason for removing from office the aged and saintly Bishop of Gozo.

In February 1929, three Anglican bishops visited the island for pastoral duties in connection with the Royal Naval dockyard, and the Governor of Malta received them in the ancient Throne Room. That a reception in this room should so offend the Vatican, and cause it to make an official complaint to Great Britain is some measure of the power of Catholic tradition on the island. The Secretary of State, Cardinal Gasparri, sent a sharp note to the British Minister complaining that it was an insult to the age-old faith of the Maltese that *Anglican bishops* should be received in the Throne Room which from time immemorial had been associated with the glorious Order of Malta and the Catholic Faith. It was this Catholic Order which had in the sixteenth century, in a heroic defence, withstood the Moslem siege and turned back the tide of Islam.[9]

It was at this point, in 1929, that the Concordat between the Vatican and Italy was signed — about which the Foreign Office commented, "It may only be a coincidence but it is certainly curious that this aggressive note from the Vatican should follow so closely on the settlement of the Roman Question with Mussolini."[10]

The British decided to ignore the note; instead, the British Minister to the Vatican was instructed to reply to Gasparri by accusing the priests in Malta of interfering in politics, and asking the Vatican to despatch an Apostolic Visitor to look into the whole matter with a view to drawing up a concordat to settle the dispute.[11] The Vatican quickly agreed, and sent the Franciscan, Mgr. Pascale Robinson, an Irish–American priest noted for his tact and diplomatic skill. The six weeks' visit of the Apostolic Delegate appears to have gone off well, relations between Lord Strickland and the Visitor being amiable, even cordial. This was duly related by Strickland to H.M.'s government, who hoped that the Vatican would now stop encouraging Italian aims in Malta. They awaited the publication of Mgr. Robinson's report with confidence.

A significant feature of Papal diplomacy is now revealed — the entirely arbitrary rule of the Pope. Pope Pius XI had been so incensed by Lord Strickland's attacks on the Church, not to mention his own person, that he was determined to break the power of the Maltese Prime Minister. We now know from what Mgr. Robinson told Mr. Ogilvy-Forbes much later that the Vatican deliberately withheld that part of his report which recommended reconciliation, and published only a garbled version with a virulent attack on Lord Strickland. "It would take too long," says Father Robinson in the report *as published by the Vatican*, "to relate the series of attacks, sometimes subtle and skilful, sometimes crude and brutal which Lord Strickland has directed against the most sacred

[9] Vatican White Book, *Esposizione della Questione Maltese*, February 1929–June 1930, Document 2, 23rd February, 1927.

[10] F.O. 371/13680, memorandum by Mr. Sargent, 13th June, 1929.

[11] F.O. 371/3680, Mr. Chilton's request to Vatican for an Apostolic Visitor, 1st March, 1929.

institutions of Malta, not sparing the venerable bishops, nor hesitating to inveigh against Religion itself. Malta is at present subjected to a reign of terror and despotism, in which the opposition in Parliament is disarmed, the press gagged, justice suspended, the Christian religion openly insulted." He finished by referring to the notes for a concordat which Lord Strickland had handed to him of which, "a superficial examination alone suffices to reveal the mentality of Erastian policy of Strickland who wishes at all costs to enslave the Church in Malta, and to turn the bishops into simple State servants". The Apostolic Delegate exhorts the Vatican to make an open gesture disowning Lord Strickland.

Such was Mgr. Robinson's report as published in the Vatican White Book. Yet on December 11th, 1931, we find Mgr. Robinson in an interview with Mr. Ogilvy-Forbes, the British Chargé d'Affaires at the Vatican, "emphasising his indignation at the publication without his consent, *and in incomplete form*, of a report which is meant to be strictly confidential". The Vatican had published, he said, only that part of his report which concerned Lord Strickland. They had omitted his recommendations on the subject of local ecclesiastical reform. It was quite true that he went to Malta with a view to drafting a concordat, in which work he had met with a large measure of success, having obtained what the Church wanted, in return for concessions to the requirements of Lord Strickland, many of which he said were of a trivial nature.[12]

That the Pope personally was behind this seems clear from the report by Sir Ronald Graham, the British Ambassador at the Quirinal. "The Pope is an obstinate combative man. Strickland has got on his nerves, and he has gone for him bald-headed, without listening to the sobering counsels of Gasparri and others of his advisers."[13]

In March 1930 the Foreign Office stated that if the Vatican would make no suggestions for a concordat as a result of Mgr. Robinson's visit, the British would put forward their own proposals. As none were received, Mr. Randall, the Chargé d'Affaires in place of Mr. Chilton (who had been sent on indefinite leave to show the displeasure of H.M.'s government) was instructed to suggest that, in return for a promise from Lord Strickland that he and his followers would not attack the Maltese clergy, the Vatican should instruct the clergy to refrain from taking an active part in politics, and not to stand as candidates for the pro-Italian party in the coming elections. This proposition was made to the Cardinal Secretary of State who said he would not accept it. "He expressed," said

[12] F.O. 371/15249.
[13] F.O. 371/13681, 26th July, 1929.

Mr. Randall, "complete scepticism regarding any verbal promise from Lord Strickland. Only deeds, not words, he said, could alter the situation. No negotiations for a concordat were possible, he said, as long as Strickland was in power."[14]

To confirm this attitude factually, the Archbishop of Malta announced in April 1930 in a pastoral letter that in the coming election it would be a mortal sin for any Catholic to vote for Lord Strickland's party. That these instructions were faithfully observed is revealed in the Governor's Report of the 26th April, 1930.[15] He states that the High Commissioner of Gozo, a responsible civil servant, was refused absolution because he admitted he voted for Lord Strickland's party. The parish priest of the village Casal Allard wrote to Lady Strickland saying that he could not bless their house, the Villa Bologna, at Easter in the normal way.

The reaction of H.M.'s government was that the Vatican was interfering in the affairs of another country and that the British Legation to the Vatican would accordingly be withdrawn. Moreover, owing to the great influence exercised by the Pastoral Letter, it was clear that the coming elections would be jerrymandered. The British government accordingly postponed them and abrogated the constitution, instructing the Governor to rule by decree. Mr. Ogilvy-Forbes explained to the Vatican that henceforth H.M.'s government would hold no communication with the Vatican until the latter "had given orders that the Pastoral Letter should be withdrawn and complete freedom restored to the electorate to exercise their political judgment in elections without clerical interference". The Secretary of State again refused. Such an action, he said, would imply an unmerited repudiation of the bishops by the Vatican. Nothing could be done as long as "those remained in power who had alienated themselves from the people and the clergy" (i.e. Lord Strickland).

This hard and fast line, stubbornly maintained by the Vatican seems at last to have broken Lord Strickland's will; moreover, the interdiction on his party had begun to affect him as a confessing Catholic. He asked a Catholic friend, Lord Howard of Penrith, who was well regarded at the Vatican, to intervene on his behalf with the Pope. In the House of Lords on the 3rd March, 1931 he said, "I am prepared to record in writing my expression of regret for anything I have said improperly in the heat of debate in the Parliament of Malta, if I may have caused offence to the ecclesiastical authorities in Malta or Rome."

[14] F.O. 371/14408, 7th March, 1930.
[15] Ibid., report from Sir John du Cane, 26th April, 1930.

But this was not enough for the Pope. Well aware of the powerful position he now occupied he said he would accept no apology until Lord Strickland had first apologised to the Bishop of Malta. Mr. Vansittart's comment at the Foreign Office was "The Pope seems to be really a full-blown idiot. This is the reaction of a Dictator rather than a nego-tiator.[16] Nevertheless on the 10th March, 1932 Lord Strickland had to complete his Canossa, writing to the Holy See — "The Undersigned begs leave to add the expression of regret humbly laid before His Holiness the Pope, and hereby also addressed to Your Grace the Bishop of Malta. We fervently implore the Apostolic and Episcopal Benediction."

Lord Strickland's daughter Mabel Strickland wrote later to Mr. Ogilvy-Forbes, "The situation was becoming intolerable for my father and his adherents to whom the bishop had forbidden the sacraments. He is an old man and a practising Catholic, to whom such a ban is a most serious matter from a spiritual point of view. Moreover, he wishes to continue in Maltese politics; it is his life hobby."[17] On the 3rd June, 1932, Mr. Ogilvy-Forbes met Cardinal Pacelli, who said the Pope had accepted Lord Strickland's apology and that the Pastoral Letter had now been suspended. The Catholics in Malta could vote for whom they liked in future elections. The controversy might now be regarded as closed. It had revealed that among a highly religious people like the Maltese, Papal interdicts and exclusions from the sacraments still retain something of the immense sanctions they had in Hildebrand's time.

The attempt by Fascist Italy to use the Vatican for furthering her expansionist aims in the Middle East was revealed once more in the twenties in the dispute over the Holy Places. The Papal claims to these dated from 1230 and the fourth crusade.[18]

In 1922 they had come for the first time in history under the control of a Protestant power, Great Britain, as a result of Allenby's conquest of Palestine. The historical claims to these Places are so complicated, and rest on such apparently insignificant precedents, that they often seem to the outsider irrelevant, even ridiculous. But to people so steeped in tradition

---

[16] F.O. 371/15249, 31st August, 1931.

[17] F.O. 371/15983, letter from Mr. Ogilvy-Forbes to Mr. O. Sargent, 25th June, 1932.

[18] The Holy Places are: (1) the Church of the Holy Sepulchre; (2) the Tomb of the Virgin; (3) the Church of the Ascension; (4) the Church of the Nativity in Bethlehem; (5) Rachel's tomb on the road to Bethlehem; (6) the Caenaculum, or scene of the Last Supper.

and religion as the Christian sects of the Middle East, historic considerations are never irrelevant. Guardianship of these shrines has always been
coveted by every Christian Church, Catholic, Orthodox, Armenian,
Coptic, Jacobite, for the immense prestige that accompanies it, and the
corresponding effect on proselytisation. The history of the British occupation until 1945 is one long story of animosities and contentions, in
which extraneous influences, such as the aims of Fascist Italy play an
increasing part, until the scenes of Our Lord's life on earth become a
political shuttlecock, and finally the cause of international conflict.

The news of the entry of British forces into Jerusalem in 1918 was
received officially at the Vatican with outward expressions of satisfaction
and a solemn Te Deum was sung in the Church of Santa Croce. To the
criticism that this contradicted the Papal policy of neutrality in the Great
War, the Vatican replied that in such matters as the recovery of the Holy
Places from the infidel, the Vatican could not fail to take sides. England,
so ran an article in the *Osservatore Romano* (December 1917), had twice
merited well of the Catholic Church; in the last century, by opposing the
eastward advance of Russian Orthodoxy (the Crimean war); and now,
by saving these shrines from the profanation of the Turk. This professed
satisfaction was, in fact, only for external consumption. The Vatican was
far from pleased at the arrival of the British with their Balfour
Declaration about "a home for the Jews in Palestine". Catholics had
learned over the centuries how to live with the Turk in Palestine; for the
Turk was indifferent to, and completely uninterested in, all other
religions apart from his own, and worshippers were allowed to do much
as they pleased provided they did not offend him. But the behaviour of
the new rulers, whose Prime Minister was a Welsh Non-Conformist,
was quite unpredictable. The Vatican had always feared that the
Protestant and Orthodox Churches might come together, at the expense
of the Catholics. Here at last were Rome's two great enemies on
common ground.

The suspicion with which England was still regarded at the Vatican was
well illustrated when the Archbishop of Canterbury announced that he
would visit Jerusalem and the Holy Places. That he was to travel there in
the yacht of, and accompanied by, Mr. Pierpont Morgan, would have an
effect on the impressionable Orientals. But what the Vatican feared most
was that the Protestant visit might result in a Protestant claim *sub jure*, after
the Archbishop had made his official entry into the Holy Places, to a share
in their occupation. The English Primate had unwisely announced that he
would be the first Archbishop of Canterbury to visit the Holy Land since

his predecessor, Baldwin, had laid his bones there in 1190 during the first crusade. The Secretary of State at the Vatican, Cardinal Gasparri, accordingly summoned the British Chargé d'Affaires, Mr. Ogilvy-Forbes, and informed him that the Vatican would not object to the visit provided the Archbishop visited the Holy Places as a *private* individual, and did not participate officially in any of the ceremonies (to eastern minds a ceremonial privilege inevitably denotes a political privilege).[19] In London, the use of the words "would not object" was regarded as a piece of gross impertinence to a sovereign power, and this caused a minor diplomatic incident. Mr. Vansittart of the Foreign Office said the words were "entirely inappropriate", and His Majesty's government lodged a formal protest at "Vatican interference in the affairs of another state". In fact, the visit of the Archbishop went off quietly and without incident. Apart from expressing admiration for his choice of company and mode of transport, the local population showed no particular sympathy for the eminent visitor or his religion.

For much of the trouble that now arose in the Holy Land, the British had only themselves to blame. During and immediately after the Great War, they had made a number of conflicting promises about it. In 1915, in order to obtain Arab support against the Turks who were threatening the Suez Canal, they told King Hussein in the notorious MacMahon letter that Palestine would be Arab; whereupon the Arabs rose against the Turks, in Lawrence's "Revolt of the Desert". In the following year, however, came the secret Sykes-Picot agreement with France by which, in the event of an Allied victory Palestine was to be divided, a part of it under French rule and a part under an international condominium. In 1917 the British, their resources strained to the limit in the third year of the war, and anxious to obtain every possible assistance from world Jewry, issued the Balfour Declaration about "the national home for the Jews". It is not surprising therefore that Palestine has often been called "the too much promised land".

For Zionism the Vatican had always displayed great mistrust. Cardinal Gasparri expressed this in a letter to the Secretary General of the League of Nations on the 15th May, 1922:

The Holy See does not oppose the Jews possessing civil rights in Palestine, which are equal to those possessed by other nations and confessions; but it will not agree to their having a privileged or preponderant position, as the Mandatory power appears to propose;

[19] F.O. 371/15332, despatch from Mr. Ogilvy-Forbes, 27th March, 1931.

and it demands that the other confessional rights of the Christians are safeguarded. The Balfour project with its National Home for the Jews appears to accord them an absolute economic administration and political preponderance. In Article 4 of the Mandate a Jewish Commission is recognised — which is no less than the powerful Zionist organisation. It will work with the British administration and is accorded considerable competence in the development of the country. In Article 6, the immigration of the Jews is encouraged. In Article 11 they are favoured in being allowed to build public works, etc., etc.

To this Great Britain replied that the Vatican had misunderstood the Balfour Declaration, which had not suggested that Palestine as a whole should be converted into a Jewish National Home, but that *such a Home should be founded in Palestine* — which was quite different. The Vatican had also misunderstood the democratic principles of the mandatory system. When Sir Herbert Samuel was in Rome he visited Cardinal Gasparri and tried to explain them. "One of the features the Cardinal could not understand," Sir Herbert wrote to Winston Churchill, then Colonial Secretary, "was why the Mandate referred in various places to the *Palestine Administration* as something distinct from the *Mandatory Power*. I explained that the distinction was due to the very principle of the mandatory system, which was not equivalent to annexation, but which contemplated a gradual progress towards autonomy."[20]

The last, and most picturesque reason for Vatican objections to the Jews in the Holy Places was given by the Catholic Patriarch of Jerusalem, Mgr. Barlassina, on a visit to Rome in May 1922 when he spoke to the German Ambassador at the Vatican, von Bergen. He referred to the immorality of the new Jewish immigrants from Europe. There were now at least twenty brothels in Jerusalem, and over 500 prostitutes walked the streets (all forbidden under the Turks); and some of the Jewish colonists lived "on Marxist lines, in unmarried love". Some of the Russian Jewish immigrants had been in the habit of bathing naked in the Black Sea; that might be all right there, but they were now doing it in the Sea of Galilee, which was causing much indignation among the more conservative inhabitants.[21]

When the British arrived in Jerusalem in 1918, six different communities

[20] F.O. 371/6389, Sir H. Samuel to Mr. Churchill, 6th July, 1922.
[21] *A.A. Pol II Stellung der Kuria zum Zionismus*, (3.20–3.36), von Bergen's despatch, 24th May, 1922.

were officiating in the Basilica of the Holy Sepulchre. To each of these certain portions of the Sepulchre were assigned, and special hours allotted for their respective functions. The Catholic, the Orthodox and the Armenians had primary rights; the schismatic Syrians, Jacobites, Copts and Abyssinians somewhat lesser ones — a chapel here, an altar there. The right to cense and light a lamp was common to all. Authority to repair a roof, a floor, a pillar or a wall implied exclusive possession of that part. Several incidents in the Holy Places between the Catholics and Orthodox, involving both Fascist Italy and the Vatican, illustrate the almost insurmountable difficulties confronting the British mandatory power.

On the morning of the 4th January, 1928, a difference of opinion arose between the respective sextons in the Church of the Nativity in Bethlehem, because the Catholic Brothers had entered the Grotto before the holy vessels had been removed from the Orthodox altar at the end of Orthodox Mass. On the morning of the 5th, this difference was no longer confined to words. The Orthodox sexton Philip Monakhas delivered the first blow, striking the Italian brother, Abel Corriola, on the face. Whereupon another Italian brother, Joseph Consiglio, went to the aid of Corriola, and in a matter of seconds three Catholic and two Orthodox monks were having a general set-to around the Grotto. Notwithstanding its holiness, both sides availed themselves freely of anything that came to hand and belaboured one another with candle-sticks snatched from the respective altars. They appear to have fought one another round the Grotto and finally tumbled, a fighting mass, into the manger. The policeman on duty, finding the affair beyond his control, ran off to obtain assistance.[22] The fight must have been particularly severe because when the British District Officer arrived, the floor of the Grotto was covered with blood. As punishment, the British debarred the five monks concerned from entering the Chapel of the Nativity for periods ranging from six months to five years.

It was now that the Vatican and Fascist Italy became involved. On being informed of these sentences on Italian priests, Mgr. Barlassina, the Catholic Patriarch of Jerusalem, stated that he refused to acknowledge them until he had communicated with the Vatican; while Mussolini's paper *La Tribuna* declared the incident a British outrage on Italian citizens (30th March, 1928). "The favouritism," it wrote, "in the sentences recently imposed by the British on Italians who had been attacked by Greeks have aroused the resentment of the entire civilised world . . . Italy will not keep silent about the blood shed by her two sons. As a great

[22] F.O. 371/13031, report by British District Commissioner, 24th January, 1928.

Catholic power, Italy will invoke the justice of Rome to claim her rights."

Meanwhile the Vatican was laying claim to the Caenaculum, for which Cardinal Gasparri had made an official request. "He told me," wrote Count de Salis, the British Minister, "that the Holy See was most anxious that the Caenaculum should be restored to Catholicism . . . They would be satisfied if the restoration took place through the Italian government." Mussolini was already engaged in his Concordat negotiations, and by offering to support the Vatican claim to the Caenaculum a valuable bargaining counter could be obtained. Moreover, his plans for expansion in the Middle East were maturing, and might be furthered by embarrassing Great Britain in this matter.

The British government's attitude towards the Holy Places had always been that there should be a commission representing all the sects to adjudicate disputes, the typical "fair play" solution which had worked so well in various parts of the Empire. They had accordingly placed a plan before the League of Nations, suggesting that the Chairman of the Commission should be an American Protestant, as he would be completely impartial in adjudicating claims (neither America nor her Protestants had any interest in the Holy Places). But this did not please the Vatican. The *Osservatore Romano* wrote, "The Catholics who for centuries have been in possession of most of the sanctuaries will now find themselves presided over by an American Protestant. The Holy See maintains that no Protestant has the same belief as a Catholic in the sanctity of the Holy Places."

As the Orthodox, the Syrians, the Copts, the Moslems and the Jews all had equally good reasons for objecting to the British proposal, the British had to withdraw it. Lord Balfour announced regretfully at Geneva that Britain now invited the Latin countries to come together and work out a solution on their own. This, after several years of wrangling, the Catholic powers proved unable to do; the French would for instance have nothing to do with anything suggested by Fascist Italy. The interested parties were still locked in interminable dispute when they were overtaken by the war of 1939–1945. This was followed in 1947 by the creation of the Jewish State in Palestine. From the point of view of the Vatican little had altered in the period between 1917 and today. The Holy Places had exchanged one set of non-Christian masters for another, the Turk for the Jew.

There can be little doubt that in the inter-war years the Fascist government used the Catholic Church to infiltrate Palestine with Italian priests. It gave free passage, for instance, to all Italian missionaries bound for the Middle East and the Holy Places. These men were to constitute the nucleus of a permanent body of Italian representatives in each country, waiting for the great day of *Mare Nostrum* and the victorious invading Italian fleets and armies (as was to be seen in 1940). Mussolini's attitude was well expressed in the famous letter of the Fascist Commendatore Fontana to Mgr. Perrin, Chancellor of the Order of the Holy Sepulchre, on the 22nd February, 1927: "It is to be noted how greatly H.E. Mussolini has at heart the prestige of Catholicism and Italy in Palestine; and how it is always the wish of the Duce to acquire greater influence through our joint institutions which have such historical and political importance."

It is also surely significant that the Italian government had earlier, just after the First World War, gone to great pains in order that the few Italians who had lost their lives in the Middle East during that war should be buried in the Palestine war cemeteries. The impression which the Fascists evidently wished to create in Italian minds was that Italy had participated actively with her armed forces in 1918 "to liberate the Holy Places from the Turk". (It has since been shown that not one of the Italians who died there during that war lost his life in the actual fighting.) Between the wars the Italian government also spent large sums on founding schools and modern hospitals in Palestine. It also subsidised financially the Latin Patriarchate of Jerusalem. Individually the priests thus became the instruments, in many cases unconsciously, of the Fascist government.

5

The Abyssinian War

––––

IF THE MALTESE AND HOLY PLACES QUESTIONS REVEALED HOW the new Fascist State was prepared to exploit the Concordat, the Abyssinian war fully endorsed these revelations. In the Fascist paper *Giornale d'Italia* (22nd November, 1935) six weeks after the Italian invasion of Abyssinia, an article entitled "To fight for Italy is to fight for Catholicism" stated that Italy's avowed aim to abolish slavery was enough to justify the invasion, *on religious grounds alone*. In a series of threatening speeches before this, Mussolini had constantly referred to "the rights of Italy in Abyssinia, in a barbarous land which still practises slavery".

The Vatican deprecates the use of military force except in a "just war"; but it had always regarded Abyssinia with its slave-owning habits as particularly suited for proselytisation, and any influence exercised there by a Catholic power such as Italy could only further that process.[1] The Belgian Ambassador to the Vatican reported that the Pope disapproved of Mussolini's methods, but that he saw no prospect at the moment of

[1] Abyssinia was Catholic from the fourth to the eighth centuries A.D. when it became Coptic — the latter Christian religion, supported from Egypt, being a greater bulwark in Africa against Islam. But the Papacy always hoped that it would one day return to the Catholic fold.

persuading him to change them, and preferred not to risk any influence he had with him by representations which might prove futile.[2] The Pope feared that if Italy went to war over Abyssinia and were defeated, the Copts in Abyssinia would be greatly encouraged in their efforts to hinder Catholic proselytising. Even worse, defeat might result in the overthrow of the Fascist regime in Italy, and its replacement by Communism, or by a return to the old Liberal, anti-clerical governments. If on the other hand Italy won the war, hatred and bitterness among the Abyssinians would be directed as much against the Catholic Church as against Italy with which they would associate it.

The Vatican is always careful never to appear to take sides in any national dispute, and is well known for its elliptical pronouncements; but none could have been more elliptical than that made by the Pope on the 28th July, 1935, three months before the invasion of Abyssinia:

> Clouds darken the sky over Italy and Abyssinia; no one should deceive himself that they may not contain dire events. We hope and believe always in the peace of Christ and his realm, and we have complete confidence that nothing can happen which is not consistent with Truth, Justice and Love. One thing however appears certain to Us — namely that if the need for expansion is a fact, we must also take into consideration the right to defence, which also has its limits, and a moderation which must be observed if the defence is to remain guiltless.

Both sides could of course interpret this in their favour. Foreign diplomats accredited to the Vatican are accustomed to decipher rather than translate Papal pronouncements. The German Ambassador, von Bergen, who had been at the Vatican since 1921, was an expert at this. In his view, the Pope was simply telling Mussolini that, although Italy certainly deserved more colonies, she should not go to war for them — "We must also take into consideration the right to defence."[3] This too is how the Fascist authorities, also well versed in Papal conundrums, understood it. Mussolini immediately sent one of his Ministers to object to the last sentence and the Fascist press omitted it from its reports of the Pope's speech. What was printed gave the impression that the Pope considered Italy's claim justified.

[2] F.O. 371/19119, C. Wingfield to Sir S. Hoare, 25th July, 1938. The latter noted, "The Pope appears to be so timid as to give the impression that he supports Mussolini."

[3] A.A. Beziehungen des Vatikans zu Abissinien, 30th August, 1935.

As matters moved towards the climax in October 1935, the *Osservatore Romano* appeared to incline towards the government view, stating that French and British colonies had been acquired by war or threat of war; it also quoted Saint Augustine that war is a punishment for the guilty, and that it may purify man. On the 1st October, 1935, it published an article claiming to present impartially the attitude of both sides; but this was couched in such abstract, philosophical language that the only deduction drawn by most readers was that the editor of the paper, Conte della Torre, was still sitting on the fence.[4]

On the 3rd October, 1935 Mussolini put an end to all this moralising by attacking Abyssinia from land and air. On the 15th November the League of Nations condemned his act and applied economic sanctions against Italy.

The Vatican had never really approved of the League of Nations which, the Vatican considered, had arrogated to itself the Papal prerogative of mediation in international disputes. For on many occasions throughout history the Vatican has mediated successfully. In 1885 Leo XIII arbitrated between Germany and Spain in a dispute involving the ownership of the Caroline Islands. In 1899, Spain appealed to Rome for settlement of her quarrel with the U.S.A. The Vatican regarded assumption of this right by the newly constituted League of Nations as supererogation. It could have little sympathy for an organisation which, in the words of the Roman newspaper *Il Messagero* (7th October, 1935), "Mimicks and adulterates a function which for centuries has been the Pope's — replacing the Universal Church's administration of Justice by a typically Anglo-Saxon substitute." The Papal interdict of earlier times, which had made kings and nations tremble, was now to be replaced by the League of Nations sanctions.

The Vatican's general attitude to the League is well revealed in a conversation which Stresemann's personal emissary, Dr. Schreiber, had with Mgr. Pizzardo, the Under-Secretary of State.[5] He reported that the Vatican made a distinction between the *political* side of the League and its social or cultural side. For the first it had little use. In the words the Pope

---

[4] Conte della Torre could be even more elliptical than his master: "War brings in its train another odious entanglement — namely, that during hostilities it is difficult, if not impossible, to speak of peace without arousing a suspicion that this ideal gift contains a hidden snare. Peace is necessary, especially when it is urgent and immediate, and not only because it is urgent, but because it is practical."

[5] *A.A. Beziehungen des heiligen Stuhls zu Deutschland*, Vol. 2, 20th April, 1926.

himself used to another German Foreign Minister, Herr Curtius, "at Geneva there are too many people talking at once for anything to be achieved".[6] But as the permanent seat for social and charitable organisations, the Vatican approved of it.

When the Vatican became aware in the early twenties that its ancient right to mediate, its healing power, had been withdrawn and transferred to a lay organisation, it was careful that an article in the Italian Concordat should absolve it in the future from any responsibility for mediation in international disputes. Critics of its conduct over the Abyssinian war (and later over the wars waged by Nazi Germany), for not pronouncing openly against Italy or Germany, must read Article 24 of the Italian Concordat: "With regard to the sovereignty which is its due in the international sphere, the Holy See declares that it desires to remain extraneous to all temporal disputes and to international congresses held to deal with such things, unless the contending parties make an appeal in unison to its pacifying mission." The words "in unison" are of particular importance.

After the Abyssinian war began, the Pope therefore made no declaration beyond the oracular one desiring "Peace based on Truth, Justice and Charity". Criticism soon came from France. "The Pope's silence," wrote L'Oeuvre on the 9th October, 1935, "is equivalent to approval of Italy's act. Does Pontius Pilate rule today in the Vatican?" The French Communists of course maintained that the Pope was working in the closest collaboration with Mussolini; L'Humanité said that a secret treaty existed between Italy and the Vatican, the latter lending money for the purchase of arms to be used against Abyssinia. In England, the Archbishop of Canterbury announced that to his call for a common declaration against the Abyssinian war by all churches "the Vatican has replied negatively". George Lansbury, the leader of the British Labour Party, stated that the head of the Catholic Church had nothing better to do than to incite Italy to make war on a small defenceless country.

Against this, the Roman Catholic Archbishop of Westminster, Mgr. Hinsley, made a gallant but not altogether happily phrased defence of the Pope. "What," he asked from the pulpit, "can the poor helpless old man in the Vatican do to prevent this or any other war? What can the head of a State with no more than a handful of Papal guards do against a neighbour possessing every modern armament?" He went on to condemn Fascism as "an example of the present-day deification of Caesarism and of the tyranny which makes the individual a pawn on the chess-board of absolutism".

[6] Ibid., Vol. 3, 9th August, 1931.

The phrase about the Pope, "a poor helpless old man", from a high Catholic dignitary gave much offence at the Vatican. But what, curiously, annoyed them even more in Archbishop Hinsley's sermon was his condemnation of Fascism. Fascism with all its faults, the Vatican considered, was preferable to what might follow its overthrow, Communism or some masonic regime. The Vatican made it clear that the English Catholic Archbishop had expressed a purely personal view. (According to the British Minister to the Vatican, this well-meant sermon cost Archbishop Hinsley the Cardinal's hat he was about to receive.)[7]

A despatch from von Bergen on the 6th November, 1935 assesses the attitude of the Vatican:

The Abyssinian affair greatly perturbs the Holy See because it fears war on an international scale, and a possible change of regime in Italy leading to a strengthening of Bolshevism. All its efforts therefore are bent towards an immediate ending of the Italo-British dispute over sanctions. During the absence of the Secretary of State, Cardinal Pacelli, the Pope is dealing with the situation himself, and he has instructed the Nuncios, of whom a large number were recently in Rome, to work unceasingly for peace. In particular, the Nuncio in Paris is said to have received instructions to contact the French Prime Minister and inform him how greatly the Pope desires peace. He hopes that France will play the role of intermediary between the League and Italy. Moreover, Laval made a very good impression at the Vatican when he was here. The Pope told his closest associates how much he admired Laval's clear conception of the problem and his practical understanding.[8]

This explains why the Hoare-Laval "compromise" offering Italy most of what she wanted in Abyssinia was approved by the Pope.

If the Vatican could not, according to its principles, take sides openly in the dispute, it could not prevent the Italian episcopate from expressing their views. A good deal of latitude is normally allowed to bishops in these pronouncements, in accordance with local conditions.[9] And here there can be no doubt as to where the sympathies of the Italian episcopate lay. In his Pastoral Letter of the 19th October, the Bishop of

[7] F.O. 371/19119(20), Mr. H. Montgomery to Mr. Eden, 28th November, 1935.
[8] *A.A. Beziehungen des päpstlichen Stuhls zu Italien*, 6th November, 1935.
[9] This independence of the local episcopate from the Curia has become even more marked since the Vatican II council (1964).

Udine wrote, "It is neither timely nor fitting for us to pronounce on the rights and wrongs of the case. Our duty as Italians, and still more as Christians is to contribute to the success of our arms." The Bishop of Padua wrote on the 21st October, "In the difficult hours through which we are passing, we ask you to have faith in our statesmen and armed forces." On the 24th October, the Bishop of Cremona consecrated a number of regimental flags and said: "The blessing of God be upon these soldiers who, on African soil, will conquer new and fertile lands for the Italian genius, thereby bringing to them Roman and Christian culture. May Italy stand once again as the Christian mentor to the whole world." This consecration of regimental colours must have embarrassed the Vatican for it announced that this, or the benediction of departing soldiers, applied only to individuals, not to the soldiers' activity in the campaign — a fine ecclesiastical distinction which was lost on the Italian people who regarded the blessing as Vatican approval of the campaign.

Sanctions were now being discussed at Geneva, and Italian episcopal utterances became even more chauvinist. The Bishop of Reggio Calabria spoke on the 28th October of "our friends of yesterday [England and France] who abandon us in our hours of need": while the Bishop of Ozieri said, "The men in Geneva are completing their shameful work, sowing the seeds of new European discord in their vain attempt to suffocate the great pioneering life force of Italy, which aspires to new fields for its historic culture in the barbarian lands." The Bishop of Foligno preached in a sermon, "In return for bringing the blessings of freedom and civilisation, Italy is to be punished, in the words of the Duce, with 'the absurd crime of sanctions' — using it for the first time to starve Italy while supplying her opponent with help and arms." Sanctions had, in fact, the effect of bringing Church and State more closely together, and Cardinal Schuster of Milan spoke of Mussolini as "he who has given Italy to God and God to Italy" (imitating ludicrously the Pope's pronouncement at the time of the Concordat).

In his long account of these episcopal utterances, von Bergen, the German Ambassador attaches importance to the utterances of Cardinal Schuster for a different reason. He was Pius XI's successor in the Bishopric of Milan and a close associate of the Pope, "a man not normally regarded as particularly well disposed towards the Fascist regime".[10] Yet on the anniversary of the March on Rome Cardinal

[10] *A.A. Beziehungen des Vatikans zu Abissinien*, 6th November, 1935.

Schuster said in a sermon that the Abyssinian war "will bring the triumph of the Cross, while breaking the chains of slavery and smoothing the way for the new herald of the Evangile". He also referred to "the intrepid army of Italy which is opening the gates of Abyssinia to the Catholic faith and civilisation". "But I hear," ends von Bergen, "that the Pope, who normally holds Cardinal Schuster in the highest esteem, has found this declaration somewhat excessive."

The patriotic statements of the bishops were soon accompanied by equally patriotic acts. Because sanctions were damaging Italy economically, the government had called for sacrifices from the people. The Archbishop of Catania and Messina formed a Catholic Action group to collect gold, coins and jewellery from the faithful and donate it to the State. The Bishop of Monreale instructed his churches to melt down gold and silver votive offerings for the Fatherland. On the 8th December, 1935 the government instituted a "Battle of the Grain", with prizes for peasants who increased their food production: and many clerics, including two bishops, worked beside them in the fields. On receiving the prize for this achievement, the Bishop of Civiltà Castellana made a speech in the presence of Mussolini in which he thanked God that he had been allowed to live through this "epic day, which will demonstrate to the entire world the unity and pride of the Italian people."

Against those who denigrate our century-old culture stands the entire Italian nation, from the King to the least peasant, crying unanimously *Frangar non flectar*! No, they will not make us yield! Nor shall we ever forget this black ingratitude of those who support the barbaric slave-dealers, talking hypocritically of the sanctity of treaties which they have arbitrarily drawn up themselves. These are the nations who now gladly repudiate other treaties which called on our brave soldiers to their help when they were in danger [he was referring to the Italian entry in 1915 on the side of the Entente]. The Italian clergy pray God to grant victory to our arms, to give His blessing to Italy, her King, her Duce.

So saying the bishop took the golden chain from his neck and offered it to Mussolini.

In view of the prominence given by the Italian press to these episcopal statements, the silence of the *Osservatore Romano* was significant. The bishops had gone too far. The paper ignored them altogether until the 7th December, 1935, and then reported the sermon of Cardinal

Schuster of Milan, only to correct the way in which it had been misrepresented in the Fascist press. On the 1st December, this press had reported that Cardinal Schuster had instructed all religious establishments to hand over to the Fascist party their gold and silver objects for melting down. Now the alienation of such objects for secular use is forbidden by canon law, and his action was explained by the *Osservatore Romano*, which said that His Eminence had merely suggested that, if the need of the poor *became sufficiently pressing*, ex-voto offerings might be sacrificed to help them. The Vatican was becoming embarrassed by its bishops. But that there was sympathy for Mussolini even in certain Vatican high places is revealed in a despatch from Mr. Montgomery. "The diplomatic methods of Mgr. Pizzardo, the Under-Secretary of State, often puzzles me," he writes, "but I am inclined to explain their apparent ineptitude by the fact that Mgr. Pizzardo, in spite of the high position he holds, is a man of very limited intelligence, who is genuinely hoodwinked by Mussolini's propaganda which is so persistently and unscrupulously levelled against Great Britain."[11]

From this it will be seen, nevertheless, that statements by the Italian episcopate do not necessarily reflect the views or policy of the Curia as many people suppose. This is well described by D. A. Binchy in his *Church and State in Fascist Italy*:

> The distinction between the Vatican and the Italian Church is too much overlaid by geographical and historical associations to be clearly visible to the average non-Catholic in other countries. A sermon in the cathedral of Milan or a speech by the patriarch of Venice (examples which are not chosen quite at random) is only too frequently mistaken by the foreign press for an authoritative pronouncement from the headquarters of the Catholic Church. Surely the danger of such confusion imposes a special duty on Italian prelates to exercise discretion in their comments on public affairs. The speech by Cardinal Schuster on the Abyssinian war had a publicity value in the world press out of all proportion to its real significance . . .

The war ended suddenly, after only nine months' hostilities with total Italian victory and the Abyssinian request for an armistice. In October 1936 the Archbishop of Rhodes, Mgr. Castellani, an ex-army chaplain and fervent supporter of the Fascist regime, was sent to Abyssinia as Apostolic Visitor to investigate the spiritual needs of the inhabitants. On

[11] F.O. 371/19162, Mr. H. Montgomery to Sir S. Hoare, 14th November, 1935.

his arrival in Addis Ababa he held a pontifical Mass during which he "saluted all the heroic soldiers of the Italian army which the world admires, but at which Heaven has no need to marvel since it is their ally". Italian Catholic missionaries now replaced all foreign ones in Abyssinia, and the foreign Protestant missions were expelled. The Bible Churchmen's Society and the American Methodists were given eight days to leave.[12] Fascist xenophobia reached its peak with the expulsion of the French bishop, Mgr. Jarousseau, who had spent fifty years in the land, and had taught Haile Selassie when the Negus was a boy.[13] The head of the Coptic Church who refused to submit publicly to the Italians was beheaded.

On the 12th February, 1937, the Pope received a telegram of congratulation on the anniversary of his accession from the King of Italy. In acknowledging this, his reply was significantly addressed to, "His Majesty Victor Emmanuel III, King of Italy and Emperor of Ethiopia", and he referred to the Queen as "the Queen Empress". Under-Secretary of State, Mgr. Ottaviani, when asked by foreign diplomats if this implied formal recognition of the Italian Empire, replied that this was not the case; but that in matters of this sort it was the policy of the Vatican "to act in accordance with realities".[14]

Mussolini's satisfaction with the Vatican over the Abyssinian war was expressed characteristically some months later to the German Ambassador at the Quirinal. Von Neurath had complained of the growing Vatican hostility to Nazi Germany; and Mussolini gave him a word of advice, from his long experience of dealing with the Vatican. Grant the Vatican, he recommended, *little* concessions, many but *little* — free tickets for priests on the railways, ringing State bells for Catholic ceremonies, tax concessions to the Cardinals, etc., etc. By these means, Mussolini claimed to have won them over completely. "Why," he said, "they even declared the Abyssinian war a Holy War!"[15]

Once the war had started, the Italian people regarded it as a crusade, as well as a colonisation comparable to that undertaken in Africa earlier by the British and French. Sanctions they saw as a monstrous injustice inspired by the jealousy of these "sated powers". Any open criticism of the war by the Pope after the 3rd October, 1935 they would have

---

[12] F.O. 371/20938, Consul Stonehewer-Bird to F.O., 22nd March, 1937.
[13] Ibid., 14th June, 1937.
[14] F.O. Annual Report for 1937 from the Holy See, Mr. Osborne to Mr. Eden.
[15] *A.A. Pol III Beziehungen des heiligen Stuhls zu Deutschland*, Vol. 2, von Neurath's despatch, 4th May, 1937.

rejected indignantly. In a secret memorandum shown to Mr. Montgomery, the British Chargé d'Affaires, the Pope explained why he could not pronounce. He was aware, he said, that he was thus laying himself open to the charge of inaction but, being more concerned with the good of humanity than with his own reputation, he was prepared to face unfavourable criticism rather than, by untimely pronouncements, to prejudice his chances of stopping the war. The memorandum added that by Article 24 of the Italian Concordat the Pope had undertaken "to remain outside temporal conflicts unless the parties concerned appeal in unison for the pacifying mission of the Holy See". On this occasion neither party had appealed. Such was the Papal apologia.[16]

Nevertheless, after the Abyssinian war the reputation of the Papacy abroad suffered from what was held to be its too great dependence on Fascism. There were many, Catholics and non-Catholics, who wondered whether the immediate and material gains of the Lateran treaty had not been too highly paid for by the loss of spiritual and moral independence, of that universality on which the authority and tradition of the Church are based.

[16] F.O. 371/19136, Mr. H. Montgomery to Sir S. Hoare. He says he cannot divulge the name of the author who has the ear of the Pope.

6

The Anti-clerical States— France, Czechoslovakia and Mexico

IN OUR TIME (1971) MAURICE DRUON CAN WRITE AUTHORITATIVELY IN *Le Monde* that "anti-clericalism has now been relegated to the museum". But in the 1920s, the main adversaries of the Vatican still appeared to be the anti-clerical States, such as Liberal Italy and Republican France (the greater danger, Russian Communism did not become apparent until about 1928).[1] The term "anti-clerical" is often misunderstood in Protestant countries, where it is taken as a synonym for "anti-religious". It is true that an anti-religious programme is by implication "anti-clerical"; but an "anti-clerical" programme is not necessarily "anti-religious", and it may even be sponsored by men like Lord Strickland who are practising Catholics. As a political phenomenon it is confined almost entirely to traditional Catholic countries, as well as to a few countries like Germany where a large proportion of the population has always been Catholic. In traditionally Protestant states it is virtually unknown; for their Churches

[1] See below, Chapter Nine, "Conversion and Persecution in Russia".

do not possess the same power. The Protestant Churches are auto-cephalous, and their dominion does not extend beyond national boundaries; nor do their members acknowledge a spiritual authority vested in a foreigner. Nor are the Protestant clergy so numerous or so well organised a corporate body as are the Catholics. The rule of celibacy also serves to place the Roman Catholic clergy in a class apart, to emphasise the difference between them and the layman. Above all, the individual Protestant cleric is not invested with the tremendous sacramental powers which the Catholic Church claims for the lowliest of its priests.

For the rulers of traditionally Catholic countries, therefore, the Catholic Church represents a most formidable institution, powerfully organised, rigidly disciplined, strong with the strength of centuries of privilege and ascendancy, and still in close touch with the ordinary people through the medium of its parish priests. In theory, the Catholic Church regards itself as a higher power than the State and rejects the notion that its activities can be regulated by the State. Nor do political and territorial boundaries represent for it anything more than a temporary administrative framework, which may well change or disappear with time.

In modern times France has always been the leading anti-clerical nation. What France does today, the world does tomorrow; and the European Free-thinkers of the nineteenth century would not have been so bold had there been no Voltaire, Rousseau, nor a French Revolution. During that Revolution the Catholic religion was almost entirely eradicated from the land. Thousands of priests were guillotined or exiled, religious statues were overturned and mutilated, churches despoiled. Towns, roads, market-places bearing the names of saints were given "rational" titles; Saint Germaine-en-Laye became Montagne-Bel-Air; Saint Tropez, Heraclee; Saint Etienne, Armes. New-born babies were "baptised" Cato, Brutus, Marat or Love-of-Satan. The seven-day week with its day of religion was replaced by the ten-day week with its Day of Joy.

Although this persecution was modified under the Empire, it was not long before the volatile French people, always avid of change, were as disillusioned with the Revolution and its atheism as with the old cleri-calism. Many of them wished to return, if not to devout belief, at least to the Catholic ethics and ceremonies of their fathers. They now preferred, it was said, "The church bells without the priests to the priests without the church bells". By the end of the nineteenth century, religion had revived in France and the Church had recaptured much of the ground lost in the Revolution.

Nevertheless, the events between 1793 and 1815 had left their mark; in no European country would there ever be so many Free-thinkers, Freemasons, Socialist Idealists, cynics, atheists and other "Progressives" as in France. These men, in the persons of the rulers of the Third Republic after 1870, saw that the Church was stealing back into its old position, and they were determined to stop it. Regarding themselves as the heirs to the Revolution, their spokesman, Emile Combes, said the Catholic Church was "organised once again in a despotic hierarchy leading the people to an ideal totally opposed to that of modern society, plotting openly the destruction of the political and social edifice constructed by the French Revolution. We have to undo in probably a very short time the clerical reaction of a century."

The Separation Laws which he introduced, in 1904, dissolved the monastic Orders once again, separated Church and State, dispossessed the former of its buildings and wealth, and abolished religious education for the young. In 1905, he denounced the existing Concordat and broke off relations with the Vatican. The ghost of Danton stalked the land, and Henri Béranger echoed the language of *La Lanterne*: "The day is coming when the police societies will hound down the traffickers in Masses like criminals... against the priest everything is permissible, the mad dog which every passer-by has a right to put down, lest its virus infects the flock..."

The State declared its complete indifference to religion, either for it or against it. Article 2 of the Law stated: "The Republic will neither recognise, support nor defray the expenses of any religious cult." Provided the various Churches, Catholic, Jewish, Calvinist, etc. did not infringe civil law, they could exist like any corporate body, the Association of Pastry-Bakers or the League of the Fishermen. Unlike the Jacobin fanatics of 1793, however, the masonic leaders of the Third Republic realised that to ignore the Church's existence altogether was Utopian and premature. They therefore made provision for worship in the confiscated churches. By the law of 1905, *Associations Cultuelles* were constituted for the respective cults, based on the unit of the parish. They were bodies of church-going laymen who were to hold and administer a part of church property, and provide from it funds for maintaining buildings and holding services; they would also pay the stipends of the clergy.

The minority faiths, Calvinist, Nonconformists, Jewish, etc., accepted this system, even seeing certain advantages in the *Associations Cultuelles*. Henceforth they could choose their own hierarchy, the pastors and rabbis, without reference to the State; their stipends would be paid and buildings maintained. But the Vatican opposed this steadfastly. It refused to recognise a system which, it contended, would reduce religion to a kind of co-operative society. The committees which ran the *Associations Cultuelles* were to be composed of laymen so that, in the words of the Italian paper *La Tribuna*, "Catholic bishops would have to take their orders from the local chemist, barber or land surveyor." To a system as hierarchical as the Catholic Church such a democratically constituted body was inconceivable; and the Vatican announced that until Catholic property had been restored, it did not intend even to discuss the *Associations Cultuelles*. In his encyclical *Vehementer* (11th February, 1906) Pius X solemnly condemned the Separation Laws; and the *Associations Cultuelles* in the encyclical *Gravissimo officii munere* (10th August, 1906): "We declare that no Catholic may join the *Associations Cultuelles*, so long as it is not laid down legally and unequivocally that the Divine Constitution of the Catholic Church, the inalienable right of the Roman Pontiff and His Bishops, shall enjoy in the said Associations complete liberty."

The Catholic clergy of France obeyed him loyally, making all the sacrifices which this entailed; for by refusing to recognise the *Associations Cultuelles*, the Church forfeited some thirty million francs annually, in stipends and money for the upkeep of its buildings. It now had to live a hand-to-mouth existence, funds being available only from charitable and private sources, or collected at services, marriages, baptisms, etc. The monastic Orders also followed the Papal ruling, remaining in their monasteries and convents until forcibly ejected. The worst incident occurred at the famous Grande Chartreuse, where the officer entrusted with the ejection of the monks gave the order to his troops — and then resigned his commission. Hundreds of peasants armed with sticks, carts, trees and rocks blocked the roads. The troops arrived to find fires burning on the hillsides and the church bells tolling. They broke down the barriers and doors, to find the monks inside at their devotions. They had to carry them bodily away, while the crowd around them sang the *Parce Dominum*.

By 1914, after a decade of the Separation Laws, many of the 10,000 parishes in France were without an incumbent. In most rural dioceses, the priests had four or five parishes to administer, so that Mass could be celebrated in each not more than once a month. Unless the priest lived among rich parishioners, he generally had to practise a side-profession, the favourite being bee-keeping. The intake of new priests declined, and until as late as 1925 the French clergy was enlisting foreign priests, particularly from Holland.

The result of all this politically was, as far as the Vatican was concerned, less disastrous. The French government ceased to have any influence in the decisions taken in France by the Church, which now looked directly to Rome. A member of Parliament, M. Meline, had warned M. Combes at the time of the Separation Laws: "The principal effect will be to make the Catholics more Catholic. The laws will increase the authority of the Pope over the clergy, making them bolder and more hostile to the Republic." Certain members of the Curia such as Cardinal de Lai actually welcomed the Separation Laws, which they considered strengthened the Pope's authority over the hitherto too independent Gallican clergy. Bishops of pronounced anti-Republican and ultramontane tendencies were now appointed to the French sees; so that by 1914 the French episcopate had become more Papal than the Pope, allied with all that was most reactionary in the Third Republic.

Between 1905 and 1914, Combes's anti-clericals could rely on the support of most of the population; *bouffer du curé* was a popular phrase. But after the war, thanks to the patriotism and heroism of the clergy, particularly at the front where they fought as ordinary soldiers, the public attitude changed. Of the 80,000 priests from all countries who took an active part in the war, 45,000 were French; and of these, 5,800 died, most of them in action.[2] This was the famous *Union Sacrée*, of layman and priest, forged by their comradeship in the trenches. The religious questions which had dominated French politics between 1900 and 1914 were replaced in the public mind after the war by the more pressing ones of reparations and reconstruction of the devastated territories.

During the war France also realised what she had lost by breaking off relations with the Vatican. Connected by bishops and Nuncios with all parts of the world, the Vatican was well informed on the progress of the war; and the Central Powers, in particular Austria-Hungary, had used Rome as a listening-post. Other countries which were not represented at the Vatican also quickly became aware of this, and established legations: Great Britain in 1914, Holland in 1917, Japan in 1917; Finland, Poland and Peru by 1919. "Why," complained the French député, Robert David, "should France not be represented in this marvellous observatory?"[3] Also, by closing the seminaries which trained her foreign missionaries France had diminished her influence in the world. For until the Separation Laws, three-quarters of the Catholic missionaries in the

---

[2] *A.A. Beziehungen zu Frankreich*, Vol. 2. The diocese of Coutances, for instance, lost 112 priests and seminaries in the war, while only five joined the priesthood.

[3] France attempted to offset this disadvantage during the war by sending the député, M. Denys Cochin, as representative to the Vatican; but, not having an official position, he achieved very little.

Near and Far East had been French; and France had always been regarded in Rome as the protector of the Catholics in these lands. In the Levant, her diplomatic representative at Catholic ceremonies was granted liturgical honours, which were withheld from other nations; and she had the right to appoint the Apostolic Visitor in Baghdad, and the Latin Bishop of Alexandria.

After 1905, the Vatican naturally withdrew these privileges. In Constantinople, it installed an Italian as Apostolic Delegate, and not the customary Frenchman; and liturgical honours were withdrawn from the French Ambassador. By 1918, French missionary influence in Iraq was almost extinct; while in Egypt, a new Franciscan college for native priests, almost entirely Italian in character, was inaugurated. In Palestine, the French religious Orders were replaced by Belgians, Americans and Germans. The Vatican was well aware of its power, and Cardinal Gasparri told the British Chargé d'Affaires, Mr. A. W. G. Randall, "It is well known that French cultural influence is bound up with the religious Orders. When I was in Lima, there were only a handful of French laymen, but many times the number of British, Italians and Germans. Yet thanks to the work of the French religious schools, orphanages and hospitals, the great prestige of the French language and culture was out of all proportion to the number of French residents.[4]

The headquarters of the Catholic missions for the Far East had been the Sainte Enfance in Lyons, where missionary contributions had been received from all over the world. After 1918, most of this money came from the U.S.A., and the American Catholic bishops now requested that, as France had no relations with the Vatican, the headquarters should be removed to Rome. The Vatican agreed, and another source of influence was lost to France.

A delegation of university professors was now sent by the French government to report on the French position in South America. Its leaders, M. Georges Dumas, a Protestant, and M. Levy Bruhl, a Jew and contributor to the Communist newspaper *L'Humanité*, reported that, if only in the interest of French foreign policy, the seminaries for training foreign missionaries should be reinstated in France. The result was that the Président du Conseil, M. Aristide Briand, now attempted to restore diplomatic relations with the Vatican. He took advantage of the canonisation of Joan of Arc in 1920 to send a delegation to Rome. The German Ambassador, von Bergen, reported: "The French are using the canonisation of the Maid of Orleans for political purposes. About a hundred

[4] F.O. 371/13348, Mr. Randall to Lord Cushenden, September 1928.

French deputies and senators have come to Rome, in special trains at State expense, together with a mass of French upper and lower clergy."[5]

Some months later Briand addressed the Foreign Affairs Commission on the subject of French religious establishments in the East, "whose influence is keenly contested by certain foreign powers".[6] He said that relations with the Vatican must be re-established, and to reassure the anti-clericals, of whom there was a large body in Parliament, he insisted that the problem was entirely one of foreign policy. He had obtained a formal assurance from Rome that the existing lay legislation in France would be respected; no question of French internal affairs would be discussed at the Vatican. The Commission was at first hostile to the proposal, the left-wing members fearing, its spokesman said, "intrigues by the Nuncio and ultramontane conspiracies". Paul Boncour in the Chambre said that "the notion of political advantage from a resumption of relations with the Holy See is erroneous"; and he implored the Chambre to "remain true to the principles of 1789". But Briand persevered and his proposal was passed by 391 votes to 179. On the 19th May, 1921, a Catholic senator, M. Jonnart, was appointed French Ambassador to the Vatican.

His immediate problem was to adapt the laws of the *Associations Cultuelles* to Vatican requirements. After much wrangling agreement was reached in July 1922, and Pius XI announced that he would accept the formation of *Associations Diocésains*, whose object "will be to provide for the cost and maintenance of religious worship, and which will be recognised by the State as possessing juridical personality".[7] The word "*cultuelle*" was replaced by "*diocésain*" to make the hierarchical character clear. In return, the Vatican agreed to recognise France's protectorate over Catholics in the East, and to give support to French ceremonies.

Opposition to this agreement came not only from the French anti-clericals but also from the French bishops who had survived surprisingly well under the Separation Laws; they found it very agreeable without a Nuncio from Rome to supervise them. They were now far from pleased that the new Nuncio, Mgr. Ceretti, attended French government ceremonies, where he received full honours. When he gave his advice about clerical representation in the Ruhr, they regarded it as "interference in our affairs".[8] The German Embassy at the Vatican reported how "Mgr.

[5] *A.A. Beziehungen zu Frankreich*, Vol. 3.

[6] F.O. 371/6984, report of speech by Lord Hardinge to Lord Curzon, 26th March, 1921.

[7] F.O. 371/10535, Sir O. Russell to Mr. Macdonald, 24th January, 1924.

[8] *Germania*, 23rd August, 1924.

Ceretti has been assiduously courting left-wing politicians in Paris . . . he travels all over the country, bestowing benedictions where the French bishops are accustomed to give them."[9]

At this point, when the fruits of the new clerical policy were beginning to be felt, M. Briand was defeated in the 1924 elections, and his moderate right-wing government was replaced by a Radical-Socialist "Cartel" under Edouard Herriot. The new President could obtain his majority only with the support of the anti-clericals, who demanded that the Embassy at the Vatican should immediately be suppressed, and the funds devoted to establishing diplomatic relations with Soviet Russia.[10] To the old criticisms of the Church they added new ones. The Pope had just addressed a letter to the French bishops containing the phrase, "The best guarantee of peace is not a wood of bayonets, but mutual trust and esteem". This, they said, was a criticism of France for sending her troops into the Rhineland; the Vatican was pro-German.[11] To the deputé David's contention that the Vatican was "a marvellous observatory", they replied, "It is no more than a concierge's lodge, the first *potinière* in the world, where you hear more gossip than information."[12] In June 1924, the French mission to the Vatican was recalled.

To justify this, Herriot launched out into a long attack on the Vatican's "pro-German policy during the war". He said that Benedict XV had tried to persuade the U.S.A. to stop sending food, weapons and munitions to the Allies; nor had he spoken up against the invasion of Belgium. The Vatican had tried to sow mistrust and discord among the Allies; for example, it had asked the French, in the event of the fall of Constantinople, to secure Haja Sophia for the Catholic Church — this being a way of undermining the French-Russian alliance. He said that, "Vatican propaganda in the Italian Army had contributed to the Italian collapse at Caporetto; that the Holy See was an uncompromising adversary of the Versailles treaty, and had opposed the French occupation of the Ruhr."[13]

Strangely, the party which seemed the least concerned by all this was the Vatican itself, and its imperturbable Secretary of State, Cardinal Gasparri. To Sir Odo Russell he said:

[9] *A.A. Beziehungen des päpstlichen Stuhls zu fremden Staaten*, Vol. 1, 17th June, 1922.

[10] *Le Temps*, 24th October, 1924.

[11] *A.A. Beziehungen zu Frankreich*, Vol. 2, Pius XI's letter, June 1923.

[12] *L'Ere Nouvelle*, 22nd September, 1924; also F.O. 371/11045, Mr. E. Phipps to Sir E. Crewe, 26th March, 1925.

[13] Commentary on this in *Osservatore Romano*, 7th February, 1925.

It was not the Holy See who raised a finger to re-establish relations with France after the long interruption. It was the French government and the French people who seized the initiative for their own political ends and approached the Vatican. As twenty-five states consider it advantageous to be represented here, it is not surprising that France dislikes the idea of remaining any longer in the cold. It is inconceivable that, after all the trouble the French took to pick up the threads, they should be so soon discarded. How will France now exercise her protectorate over Christians in the East — a question which will become even more acute when, as will shortly be seen, the Holy See despatches its Internuncio to China? The French will view that act with disapproval — but who will there be to protest, if they have no Ambassador here? Never in the history of France has she been more in need of support to maintain her international prestige; but if, as M. Herriot threatens, the law against the Congregations is applied, France will instantly lose a large measure of that moral support and sympathy which would otherwise flow to her through Catholic channels from abroad. There are many in France who will realise the futility of the course pursued by M. Herriot. If however, in spite of these disadvantages, France decides to cut the knot, let her do so. She alone will suffer, not the Holy See.[14]

If the Vatican remained unperturbed, the French bishops were delighted that the French government had committed another blunder, and they issued one of the most strongly worded declarations ever uttered by churchmen against the civil power. They recommended the Catholics of France to "imitate the Communist methods" and go on strike to ruin the economy of the country. The Communist strikers, they said, went *en masse* to the doors of the Mairies, Ministeries and Prefectures, where they presented their ultimatum. The Catholics should do the same. "What we Catholics have lacked — and surely we can do better than the Godless do? — is unity. Let us unite! Never in fifty years has the moment been more auspicious. Let us act now!"[15]

Faced with this, Herriot introduced a motion in the Chambre censuring the bishops' declaration as a call to civil war (19th March, 1925). He contrasted the pure "Christianity of the catacombs" with the modern "Christianity of the bankers", identifying the bishops with the latter. This remark in the tensely wrought Chambre acted like a bombshell, and pandemonium broke loose. The right-wing deputies began banging the

[14] F.O. 371/10535, report of conversation with Cardinal Gasparri, 7th June, 1925.

[15] Reported in *L'Action Française*, 12th March, 1925.

lids of their desks to drown the rest of Herriot's speech; while those of the left rose at intervals to acclaim him. They soon came to blows, and the whole Chambre was a seething mass of furious, struggling humanity. Painlevé, the President, was so overcome that he forgot to put on his hat, which would automatically have suspended the sitting; he stood surveying the scene in bewilderment hopelessly waving his arms. The Marquis de la Ferronaye, who used a gross word to Herriot, was removed from the hall *manu militari*.[16]

Three weeks later, the peripeteia of democracy operated again, this time in favour of the Vatican. Herriot had barely passed three-quarters of his anti-clerical legislation when, just before Easter 1925, his government fell on a relatively unimportant tax issue.[17] A new government was formed under Painlevé, who managed to obtain a majority without the help of the Left "Cartel" and the anti-clericals. He immediately announced that the Embassy at the Vatican was to be re-established; and M. Jonnart returned to Rome. With this, Franco-Vatican relations entered, after over twenty years, into calmer waters.

To dismantle the Combes anti-clerical legislation took another three years and, in face of a sizeable left-wing minority in the Chambre, all manner of subterfuges had to be employed. Any attempt at introducing a direct bill, granting the restoration of Church property to the diocesan associations, or re-establishing the missionary colleges in France, was met with such opposition that finally the Government had to slip two articles dealing with it, numbers 70 and 71, into the annual Finance Bill. The manoeuvre was successful. Of the twenty anti-clerical members on the Finance Commission, only six were present when Articles 70 and 71 came up for the vote. They were hastily passed before the other fourteen anti-clericals could return to veto the measure. The Finance Bill had been lying on the consultation table for the customary six weeks before the vote, but they had not taken the trouble to read as far as Articles 70 and 71.

Apart from the Action Française affair (see below, Chapter 7) relations between the Vatican and the French State now remained undisturbed until the Second World War. The ghost of Combes walked once again in 1928, when Edouard Herriot unveiled a statue to him, and its nose was knocked

---

[16] F.O. 371/11045, debate reported in despatch from Mr. E. Phipps to Sir E. Crowe, 22nd March, 1925.

[17] F.O. 371/11050, April 1925. Cardinal Gasparri's comment on hearing of the fall of Herriot at this auspicious season of the year was, "The Holy See could not have had a better Easter egg," adding, "If M. Herriot's successor is not much better, he cannot be much worse."

off by youths of the Action Française. The last word belongs to the imperturbable Gasparri. The German Ambassador told him that France would now exercise great pressure on the Vatican through her skilful new Ambassador, the Vicomte de Fontenay; von Bergen wondered if the Vatican would be able to resist his blandishments. Cardinal Gasparri replied, "I think I should know how to defend myself by now, don't you?"[18]

It is well known that the new Czechoslovak State created at Versailles modelled itself proudly on the French Third Republic. Winston Churchill in *The Second World War* writes, "For twenty years Masaryk and Benes were the faithful allies, almost the vassals, of the French. They always supported French policies and French interests at the League of Nations and elsewhere." So great was this Czech admiration for all things French that Masaryk and Benes, who were Free-thinkers, introduced into their new state the same anti-clerical laws which were in force in France between 1904 and 1925.

These two Czechs had good cause for disliking the Vatican. During the preceding three hundred years since the Battle of the White Mountain which had obliterated their State, the Habsburgs had ingeniously used the Catholic Church to keep them in bondage. A devout peasantry had followed the rulings of the priests, who in turn had followed those of the bishops who, thanks to a concordat with Rome which was most favourable to Austria, were nominated by His Apostolic Majesty in Vienna. That the mark left on Bohemia, particularly in the capital Prague, by the Habsburgs is more religious than secular can still be seen today in the magnificent baroque churches built by Fischer von Erlach and other Austrian architects. Even today, the people of Prague still ruefully refer to the baroque as "the Jesuit style". After the Austrian victory at the White Mountain in 1620, the captured Czech flags were sent to Rome, where they remain to this day in the Church of Santa Maria della Vittoria, an ever-present reminder to the Czechs that the Habsburg State and the Vatican were once allied in the overthrow of their liberties. The biggest blow of all was the immolation at Constance in 1415 of the Czech national hero, John Hus, as a heretic.

When therefore the Habsburg monarchy fell in 1918 and the Czechs regained their liberties, it is not surprising that the Head of the new State, Masaryk, declared, "We have got rid of Vienna. Now we will get rid of Rome!" And having passed the Separation Laws on the French model, he resurrected in 1925 the Hussite or Czech National Church. This had been

[18] *A.A. Beziehungen zu Frankreich*, Vol. 4, von Bergen's despatch.

founded in the fifteenth century by John Hus. Its four articles were: the word of God to be freely preached; the sacrament to be in both kinds; priests and monks to be deprived of their worldly wealth; mortal sins of clergy to be punished in civil courts. Its avowed intention was to discard traditional Catholic dogma and conform to the teaching of modern thought. Obliterated after the Battle of the White Mountain it was formally resurrected on the 6th January, 1925 in the Church of St. Nicholas, Prague, when three Czech bishops were installed in the presence of representatives from the Ministry of Education, the Hus Theological Faculty and other prominent laymen.

The new regime was supported in this anti-Catholic policy by a number of the Catholic clergy themselves, intoxicated like everyone else with the new independence. These Catholic priests demanded that Czech should be the liturgical language, and they announced that they intended to marry. It was a married Catholic priest, the defrocked Zahranik, who first celebrated Mass in the vernacular in the same church. Another new law enacted that where more than half the population of a village were in favour of the Hussite National Church, the Catholic Church's property in that place became Hussite. By the end of 1925, the Hussite Church had 200,000 members, all lapsed Catholics, and 150 parishes. In some places Catholic schools were forcibly closed, in others Catholic Orders forcibly ejected from their monasteries. The spirit of Combes, the French hammer of the Church, had returned in another land. In their blind admiration for all things French, however, the new leaders of Czechoslovakia seemed to have forgotten that much had changed in France since 1904.

The next attack was on Church lands. One of Masaryk's maxims was "The land belongs to the people, and will be returned to the people". Sequestration laws were therefore passed, and a tax of 140 million crowns a year levied on Church property. The Church was forced to sell works of art in order to pay it. The tension increased until a direct collision with the Vatican became inevitable. It occurred on the occasion of the anniversary of the death of John Hus.

The Czechs do not possess a large selection of figures capable of fulfilling the role of national hero, around which tradition can crystallise. The Frenchman bows at the Invalides, the American feels inspired before Mount Vernon, the Englishman hangs about Trafalgar Square. The Czech now went to the John Hus memorial, a piece of flamboyant modern sculpture in the Old Town square. The government proposed to make the anniversary of Hus's immolation at the hands of Rome a national holiday and day of commemoration; and in the presence of representatives of many

Protestant nations, the Hus celebrations took place on the 6th July, 1925. Wreaths were deposed around his statue in the Old Town square, and eulogies about "the Czech martyr" pronounced. A Danish visitor declared that the object of the commemoration was "to condemn the Holy See as the irreconcilable enemy of civilisation and the Bohemian nation, both of which are incarnated in the person of the glorious martyr of Constance".

Further insult to the Vatican was seen in the ostentatious hoisting of the Hussite national flag on the Hradcin opposite the palace of the Papal Nuncio. It displayed the chalice of the Czech National Church. When the Nuncio made a formal protest to the Foreign Minister, Dr. Benes, about the presence of the Czech President at this anti-Catholic ceremony, Dr. Benes replied that the President had attended in a private, not an official capacity. This explanation was judged inadequate by the Vatican which regarded the whole affair as a studied insult. It accordingly broke off all relations and recalled the Nuncio from Prague.

The Secretary of State at the Vatican, Cardinal Gasparri, took all this with his usual calm, observing to the British Minister that the reformers would almost certainly overreach themselves. "Let them go ahead," he said. "The Church will not be the one to suffer from such a policy."[19] He added that although the new men who had come to the helm in Czechoslovakia had any amount of self-confidence and theories of perfection, they possessed neither knowledge nor experience of government. He was soon to be proved correct.

The new Czech National or Hussite Church had not been in existence more than three years before it began to show signs of schism. One group headed by Archbishop Pavlik of Olmütz, was in favour of joining the Orthodox Church; while another around Dr. Farsky, Archbishop of Prague, wished to join the Methodists. Once the first enthusiasm for the Czech National Church had worn off, it did not develop as its founders had planned. It remained no more than a large sect, without making any impression on, let alone eradicating, Catholicism, particularly among the devout Slovak peasantry. On the contrary, the Catholic element was represented with increasing weight in Parliament by the Christian Social party, which was biding its time. This came in 1926 with a radical change in the political situation. The All-National coalition, with its strong anti-clerical basis, collapsed, chiefly out of inertia after ruling for so long. Masaryk and Benes were now faced with the alternative, if they were to remain in power, of enlisting either the help of the powerful Sudeten-German party (three million in a state of only nine million), or the

[19] F.O. 371/10677, despatch from Sir O. Russell, 10th July, 1925.

Christian Socials (Catholics). They did not hesitate. The Sudeten-Germans had long been noisily proclaiming their intention of destroying the State created by Versailles and reverting to Germany (which with Hitler's help in 1938 they were to do); while the Christian Socials were at least patriotic Czechs and Slovaks. In the new government, the Christian Socials were given six portfolios. As Mr. Charles Dodd of the British Embassy reported to Sir Austen Chamberlain, "This has shown that not only is Czech nationalism as strong as ever, but also that anti-religious passions will bow before the material interests of the country."[20]

The Vatican could now make some reply to the attacks it had, impotently, had to withstand for the last six years. On the 6th March, 1926, in a Pastoral Letter read from all the pulpits in Bratislava, the Catholic episcopate excluded Communists, Socialists, Freemasons and sundry Liberals from the rites of baptism, marriage and burial. A howl of rage went up at this from the Socialists and Reformers. They called on the government to discipline the bishops by applying the land reform in all its vigour to the Church estates. So loud was their protest that the Archbishops of Prague and Olmütz, to show their support for those of Slovakia, issued a statement defending the Pastoral Letter. Nevertheless, in some hundred places in Slovakia, where priests had read the Letter from their pulpits, they were indicted before the courts.

The Vatican was fully aware that the Slovaks were a highly religious people, and Gasparri had carefully studied the new Czech Constitution. Still much influenced by the French brand of democracy, the new Czech leaders had enacted that in the voting for the President every seven years, a three-fifths majority in Parliament was necessary. The time for the new presidential election was approaching, and a majority of this size in favour of Masaryk could be obtained only, once again, with the support of either the Sudeten-Germans or the Christian Social party. Again, the leaders did not hesitate. This, in the simplest terms, explains why Dr. Benes suddenly appeared in Rome to discuss a modus vivendi with the Vatican. It was ironical that now, when he and Masaryk would have welcomed a concordat, their own constitution rendered it impossible — for this too would require a three-fifths majority in Parliament; and this the Left-wing parties would frustrate. If ever men were "hoist with their own petard" it was the group of Socialist Progressives who had come to power with Masaryk. He had to eat his words of 1919 — "We have got rid of Vienna; now we will get rid of Rome."

[20] 6th March, 1925.

The Vatican was in no hurry, particularly in dealing with a State which it saw was not properly consolidated, and Benes was made to cool his heels for a while. It was no longer a question of separation of Church and State, but of what form an agreement with the Vatican would take. As a concordat could not obtain the necessary parliamentary majority in Prague, a compromise was reached in the so-called modus vivendi with the Vatican, which did not require parliamentary approval. It contained six main clauses and was signed by Cardinal Gasparri on the 2nd February, 1928, three years after the withdrawal of the Papal Nuncio from Prague at the time of the Hus celebrations. The principal concession to the Church was that the property confiscated in the land reforms was restored; and the State renounced all claims as heirs to the Habsburgs in the nomination of bishops. The Nunciature in Prague was filled again, in the person of Mgr. Ciriaci; and on the 10th June, 1928 Redinski, the new Czech Minister to the Vatican, presented his credentials and expressed President Masaryk's esteem and regard for His Holiness. Cardinal Gasparri told Sir O. Russell, "The controversy over John Hus has been relegated to oblivion, where it always belonged."[21]

Relations between Church and State now remained tranquil until the Sudeten-German problem momentarily bedevilled them in 1931. Of the three million Sudeten-Germans, ninety-five per cent were Catholic; hence the interest of the Vatican in what was to become known as "the Sudeten problem". With Hitler in power across the frontier, these Sudeten-Germans, noisy enough at the best of times, became overweening, occupying the political platform increasingly and attempting to seize every lever of power. One of these was the bishopric of Leitmeritzer, for which they persuaded the Archbishop of Prague to support their candidate. The Papal Nuncio, acting on instructions from Rome, opposed this because, "the Sudeten-Germans are proposing this candidate less on religious grounds than from a political and nationalist consideration".[22] (This sentence may sound mild enough, but it is significant as revealing that the Vatican was well aware, as early as 1931, of the Nazi methods, which were to become so familiar throughout Europe.) The Sudeten candidate was vociferously supported by the German Catholics in the Sudetenland, whose powerful local press attacked the Nuncio in the grossest terms. To this the Vatican reacted with unusual vigour and promptitude. The

[21] F.O. 371/12951, despatch from Sir O. Russell, 10th June, 1928.
[22] A.A. Pol III Beziehungen des heiligen Stuhls zu Tschechoslovaakei, despatch dated 17th October, 1931.

Nuncio, who had been recalled once again to Rome, returned with plenary powers to deal with the pro-Sudeten Archbishop of Prague. He convened a bishops' conference at Olmütz which pronounced an anathema on the Sudeten Catholics and their press. Catholics were forbidden to read the two main Sudeten newspapers, *Deutsche Presse* and *Egerland*; and the priests who had written articles in them against the Nuncio were suspended *a divinis*. The professor of the Czech Catholic Theological Institute, who had supported Sudeten-German demands, was relieved of his professorship. The *Osservatore Romano* published the text of the Pope's letter to the Olmütz Bishops' Conference fully approving their decision, and stating that the Sudeten Catholics, in supporting the Archbishop of Prague, had erred. The result was that the pro-Sudeten Archbishop of Prague announced his retirement. Once again the Vatican had triumphed.

This may be regarded as the Vatican's first brush with the Nazis. It was the forerunner of many to come. The Nazi press in Germany took up the challenge, castigating the Vatican for "interfering in Czech internal affairs". The *Völkischer Beobachter*, which could always be relied on to produce something sensational, reported that the Pope, Dr. Benes and Litvinov, the Russian Foreign Minister, had met secretly in Prague to bring about a Habsburg restoration, which the Russians would welcome as directed against Germany. Even more sensational, a week later it reported that the Pope and Stalin had met on a boat in the middle of the Marmora Sea near the island of Prinkipo, "the Pope dressed as a simple priest", having been flown to Turkey in an aeroplane lent by the Italian government. Stalin and the Pope had agreed to provide Hungary with heavy armaments from Russia, for which the Vatican would pay, to bring about a Habsburg restoration and destroy Czechoslovakia. In view of the much worse fate which was to befall this unhappy land in 1938, many Czech patriots may since have wished that this German fairy-tale was true.

The anti-clerical movement of the twenties was a serious challenge to the Church. But it was not violent; no one was killed by the Separation Laws in France or Czechoslovakia. In Mexico in 1926, the movement became revolutionary and many thousands of people died violent deaths during its three years; for Spanish violence and intransigence are combined in the Mexican mestizo with Indian lack of self-restraint to produce a highly inflammable mixture.

The quest for gold and the propagation of the faith were the principal objects of the conquest of Mexico begun in 1519 by Cortes. In the early days, the worldliness and greed of the conquistadores was matched by the good works and devotion of the priesthood. The achievements of the Spanish missionaries, who at the risk of their lives converted savage and remote tribes, was no less courageous than the feats of arms by which Mexico was won. Equally admirable were the humbler village priests who later devoted their lives to the service of the poor and scattered Indian communities in a country and among a people which must have remained for ever strange to them. But as colonisation advanced, and with it prosperity, the Catholic clergy appear to have lost their altruism. "We could not fail to note," wrote the English Dominican priest, Thomas Gage, in 1625, "that the life and customs of the clergy were most dissolute, and that their conduct completely belied their vows and calling." Like almost every other independent observer, he contrasted the wealth and magnificence of the Church with the poverty of the masses.

Two and a half centuries later, Lord Acton, himself a Catholic, wrote:

The largest land-owner in Mexico is the Catholic Church; and as there is no religious toleration, it is the Church of the whole nation, the only giver of the moral law to the natives, the sole channel through which the majority have access to the civilisation of Christendom. The clergy therefore enjoy an influence of which there has been no example in Europe for the last five hundred years, and have formed a strong basis of aristocracy and the most serious barrier to the realisation of the democratic principle. To establish a real democracy, the first thing to do is to reduce this immense and artificial influence. For the last twelve years this has been the one constant object of the Democratic party. It is a war of principles, a struggle for existence on either side, in which conciliation is impossible, and which can only be terminated by the ruin of one of the contending forces.

Another acute observer of the Mexican scene, Miss Joan Haslip, writes "Power breeds corruption, and there was little connection between the early monks and the Mexican clergy at the end of the eighteenth century."[23]

As late as 1870, the Catholic Church still owned a quarter of Mexico. It had amassed great wealth at the expense of the poorer classes and had done little for education and enlightenment. Church marriage was still expensive, the priests demanding exorbitant fees and expecting offerings to be made to the local Virgin. The peon had no idea of civil marriage and the registry office did not exist; so he took a wife and begot children

[23] Joan Haslip, *Imperial Adventurer* (Weidenfeld and Nicolson, 1971).

without the sanction of the Church. Later he hoped to save enough money to pay the priests and thus obtain legitimisation for his wife and children.[24]

But, as Lord Acton had foreseen, a "Democratic party" came to power at last, and in 1917 passed the Queretaro Constitution, enacting anti-religious legislation on the lines of the French Separation Laws of 1904. The Jesuits were outlawed and all Spanish priests expelled. Churches became the property of the State, which selected those that might remain open for worship. All other religious establishments such as monasteries, convents, church schools, orphanages, hospitals and almshouses, were sequestered. No religious act or procession might be celebrated outside a church.

Yet once again, as in Czechoslovakia, these measures proved premature. Mexico was not at the same stage of political and social development as France. Of Mexico's fourteen million inhabitants, eleven million were mestizos, or half-castes, whose only notion of right and wrong still derived from the village priest. The Virgin was still their most beloved figure, and the Crucifix at the street corner still had its daily offering of flowers. In the village churches candles still burned at the altar. To rob the peon of his sources of consolation in this life, and to cast doubts on his hope of salvation in the next, seemed sacrilegious to most Mexicans. The result was that for nine years, until 1926, the new laws were not properly applied; they were regularly and openly flouted — rather as the Prohibition Laws were in America. One example of how the law proscribing "religious acts or processions outside a church" was flouted during this period reveals how premature these laws were.

In January 1923, a monument to "Christ the King of Mexico" was unveiled on a lofty peak, the Cerro del Cubilete, in the geographical centre of the country. In spite of the law an elaborate procession of some 40,000 peasants carrying Crucifixes, images of saints, banners and lighted candles, went up the mountain to the shrine. On its slopes the stations of the Cross were enacted. Four archbishops and eight bishops wearing their episcopal robes also ascended the mountain on palfreys, and the Papal Delegate, Archbishop Filippi, was present. As he went up the mountain old men, women and children knelt and kissed the ground over which he passed. After the unveiling and blessing, he announced that the Pope had granted indulgences to all who had come. At this the multitude broke into cheers for Christ the King, the Virgin of Guadalupe, the Pope, the Apostolic

[24] F.O. 371/11146. Many of these priests were Spaniards. Mr. Ovey, the British Minister to Mexico, wrote in 1926, "The Spanish priests have obtained the easiest and most lucrative livings."

Delegate and the local bishop. They intoned sacred chants, let off fire-works and danced. At eleven o'clock the bishop addressed the crowd, explaining the importance of this ceremony which crowned Christ King of Mexico. The image of Christ on one of their highest mountains would guard and watch over all Mexicans.[25]

In this case the government could not ignore such open defiance of the law, particularly as the ceremony was patronised by the Pope's personal representative. They regarded this and similar incidents as part of a campaign by the Vatican to retain its old domination over the minds of the people. Instead of being simply a religious symbol, "Christ the King of Mexico" had been depicted as the supreme power of the land. Equipped with this tremendous sanction, the Vatican could always make its will felt before that of the State. The Papal Delegate was accordingly expelled.

This took place in the relatively indulgent days of 1923. But they were numbered, for in 1926 a fanatical anti-clerical and Socialist, Plutarcho Calles, became President. He immediately enforced the Queretaro Laws to the letter. Mr. Ovey, the British Minister to Mexico, described him as "the driving force against the Catholic Church, a man who sees red at the very mention of a priest". Within a few weeks of his election, seventy-three convents, ninety-two churches and 129 religious colleges had been closed, and 185 Spanish priests expelled. That any resistance to this was savagely repressed is proved by the remark of the Soviet Ambassador to his German colleague that "in its anti-clerical policy today the Mexican government is going far beyond my own".[26] In Calles's own words to a foreign journalist, "Mexico is engaged today in a struggle to establish the supremacy of the civil government. Our laws will be enforced. We are determined that no religious body shall thwart them. Mexicans own only one-third of the wealth of their country [he was referring to the big American foreign investments], and of that third the Catholic Church owns two-thirds. Foreign priests spell calamity for us. Our law forbids them to officiate in Mexico, and about a hundred have left the land . . ."[27]

The Vatican was not slow to retaliate; and in Mexico it was probably more powerful than anywhere else in the world. As no positive counter-measures were possible, the Vatican instructed the Mexican clergy to comply literally with the law, by simply refusing to officiate. Henceforth, the priests were to take no part in religious services. Baptism, Holy

[25] *Excelsior*, 12th January, 1923.

[26] A.A. *Pol Beziehungen des heiligen Stuhls zu Mexico*, report by the German Ambassador, Herr Will, 18th May, 1925.

[27] Interview with J. Mason of the *Daily Express*, 10th April, 1928.

Communion, marriage and burial would, if necessary, be administered by laymen. The churches which were now, theoretically, the property of the State could be run by the State. They therefore stood empty or, in the words of Mr. Ovey, "the churches are open but priestless".[28] On a highly religious people these retaliatory measures by the Church had an immediate effect. In the capital of the State of Colima, a crowd of 3000 demonstrated outside the Governor's palace calling on the government to rescind the anti-clerical laws or resign. In Michoacan, a clash took place between a crowd of Catholics and the police, resulting in a number of casualties. A "National League for the Defence of Religious Liberty" was founded, which distributed leaflets all over the country, urging Catholics to abstain from travelling, from all festivities and the purchase of luxury goods in order to weaken the government's economic situation through the loss of revenue from indirect taxes — a measure which proved to be remarkably effective. In Guadalajara, the capital of Jalisco, the sale of clothes fell by eighty per cent; in Mexico City, sales of motor-cars and their accessories fell by a half. But this was only the beginning. Catholic opposition to the government soon took the form of open revolt, especially in the western states where the government forces were soon fighting some 40,000 Cristeros, as the Catholics called themselves (followers of "Christ the King"). Their battle cries were, "*Viva Cristo Rey!*" and "*Viva la Vergen, Reins de Mexico!*" The Archbishop of Guadalajara took to the hills and, if he did not actually lead the Cristeros, inspired them to battle. The same could be said for Mgr. Hidalgo, the Bishop of Huejuthla, who was captured and imprisoned on charges of rebellion and sedition. Soon the government controlled nothing in Jalisco except the lines of communication, on which the Cristeros attacked trains and military convoys. Some idea of the bloodshed is revealed in the casualties published between January and May 1928. On the government side, killed — two generals, 324 officers and 2892 troops; on the Cristeros side, killed — forty-eight leaders and 6148 others.

These people were the descendants of the contemporaries of Cuanhtemotzin, the last native emperor, whose priests tore out the living hearts of their victims; and as Graham Greene has shown in his novel *The Power and the Glory*, they lived up to this tradition. At Toluca, a young Catholic priest was nailed to a cross, soaked in petrol and burned alive. In Mexico City, seventeen priests were taken to a cemetery and shot in front of an open grave into which their corpses were then thrown. A priest in Guadalajara was bound hand and foot and thrown on to a dung heap

[28] F.O. 371/11146, report by Mr. Ovey to Sir A. Chamberlain.

where he remained for three days before being despatched. About the most notorious execution of all, of Father Pro, a Jesuit priest accused of being involved in a bomb attack, the German Minister, Herr Will, reported, "The execution without trial was so hasty that everyone thinks the government has something to conceal."[29]

The Vatican drew up a list of these atrocities which it circulated to foreign countries, asking them to complain officially to the Mexican government. The Pope also issued an encyclical in which he said, "The Mexican government has reduced ministers of religion to the level of outlaws and criminals, and made the preaching of religion a crime." To this, the Mexican government retorted that the Cristeros had committed atrocities. The Mexican city newspaper, *Excelsior*, reported that fifty Cristeros shouting "Long Live Christ the King!" raided the town of Parras de la Fuente where they put the Socialist leader, Rafael Delgado, to death.[30] On the 21st March, 1927, the *Associated Press* reported that twenty Cristeros shouting the same battle cry attacked the Mexico City–Laredo train, in which they murdered the conductor and guard, and stole $18,000 of State funds. On the 20th April, 1927, some three hundred Cristeros, headed by four priests attacked the Mexico City–Guadalajara train and killed about fifty travellers, including several women and children; they then poured kerosene on the coaches and set fire to them. Mr. Gallup of the British Foreign Office reports that the Cristeros were intolerant of lay school-mistresses, particularly those who "teach socialism and sex education". About eighty of these unfortunate "progressive" women were murdered, and in some cases first their ears were cut off.

The only countries which responded to the Pope's appeal for condemnation of the governmental atrocities were Mexico's South American neighbours. In Chile two monster demonstrations were held in support of the Catholic Church in Mexico. The President of Peru sent a telegram to President Calles asking him to mitigate the anti-religious laws; and the British Ministers in Lima commented, "It is to be presumed that the President did not despatch the message on his own initiative, but that it was inspired by the Vatican. The Roman Catholic Church still enjoys considerable prestige in Peru and, although it does not interfere actively in political matters, its influence is such that it is advisable not to disregard it."[31] In Brazil on the 2nd August, 1926, the Catholic Confederation of Rio de Janeiro held a general assembly presided over by the Vicar General

[29] A.A. Pol III *Beziehungen des Vatikans zu Mexico*, 16th October, 1926.
[30] *Excelsior* article reported in the *New York Herald Tribune*, 4th January, 1927.
[31] F.O. 371/11147, despatch from Mr. Harvey, 13th August, 1926.

at which a unanimous resolution was passed demanding the pacification of the religious strife in Mexico, and conveying to their brethren, the Catholics of Mexico, their affection and sympathy, exhorting them to "stand firm in the Faith, preferring suffering and martyrdom to a vile and sinful apostasy".[32]

The reaction of the European powers to the Papal appeal was very different. They did nothing. The principal reason for this was that most of them had financial assets in Mexico and they did not wish to alienate President Calles, a Socialist as well as an anti-clerical, who was threatening to nationalise foreign interests as well as Church property. When asked by the Vatican to make a formal protest, the British government suggested that the Catholic powers should be approached first.[33] The country from which the Vatican might have expected most support was Spain, which had been humiliated by the expulsion of her own priests from Mexico. But in spite of every effort, all the Vatican could obtain from Spain was a mild note to the Mexican government drawing its attention in a purely unofficial way to the existence of a large number of Spanish subjects in Mexico, to whom the Catholic religion was a matter of considerable concern.[34] Spain added that by this she did not wish to criticise legislation which the Mexican government, in the exercise of its sovereign right, had passed. At the Vatican, Cardinal Gasparri complained bitterly to the British Minister that the Spanish press "probably for commercial reasons, was not allowed to criticise the Mexican government and its detestable methods".[35] The French and Italian reactions were much the same, and Mr. Vansittart at the Foreign Office commented drily, "If the Catholic powers have proved so cautious, it is well indeed that we are. If we protested to the Mexicans we should be met by some such retort as that the Church has been supreme for 400 years there, and that over ninety per cent of the population are still illiterate."[36] The British diplomat, Mr. T. M. Snow of the Foreign Office, commented on a despatch from Rome:

The Holy See have asked us to "find a means to remonstrate in the name of civilisation with the Mexican government". No doubt, however, the Mexican government sincerely believe that their anti-

[32] Ibid., Mr. Alston to Sir A. Chamberlain.
[33] F.O. 371/12767, from the British Minister to the Vatican.
[34] F.O. 371/12004, report from Sir H. Rumbold in Madrid.
[35] F.O. 371/12767, from the British Minister to the Vatican.
[36] F.O. 371/12004, 4th February, 1927.

religious law is in the interests of civilisation, and regard the Church as a body of obscurantists exploiting the superstition of the masses and responsible for the backward condition of the country. It is evident that if H.M.'s government accede to the Vatican request we might forfeit at a blow, and with little advantage to ourselves, the whole of the position we have managed to establish in Mexico. Moreover, we have not ourselves at present any serious objection to the Queretaro laws.[37]

The Germans took much the same line. The German Counsellor told Mr. Vansittart that Germany would do what the other countries did, although she would prefer not to protest because this would damage her commercial interests in Mexico.

The very pragmatic attitude of the British government may have been due in part to President Calles's care not to offend the religious susceptibilities of a Protestant country. The Church of England cathedral in Mexico City was not closed, nor were any of the clergymen administering it expelled (as were the Catholic foreign priests). The General Superintendent of the Methodist Church was allowed to enter Mexican territory whenever he wished, and attend to the spiritual needs of British Honduras subjects working on the Mexican side of the border.

The Vatican showed pained surprise at the supine reaction of the great Christian powers. The *Osservatore Romano* warned that the worst of the anti-religious laws were clearly inspired by the Bolshevists and the nationalisation of Church property would soon lead to measures against foreign capital. The Mexican government, it said, had actually asked the Russian Soviets for a copy of their penal laws. However, where even Spain had not seen fit to speak up, they could hardly expect other countries to take a firm line.[38] Sadly, the Cardinal Secretary of State told Mr. Randall of the British Legation that the struggle must remain one between the Mexican Catholics, supported by the moral encouragement of the Vatican, and the Mexican government.

There remained, however, the most important foreign influence of all, the United States. The Catholic organisations in North America had contributed generously to the relief of the Church in Mexico; but in a largely Protestant land the voice of these isolated groups, mostly Italians, Spaniards, Irish, etc., was not very loud. Vatican diplomacy worked unceasingly on the State Department, who were also beginning to find

[37] Ibid., 17th January, 1927.
[38] *Osservatore Romano*, 18th August, 1926.

that two years of religious strife were affecting American commercial interests. The American Secretary of State issued a warning to Mexico about the land nationalisation: "We insist," he said, "that adequate protection under the rules of international law be afforded to the property of American citizens." He was referring to Calles's Agrarian Law by which foreigners were deprived of some 470,000 acres without compensation, and to the petroleum laws about the ownership of the subsoil, much of which was in American hands. To nothing do the Americans react more sharply than to anything connected with oil. Mesmerised by his success with the Church confiscations, Calles appeared to have overstepped himself.

President Hoover sent as Ambassador to Mexico Mr. Dwight Morrow, a banker who had worked with J. P. Morgan, to persuade Calles to moderate his persecution of the Church, or to risk economic sanctions. This proved to be the correct treatment. By threatening withdrawal of economic support, he soon obtained permission for the Archbishop of Mexico City, who was in exile, to return for a secret interview with the government. After much bargaining their efforts were successful, and an agreement was drawn up, of which the main clauses were that henceforth the Mexican prelates would nominate the priests who were allowed to register according to Mexican law. Church property would be restored. Religious instruction, while not permitted in schools, could be given in Church buildings. The bishops now reappointed to their cures the 4000 priests who had scattered far and wide, many of them in exile; and on the following Sunday crowds poured into the churches to offer thanksgiving.

Nevertheless, it was really a victory for the government. Most of the Church lands remained in its hands, and the whole episode had greatly weakened the hold of the Church on the Mexican mind. Vatican diplomacy has, in the other controversies examined here in the twenties, in France, Malta and, to a lesser extent in Italy, on the whole been successful. In these countries the priesthood was composed of an intellectually evolved rank and file. But most of the Mexican priests, mestizos themselves, were quite unreliable, and in some cases semi-literate. They did not give, or probably were incapable of giving, the information required by the Vatican for the proper handling of the situation. As a result, the Secretariat of State at the Vatican never seems to have been aware of the need for reform nor understood anti-clericalism in Mexico.

7

Papal Condemnation of the Action Française

———

When Pius XI came to the throne in 1922, he gradually withdrew his support from Catholic political parties, which he believed were not in accord with the spirit of the times. For lack of his support, Don Sturzo's Popular Party in Italy collapsed. An analogous, if not similar, situation arose in France in 1926 over the Action Française party which had also championed Catholicism against the onslaughts of the twentieth-century Liberals.

Founded in 1899 by the brilliant polemical journalist, Charles Maurras, its avowed aim was the overthrow of the Third Republic and the restoration of the monarchy in France. Maurras scorned petit-bourgeois democracy and liberalism, maintaining that only a return to the monarchy which had made France glorious and respected for eight centuries could restore the country's fortunes. Authority, he contended, was more important than the "Liberty" of the Democrats, which led only to corruption and parliamentary anarchy. His newspaper, L'Action Française, which at the height of the movement was one of the most influential in France, bore as sub-title, "*organe du nationalisme intégral*", with beneath it the battle cry of the Duc de Guise, pretender to the throne: "As head of the House of

France, I revindicate all rights, I assume all responsibilities, I accept all duties. I, the Duc de Guise, heir to the forty kings who, in a thousand years, made France."

The Catholic Church had suffered much under the Liberal regimes of the Third Republic, and it was Maurras's attack on this form of government rather than his insistence on monarchy which attracted Catholics. His greatest following was in the old Catholic military families; for successive Third Republic governments had axed the armed forces, victimising officers of Catholic faith or descent. Maurras advocated a strong army to protect France from her powerful neighbour across the Rhine, and he preached a form of extreme nationalism which had not been heard since the days of the first Napoleon. In place of what he considered the mediocrity of the Third Republic he offered again *la gloire*. He ingeniously associated his programme with the Catholic Church which, thanks to its hierarchy, discipline and tradition, he regarded as a bulwark of the social order. One of the sights in Paris in the first years of this century was the groups of well-dressed young men selling his party paper, *L'Action Française*, at the church doors as the worshippers emerged, crying under the very noses of the Republican police: *"Action Française! Journal Royaliste!"* In defiance of the law against religious celebrations in public, the Action Française also resurrected the annual procession in honour of Joan of Arc who, although not yet officially canonised, was a religious as well as a patriotic symbol to all Frenchmen.[1] This procession became the annual scene of battles with the police, broken heads and young men bearing some of the proudest names of France being hauled off to prison because they had laid a wreath at the foot of her statue.

Of the seventeen Cardinals and bishops in France, eleven publicly sympathised with Maurras, and his following among the minor clergy was even greater.[2] Belonging himself neither to the Church nor the aristocracy, he assumed with sublime arrogance the role of high prophet of Catholic conservatism. Such was the dialectic brilliance of his writing that, within a decade of founding his party, he had persuaded most of France and Europe that the Pope was his spiritual patron.

It might be assumed from all this that the Vatican would be grateful for having such a vigorous ally in its battles with the Third Republic. In the early days, until about 1910, this was the case, and Pius X told a visitor, M. Bellaigue, "M. Maurras is a great defender of the Church". Maurras

[1] She was canonised in 1920.
[2] It has already been seen that the French clergy had tended to become, as a result of the Separation Laws, excessively conservative and ultramontane.

himself later produced a series of testimonials by persons to whom Pius X had spoken favourably of the Action Française, among them his own mother to whom the Pope had said, "I bless his work". But in the years immediately before the First World War, the Vatican became increasingly aware that the support his movement gave the Church had little to do with religion. In its desire to achieve political power, the Action Française had coined the catchword *"Politique d'abord"* and it cynically instructed its members, "All means are permissible, even legal ones." It soon became clear that the Church was to be one of these "means", to impose authority and advance policy, on the lines of the Napoleonic maxim, "Religion is not the mystery of the incarnation, but the secret of social order." This was of course a travesty of the Church's conception of itself — a divine organism entrusted with the direction of men's souls towards a super-natural end. The Action Française's annual presence at the festival of Joan of Arc, the battles with the police, the ostentatious selling of the party newspaper at the church doors, were now seen at the Vatican to be purely political acts.

Nor did Maurras make any attempt to conceal these motives in his writings, frequently referring to the "wonderful organisation of the Church of Rome". Although he had been brought up as a Catholic, he had since become a disciple of the positivist, Auguste Comte, who had venerated the pagan world of Greece and Rome. The latter city, Maurras contended, had bequeathed to the Catholic Church its "wonderful organ-isation", and he acclaimed the Roman emperors who had "subordinated the Christian conception of the supernatural to material discipline". The life of Christ appeared to mean little to him. In his books, *Anthinea* and *Le Chemin du Paradis*, he regretted "the night with which the Cross of a suffering God had cloaked the modern world". The Catholic Church he described as "clad in a mantle of purity, of order and harmony, which it has stretched out over the existing Jewish and barbarous anarchy". He respected it only in so far as "its humanity veils its divinity, that is when it ceases to be the messenger of the Hebrew Christ who is a dangerous dreamer". Here was the anomaly, Maurras's claim to be the champion of the Catholic Church in France, and yet at the same time being a pagan and a positivist.

His writings had been known to the Church for some years, but the Vatican is reluctant to condemn if there is any hope of recantation. More-over, the Action Française was not an enemy like Liberalism or Socialism, nor a sect within the body of the Church preaching a false doctrine. Con-demnation would be not of a man who opposed the Church, but of one who supported it, and of whose support it had originally been grateful. Nevertheless, to a transcendental Church, an avowed positivist cannot remain an ally however much he may support it. Pius XI said in a private audience to Henri Bordeaux, "M. Maurras has one of the finest minds alive today. No one knows that better than I. But it *is* only a mind . . . Reason is not enough; it has never been enough. Christ is completely unknown to him. He sees the Church from the outside, not the inside. He attempts to bring French policies and the Church together. But he puts politics before the Church. Does he not say, *'Politique d'abord!'* " When Bordeaux suggested, "Because, Your Holiness, politics should defend religion and Christian ethics," the Pope replied, "No, precisely the contrary is the case. It is religion which defends politics. And every time politics ignores the lessons which religion teaches, it becomes bad politics." The Vatican was also aware that the strong nationalist feelings stimulated in France during the Great War were abating, and that the chauvinism of the Action Française was losing its appeal to the French people. The number of practising Catholics who were politically moderate was increasing.

As early as 1914, Pius X had considered condemning the Action Française: *"Damnabilis non damnandus,"* he had said. But war broke out before he could do so, and he did not wish to inflame passions further. After the French victory he hoped that Action Française would moderate its chauvinism. Instead, Maurras and his party were among the first in 1919 to demand the economic destruction of Germany and the fullest application of the Versailles penal clauses. Léon Daudet, Maurras's closest collaborator, commenting in their paper on the appalling conditions in Germany caused by the Allied blockade wrote, "I applaud the German famine."

At this time Pius XI was giving grants to the suffering and starving masses in Germany, and he never ceased preaching reconciliation between France and her defeated enemy.[3] When, under Aristide Briand in 1926, the first steps in that direction were taken at Locarno, his Nuncio in Paris, Mgr. Maglione, was the first to congratulate the French government publicly. At the New Year ceremony in the Elysée attended by the diplomatic corps he made, as doyen, the annual speech to the President of the

[3] His encyclical, *Ubi Arcano Dei,* issued at Christmas 1922, caused resentment in France because he said that the Versailles and Trianon treaties were too harsh. His predecessor, Benedict XV had even admonished the Cardinal Archbishop of Paris, Amette, and the Belgian Cardinal Mercier for their nationalistic behaviour. *A.A. Beziehungen zu Frankreich,* Vol. 1, despatch from von Bergen, 28th August, 1920.

French Republic. His words, although mild enough, almost created a diplomatic incident. "The diplomatic corps," he said, "expresses its sympathy and satisfaction for the efforts accomplished by France in the pacification of the nations. We are convinced that her government will continue this good work, worthy of her humane traditions, of the noble heart and magnanimous soul of this great country. The full confidence we have always placed in France has recently been confirmed by the projects which your Foreign Minister announced three months ago to the representatives of so many nations at Geneva. No one can recall without emotion the speech he made on that occasion . . ." The speech he referred to was Briand's, proposing that Germany should be admitted to the League.

The Action Française and its newspaper now turned on the Nuncio and M. Briand with extraordinary ferocity, describing the latter as "the crookedest and vilest politician ever produced by the rottenness of Democracy, a traitor and a public enemy". In a sarcastic aside aimed at the Vatican, it referred to him as "Saint Aristide". At Locarno, the paper said, Briand had disarmed France and deprived her of her guarantees against Germany; he was preparing "a new hecatomb". The Nuncio, Mgr. Maglione, was described quite simply as "a German agent", and the paper accused the Vatican of planning the resurrection of the Holy Roman Empire, a Teutonic Catholic State created by the union of Austria and Bavaria, together with the non-German Rhenish lands, and the "Flamingant" districts of Belgium. The inclusion of these areas in the Reich would, it said, not only create a solid Catholic block in the centre of Europe (Austria, Bavaria, the Rhineland, Belgium), but would make this State the largest and most powerful in Europe. It would reinforce the German Centre (or Catholic) political party to such an extent that it could control the whole of German life. The subservience of the German Centre to Rome was, the Action Française said, notorious. Hence the Vatican plan for the subjugation of Europe had become clear! The *Osservatore Romano* should be called the *Osservatore Tedesco*. Nor did the Action Française hesitate to use physical means against the "traitors". M. Sangnier, a deputy who supported Briand's policy, was assaulted by the Action Française Youth Association on his way to a League of Nations meeting, and well dosed with castor oil.

Matters came to a head when the Belgian *Cahiers de la Jeunesse Catholique* organised a referendum on the question, "Whom do you consider the writer who has influenced you most in the last twenty-five years?" The Catholic youth of Belgium selected Charles Maurras by 174 votes to Bourget's 123 and Barres's 91, describing Maurras as "a giant in the realm of thought, a lighthouse to our youth". The implications of this were considered by the Vatican too dangerous to the Catholic Youth of Europe as a whole, and the Pope now decided to act. Condemnation, he considered, would come best from a French bishop, preferably one who sympathised with the Action Française. That several French bishops who were approached excused themselves on various pretexts was significant; the Gallican episcopate was "still more papal than the Pope". Finally, the elderly Archbishop Andrieu of Bordeaux agreed to pronounce the anathema. On the 27th August, 1926 the weekly paper of his archdiocese, *L'Aquitaine*, printed his formal reply to "a question asked about the Action Française by a group of young Catholics". In it, he denounced the movement and its leaders whose teachings were "atheism, agnosticism, anti-Catholicism and anti-Christianity, amoralism for the individual and society . . . the restoration of paganism with all its violence and injustice."

The directors of the Action Française refer to God [Cardinal Andrieu wrote] yet they regard God as unknowable and non-existent. In spite of their praise of the Church, they deny that it is a divine institution. They are Catholics not by conviction, but out of interest . . . they wish to use the Church for their own ends . . . they ignore the distinction between Good and Evil; for virtue they substitute aestheticism or the cult of Beauty, and epicureanism or the cult of Pleasure . . . they replace our moral laws by a pagan social organisation in which the State is all and the individual nothing.[4]

At first the statement passed almost unnoticed in the Paris press; but when the Pope himself wrote an open letter to the Cardinal of Bordeaux approving his words,[5] French Catholics realised that they represented more than the purely personal opinion of one bishop. "In the publications of the Action Française," His Holiness wrote, "is evidence of a new religion, a new moral and social system, a new approach to the subject of God, the Incarnation, the Church and, generally, to the dogma and Catholic moral, principally in relation to the political, which is logically subordinate to the moral. There is clear evidence of a revival of paganism, which is closely linked with naturalism . . ."

[4] The Action Française had become the French brand of Fascism; and had the movement achieved power, it seems likely that a dictatorship, rather than a monarchy, would have been installed in France.

[5] *Osservatore Romano*, 8th September, 1926.

In spite of this anathema, Maurras refused to recant. On the 24th December, 1926 under the heading "*Non Possumus!*" his newspaper published defiantly:

The intention of the Holy See is clear — to decapitate the Action Française and simultaneously persuade Catholics to unite on republican terms . . . this is no longer a question of morals or faith, but of political life or death . . . If the Holy See has its way, the Action Française will be suppressed and the safety of France jeopardised. To allow such a thing would be a betrayal of the fatherland. We will not betray. The father who asks his son to murder his mother, or what comes to the same thing, to cause her to be murdered, may be listened to respectfully; but he cannot be obeyed. *Non possumus!*

Even Mussolini was shocked by the last phrase: "To say '*Non possumus*' to the Pope!" he said to a friend. "No, no, one does not say '*Non possumus*' to the Pope!" On Sunday the 23rd January, 1927, a pastoral letter from the Archbishop of Paris was read in all the churches in his province prohibiting the faithful from reading *L'Action Française* which was now, together with the works of Charles Maurras, placed on the Index.

Uncontrite as ever, the Action Française only continued its campaign against the Vatican. A close connection, it declared, existed between this papal anathema and the Nuncio's speech at the Elysée on New Year's day. These two incidents were links in the same chain, part of the Vatican's plan for the German hegemony in Europe. The Vatican was working closely with M. Briand, whose policy of Franco-German rapprochement would be fatal to the interests of France. The placing of *L'Action Française* on the Index was depicted as an attempt by the Vatican to undermine French patriotism. Readers of *L'Action Française* were urged to disregard the Pope's ruling and to put their duty as patriotic Frenchmen before their obligations to the Church.

The Duc de Guise, the Pretender to the throne and patron of the Action Française, avoided expressing any opinion on the controversy. He merely telegraphed to M. Maurras, "Deeply affected by the decision which strikes you and your paper. Aware of your respect for religion and your patriotic devotion to national interests, I assure you of my entire sympathy." Had the monarchists really represented an important body of public opinion in the country, the banning of their paper might have affected the Catholic religion adversely; but this was not the case.

An edict was now issued by the Vatican to the French Cardinals and bishops formally forbidding them or their clergy to baptise, marry, confess or bury persons subscribing to, or reading, *L'Action Française* newspaper.[6] This order was, with one or two exceptions, faithfully carried out. Jacques Bainville, the well-known Academician, a Catholic and a member of the Action Française, was refused a religious funeral by the Archbishop of Paris. The Princess Anne, a member of the Guise family, was about to marry into the Italian Royal house, and the ceremony was to be conducted by the Cardinal Archbishop of Naples. She was unwise enough a few weeks before to write to Charles Maurras, thanking him for the support he and his party had given her family. The Pope accordingly instructed the Cardinal Archbishop not to officiate at the ceremony, and it was conducted instead by the local priest.[7] Pius XI was adamant. He even compelled the Cardinal who had placed the tiara on his own head at his Coronation, the French Cardinal Billot, to resign his biretta, because Billot opposed the Papal condemnation of the Action Française.

Nevertheless, faced with these sanctions, the Action Française still refused to retract. Its paper contended that in return for the Articles 70 and 71 in the Finance Bill which restored the Church property, the Vatican had agreed to condemn the Action Française. The Pope had been the victim of an unholy plot concocted by the Christian Democrats, Briand and the Germans.[8] It attacked the *Osservatore Romano*, "the infamous Vatican newspaper which should be called the *Diffamatore Romano*". It published articles about historical figures and events which reflected adversely on the Curia: Galileo, the Saint Bartholomew massacre, Alexander VI and his bastards, the Bishop Cauchon, etc. Later it even contrived to use the Italian air manoeuvres over Rome for criticising the Vatican.[9] During a practice nocturnal air-raid, the Vatican had agreed to a black-out. "Can the Vatican," asked *L'Action Française*, "really call itself neutral, as it claims to be after the Concordat? This black-out presupposes Franco-Italian hostilities, and the Vatican is clearly taking the side of Italy." Even more grotesque, the paper accused the Vatican of "consorting with Radicals and Freemasons". It said that among the guests at the Nuncio's reception on the anniversary of the Pope's Coronation, the 13th March, 1927, were Mesdames Herriot and Berthelot, both wives of prominent Freemasons.

---

[6] Published in *La Croix*, 29th March, 1929.

[7] F.O. 371/12626, report of 3rd November, 1927.

[8] Ibid., November, 1927.

[9] *A.A. Beziehungen zu Frankreich.* Reported from *Kölnischer Zeitung*, 9th October, 1932; also in *L'Action Française* and *L'Echo de Paris*.

"And so," said *L'Action Française* "we see these pretty atheists drinking champagne in the company of soberly clad Franciscan monks."

Although the condemnation of the Action Francaise was due primarily to the anti-Christian attitude of its leaders, this moment was also chosen by the Vatican to give moral support to the French government and Briand in whose hands, the Pope considered, the cause of international peace was safer than it had been for years. He was determined, as the *Osservatore Romano* wrote, to play what part he could in the progressive "disarmament of the minds of the people of Europe"; and he was determined to support Briand's Locarno policy, by which it seemed the Franco-German feud might at last be settled.

For some years the quarrel lingered on, and Lord Crewe, the British Ambassador in Paris, wrote that he could see no end to "an affair which seems likely to last as long as the Jansenist heresy".[10] In 1932 the Action Française was still accusing the Nuncio in Paris, Mgr. Maglione, of having been a spy in the pay of the Germans when he was in Switzerland during the war. At a student meeting in Paris, the Nuncio was unable to speak because members of the Action Française shrieked, "German spy!" "Send him back to Berlin!" "Give him his papers!"

But these were isolated incidents. With every year the membership of the Action Française diminished and its newspaper lost subscribers. Its attempt to envenom relations between the French Republic and the Vatican had failed completely; for on the 15th January, 1935, the Pope received Pierre Laval, the French Foreign Minister, the first Republican Minister to visit the Vatican officially since the foundation of the Third Republic. Pius XI conferred on him the Grand Order of the Cross of Pius XI, and on President Lebrun the Supreme Order of Christ, the highest Papal decoration. In making its peace at last with the French Republic, the Vatican had tacitly admitted that the cause of the monarchy in France was lost. The ways of God are indeed strange. In the churches of France now hung, not the white lilies of the Bourbons, but the Tricolours of the Republic.[11]

[10] F.O. 371/13348, September 1928.

[11] It may appear inconsistent that the Vatican should condemn nationalism in France, in the form of the Action Française, but condone it in Italy under Mussolini. The explanation is that in France the Action Française was in conflict with the Republic — a Republic which the Vatican now saw had public support and was there to stay — whereas in Italy the Nationalists and Fascists were the government, equally solidly based.

8

The Papacy and the Spanish Imbroglio

ANTI-CLERICALISM IN SPAIN WAS NEVER AS STRONG AS IN THE other Latin countries. Isolated from the rest of Europe by the barrier of the Pyrenees, the peninsula retained, almost until the 1920s, much of its medieval character. Throne and Altar were closely associated. Yet in a country like Spain, where the population was largely uneducated and illiterate, and bearing in mind the inflammable nature of the Spanish character, the transition from medieval Catholicism to rank atheism proved easier than might be expected. The desire for a fanatical faith, without which the Spanish soul seems unable to exist, found it when the Throne collapsed, in Anarcho-syndicalism, one of the most violent attacks on the Altar that the twentieth century has seen.

At the opening of that century clerical influence still pervaded the Court and the aristocracy, and the Church had official connections with all important branches of public life. Twenty thousand monks and three times as many nuns were enrolled in well-endowed orders, of which the Jesuits were the most prominent. They possessed a near monopoly of education, and youths who passed through their schools joined organisations which prolonged their contact with ecclesiastical circles for the rest of their lives. The daily newspapers, *El Debate* of the Jesuits, and *El Siglos* which was closely connected with the Cardinal Primate, had the largest circulation in the land. The sparsely scattered Labour organisations were amenable, if not subordinate, to clerical pressure. While the women of Spain, as devout as any in the world and ever open to the suggestions of their spiritual advisers, voted against the Female Suffrage bill.

Nevertheless, certain signs of change had begun to appear after the First World War. If only as a result of improved communications, the rampart of the Pyrenees no longer shut Spain off from the rest of Europe. The mists of Spanish obscurantism were gradually dispersing, and an indigenous class of revolutionary with the sesquipedalian name of "Anarcho-syndicalist" had appeared, preaching that Throne and Altar were a satanic alliance which must be exterminated. Aware of these new trends, the Right-wing governments of the early twenties tried to introduce certain overdue reforms connected with the Church. The year 1923 opened with two disputes with the Vatican.

In an attempt to assess the immense wealth of the Spanish Church, the government proposed that all art treasures in churches should be placed under State protection, and that an inventory should be made. The Vatican instructed its Nuncio to make an official protest, on the ground that this was the first step towards sequestration of Church property. So powerful was the Church in Spain that the government immediately yielded and withdrew the legislation. The second dispute concerned Article 11 of the Spanish Constitution granting Catholicism a privileged position in Spain. It read: "The Apostolic and Roman Catholic religion is the State religion ... No public ceremonies or manifestations other than those of the State religion shall be permitted." The reformers' modest proposal was that the last sentence should be deleted, thereby permitting a certain liberty to other denominations, insignificant as they were. This too led to protests from the Nuncio that any change in Article 11 implied denunciation of the Concordat (1880). Again the government yielded.

So supine a regime could hardly last, and a few months later it fell over a much more serious issue. General Silvestre's military adventure in Morocco against the Riffs had ended in disaster, with the loss of thousands of troops and much territory. Governmental corruption as much as ineptitude was responsible, and a search was made for scapegoats. While recriminations among the Ministers about who was to blame were in progress, the country was suddenly roused from its summer siesta by the news that General Primo de Rivera, Captain General of Catalonia, had declared martial law in his province, and demanded that the King should dismiss the corrupt Ministers responsible for the Moroccan disaster. The important region of Catalonia was entirely in his hands and the government, being powerless to wrest it from him, resigned. No parliamentary leader appeared capable of forming a new government, so the King, Alphonso XIII, impressed by Primo de Rivera's forthright methods, invited him to form one. The General agreed, but only on condition, that he should rule by military decrees. He had no faith in parliaments.[1]

He was well aware, however, of the power of the Church, and one of his first acts was to arrange an official visit by King Alphonso XIII to the Vatican. He intended thereby to retain the support in Spain of the powerful clerical and conservative circles which still condemned the Italian Savoyards for having dispossessed the Pope of his Papal States in 1870; and he let it be known that he considered King Alphonso's visit in Rome to the Vatican more important than the one to the Quirinal. That the King's audience with the Pope was most ceremonious caused some irritation in Italian Fascist circles (it must be remembered that the Concordat with the Italian State had not yet been made; Vatican and Quirinal still did not officially recognise one another). The King of Spain and his Queen made three genuflections to the Pope, kissing his foot and hand; whereupon the Pope embraced them on both cheeks. Alphonso then read a speech full of references to Spain's historical struggle in support of the Catholic faith against Islam and the heretics. He spoke of Lepanto, the dunes of Flanders, the banks of the Elbe. He even offered, should His Holiness so desire, to become another Urban II, and lead a crusade against the new enemies of the Church.[2] The British Chargé d'Affaires reported that "many people including the Vatican would have preferred the audience to have been less formal, because it gave offence to the King of Italy and Mussolini".[3]

With these and other methods for enrolling the support of the Church, Primo de Rivera governed for six years until 1930. As dictators go, he

---

[1] F.O. 371/9493. Cardinal Gasparri told Mr. Dormer of the British Legation on the 21st September, 1923 that Primo de Rivera's military regime "might well produce a more healthy atmosphere". He added that Spain had until now been governed by "political cliques who took it in turns to form Ministries, one worse than the other".

[2] Further reference by the King in the speech to "the barbarians of Islam in Morocco" did not improve Spain's relations with that country. The Turkish Ambassador in Madrid also showed his annoyance. Lord Curzon's comment on the speech was, "The King of Spain's speech at the Vatican reminds one of the Kaiser at his best — or worst." F.O. 371/9493, 7th December, 1923.

[3] F.O. 371/9493, report to Lord Curzon.

was a mild man, more concerned with the pleasures of the table and the bed than with ruling. (He once said, "Had I known in my youth that I would one day have to govern this country, I would have spent more time studying, and less fornicating.") He fell largely because his rule, like all governments in Spain which last more than a year or so, had become corrupt. The administration, whether he liked it or not, was soon filled with sycophants and other time-servers. Moreover, a monarchy supported by a military dictatorship and a reactionary Church was becoming increasingly more repugnant to the rising middle and educated classes who, in a series of epigrams and witticisms, ceaselessly attacked Church and Throne. This seems to have undermined Primo de Rivera's self-confidence, because he suddenly, of his own free will, resigned and emigrated to Paris (where he later died in a night-club). The way was now open for the rising Liberal and Socialist reformers who were clamouring for a republic on the French lines. The Monarchists had been incapable of governing in 1923, when their only recourse had been to the soldier's sword. Now when the soldier had laid down his sword, they could do nothing to save the monarchy. Faced with the prospect of civil war, Alphonso XIII abdicated. The Republic was declared on the 14th April, 1931.

True to its Socialist principles, the new government immediately introduced legislation separating Church and State, again on the well-tried French model. The Jesuits were, as usual, expelled first, and their property confiscated. The Catholic Church was declared a corporation in public law, without privileges of any kind. Religious instruction was no longer made compulsory in State schools. Civil divorce was introduced. Religious processions and demonstrations in public were forbidden. Azaña, the Socialist leader and Prime Minister, made the momentous statement in Parliament, "And with these measures Spain ceases to be Catholic."

Azaña was a well-intentioned idealist much concerned with social progress who, when he made this remark was, like Masaryk in Czechoslovakia, quite unaware of the explosive forces he was unleashing. Mr. Hugh Thomas, in his well-documented and impartial *The Spanish Civil War*, says that these anti-clerical measures were political folly because they were premature. It would have been wiser for instance, he says, to have waited until the Jesuit schools had been replaced by lay schools of similar quality; for the Orders, whatever their shortcomings, had founded the best, and in some places the only, schools in Spain. Moreover the Socialist government proved incapable of controlling its extremist allies, the Anarcho-syndicalists. Within a matter of days after the promulgation of the anti-clerical laws, they had become the excuse for unbridled plundering and destruction by these extremists of churches, monasteries and convents all over Spain. The Jesuits' principal establishment in Madrid was sacked and their training college, where free technical training was available to working men, was burnt to the ground. From Malaga, the British Consul reported that the mob had sacked the Bishop's Palace and the offices of a paper with Jesuit affiliations.[4] Similar attacks were reported from Seville, Cadiz, Saragossa, Alicante and Murcia.

The immediate reaction of the Vatican was curiously mild, especially when compared with its resolute opposition to earlier, less violent, anti-clerical measures in Italy, France and Czechoslovakia. In fact, neither the Vatican nor its Nuncio in Madrid, Mgr. Tedeschini, had been taken unawares by the Royal abdication and the establishment of the Republic. Since the First World War, the Vatican had foreseen that the days of the King and his supporters were numbered. The Church may abominate Liberalism, but it knows when it has to come to terms with it; and Mgr. Tedeschini had been instructed to establish good relations with prominent members of the Republican party before it came to power. This he had done. Von Bergen reported from Rome, "the Vatican appears not at all surprised, or perturbed, by the fall of the Spanish monarchy. It appears that Azaña, the new President, has assured them that he will not disturb the good relations existing between the Spanish episcopate and Rome. And the Vatican believes him."[5] The Vatican was, in fact, prepared to regard the vandalism and destruction of Church property as the work of extremists, the Anarcho-syndicalists, whom Señor Azaña himself condemned.[6] In May 1933, the Pope issued his encyclical on Spain, *Dilectissima Nobis*, in which, while condemning the vandalism severely, he was careful not to say anything against the Republic. He made it clear that he was concerned with religious liberty, not with the form of government.[7] The Papal Nuncio now began to visit the new Cabinet Ministers regularly, and they soon showed considerable respect

---

[4] F.O. 371/15774, reported by the Consul, Mr. D. Young, 30th May, 1931.

[5] *A.A. Beziehungen des heiligen Stuhls zu Spanien*, 15th April, 1931.

[6] Ibid. Graf von Welczeck, the German Ambassador in Madrid, reports that three of the leading Spanish intellectuals, Ortega y Gasset, Marañon and Perez de Ayala, maintained that the Republicans had nothing to do with the vandalism.

[7] The Spanish government also wished to avoid a clash with the Church such as had occurred in France after the Combes Separation Laws; it attempted to carry out the anti-clerical programme to which it was committed as unostentatiously as possible.

for him. He also persuaded the Spanish episcopate to be patient and avoid recriminations. This last recommendation was, however, thwarted by the Primate of Spain, Cardinal Segura, an intransigent Monarchist who had already had several clashes with the Republican leaders. The career of Segura throws a revealing light on the independence of the local episcopate from the Vatican.

This remarkable prelate, of peasant origin, owed his advancement to the highest clerical office in Spain at the early age of forty-eight to King Alphonso, who had discovered him when he was Bishop in Extremadura. By a not unusual quirk of human affections, the voluptuary King took a liking to the ascetic priest, who wore a hair shirt next to his skin, and believed that a bath was a heathen invention. The two men were frequently in consultation, on terms even of intimate friendship. When the monarchy fell, Cardinal Segura did not wait for instructions from Rome, but roundly condemned the new Republic and its leaders from the pulpit. He also issued a pastoral letter containing the inflammatory words, "If we remain quiet and idle, if we allow ourselves to surrender to apathy and timidity, to those who would destroy religion . . . we shall have no right to lament when reality reveals that we had victory in our hands, but knew not how to use it." As a result of this letter and his close friendship with the King, the Republican government informed Cardinal Segura that they could not be responsible for his safety, nor protect him from public insults, and they requested him to leave the country. The Cardinal refused, whereupon he was escorted, politely but firmly, to the French frontier and ejected.[8] Nothing daunted, he returned clandestinely two weeks later, avoiding the Customs posts and reaching Guadalajara before being arrested again. This behaviour was a source of considerable embarrassment to the Vatican which informed him, when he arrived back in Rome for the second time, that he must bear full responsibility for any incidents caused by his return to Spain. As a result presumably of these Papal remonstrances, he resigned as Primate of Spain and became a Curia Cardinal. According to the German Ambassador in Madrid, Azaña took the whole affair as calmly as did the Vatican. "The new Prime Minister of Spain," he wrote, "is a sworn enemy of radical measures, and he does not subscribe to the view of some of his colleagues that, if a satisfactory explanation of Segura's conduct is not forthcoming from the Vatican, relations with the Holy See should be broken off."[9]

It was soon clear that the flexible policy adopted by the Vatican was

---

[8] Account in *Osservatore Romano*, 17th June, 1931.

[9] *A.A. Beziehungen des heiligen Stuhls zu Spanien*, October 1931.

beginning to yield dividends. Within a year of the proclamation of the Republic, a new Catholic Republican Party, the Accion Popular, had been founded, a modern party based on the principles of Pius XI's encyclical *Quadragesimo Anno*. One of its principal aims was to attract the working classes into the Catholic Labour Unions, and it was led by an energetic young lawyer, Gil Robles. He had the full support of the Vatican because he was well aware of modern currents of political thought and, although he had been a Monarchist, he believed that the Republic had come to stay, at least for the foreseeable future. He announced that there was nothing anomalous about a strong Catholic Church within a republican state. The Monarchists naturally regarded him as a traitor, and the British Ambassador in Madrid reported that ex-King Alphonso, who was in exile in Rome, had tried on several occasions to influence the Pope against him, but without success.[10]

Similar unsuccessful attempts by the Spanish Monarchists to enlist the Vatican's support were illustrated on one notable occasion in Rome, at the wedding of King Alphonso's daughter, the Infanta Beatrix, to the Italian Prince Torlonia. It was celebrated with great pomp in the Church of the Gesù by Cardinal Segura himself, in the presence of King Alphonso and his family, the King and Queen of Italy, the aristocracies of both countries and several hundreds of Spaniards of all classes who had come to demonstrate their loyalty (the journeys of the poorer being paid by the Spanish Monarchist press). In his advice to the married couple, Cardinal Segura emphasised the importance of Spanish patriotism, and he particularly urged the Infanta never to forget her Spanish birth and upbringing.

The Vatican was not pleased by this, nor by these demonstrations of Spanish Monarchists in an Italian church. The Spanish Republican government made representations through its Ambassador to the Vatican, Señor Pita Romero, who asked why Cardinal Segura had been allowed to officiate. The Pope had of course not sanctioned this; but all he could do to show his disapproval was to reply coldly to the request by the Spanish grandee visitors for an audience. Any courtesy he extended to them would have confirmed what Gil Robles was attempting to refute — that the cause of the Church in Spain was the cause of the Monarchy. Had he granted an audience to the Monarchist visitors they would certainly have offered loud cries for Pope and King, Throne and Altar, which would have placed him in an invidious position. The distinguished Spanish visitors and their wives were therefore made to

[10] F.O. 371/19735, Sir G. Grahame to Sir J. Simon, 15th February, 1935.

wait, not in one of the usual Vatican audience halls, but outside in the Cortile di San Damaso where, after standing for nearly an hour in the rain, in an icy January *tramontana*, they were only favoured with a brief appearance of the Pope at an upper window.

The Pope's official reason for this inhospitality was that the Vatican possessed no room suitable for so large a gathering. An eye-witness said, however, that when the Pope appeared at the window and gave the blessing to the Spanish grandees he was "not himself at all, changed in countenance, pale, agitated, his face distorted".[11] Von Bergen reported that the incident gave much satisfaction to the Spanish Republican government, which offered to return the confiscated houses of certain Jesuits, and asked the Vatican to fill six bishoprics.[12]

Whatever may have been the embarrassment caused at the Vatican by this and similar Monarchist incidents, the new policy towards Spain adopted by the Vatican in favour of the Republic seemed to be completely vindicated; because at this point the Socialists, who had dominated the Spanish Parliament in 1931, lost their majority in the 1933 elections. Of the Right-wing parties who now gained control, the largest element was Gil Robles's new Catholic Party, the Accion Popular. By making an alliance with the Radicals, he was soon strong enough to introduce legislation to compensate the Catholic clergy who had been dispossessed of their benefices by the 1931 laws. Although the Socialists contested this energetically, the measure was passed and six-teen million pesetas was assigned annually by the State to compensate the clergy. Señor Romero was sent to Rome to open negotiations for a new concordat. The British Ambassador in Madrid, Sir G. Grahame, reported, "this looks like the thin end of the wedge, which might restore the Church to something approaching its old position". He considered that Gil Robles's aim was "to gain increasing power in this essentially Right-wing government, to time elections favourably, and then to alter the Constitution by eliminating its present anti-clerical provisions".[13]

Some idea of the growing power of Gil Robles's Accion Popular was revealed at a meeting held in the great square of the Escorial in April 1934 attended by some 20,000 people who came from all over Spain. It began with an open-air celebration of Mass, and then Gil Robles spoke. He said that his party would take power only when the time was ripe, not before. He emphasised that the Accion Popular had no connection

[11] F.O. 371/19735, despatch from Sir C. Wingfield, 22nd January, 1935.
[12] *A.A. Beziehungen des heiligen Stuhls zu Spanien*, 29th January, 1935.
[13] F.O. 371/18595, despatch from Sir G. Grahame, 10th March, 1934.

with Fascism or Nazism; they were patriots who had no intention of imitating other nations, either those who sought to revive the Roman Empire (Fascist Italy) or those who extolled the virtues of race (Nazi Germany). The strength of the Accion Popular lay, he said, deep in the Spanish soul and its Catholic past; the more they were Catholic, the more they were Spanish. That evening the spleen of the Left-wing extremists at the success of this rally vented itself in Madrid in a strike of trams, buses, restaurants and bakeries, and in the burning and overturning of the buses and cars of those who had attended the meeting.

A minor incident in connection with the Concordat negotiations now in progress in Rome reveals the skilful and patient diplomatic methods which the Vatican was now employing to retrieve its position in Spain. Señor Romero, the Spanish Ambassador, had been negotiating in Rome for six months, but without success; the Vatican Secretariat of State under Cardinal Pacelli was more than usually evasive, accepting a point one day only to modify it the next, being ingratiating in the morning and refractory in the afternoon. A few days before Señor Romero was due to return to negotiate for the fifth time, Mgr. Tedeschini, the Papal Nuncio in Madrid, telephoned a priest who worked at the Secretariat of State in the Vatican to instruct him how to deal with Señor Romero in the next round of negotiations. By a coincidence, the name of the priest at the Vatican with whom he wished to speak was the same as that of a Spanish attaché at the Spanish Rome Embassy; and owing to an error at the Rome telephone exchange, Mgr. Tedeschini was connected with this Spanish attaché and not with the priest at the Vatican. Unaware that he was talking to the wrong man, the Papal Nuncio immediately gave instructions on how Señor Romero was to be given every hope of an early signature of the Concordat — *but that the actual signature was to be delayed as long as possible.* The reason for this, he confidentially explained to the astonished Spanish attaché, was that Gil Robles, the Spanish Catholic leader, would soon be Prime Minister. The Concordat could then be negotiated on terms far more favourable to the Vatican.

The Spanish attaché hung up the receiver without revealing his identity, and immediately telephoned the Madrid Foreign Office, to whom he gave an account of the Papal Nuncio's words. Whereupon the Spanish Foreign Minister, Señor Rocha, telephoned the Nuncio and asked to see him. At their meeting, the Nuncio at first expressed his confidence that the Concordat would shortly be signed. Señor Rocha

cut him short by showing him the text of his own telephone instructions to Rome that morning. Despite the Nuncio's great diplomatic
experience, it was some time before he gained his aplomb.[14] He had to
explain lamely that he had only acted on Gil Robles's confident
assertion that at the coming elections the Accion Popular was bound to
win. This telephonic comedy of errors caused some mirth in Madrid,
where the Socialists demanded the rupture of negotiations on account of
the Vatican's "duplicity".

Nevertheless, relations between Church and State continued steadily to
improve. In the Pope's annual New Year Address to the College of
Cardinals, Spain was no longer listed, together with Mexico, Russia and
Germany, as a source of sorrow to His Holiness. Perhaps, it was hoped
at the College, Spain might at the end of the coming year be listed
among His Holiness's sources of joy. The Cardinals were to be sadly
disappointed.

At the beginning of 1936, Spain was preparing for a general election in
which it was expected, as Gil Robles had confidently predicted, that the
Right would attain power. Both sides were split — the Left into Radical,
Socialist, Communist, all on the worst terms with each other; the Right,
although consisting entirely of Catholics, into Royalist and Republican
groups, each of which held that with it alone lay salvation, and that the
other was betraying the Catholic cause. Indeed, many prelates of the old
school now exiled in Rome with Cardinal Segura declared that Gil
Robles's Catholic Republicanism was sacrilegious, that no political
advantage could possibly justify the abandonment of the monarchy.
However, most of the Spanish clergy, particularly the lower ranks,
sympathised with Gil Robles, whose party was of course favoured by the
Vatican.

Although everyone had expected that the Right would win the
election, by a quirk of parliamentary democracy (not uncommon in
England and the U.S.A.), the Cortes was furnished in February 1936
with a sizeable Left-wing majority — although the aggregate poll for the
Right was larger by several hundred thousand votes. Here was the first
of the factors leading to the civil war six months later. Although the
system of election by constituencies could of itself have accounted for this
anomaly, it was alleged by the Right that the results had been falsified;
otherwise, it would have had a majority in Parliament as well as in the
country. When the Nationalist insurrection took place six months later,

[14] F.O. 371/18596, report from the British Embassy, Madrid.

General Franco contended among other things that he had been summoned to depose a government which had not been constitutionally elected.

The Popular Front government now took office under Señor Azaña. It consisted of the Socialists, the Republican Union, the small Communist party and the large Anarcho-syndicalist group. In fulfilment of his election pledge that political prisoners would be released if the Left won the election, Azaña immediately declared an amnesty. Out of the prisons marched thousands of Anarcho-syndicalists, often accompanied by common criminals; and two days later the churches and convents were again going up in flames all over Spain. The Anarcho-syndicalist interest in the Popular Front government was now over; it had served its purpose. From now on, the fires died down in one place only to be lighted in another; the gunman worked unchecked, the bombing squad unhindered. Señor Azaña and his Socialists had let loose a juggernaut which, in spite of their pathetic appeals for order as the surest proof of Democracy, they could not stop.

Spring turned to summer, the daily tale of murder and arson continued, with the destruction of churches, convents and monasteries. Tension was further increased by the news that Bela Kun had arrived in Barcelona, "the sanguinary hero of the Hungarian revolution and Professor in Terrorism": he had come to give lessons on the theory and practice of his sinister creed. On the 24th March the Papal Nuncio, Mgr. Tedeschini, told the British Embassy that the situation was far more dangerous for the Church than in 1931 and, fearing for his life if civil war came, he asked if he might take asylum in the Embassy.[15]

In the mid-summer of 1936, the long series of political killings came to a climax with the murder of José Sotelo, a prominent member of the Falange. Four days later, on the 17th July, a number of regiments in Spanish Morocco mutinied, and General Franco flew there to raise the Falangist standard. With the backing of the Foreign Legion, Moorish contingents and the regular troops, he was soon master of Spanish Morocco. The following day the rebellion spread to the peninsula; and by the 19th July, garrisons all over Spain had risen in sympathy with him.

Where did the Vatican stand in the coming struggle? It has often been placed in the "Fascist" camp. On the contrary, as we have seen by the end of 1935, the Vatican had reached a modus vivendi with the

[15] F.O. 371/21164, Mr. Osborne to Mr. Eden, Annual Report for 1936 from the Vatican.

Republican government, and would have been quite content for this state of affairs to continue. On three occasions during the civil war Franco attempted to obtain Vatican recognition of his regime; and on three occasions it was refused.[16] As soon as the war began, the Falangist displayed a marked religious ardour which they had hardly shown before. Their members had, in fact, been expressly instructed to attend Mass, to confess and communicate. In the words of Mr. Hugh Thomas "Their propagandists represented the ideal Falangist as half-monk, half-warrior; while the ideal female Falangist was described as a combination of Saint Teresa and Isabella the Catholic." At first Franco described himself as "*El Generalisimo Cristianisimo de la Santa Cruzada*"; but when he realised that the Vatican was by no means certain yet that his was a "Holy Crusade", nor that he was so "very Christian", he dropped the title.

The official view of the Church may be deduced from an article in the *Osservatore Romano* (21st October, 1937) under the heading, "The Two Wars".

It is quite erroneous to suppose, as do many people today in France and England, that there are simply two camps in the Spanish civil war — the one the Reds, the other the Nationalists who are supported by the Vatican. The Church does not belong to any political or social camp. It is not a combatant, but a martyr. The various national States in the world can take one side or the other; but religion stands above the conflict — which public opinion has not understood. The campaign in Europe against the Church has nothing to do with the Spanish civil war — something which is merely being used as a further pretext and opportunity to attack the Church.

Elliptical as usual, the paper seems here to pronounce the lofty principle of *audessus de la mêlée*. But as the civil war continued, and the physical attacks on the Church by extreme Left-wing groups increased in severity, the sympathies of the Vatican inevitably inclined towards their opponents. Mr. N. King, the British Consul-General in Republican Barcelona, scene of some of the worst atrocities, reported that already

---

[16] F.O. 371/21289, Mr. Chilton to Mr. Eden, 10th April, 1937. Also *A.A. Büro des Staatssekretärs*: despatch by the Graf du Moulin, 3rd March, 1939. German disapproval of the tardiness in recognition is described in the Graf's confidential despatch about Cardinal Pacelli; "he must be blamed for this, it took him over a year to recognise the Franco government."

before hostilities had begun a number of anti-religious measures had been introduced by the Catalan authorities. The word "God", he says, was abolished, and anyone pronouncing "*Adios*" in the street was liable to be stopped and told to say "*Salud*", for "there is no God". Names of places called after saints were changed. Christian festivals were suppressed. Sacred pictures, images, books or other articles connected with the Faith were thrown on to bonfires in the streets; if found in the luggage of travellers at the Customs, they were confiscated; possession might mean imprisonment, even death.[17] In July 1936 he reported that all churches, convents and religious buildings in Barcelona except the cathedral had been burnt.[18] The churches were also destroyed in Tarragona — except the cathedral which was used as a store-house. At Bujalance, the church was turned into a cinema; at Carpio into a market-hall; the cathedral at Malaga was used as a manure dumping ground. Some churches were spared because their towers were in a commanding position, and could be used as machine-gun emplacements. The *Osservatore Romano* of the 28th April, 1937 reported, "The church of the Carmine at Manresa, a fine twelfth-century monument, created by the art and piety of past generations, has been destroyed, not in a moment of blind unconsciousness, but coldly, stone by stone, during weeks and months, out of a deliberate desire for a continuous, savage destruction unparalleled in history."

As for the murder of clerics, Franco's Nationalists published after the war the figures of 7937, including twelve bishops, 5255 priests, 2492 monks, 283 nuns and 249 novices. The *Osservatore Romano* gives a higher figure, of 16,500. Mr. Hugh Thomas in *The Spanish Civil War* says the Nationalist figures are probably correct, "although certainly not an under-estimate". These killings of priests were accompanied by that brand of cruelty peculiar to civil war — as at Bellmut del Priorat, where the curé and his housekeeper were taken to church, made to go through a form of marriage ceremony, then shot together, after which a ball was given in the church. The Bishop of Siguenza was led out naked in front of the nuns of the Immaculate Conception to his execution. Mummies and skeletons of nuns were dug up in Barcelona and exposed in the streets in grotesque attitudes, football being played with their skulls. Mr. Thomas relates that the parish priest of Navalmoral when arrested told his inquisitors, "I wish to suffer for Christ." "Oh, you do, do you?" they said. "Then you shall die as he did." They stripped him and scourged

17 F.O. 371/21239, his report to Mr. Roberts, 2nd March, 1937.
18 F.O. 371/20525, his report to Mr. Eden, 29th July, 1936.

him, fastened a beam on his back, made him drink vinegar and crowned him with thorns. "Blaspheme and you shall be spared," said the leader. "It is I who forgive you and bless you," replied the priest. Some of them wished to nail him to a cross, but in the end they simply shot him. His last request was to be shot facing his torturers, so that he might die blessing them.

Atrocities were also perpetrated, and executions carried out, by the Nationalists; but except in the Basque country, where the priests often sided with the government because they believed the Republicans were more likely to grant them autonomy, they were not committed against the Church. Freemasons, members of the Popular Front parties, trades unions and in some cases anyone who had voted for the Popular Front in the February elections, were arrested by the Nationalists and generally shot. After the war, the Republicans made the astronomical claim that Franco's men executed 750,000. Mr. Thomas, after having gone into the matter carefully, suggested a figure around 40,000.

The tale of these atrocities could be continued indefinitely in this cruellest of civil wars. The few examples have been selected here only to show that, if the leaders of Republican Spain, such as Azaña, were sincere, well-intentioned social workers with whom Mr. Attlee and British Protestant bishops could sit at a table and talk reasonably, they had no control over their extremists. And why should they have had any? They were intellectuals, unaccustomed to the exercise of power — lawyers, philosophers, doctors, logicians, poets, chemists. Once in the political arena, they found its discussions very different from the arguments in academic circles; they found hatred, intrigue, ambition, internecine destruction of comrades, political assassination.

Yet it was with these anti-clericals and free-thinkers, as we have seen, that the Vatican had been prepared to come to terms, realising that monarchism as a political force in Spain was spent, and believing that these were the men of the future. But collaboration with them demanded two essential conditions — one, that the Republican government should maintain law and order, and the other, prevent the anti-religious excesses of their extremists. Neither of these conditions were they able to fulfil. The pyromaniacs who destroyed the churches and convents also destroyed the Spanish Republic. The Vatican at length turned against the Republicans, with all that this meant in a Catholic land like Spain. Only to this extent then was the Catholic Church, as its enemies never tire of repeating, "Fascist" in the Spanish civil war.

As the civil war continued and the Nationalists gradually occupied more and more territory, the Church came back into its own. Mr. Thompson, the British representative with the Nationalist forces, reports somewhat sarcastically that the Festival of the Sacred Heart was again being celebrated throughout the Nationalist zone with "the clergy exploiting the superstition and emotional character of the crowd, who chant with the right arm extended heavenwards, '*Viva Cristo Rey!*' in unison with '*Viva Franco!*' " At Burgos two decrees were passed, one suspending civil divorce and the other reintroducing the law against blasphemy. On the walls of the schools the portrait of the Immaculate Virgin again occupied the place of honour. Also reintroduced were the rosary prayers and the salutation "*Ave Maria Purisima*", obligatory religious instruction and a daily school service. In the first flush of restoration, the Spanish priesthood seems to have gone further than the Vatican would have wished — from the renewed censorship of obscene and atheist works to the issue of strict instructions concerning bathing-dress. A man might perform his natural functions openly, but a boy of five might not enter the sea without a costume to cover his chest.

In 1938 Franco issued his "Latin Charter" based on Leo XIII's famous social Encyclical *Rerum Novarum*. The Charter enshrined "the Christian concept of labour, in opposition to the merely material concept of labour as an article of merchandise". In plain words, this meant Labour Tribunals to deal with strikes and lock-outs; a minimum wage "to assure the worker a worthy and moral existence"; respect for small craftsmen; and "the recognition of the family as the basis of society". Much was also made of Leo XIII's substitution of the principle of hierarchy and corporate economy for the old Liberal laissez-faire and competition. The Charter was declared the basis of Falangist social and economic policy.

If Franco made these concessions to the Church, his reasons must have been largely pragmatic, because he spoke in a very different tone to the German Ambassador in May 1937. Strongly deprecating "all Vatican interference in his peace negotiations with the Republican government", he told the German diplomat that during Spain's greatest historical period, under Charles V and Philip II, clerical influence had been at its lowest; conversely, in Spain's weakest period, Vatican influence was at its peak.[19] It is unlikely that Franco approved of these activities of the Spanish clergy as they returned to power; but in a country like Spain he had to permit them. After his victory in 1939, the Vatican had no hesitation in condemning certain features of his rule, such as the education of the youth on totalitarian lines. The irrepressible Cardinal Segura

[19] *A.A. Beziehungen des heiligen Stuhls zu Deutschland*, Vol. 2, 23rd May, 1937.

returned as Archbishop of Seville and was soon in trouble again, this time with Franco and the new government. He refused to allow a plaque commemorating the founder of the Falange, Jose Antonio Primo de Rivera, to be placed in the interior of his cathedral. When the governor insisted, Segura threatened to excommunicate him, and was only dissuaded from doing so by specific instructions from the Vatican. He also refused to recognise that Franco had inherited as Head of State the ex-King's right to nominate bishops, and he was not afraid to insult the Dictator openly. Invited by Franco to a reception, he said he was too ill to attend, and then ostentatiously celebrated a special High Mass in his cathedral. In 1940, the civil Governor of Seville enacted that "the names of all those who fell during the civil war shall be inscribed on the walls of the parish churches". To this Segura replied that it was against the Code of Canon Law "preventing the Church building from being put to any use that might detract from its religious character". He announced solemnly "His Eminence will fulminate the most grievous canonical penalties against those who directly or indirectly may be considered perpetrators of such sacrilege."

Another Spanish bishop, Martinez, in his Pastoral Letter of November 1942 not only attacked Communism, which he said really no longer presented any serious danger, but "the creation of a new ruling class in Spain today which introduces racial laws which are manifestly and unequivocally anti-Christian". The Jesuits also contrived to prevent the pro-German Bishop of Valencia, Miguel de los Santos, from obtaining the important see of Barcelona. Not only had Franco and his regime to swallow these insults, they even had to be obsequious to Segura. At the Holy Week celebrations in Seville in 1940, Franco and his whole entourage were marched about in the cathedral by his bishops, finishing up by doing the Stations of the Cross on their knees.[20] As Herr Dieckhoff, the German Ambassador in Madrid, reported ruefully in December of that year, "Everyone here who is not a Catholic is regarded simply as the Devil."[21]

When Franco set up his totalitarian State he fully appreciated the influence of the Catholic Church, which had been a decisive factor in the civil war, and which he intended to retain as a support for the Falange

[20] F.O. 371/24507, report from Sir M. Peterson, 27th March, 1940. "It all recalled," writes Peterson, "the days of the Holy Roman Empire and the struggles between Pope and Emperor."

[21] A.A. Akten Repetorium, p. 0030, Spain '42–'44, from the German Ambassador in Madrid, 21st December, 1943.

regime. For the attainment of this unspiritual goal he offered generous subsidies for the reconstruction of the devastated ecclesiastical buildings. He intimated that provided the ministers of the Church were subservient to the party, they would be given every opportunity of exercising their authority and influence throughout the country. He was also determined to be consulted over the appointment of bishops; and negotiations over this with the Vatican were begun immediately after the civil war. It was not until 1941 that they were completed, when arrangements were made for filling the twenty-five vacant episcopal sees. One of Franco's provisions was that every consecrated bishop must take an oath of allegiance to the State — which resulted in the nomination generally of "safe" men, sycophants of Franco. In spite of this provision, the Vatican managed to reject seven notorious Falange clerics whom Franco wished to raise to the episcopal rank.

The prerogative of episcopal nominations by the Vatican might not appear to the lay mind a matter so important as to provoke a crisis with Franco. But students of Spanish history know well the harm caused to the Church by the system known as "Regalism", which aimed at increasing the supremacy of the State at the expense of the independence of the Church. The attitude of the Vatican was not so much that they would accord this right only to a monarch, but that they had even gone too far with this medieval privilege under King Alphonso; and they had no intention now of returning to a practice from which the Republic had freed them. For this authority, granted to Ferdinand and Isabella (whose religious convictions were beyond suspicion), had become in the hands of certain of their successors a weapon used against the spiritual authority of the Roman Pontiffs. Indeed Charles III, in everything pertaining to the government and administration of the Church in Spain, actually supplanted the authority of the Vatican. By his royal decree a Roman brief required a *regium exequatur* before it could be published in Spain, and no Papal appointments were regarded as valid unless they obtained the Royal assent.

The attitude of the Vatican was now shared by most of the Spanish bishops, including Cardinal Goma, the Primate, the Bishop of Avila, whose Advent Pastoral Letters were suppressed by the government, and of course Cardinal Segura. In opposition to them were half a dozen bishops who contended that Generalissimo Franco (whose religious convictions were also beyond doubt) would never allow any privilege to operate against the interests of the Church he had so loyally and devotedly served. They advised a practical recognition of his services to religion by granting the right of a prerogative which, while exercised by the saviour of the Christian faith in their land, could never be injurious to the Church. These dissenting prelates also believed that the Falange administration was the only hope for Spain, that safety lay only in supporting the new regime wholeheartedly, and that any neo-pagan influences imported from Franco's ally, Nazi Germany, would always be neutralised by "the staunch spirit of Catholic Spain". Any trouble with the Vatican, they contended, would only discredit the regime which was still surrounded by enemies, and thereby expose the country to another period of disorder and chaos.

But the Vatican and Cardinal Goma set their faces steadfastly against regranting the prerogative of the episcopal nominations, and General Franco was again rebuffed. In retaliation the government attempted to neutralise the power of the Church by absorbing all social, educational and religious organisations of the Catholic Action type. Membership of the "Sindicato Español Universitario" was made compulsory for all students, thus striking a powerful blow at the Catholic Youth Associations. A compromise was finally reached, the Head of State acquiring certain privileges formerly held by the Crown, the *derecho de presentacion*, but no candidate could be presented without the previous consent of the Vatican.

But the last word belongs to Cardinal Segura, who preached a much-discussed sermon in Seville Cathedral on the text, "Beware of wolves in sheeps' clothing." It contained references to the subtle methods of political systems which used the mantle of religion for the furtherance of their political ends. This great enemy of the Republic had now become a thorn in the side of the Falangists.

9

Conversion and Persecution
in Russia

IT MAY SEEM STRANGE TODAY TO REALISE THAT THE NEW
Soviet rulers of Russia in 1918 were at first regarded by the Vatican
without undue apprehension. Admittedly, they openly preached atheism; but owing to the chaos prevailing under their rule, their
ignominious submission at Brest-Litovsk and failure before Warsaw, the
powerful foreign contingents under Wrangel and Denikin threatening
their frontiers, their hallucinatory and impractical economic theories, the
Vatican was convinced, like most other states, that Bolshevism could
not last.

On the contrary, the Vatican regarded the situation under the
Bolshevists as most favourable for proselytisation. The return of the
Eastern Churches to the Catholic faith has been for a thousand years
one of the most cherished aims of the Vatican. Under the Czars, the
twenty million Catholics in Russia had been placed in a position of
abject inferiority with respect to the Orthodox Church which enjoyed
all the advantages of a State religion. But now the Soviets stated that all
religious denominations — in so far as they meant anything to a good
Bolshevist — were on an equal footing. A Russian Catholic priest,

Father Rederov, summed it up: "In the time of the Czars we were subjected to much persecution . . . All of us Latin Catholics breathed a sigh of relief when the Revolution took place in 1917. We were then put on a footing with the Orthodox Church."

A further reason for optimism was the abysmal condition of the Orthodox priesthood in Russia, and the clamouring by most educated Russians for something more cultivated. For two hundred years, since Peter the Great abolished the patriarchate, the Orthodox priests had come to regard themselves as a kind of civil servant. Confronted with any difficulty, the Orthodox priest was apt to send for the police, or report to some higher State official, instead of suggesting his own solution. Often as uneducated as his flock, he could hardly offer the spiritual consolations required from a cleric — and the Russians are a mystical people. The few Orthodox priests who were educated had always envied the Catholic priests such as the Jesuits, who knew exactly what to do in any situation, however unforeseen. Here then, contended the Vatican, was an excellent field for its missions, which would be welcomed by millions of Orthodox starved of a true faith. Roman Catholicism would fill the spiritual vacuum created by the decay of the Orthodox Church. Here was a chance in a thousand years.

After the Revolution of 1917, both Benedict XV and Pius XI immediately apportioned large sums for the conversion of these Orthodox Slavs. Missionaries were to be trained, and a special Pontifical Oriental College was founded in Rome for the study of the Greek Orthodox Church and the Slavonic languages. A bi-monthly periodical *Stoudion* was issued to make the East, its rites, theology and customs familiar to the Western world. In the mid-twenties, the Vatican founded colleges in Belgium for priests who would later enter Russia to proselytise (reminiscent of the sixteenth-century recusants in Louvain and Douai trained to infiltrate England).

Immediately after the Great War, both the Soviets and the Vatican were aware of the advantages of establishing normal diplomatic relations. It is indeed questionable which party desired them most — the Vatican for proselytising, the Soviets because official recognition by Rome would be an important step for them internationally. In 1922, when the Conference of Genoa was convened to consider the situation of the defeated powers, the Pope sent an envoy, Mgr. Sincero, to meet the Russian delegate, Chicherin. He hoped to discuss how Catholic missions might work in Russia. Chicherin appeared most amenable and, at a reception given on the Italian warship *Dante Alighieri*, the two men drank toasts to Soviet-Vatican collaboration.[1] No agreement was reached however, because the Soviets insisted on official Vatican recognition of their government first, before they would guarantee conditions for Catholic missions in Russia. For the Vatican, acceptance of this condition would have meant using their best bargaining-counter too early. But they did not abandon hope, and before the Genoa Conference adjourned the Pope sent another delegate, Mgr. Pizzardo, with a memorandum addressed to all the Powers at the Conference. Its aim was to persuade them to recognise the U.S.S.R. *only* if the Soviets guaranteed religious freedom in Russia. As is known, the Conference came to no conclusion because Chicherin suddenly left in the middle for Rapallo, where he signed the notorious agreement with Germany. In the final communiqué of the Conference, therefore, no mention was made of the Vatican's request for the religious clauses. Somewhat later Count Brockdorf-Rantzau, the German Ambassador in Moscow, reported that Chicherin said to him of this Conference, "Pius XI flirted with us at Genoa, in the hope that we would break the monopoly of the Orthodox Church in Russia, and open the way for him."[2]

The first opportunity for a Papal mission in Russia occurred when the civil war was ending. To its ravages was added in 1921 the failure of the harvest. The south of Russia was afflicted with one of the worst famines in modern history. Hundreds of thousands starved to death. On the 5th August, 1921, Benedict XV wrote to Cardinal Gasparri, the Secretary of State, "We are in the presence of one of the most fearful disasters in history. From the Volga basin to the Black Sea, tens of thousands of human beings destined to the cruellest death cry out for help." He immediately offered to send a relief mission with food and clothing.[3]

The Soviet government accepted, but only after long negotiations between their representative, Woronsky, and Cardinal Gasparri, in which the latter agreed that the mission would take no part in "Apostolic activity". Other foreign relief missions were already at work in southern Russia, the Quakers, the German Red Cross, the Baptists, the Jews, the

---

[1] In Russian émigré circles the Vatican was much criticised for this, for having "shaken the blood-stained hand of the Soviets".

[2] *A.A. Beziehungen des Vatikans zu England (geheim)*, despatch from Brockdorf-Rantzau, 29th August, 1927.

[3] Mgr. d'Herbigny, "L'aide pontificale aux enfants affamés de Russie", *Orientalis Christiana*, IV, 1925.

Memnonites and, the richest and therefore the most welcomed by the Soviets, the American Relief Administration. To this last the Papal Mission was affiliated; and on the 29th September, 1922, its nine priests and three laymen under Father Gehrmann landed at Odessa. They immediately began distributing food and clothing without distinction of nationality or confession. On each packet for the children were the printed words, "To the children of Russia from the Pope of Rome".[4] Was this, or was it not, "Apostolic activity"? The Soviets later contended it was.

The Papal Mission soon installed camp kitchens throughout the area (in one day, ninety-two field-kitchens in the district of Eutropia alone). It set up clothing and shoe-making factories, field-hospitals were opened, and in the malarial districts quinine was distributed. Between September 1922 and February 1923, 2400 tons of food were imported, and the Vatican Mission was feeding some 25,000 people daily. In the Russian press long columns were devoted to the energetic measures taken by the Soviets to relieve the famine, but no mention was made of the Vatican Mission.

It is significant that as conditions improved (a better harvest the following year), the Soviet authorities became less amenable. They now confined the activities of the Papal Mission to the Crimea, and suggested that all its establishments should be taken over and run by the local Soviets. To this demand the Vatican could not agree, and their Mission was given two weeks' notice to leave the country. On its departure, the Soviets took over all its supplies. When he reached Rome, Father Gehrmann reported to the Pope that the Mission had been of great value, not only because of its relief work, but on account of the knowledge it had gained about the new Bolshevist regime. He was sorry to disabuse the Vatican, but he saw no possibility of it collapsing in the foreseeable future.

Nevertheless, the Vatican still did not wish to lose contact with Russia, because a large number of Catholics from what were now Polish territories had been sent to Siberia, where they were entirely without priests or the consolations of religion. Count Brockdorf-Rantzau, the German Ambassador in Moscow, reported on the 31st July, 1924 that, "Mgr. Pacelli, the Papal Nuncio in Berlin, is having conversations with the Soviet Ambassador about sending an Apostolic Delegate to Russia to care for Catholics."[5] These negotiations were successful, and in October 1925 the Jesuit Father, Mgr. d'Herbigny, was allowed to enter Russia. Here he met

---

[4] L'Information, 17th August, 1928.

[5] A.A. Beziehungen des päpstlichen Stuhls zu fremden Staaten, Vol. 3, telegram from Brockdorf-Rantzau, 31st July, 1924. Confirmed in Beziehungen des Vatikans zu Russland, Vol. 1, Meyer's telegram from the Vatican, 10th February, 1925.

Chicherin, the Foreign Minister, who showed an unexpected respect for the Vatican and the Catholic Church — although not perhaps in quite the way the Pope would have wished. "We Communists," Chicherin told Mgr. d'Herbigny, "feel pretty sure we can triumph over London capitalism [sic]. But Rome will prove a harder nut to crack. If Rome did not exist, we would be able to deal with all the various brands of Christianity. They would all finally capitulate before us. Without Rome, religion would die. But Rome sends out for the service of her religion propagandists of every nationality. They are more effective than guns or armies . . . The result of the struggle, my friend, is uncertain. What *is* certain is that it will be long."[6]

Such was the Vatican's insistence on being represented in Russia to cater for the spiritual needs of the Catholics, that it was prepared to swallow insult after insult rather than abandon the struggle. In the words of the German Chargé d'Affaires at the Vatican, Herr Meyer, "The Vatican will not give up its long-term goal — totally independent of personalities and regimes — of retaining some sort of relationship with Russia, while awaiting the favourable moment."[7] Pius XI was most optimistic. He told Sir Odo Russell, the British Minister, that it was "a source of pleasure to read more than once in the reports of the Soviet authorities themselves that the Church of Rome remains the most formidable barrier to the progress of revolutionary ideas, and that so far no breach in Russia has been made in its position".[8]

In 1925, the Soviets handed to Mgr. Pacelli, the Papal Nuncio in Berlin, their plan to regulate conditions for the Catholics in Russia. Among their conditions was the extraordinary one that all correspondence between Rome and its priesthood in Russia should be censored. The Vatican, still hoping for an agreement, perhaps in the form of a concordat, agreed, if unwillingly. But it soon became clear that the more the Vatican conceded, the more Moscow demanded. After interminable discussions between Mgr. Pacelli and the Soviet representative in Berlin, the crisis came to a head, when the Soviets suddenly announced that there could be no question of a concordat; they intended henceforth to deal with all Catholic problems, Church property, religious education, priest's stipends, etc., by unilateral legislation. The Vatican would not even be consulted.

[6] *A.A. Beziehungen des Vatikans zu Russland*, Vol. 1.
[7] *A.A. Beziehungen des heiligen Stuhls zu fremden Staaten*, Vol. 3, 27th September, 1924.
[8] F.O. 371/12582, despatch from Sir O. Russell, 28th December, 1926.

What had happened is quite simply explained. In 1933 the Soviets had been officially recognised by the United States; and the other nations would soon follow suit. The Soviet Union now had no need of Vatican recognition. Thus ended the Papal-Soviet negotiations which had opened so auspiciously with Chicherin five years before in Genoa.

It was now that the Vatican began to realise that its principal enemy in the post-war period was Communism, which had come to stay in Russia, at least for the foreseeable future, and which was now carrying on a systematic persecution of the Churches. This persecution may be divided into three periods. The first lasted from 1918 to 1923 when, in the first flush of iconoclast delirium, the Bolshevists confidently believed that religion could be eradicated overnight, as in the days of the French Convention. The second period lasted roughly from 1923 to 1928 when, in the ecclesiatical as well as the secular domain, the milder policy of Lenin's NEP prevailed. The third period began in 1928, when the Soviet regime was firmly established and could attack religion "scientifically", on a long-term basis, avoiding the excesses of the first period, which had proved ineffective. That there was more actual physical persecution in the first period should not obscure the fact that it was, in the eyes of the Vatican, the least dangerous. Since Tertullien said *sanguis martyrum semen Christianorum*, the Church has become well accustomed to martyrdom, has indeed often thrived on it. The second and third periods really overlap, and a clear demarcation cannot be made.

The first period, 1918–23, was marked, as almost always in revolutions, by the inability of the new regime to control its extremists. Thousands of priests, monks, nuns and other members of the various Christian communities in Russia were done to death in a variety of brutal ways, from judicial murder to bush justice and slow starvation in Siberia.[9] Other priests were held as hostages to be exchanged against Communist agitators imprisoned abroad. One of the heads of the Catholic hierarchy in Russia, Bishop Ropp, was arrested by a local Soviet on some trumped-up charge. His subordinates immediately made representations, but they were not allowed to visit him in prison. Whereupon they went to Moscow and managed to get as far as Lenin's office; but Lenin refused to

[9] *A.A. Beziehungen des Vatikans zu Russland*, 18th April, 1929. Von Bergen reported from Rome that Catholic priests were often banished to the notorious island of Solovetzky in the White Sea where "they are said to work on cutting ice blocks while standing up to their knees in water."

receive them, saying he knew nothing of the matter. They were referred instead to the Commissariat of Nationalities, where they were received by one Joseph Stalin; but he too professed to be completely ignorant of the affair. The bishop managed to escape only thanks to the good offices of the Persian Carpet Company, which conveyed him secretly in their transport to Tabriz. The whole topsy-turvy incident, the arbitrary arrest and peculiar escape, the apparently easy access to the leaders of the Revolution, seem typical of those early days of revolutionary chaos.

In these days, too, the "Union of Militant Godless" was very active. In Moscow, it organised a procession of all the Gods and Prophets, including Buddha on horseback in a priapic posture; the Virgin Mary lying on her back, also in a suggestive attitude; and a repulsive-looking Catholic priest making overtures to a beautiful girl. In December 1922, it erected in Leningrad a scaffold in the middle of the Nevsky Prospect on which effigies of the Pope, the saints and prophets were beheaded and burned. The clergy of all faiths were also attacked for their alleged gluttony and the drunkenness which accompanied religious festivals. A shop-window in Moscow was decorated at Easter with a wax-work of six priests in a small boat swilling vodka, with a number of empty bottles littered around them. Another showed a smart new Soviet tractor being driven over a Catholic priest, a Jewish rabbi and a Moslem mullah.

The first period was also one of the confiscation, and often wilful destruction, of Church property. All churches with everything they contained, such as sacred vessels, liturgical vestments, church bells, etc., were proclaimed national property. Many were pulled down, even those of architectural value, the pretext generally being road-widening or metro construction. In July 1922, the Pope offered at the Genoa Conference to buy back all the valuables taken from the churches, at a price fixed by the Soviets. The offer was refused.

The second period, 1923–9, which coincided with Lenin's New Economic Policy, witnessed a slackening of these severities. It was also the time when the Soviet State made the experiment of creating, in rivalry to the existing Churches, a Church of its own, "The Living Church", under Bishop Antonin. This consisted of a small group of priests who had withdrawn their allegiance from the Patriarch, and who professed a kind of formal acceptance of the principles of Communism — having something in common with the *assermentés* priests of the French Revolution. "The Living Church" defended the existence of God and Christian principles, but without much conviction. It proved, in fact, a "Lifeless Church", and it lasted only five years.

A certain astuteness in Bolshevist thinking in the second period warned against any more cases of open persecution, and in official statements the excesses of the early period were condemned. One of the great slogans at the time was the "liquidation of the kulak as a class", but the Bolshevists were now careful not to talk about "liquidating the priests as a class". It was about this time that Lunacharsky pronounced his famous apothegm, "Religion is like a nail. The more you hit it on the head, the more it sinks in." This second or milder period is here arbitrarily situated as beginning in 1923 because in that year a circular containing instructions about how to deal with religion, issued by the Central Committee of the Communist Party in the Ukraine, came fortuitously into the possession of Mr. R. M. Hodgson, the British Chargé d'Affaires in Moscow. It left no doubt about the intention of the party to eradicate religion, which it described as "an evil no less pernicious than alcoholism or prostitution". But it stated textually that direct persecution was to be avoided, primarily on account of the outcry which might arise in foreign countries whose sympathy the Soviet Union wished to enlist at this difficult period in its early life. The campaign of anti-religious propaganda, stated the document, as conducted by the Besboshnik and the Communist Youth was defeating its own ends. Ribald parodies of sacred themes and personalities were to be replaced by lectures, discussions and arguments based on scientific exposition. The process of quietly fostering antagonism between religious sects and creeds was recommended as more likely to yield results. The two thousand-year reign of the Church over the minds of men could not be overthrown by stump oratory. A sign of the improvement was also seen in a despatch from the German Consul, Herr Grosskopf, from Nowosibirsk (22nd March, 1930), reporting that in country regions the closing of the churches had been suspended, and that at Issil-Kel in the district of Omsk, the church bells recently confiscated had been rehung.[10]

Persecution became administrative rather than political. Priests were now less likely to be arrested and tried arbitrarily than to find it difficult to obtain board and lodging, for which every Soviet citizen required a ration card. According to Communist classification, priests do not belong to the working community, are attached to no trade union, and are therefore not entitled to ration cards. They are free to buy their food on the open market which, owing to the acute food shortage in Russia at the time, was prohibitively expensive. They therefore had to live on the charity of parishioners. The Churches were no longer destroyed materi-

[10] A.A. *Beziehungen des Vatikans zu Russland*, Vol. 3.

ally, or even turned into cinemas, but simply closed on the ground that there were not enough faithful in the neighbourhood to warrant their upkeep. One method was to detain the priest on some petty charge, such as drunkenness or peculation, and then to close the church on the ground that there was no one to officiate.

Until about 1928 the Vatican was still negotiating through Mgr. Pacelli, the Nuncio in Berlin, for a modus vivendi with Soviet Russia leading perhaps to a concordat which might allow a measure of penetration, even proselytisation. But when it at last became clear that Bolshevism was not going to collapse, and that the anti-clerical persecution, although abated physically, was becoming more dangerous and insidious, the Pope decided to speak up before the world. It was at once his recognition of defeat and declaration of war. On the 2nd February, 1930, in an open letter to Cardinal Pompili, the Vicar-General of Rome, he protested against "the horrible and sacrilegious outrages being perpetrated against the Catholic Church in Russia". He told of children who were brought up, and encouraged, in unchastity; of the anti-God processions, and of workers who had to declare their hatred of God if they were to retain their jobs; of the arrest and murder of Catholic priests, etc.

His words had an immediate effect throughout the world. Meetings to discuss the persecution of the Catholic Church in Russia took place in almost every country with which the Vatican had diplomatic relations. At the same time, the Pope declared a solemn expiatory Mass for Russia and its persecuted Catholics in St. Peter's on the 19th March, 1930. Von Bergen reports that it was attended by 50,000 people, including many non-Catholics and Russian emigrants, amid scenes of wild emotion. The diplomats of all the countries represented at the Vatican were invited, and it was significant that those who had already recognised the Soviet Government did not attend. Von Bergen, for instance, was instructed by his government to absent himself, so that "German-Soviet trade relations might not be endangered". Only those countries which had not yet recognised the Soviet Union sent their representatives — a small contingent, Spain, Belgium, Hungary, Chile, Venezuela and Nicaragua. But the expiatory Mass had an effect far beyond the bronze doors of St. Peter's. All over the world similar Masses were said in Catholic churches, imploring God to send means to repair wrongs done to the Church by the Communists. The *Civiltà Cattolica* of the 5th March, 1930 wrote that the Pope had spoken for all Christianity, not only for Catholicism. It asked if other lay governments had done as much against the Communist danger.

His words provoked a storm of abuse in Russia itself. Bukharin dug up all the old Papal skeletons, Alexander VI, the Inquisition, the immolation of Giordano Bruno, Cesare Borgia, Galileo, etc. The Pope was accused of plotting with Kerenski and the Wall Street bankers. The Pontifical Oriental College in Rome was described as the "cradle of a Holy War to be waged on Russia in the form of a White Army under Prince Wolkonsky".[11] It was clear that the Soviets, too, now recognised who was their principal enemy. Litvinov declared at Geneva, "The motive force behind any anti-Soviet crusade will henceforth be the Vatican."

"The Pope," wrote von Bergen, "has taken a very strong line. He calls for the unity of all Christian peoples in the face of a movement aimed at shaking the very foundations of Christian culture. He even criticises the nations which have recognised the Soviets."[12] The *Osservatore Romano* wrote very sharply about the negotiations between the Soviet Union and the United States of America, "So the emissary of Moscow, Litvinov, well versed in every diplomatic ruse, shakes hands with the representative of the most bourgeois and capitalist country in the world. At any moment now Roosevelt will pronounce the *de jure* recognition of the atheists. The Russians have completely duped Roosevelt."[13]

But there was little that the *Osservatore Romano*, or indeed the Pope, could do. Communism had arrived in Russia. The Vatican would now have to wait until in some future war a powerful State defeated it and reinstalled the Christian Faith. That, too, was to prove between 1941 and 1945 another tantalising but vain chimera.

---

[11] *A.A. Beziehungen der Vatikans zu Russland:* vol. 3, von Bergen reports on this, 15th October, 1929, adding "this can be taken seriously only in the mind of a Russian moujik."

[12] *A.A.* ibid report from von Bergen, 9th April, 1931.

[13] To give Mr. Roosevelt his due, he insisted, when granting recognition, on a clause being inserted in the agreement guaranteeing religious liberty in Russia. He even sent Mr. Sarley, a Catholic, to see Litvinov in Geneva about it.

10

The Habsburg Secession States

In 1918 the fall of the Habsburg dynasty with which the Catholic Church had for so many centuries been closely associated, the dismemberment of the Austro-Hungarian Empire and its replacement by a number of small republics was, to the Vatican, most unwelcome. It feared that these new States might one day form a confederation which would come under the influence of Russia. Except that its fear was of a revived Czarist and Orthodox Russia, this proved a remarkable prognostication. The Vatican could hardly have then foreseen the Second World War, the victory of Russian Communism, and the "Satellite States" of Eastern Europe.

Before 1918, the close links between Throne and Altar in Austria-Hungary had enabled the Catholic Church to influence policy more effectively than in any other country. "Nowhere else," wrote Joseph Lehrl, "has the corpus of Catholic teaching become so deeply embodied in the historical consciousness of a people as in Austria. The relations between Rome and the State have always differed radically from those in other countries. The two were not simply parties to a legal contract (the Concordat), but two different expressions of the same idea, each moving in its own manner towards a common goal. Church and State were not two independent powers, but members of a common Christian entity."[1]

There was much talk in the early days after the First World War, particularly in France, of a Habsburg restoration, enjoying the full support of the Vatican. It is no doubt true that, on traditional grounds, the Papacy would have welcomed the restoration of what was until 1918 the principal Catholic dynasty in Europe. In other words, if a Catholic restoration had become practicable, it would have been impossible to imagine the Papacy opposing it. But Pius XI was not a traditionalist. With him, dynastic interests were nothing compared with the interests of the Faith, and if he had to choose, he preferred a safe Catholic republic to a precarious clerical monarchy. Von Bergen, the German Ambassador at the Vatican, was asked by the Wilhelmstrasse what would be the Pope's attitude towards a Habsburg restoration. He replied that although the Pope was well disposed towards the Habsburgs, he would maintain complete neutrality in the matter, because "the present Austrian government is excellent, corresponding exactly to the requirements of the Vatican" (this was Dollfuss's Corporate State of 1933), and that a restored monarchy could not improve matters. On the contrary, the Josephinist tradition might still be alive in certain members of the Habsburg family;[2] whereas with the present Austrian government there was no sign of that. Further, the Vatican did not intend, simply in order to please the Habsburgs, to impair its present relations with France and Czechoslovakia, both of which were naturally opposed to a Habsburg restoration. Finally, von Bergen reported that the Pope considered the Austrian Pretender, the Archduke Otto, too young and inexperienced to become Emperor; the Pope had advised him to take a wife and "make a position for himself".[3]

In the Habsburg days before the First World War, the strength of the Church in the Dual Monarchy had lain in the countryside among the peasantry, of whom ninety per cent were Catholic, most of them devout. A recruit for the police, for instance, required the recommendation of the village priest before he could be considered. The strength of the Socialists, on the other hand, lay almost exclusively in Vienna, "Red Vienna" as it came to be called. Its post-war Socialist municipality, using an ingenious system of doles, subsidies and free passes on the trams and

[1] Joseph Lehrl, *Bildungskräfte im Katholicismus der Welt* (Herder, 1936).

[2] Joseph II, the Emperor of the *Aufklärung*, who, alone of the Habsburgs, had put certain impediments in the way of the Catholic Church in Austria.

[3] *A.A. Pol II Beziehungen des Vatikans zu Österreich*, Vol. 1, despatch from von Bergen, 5th January, 1936.

railways for the working classes, soon began to make extensive conversions from the Catholic faith. They offered a Socialist paradise for all who joined the party, with Socialist hiking tours in the Vienna Woods and Socialist holidays in the mountains; they organised Socialist philatelist clubs, Socialist pigeon-fanciers' clubs, Socialist weight-lifting clubs. Their members worked together, played together, read the Socialist press together, and when they died were incinerated in the municipal crematorium together. Soon the Church was losing some 30,000 Catholics a year in the little rump state of Austria, which now numbered only six million souls.

As this continued, Austrian Catholics became alarmed that worse might lie ahead; the Liberal-Socialist State of the Girondins might be replaced by the absolutist State of the Jacobins. Already on their own frontiers the Bolshevists, Bela Kun in Hungary and Eisner in Munich, were announcing that they were ready to help the Austrian comrades. Already certain Austrian Socialist leaders like Bauer boasted of their "Austro-Marxism", of establishing a dictatorship of the proletariat. The special position the Austrian Catholics had enjoyed under the Monarchy seemed more than threatened. Yet during the next two decades, thanks to the political skill of two Catholic politicians, Mgr. Seipel and Dr. Engelbert Dollfuss, these fears were dispelled. Throughout the twenties and thirties the Socialists, although the largest party in the land, never came to power again, as they had in 1919. Until 1938, Austria was governed by a series of Catholic-dominated coalitions.

We have seen that the Pope had discouraged priests from taking part in politics unless "Altar or Family were threatened". The anti-clerical situation in Austria was so threatening in the early twenties that he made an exception, and turned a blind eye on the cloth of the most accomplished politician of his time. Ignaz Seipel was born in Vienna in 1867, the son of a Variety Theatre doorkeeper. As a young parish priest in Vienna, he observed the evolving Socialist methods for detaching Catholics from the Faith, and he took every opportunity of studying working-class conditions. After becoming a doctor of theology, in Salzburg, he entered politics, rising to the top in a remarkably short time. Such was the simplicity of his life that, during the whole period when Seipel was Chancellor of Austria, he lived in the Convent of the Sacred Heart, of which he was an almoner. He rose at 5 a.m. and celebrated Mass before going to work in his office in the Ballhausplatz, to which he took a tram. He dismayed his staff by travelling second-class to Geneva to represent his country at the League of Nations. Throughout his political career, he always wore clerical garb. In June 1924, an unemployed railwayman tried to assassinate him, and his life was in danger for several days. It was typical of Seipel that he supported the parents of the would-be assassin financially while the man served his gaol sentence.

With this outward simplicity went a cunning, even Machiavellian, intelligence. Sir Eric Phipps, the British Ambassador in Vienna, who clearly did not like him, referred to "this over-subtle, tortuous priest . . . first and foremost a priest, and as such unduly obedient to inspiration from the Vatican".[4] Undoubtedly Mgr. Seipel worked unceasingly to maintain the prestige of the Catholic Church in Austria, and he accepted the Chancellorship, convinced that through his Faith he could also serve his country. Von Schuschnigg wrote of him, "Above all Seipel was the priest — he saw everything *sub specie aeternitatis*. In the manner and style of his life, in every situation, he brought his actions and decisions into relation with the sanctity of his original calling."[5]

Seipel's great achievement in internal politics was to secure the continuous support of the other bourgeois parties in a series of coalitions with his Catholic party, the Christian Socials, thereby always outvoting the Socialists. In foreign affairs, he regarded Austria as not German, but as Central European, and he intended it to act as a link between the German and Danubian States. He skilfully played off Czechs, Hungarians and Italians against one another, and was accused of using the French and English fear of an *Anschluss* with Germany to extricate loans from them for his impoverished country. Sir Eric Phipps wrote again, "While there is no doubt some justification for this charge, it certainly does not reveal his dominant motive, which is invariably an inordinate preoccupation with the interests of the Holy See."[6]

This is an exaggeration for Pius XI, on the contrary, disapproved of priests in politics. In Italy he had preferred Mussolini to the priest Don Sturzo; and had Austria been able to produce a strong man, a Mussolini, to deal with the Marxists, he would no doubt have treated Mgr. Seipel as he had Don Sturzo. But until the arrival of Dollfuss in 1933, no such strong man existed. The only politician capable of confronting the powerful and numerically superior Austrian Marxists was Mgr. Seipel. It is significant that when, after Seipel's death, Dollfuss became Chancellor, the Vatican immediately instructed the Austrian priests no longer to take part in politics. The interests of the Church were so well served by Dollfuss, a

[4] F.O. 371/14311.
[5] Kurt von Schuschnigg, *Dreimal Österreich*.
[6] F.O. 371/14311, Annual Report for 1929 to Mr. A. Henderson, 15th February, 1930.

devout Catholic, that their participation was no longer necessary. On the 5th December, 1933, the Austrian Bishops' Conference announced that all clerics with parliamentary mandates — there were eighteen in Parliament — were to lay them down.[7] Pius XI thus returned to his basic policy. The Christian Social party which Mgr. Seipel led in the twenties had, in spite of its name, nothing Socialist about it. It was a clerical party combining politics with religion even more intimately than did the Popular Party in Italy or the Centre Party in Germany. It included anti-Socialists of all shades, from near-Fascists and big industrialists to social reformers and the Christian trades unions, with names such as Heimatblock, Landbund, Heimwehr, Agrarien, etc. All these variegated groups were welded together by the skill of Mgr. Seipel. Although the largest party in Parliament was the Socialist with seventy-two mandates (the Christian Socials had sixty-six), Mgr. Seipel always combined with the other bourgeois parties to obtain a majority. When he came to power in 1920, the Socialists were unaware that they were now to be permanently in opposition. Convinced that it was only a matter of months before Austria followed the example of her neighbours, Bela Kun in Hungary and Eisner in Munich, the Socialist future seemed bright. So confident were they that when Mgr. Seipel, by his ingenious political combinations, became Chancellor they were convinced that he could not last, and their rowdies, like the French mob of the Convention, invaded Parliament and threatened the members. The Chamber resounded to their abuse for months until, when they realised that Seipel and his coalition were well installed, they abandoned constitutional methods, and formed their own private army, the Schutzbund, and resorted to physical violence. In 1927, being displeased with a legal verdict against a member of their party, they burned down the Vienna law courts. An Italian cleric, Mgr. Faidutti, who visited Vienna at this time, told von Bergen, the German Ambassador to the Vatican, that Viennese Socialism had now become "Bolshevism pure and simple", and he described the terrorist methods used to intimidate Parliament, their propaganda against religion and morals, their boasts of "emancipating the family from the religious yoke and returning to the natural condition of man". The principal reason for all this, said Mgr. Faidutti, lay in the tolerant good nature, the *Schlamperei*, of the Viennese, who were fundamentally religious.[8]

[7] *A.A. Pol II Beziehungen des Vatikans zu Österreich*, Vol. 1, despatch from the German Legation in Vienna, 6th December, 1935.

[8] *A.A. Pol II Beziehungen des Vatikans zu Österreich*, Vol. 1, von Bergen's report of conversation with Mgr. Faidutti.

Thanks to his political skill, Mgr. Seipel managed to keep the Socialists out for nine years. But he knew that with the mounting unrest on the streets created by the Schutzbund and the emerging Austrian Nazi party, the days of parliamentary government in Austria were numbered. He was getting old, and although confidence in him personally remained, the government seemed incapable of maintaining order. Many Catholics began to look for protection against the Socialists and Nazis in a paramilitary body of their own, the Heimwehr. It was ostentatiously Catholic, its flags and guidons being blessed in church, and its military exercises were always preceded by a *Feldmesse*.[9] To the Vatican, it was something of an embarrassment, and the Pope did not recognise it officially.

The continual marchings and counter-marchings of these rival private armies were a permanent threat to civil peace; and on the 18th August, 1929 a regular battle took place between the Schutzbund and the Heimwehr in the village of St. Lorens in Styria, in which thirty-two men were killed. Then on the 13th September, the Heimwehr attempted a full-scale putsch aimed at occupying Vienna and installing a totalitarian government under their leader, Major Pfrimer. It failed, but it convinced Mgr. Seipel that as parliamentary methods could no longer function under these conditions, some new form of government must be devised. As early as 1927 he was working on a scheme for constitutional reform, a corporate State on the Mussolini lines. He had a further reason for wishing to modify the existing parliamentary system. On the 24th April, 1932, the Austrian Nazi party did surprisingly well in the local elections in the important Bundeslander, Vienna, Lower Austria and Salzburg; and it appeared certain that if there was a general election, they would play a dominant part in the new Parliament. In view of what was happening next door in Germany, Seipel saw very clearly where this might lead.

At this point another event occurred which confirmed Seipel and the man who was to be his successor when he died, Dollfuss, in the conviction that a new constitution was necessary. On the 15th May, 1931, Pope Pius XI issued his famous social encyclical, *Quadragesimo Anno*, which condemned modern capitalism as practised in the parliamentary democracies, and demanded a new system to "replace individualism, whose economic unsoundness and heartlessness have clearly been shown". Austrian Catholics could easily relate this criticism to their own society for, as in all Western democracies after 1918, immense fortunes had quickly been made by dubious means. Parliamentary democracy was proving to be the rule of

[9] Mussolini approved of the Heimwehr's similarity with his Fascists; he supplied it with funds and propaganda material.

a monied oligarchy aided by unscrupulous demagogues. The Pope's cure for this was a State founded on the old *Ordines*, or vocational groups, among whom it would be the State's duty to foster harmony. "When we speak of reform of the social order," wrote the Pope in his encyclical, "it is principally of the State that we think because, on account of the evils of Individualism things have come to such a pass that the highly developed social life which once flourished in a variety of prosperous institutions organically linked has been ruined, leaving virtually only the individual and the State." This "Individualism" the Pope regarded as largely responsible for the evils of class warfare, because it assumed that free enterprise and the open market alone could produce the best economic results. The system he now advocated existed already to some extent in Italy, for the Fascist State was divided economically into thirteen corporations, according to trades or professions. But the Austrian Constitution which Seipel now outlined, and which his successor, Engelbert Dollfuss, elaborated, came even closer to the Pope's conception of a corporate State. As Mr. Gordon Shepherd says in his biography of Dollfuss, "It was drawn less from Mussolini's contemporary Fascist State than from the ancient vision of St. Augustine's *Civitas Dei*." It was to be governed by one man, the Chancellor, assisted by a Council of State of some fifty men whom he would nominate. It was in fact a dictatorship; but what distinguished it from other contemporary dictatorships was its insistence on Christianity, and in particular *Catholic* Christianity. The preamble of the Constitution included these remarkable words, "In the name of God the Almighty from whom all justice flows, the Austrian people accept this Constitution"; and Dollfuss said, "We Catholics must renew the life of Austria. When the rest of the world sees that this people is better, more honest, more capable of sacrifice, we shall have made propaganda for the Catholic conception of life."

Another Catholic feature was that the Austrian Concordat, which was signed with the Vatican on the 1st May, 1933 was actually incorporated into the new Constitution. This Concordat fully satisfied the Vatican's requirements about marriage, education and canonical law. Matrimonial questions, for instance, were to be regulated according to canonical, and not civil, law. In a notable case two years later, a husband demanded a divorce on the ground that his wife had given birth six months after their marriage, and that he had had no carnal relations with her before marriage. In Austrian civil law, because the wife had not told him the child was by another man, he could have divorced her. But canonical law does not recognise these grounds, and under the new Constitution he lost the case.[10]

[10] See *Agentum des deutschen Nachrichtenburos*, No. 113, 23rd April, 1936.

The Austrian Concordat was, from the Vatican's point of view, the most satisfactory made with any country between the wars. Other points favourable to the Church were: the Pope could appoint bishops as he pleased; full freedom was guaranteed to Catholic Action and the Catholic press; and the State increased its financial aid to the Church.

The Socialists naturally attacked the Concordat and savagely, but they now had no parliamentary platform and their attacks had to be confined to press articles and caricatures. Their newspaper showed God in a dressing-gown with a long pipe and beer-mug being asked by St. Peter when he will put an end to these antiquated marriage laws. God's answer is, "I'd certainly like to, but Mgr. Seipel won't." This "Vaticanisation" of Austria, as its opponents called it, was attacked not only by the Socialists, but by the quasi-Fascist Heimwehr, the private army which, with its *Feldmesse* and consecration of flags and symbols, had always prided itself on its Catholicism. In a speech in Linz, one of its leaders, Count Revetera, said that the Catholic priesthood in Austria had now been given a political power they had never possessed before; *Österreich* should be called *Klosterreich*.[11]

Dollfuss's exemplary Christian life was as much approved by the Vatican as were his policies. When the Austrian President, Miklas, invited him after the death of Siepel to become Chancellor he did not accept immediately but spent the night in prayer in a church in one of the poorer quarters of Vienna before reaching his decision. The *Osservatore Romano* likened him to "a crusader dedicating himself as he girds on his sword"; and the Pope conferred on him the Order of the Golden Spur for his "well-known devotion to the Catholic religion". In a speech of welcome to Austrian pilgrims under Cardinal Innitzer at Easter 1933, the Pope referred to Dollfuss as "the illustrious man who rules Austria so well, so resolutely and in such a Christian manner. His actions are witness to Catholic visions and convictions. The Austrian people, Our Beloved Austria, now has the government it deserves. We beseech the Almighty to accompany His blessing with the fullness of His grace and always to support such a Christian, giant-hearted man as the Chancellor, to protect him from all evils and dangers so that he may long strive and delve fruitfully for Our Beloved Catholic Austrian people."[12] But it was not to be. Hitler's accession to power in Germany at the same time as Dollfuss became Chancellor was to render all the

Austrian efforts vain, and before the next year was out to rob him of life itself.

After his murder by the Austrian Nazis in 1934, a special Requiem Mass was held for him in the Church of Santa Maria dell' Anima in Rome, at which the entire diplomatic corps were instructed to attend in uniform; and the absolution was pronounced by the Secretary of State, Cardinal Pacelli, himself.

We have seen that France had always contended since the war that the Vatican supported an Austrian *Anschluss* with Germany because the Church might turn it to good purpose—a Catholic bloc with Bavaria and the Rhineland, both eminently Catholic lands, in Central Europe. Until the arrival of Hitler in power, there was some truth in this. The Vatican believed that Austrian Catholics would strengthen the already favourable position of the Catholic Church in Germany under the Weimar Republic. But after Hitler arrived, the Vatican opposed this on the very good grounds that Hitler's Germany was proving to be, in spite of the Concordat made with Nazi Germany (see Chapter 12), an anti-Catholic and pagan State. There was little, however, the Vatican could do to influence events in Austria beyond using its new prerogative under the Austrian Concordat to nominate to positions of authority bishops who were known to oppose the *Anschluss* with Germany. In December 1934, it appointed to the important see of Salzburg Dr. Sigismund Waitz, who had preached a number of eloquent sermons against the *Anschluss*. Von Papen, the German Ambassador in Vienna, reported indignantly that "the selection of this prelate by the Vatican was totally unexpected here; he is known to be an inveterate enemy of Germany". Von Papen also pointed out that only a year before Dr. Waitz had been made Papal Throne Assistant and a Papal Count, "distinctions granted only for achievements which go well beyond the scope of diocesan work".[13]

The Vatican was particularly pleased that Mussolini had condemned the project of an *Anschluss*. In his paper, the *Popolo d'Italia* (13th February, 1935), he wrote himself:

The traditional devotion of the Austrian people is to the Catholic religion. To be Austrian is to be Catholic — and a devout Catholic at that, firmly attached to the Apostolic Church of Rome. Since the war Catholicism has shown how deep are its roots in Austrian soil. The great

[13] *A.A. Pol II Beziehungen des Vatikans zu Österreich*, Vol. 1, von Papen's despatch from Vienna, 20th December, 1934.

Austrian Chancellors, Seipel and Dollfuss, were good Catholics. Schuschnigg is a good Catholic. Seen from Rome, Austria appears as the great Catholic barrier in the Danube basin, on whose banks the waves of Slavonic Orthodoxy and the German Reformed Church break in vain. The tasks of Austria are therefore twofold; first, defence of the values of Teutonic culture, humanised through its contact with Latin culture; second, to act as the vanguard of Catholicism in north-east and central Europe. In this sense, Austria performs an enormous service to European civilisation. Her absolute independence is therefore of the highest importance.

These hopes were brutally shattered in February 1938 when Hitler summoned Schuschnigg to Berchtesgarten. The Under-Secretary at the Vatican told Mr. Osborne, the British Minister, that "what is now happening is a disaster caused by German vainglory, Italian folly and Anglo-French weakness".[14] When Schuschnigg announced his intention of holding a plebiscite, the *Osservatore Romano* published an article in defence of Austria's independence referring, as Mussolini had, to the historical, cultural and religious grounds for that independence. Almost to the last the Vatican hoped that France, England and Italy would prevent the *Anschluss*. Once it had taken place, however, the Vatican refrained from further comment; nor was there anything more that the Austrian episcopate could do. This may have influenced Cardinal Innitzer, the Primate of Austria, when he made his notorious profession of loyalty to the new German Reich, and wrote the letter to the Nazi Gauleiter of Vienna, Bürckel, finishing with the words, "Heil Hitler!" He was also unwise enough to visit Hitler in the Hotel Imperial soon after the Führer's arrival in Vienna where, according to von Shirach, he gave Hitler the *"Deutscher Grüss"*.[15] The Vatican immediately dissociated itself from this, and the *Osservatore Romano* stated (2nd April, 1938), "The declaration of the Austrian episcopate was drafted and signed without the previous knowledge or approval of the Holy See." The Under-Secretary of State, Mgr. Pizzardo, was clearly ashamed of the Austrian bishop's behaviour because he tried to gloss it over when he told Mr. Osborne,

The Innitzer declaration has been extracted from the Austrian bishops by a typically Nazi manoeuvre. They threatened, terrified and then assured them that a reasonable show of collaboration would be reci-

[14] F.O. 371/21641.
[15] Baldur von Shirach, *Ich glaubte an Hitler.*

procated in Church matters. It was for them to choose whether to wage a hopeless battle or, by collaborating, to preserve the rights and liberties of the Austrian Catholics. Then, when the Innitzer declaration was published in the press, the Nazis suppressed certain passages about rendering unto Caesar and unto God, etc., which would have qualified it considerably.[16]

Cardinal Innitzer was summoned to Rome where, by all accounts, he was lectured very severely by the Pope; after which he signed a statement which appeared in the *Osservatore Romano* that the Austrian bishops' profession of loyalty to the Führer must not be interpreted as expressing anything incompatible with the laws of God, and with the liberties and rights of the Church. He added that in future the Austrian bishops would insist that in all matters concerning the Church in Austria there could be no question of any modification without previous approval of the Vatican, and that in particular the religious education of the young would at all costs be protected (this no doubt in view of what was happening to the south of Germany).

The German Ambassador to the Vatican, von Bergen, stated however that he had always known that Cardinal Innitzer adopted a "Greater Germany attitude". "I had the impression," he reports, "that he had a most disagreeable audience with the Pope. It seems that pressure has been brought to bear on him to make this recantation in the *Osservatore Romano*. Once again the Pope has allowed himself to be swayed by his morbid resentment of German success. I suggest," finished von Bergen, "that we continue to show confidence in Cardinal Innitzer and stand by him."[17]

The Innitzer episode had a curious sequel, connected with the Vatican radio station. For reasons which have never been fully explained, this station had, since its inauguration in 1923, always been controlled by the Jesuits; and it was not subject to any supervision by the Secretary of State. Immediately after Cardinal Innitzer's unfortunate profession of loyalty to the Third Reich had been published in the Austrian Nazi press, the Vatican Radio broadcast a violent and scurrilous attack on him personally, his

---

[16] F.O. 371/21641, Mr. Osborne to Lord Halifax, 29th April, 1938.

[17] *A.A. Büro des Staatssekretärs*, Vol. 1, 6th April, 1938. In an interview after the war with *Agenzia Romana Informazione* (see F.O. 371/46674) Cardinal Innitzer described what Pius XI had said to him at the audience. "It was very simple-minded of you," he said, "to believe in any promise made by Hitler." Innitzer then admitted that he had been persuaded by von Papen that under the Nazis the Church would be able to carry on its activities better than before.

morals as well as his ethics. The Vatican was not in the habit of using suc means, even when rebuking a subordinate, and the Secretary of State Cardinal Pacelli, asked the Jesuit Father Soccorsi, the Director of th Vatican Radio, for an explanation. Father Soccorsi said he had been o holiday from Rome at the time, and knew nothing about it. Furthe enquiries revealed however that the broadcast had been written an introduced surreptitiously into the radio programme by the ex correspondent of the *Weiner Reichspost*, a baptised Jew called Hein Ludwig living in Rome, and who was occasionally engaged by th Vatican Radio on account of his knowledge of German affairs. Befor 1933, he had been a journalist in Berlin on the *Berliner Börsenzeitung*. In tha year when Hitler came to power he hastily removed to Vienna, where h assumed Austrian nationality, only to have to move again when the Nazi threatened Austria. He then moved to Rome, where he was baptised. Her he found his way into Vatican journalist circles, first by working for th *Illustrazione Vaticana*, then for the *Osservatore Romano*, and finally for th Vatican Radio. The incident is related at some length by von Bergen, wh adds irritably, "We have already had enough trouble with this mis chievous little Jew, who was guilty during the Saar plebiscite of the mos pernicious propaganda against Germany. I suggest we withdraw hi Austrian nationality from him."[18]

In spite of Cardinal Innitzer's attempts at conciliation with the Nazis, h gained no advantage for the Catholic Church, and lost much of th prestige and influence he had among his own people. The Nazis certainl did not respect him, and Gauleiter Bürckel said how surprised he was tha Cardinal Innitzer had "offered us his assistance and abandoned hi friends".[19] Worse was to come. One evening in October 1938, a numbe of Hitler Youths smashed the windows of Cardinal Innitzer's palace in th Stephensplatz, and entered the first floor by ladder. They destroyed any works of religious art they could find including some busts of the Popes stole valuable chalices and episcopal rings, and threw the robes and personal effects of the Cardinal (who had taken refuge on an upper floor into the street, together with several pieces of furniture, to which they se fire. A priest belonging to the Cardinal's household who tried to restrair them was attacked with a broken bottle and had to have five stitches in hi head. Another priest was thrown out of the window and broke his leg The police who had immediately been summoned did not arrive until i

[18] *A.A. Büro des Staatssekretärs*, Vol. 1, despatches from von Bergen, 2nd April and 5th April, 1938.
[19] *A.A. Beziehungen des heiligen Stuhls zu Deutschland*, Vol. 5, 8th October, 1938.

was all over. Whereupon the leader of the young Nazis blew a single blast on his whistle, at which they formed into a column and marched off unapprehended by the forces of law and order.

When the Vatican complained officially about this, the authorities shed some crocodile tears and said the culprits would be punished, adding however that Innitzer had only himself to blame. The Hitler Youth had been incensed by a speech he had recently made to the Catholic Youth of Vienna, who had acclaimed him with cries of "Innitzer orders, we follow!" and "Christ is our Führer!" The Nazi youth had naturally retaliated to such an insult to their Führer![20]

This was only one of the incidents which revealed the attitude the Nazis intended to adopt towards the Catholic Church in Austria. By the end of 1938, they had expropriated the College of the Capucin Fathers in Vienna, and expelled the monks from the monastery of St. Lambrecht, which they turned into a Hitler Youth hostel. The clerical training schools and theological faculties at Innsbruck and Salzburg were closed. The Jesuit Institute at Feldkirch was sequestrated, as was the Benedictine monastery at Innsbruck. The Catholic Women's and Girls' associations were dissolved. The Catholic press was proscribed, its editors and journalists dismissed, in some cases arrested. Respect for episcopal dignity was derided, and the Archbishop of Salzburg was bodily searched for incriminating documents before he set off for a bishops' conference. The new ruler of Austria, Gauleiter Bürckel, publicly announced that he hoped to be able on the 20th April, 1938, the Führer's birthday, to make him a present of a *klosterlos* Austria, an Austria free of monasteries and nunneries.

Three other States arose in 1918 out of the ruins of the Habsburg Empire, Poland, Czechoslovakia and Yugoslavia. The new Poland was a mosaic containing, besides Poles, large numbers of Germans, Lithuanians and White Russians, from areas of former Austria, Prussia and Russia. Its new frontiers played havoc with the old dioceses; and Pius XI had been sent in 1921, when he was Mgr. Ratti, to unravel this tangled skein. Techen, for example, formed part of the diocese of Breslau, as did the whole of Upper Silesia. Were the parts of both these districts now allotted to Poland to remain ecclesiastically under the control of a German bishop? Again, certain parts of the diocese of Gnesen were still German. Were they to remain under a Polish archbishop? And then Danzig — the city itself was in one diocese, while its territory between the Vistula and the Nogat

[20] Ibid., report by Muller. Within six months of the *Anschluss* the Hitler Youth movement had been introduced on a vast scale.

was in another. It may be objected — who, except the bishops, cares about diocesan frontiers? As will be seen, in countries such as Poland containing a large number of devout Catholics, who suddenly find themselves under a foreign bishop, many people care.

The dangers in all these new boundaries had been foreseen by the Vatican as early as 1920. Cardinal Gasparri wrote an article in the *Osservatore Romano* (14th August) entitled "the Vatican and Poland", in which he said, "What we can state without fear of contradiction is that the Holy See, since the days when Poland became a sovereign State again, has never ceased warning Poland to be moderate in demanding and accepting territories containing a majority of peoples of other nationalities. These warnings have been pronounced on several occasions, both in Warsaw and in Rome." It is some measure of Mgr. Ratti's diplomatic skill that he managed, after two years' hard work, to arrange the diocesan boundaries so that they gave at least minimum offence to the minorities concerned.

The biggest problem however concerned members of the Orthodox Church now incorporated in the new Polish State, some three million White Russians and Ukrainians — a fair proportion in a country of thirteen million Catholics. Poland, a fundamentally Catholic country, in tradition as well as population, now ruled over a large number of persons of the Orthodox faith. Here lay the seeds of discord between the Polish State and the Vatican. The Vatican saw in the new situation a most fruitful field for proselytisation — as it had in 1918 in Russia (see Chapter 9). It was soon in dispute with Pilsudski about the best way of converting these Orthodox who were now Polish citizens.

It might be supposed that the Vatican, with complete freedom of movement for its missionaries in Poland, would have undertaken direct conversion to Rome. This was not the case. The Vatican considered that the best way of converting these, for the most part primitive, peasants was to bring them back first into the Uniate or Greco-Roman Church to which they had belonged for centuries. The Uniate Church recognises the Pope in Rome as its head, but its ceremonies are conducted according to the Orthodox rite. It was considered in Rome that this method, a kind of half-way house, was the best way of converting a peasant population very set in its ways. They would continue to practise the rites of their fathers, while turning their faces not towards the synod in Moscow, but to the Pope in Rome.

Marshal Pilsudski, the uncrowned Dictator of Poland, opposed this vigorously. He was a practising Catholic; and he too was well aware that the new Orthodox population in his State had looked in 1918 to Moscow as their spiritual capital. This for the new Polish State, which had just shaken off the material bonds of Moscow, was clearly undesirable. He wished therefore to create an autocephalous Orthodox Church for these Orthodox on the lines of the autocephalous Churches in the Balkan countries. He and most Polish leaders believed that only in this way could the three million Orthodox be weaned from Moscow and made contented with their lot in the new Poland. He was also convinced that a Uniate Church resurrected in these new eastern territories would at best be a makeshift arrangement. The former Uniate Church had collapsed igno-miniously in the nineteenth century in the face of Russian persecution, and there was no reason to suppose that a revived Church of the same character would have any more power of resistance. Faced with his immediate political problems, Pilsudski could not share the long-term view of the Vatican that conversion to Rome would go deeper, and be firmer, if it were carried out by stages. His was a political as distinct from a religious solution.

In spite of his objections, the Vatican continued with its plans and announced that Uniate bishoprics would be created in the eastern marches; and it entrusted a group of Polish Jesuit priests with the task. They went about dressed as "Popes" (Orthodox priests), bearded and wearing their hair long. Their churches were accoutred in the Orthodox style, priests and congregation being separated into two distinct areas, the door being closed during the service. On the altar stood the Greek Cross, and Mass was said not in Latin, but in Old Slavonic. The sacrament was adminis-tered with a spoon, and the faithful received it in the Eastern manner, standing, their arms folded over their breasts. The sign of the Cross was made from left to right, and the faithful greeted one another with the kiss of peace. The Jesuit taking the service repeated at intervals the words, "Let us pray for the All Holy World Patriarch, Pius Pope of Rome, and for his bishops."

Mgr. d'Herbigny, the eminent Jesuit in charge of the proselytisation in Russia and the Slavonic lands, describes the effect of these methods on the guileless Orthodox population of the new Poland, and on their equally guileless clergy.[21] One man, he says, expressed some fear that he (d'Her-bigny), "the learned Jesuit had come to pick up Masses in the abandoned field of Russian Orthodoxy" — which was precisely what he was doing. Another became suspicious because Mgr. d'Herbigny wore his hair long, not short like the ordinary Catholic priests. Was he not doing it deliber-ately, to attract the people? Again, this was perfectly true; but d'Herbigny

[21] *Orientalis Christiana*, V, 20; reprinted in *Osservatore Romano*, 9th April, 1926.

replied, "No, I wear it long like this to avoid catching a cold in your damned climate." The question of the length of hair appears to have preoccupied these people. That all good priests should be "Nazarenes", that is, bearded and with long hair like Jesus, was a part of their dogma. "They condemn the Catholic clergy," writes d'Herbigny, "for failing in this respect, for destroying God's work in order to appear younger, more graceful, with a feminine face. This, they believe, is sinful because the beard is what distinguishes the male from the female countenance." These incidents reveal that the Vatican's "half-way house" manner of conversion was based at least on a sound knowledge and experience of the Slavonic character.

But Pilsudski remained adamant. He retaliated by announcing that the Polish government would not recognise the existence of Uniate priests. A book was published by his Secretary General, Count Lubienski, entitled *Rome's Road to the East*, which strongly criticised the methods of the Uniate Church and the "hypocrisy" of the Vatican in employing them. The book was immediately proscribed by the Archbishop of Warsaw; whereupon the entire Polish press took up the cry, publishing a series of attacks on the Vatican. The Pope's infallibility, which among this very Catholic people had always been accepted, was also impugned.

Faced with this onslaught, the Pope did not remain silent. He instructed the Archbishop of Warsaw to declare that any Pole who attacked the Church's Uniate policy in the Eastern territories was a bad Catholic. The Catholic Church would not allow her Faithful to place themselves in the role of judges and condemn the methods she chose to employ. The Vatican had no intention of being diverted by short-sighted Polish national considerations. In spite, therefore, of every obstacle placed in their way, the Jesuits continued their work of conversion to the Uniate Church. After ten years, by 1935, they had made some 30,000 conversions which, in a population of three million Orthodox was, the Vatican admitted itself, not very great. But to a Church which sees the future not in terms of decades but of centuries, this was no reason for despondency.

When Pilsudski died in 1935, his shade continued to pursue the Vatican from the grave. He was buried with great pomp in the Polish Pantheon, the Cathedral of the Wavel; but two years later the Bishop of Cracow, Prince Sapieha, took the unprecedented step of transferring his remains to a crypt outside the cathedral precincts. He did this, he explained, because the body was suffering deterioration from the damp, and also because the constant influx of visitors to Pilsudski's tomb interfered with the cathedral services. Everyone knew that Bishop Sapieha had often criticised

Pilsudski, and this was taken by the Polish nationalists as a deliberate insult from Rome. Polish ex-legionaries from all over the country, to whom Pilsudski was the greatest national hero since Sobieski, came to Warsaw and denounced the Pope, passing resolutions that Bishop Saphieha should be deprived of his citizenship, even expelled from Poland. Passions gradually cooled, but the affair rumbled on for months until it was enveloped and forgotten in the direr events of September 1939.

The collapse of the Habsburg Empire brought with it another kind of problem for the Vatican in the Balkans which, unlike Poland and Czechoslovakia, had known for centuries virtually only one Christian Church, the Orthodox. After 1918 and the treaty of Versailles, Serbia found herself engulfed in the hybrid State of Yugoslavia in association with an almost equal number of Croatian Catholics (six million Orthodox Serbs to five million Catholic Croats). Whereas in the Balkan countries the head of the Orthodox Church is always a citizen of the land in question — and a government nominee — the head of the Catholic Church is a foreigner. The Orthodox looks for spiritual guidance to his own capital; the Catholic looks to Rome. It requires no effort of the imagination to understand that religious passions ran high when the new Yugoslav State was born; and that the phrase *odium theologicum* is not an empty one.

King Alexander, an Orthodox Serb, was a man of great integrity and personal courage. He was quick to see the dangers of a situation in which the Catholic Croats would resent what they regarded as rule from Orthodox Belgrade. He immediately opened negotiations with Rome for a concordat, to regularise their position and guarantee their religion. He was also well aware that the Catholic Croats were more highly educated than his own Serbs; and he believed that the Catholic Church provided the surest bulwark against Communism. His was a superhuman task. As an Orthodox Serb, his first loyalty had to be to his own people; and they rendered most of his attempts at conciliation vain. Beginning as a constitutional monarch, he was gradually forced into the unwilling position of governing, as Dollfuss had in Austria, as a dictator. Like Dollfuss, too, he was assassinated when it seemed that at last his plans were maturing.

When he began the Concordat negotiations with Rome, a howl of fury went up from the Orthodox clergy. They told the Serbian peasants that if a concordat was signed, they would be compelled to become Roman Catholics, to change their Serbian Orthodox names to those of Catholic saints, and to forego their *Slavas* — the annual name-day holiday. Nevertheless, King Alexander persisted in the negotiations with the Vatican. The latter, for its part, was in no hurry, well aware of the value, indeed necessity, of an agreement for the King to govern the new Catholic element representing nearly half his Kingdom. The Orthodox fury was regarded with equanimity by Cardinal Gasparri; and the Nuncio in Belgrade, Mgr. Cherubini, told the German Ambassador, von Kessel, "The Orthodox should not go too far with us. If there is a struggle, they will not be the victors."[22] To the usual questions in a concordat of religious education, the appointing of bishops, the payments of priests' stipends, etc., were added the specifically Yugoslav ones of the use of the Old Slavonic language (Glagolithic) in the litany; and the curious one of the Institute of St. Jerome of the Slavs in Rome.

The problem of the Glagolithic in the Litany was familiar to the Vatican. Certain churches in Dalmatia already enjoyed the privilege of celebrating the litany in the Glagolithic; but the demand by the Yugoslav government for the extension of this concession to the whole country caused some concern at the Vatican. The Pope feared that if the Church gave way further, other countries might demand the same right — with a corresponding weakening of the ties with Rome.

The other problem concerned the Institute of St. Jerome of the Slavs. This had been founded in 1901 by Leo XIII in his Bull *Slavorum Gentem*, for the education of Croatian priests of the then Austro-Hungarian Empire; and the Vatican had always regarded this building in the centre of Rome as its property. During the 1914–1918 war the Italian government (which then had no relations with the Vatican) announced that they regarded the Institute as enemy (Habsburg) property, and they accordingly sequestered it. After the war however they signed the Treaty of Nettuno with the new Yugoslav State (1924), one of the provisions of which was that the Institute of St. Jerome of the Slavs should be handed over to the new Kingdom as Yugoslav property. The Yugoslav Minister in Rome accordingly moved his Legation lock, stock and barrel into the Institute, where he took up his quarters. Whereupon the Pope nominated a rector — as he claimed was his right since the Leonine foundation — and instructed him to move in too. When this Rector, Mgr. Nardone, carried out these instructions, he occupied another part of the building with his students, locking the doors connecting them with the self-styled Yugoslav Legation. The

[22] A.A. Pol III Beziehungen des päpstlichen Stuhls zu fremden Staaten, Vol. 1, despatches from von Kessel, 19th February, 1921 and 4th July, 1922.

Yugoslav Minister replied to this in the middle of the night by smashing down the communicating doors, and preventing the students from entering their dormitories, which he declared were the property of the Yugoslav State.

The Yugoslavs complained to the Italian government, assuming that they could be sure of its support, physical as well as moral, in any trial with the Vatican. But here they were not aware that Mussolini was just beginning his negotiations for the Concordat. They did not realise that the era of the old Liberal, anti-clerical regimes was passing in the Latin countries. Mussolini said the question did not concern Italy, and that the Yugoslavs and the Vatican must settle it on their own. It took five years before this ridiculous affair was settled — the refractory Yugoslav Minister being replaced by a man more agreeable to the Vatican, and the Rectorship of the Institute being filled by a Croat, Mgr. Cuca, the Canon of Split. The Institute of St. Jerome of the Slavs was to remain Vatican property, but the Yugoslavs were to be consulted about the nomination of its rector.

It is some measure of the stubborn bargaining power of the Vatican that another five years elapsed before it was satisfied with the conditions for a concordat. For the Vatican had foreseen that, in order to preserve some sort of civil peace with the Croats, the Yugoslav government would inevitably be forced to come to terms. In return for recognising the Glagolithic as the liturgical language, the Church obtained almost everything it wanted. Catholic Action was to be instituted with complete freedom to develop its educational and charitable organisations. The Catholic clergy would be allowed to teach freely in the schools. The possessions and institutions of the Catholic Church were declared inviolable.

The Concordat was initialled by both parties; but it was soon evident that the Orthodox Church would do all in its power to prevent ratification in the Skupshtina, the Yugoslav Houses of Parliament. On the 20th July, 1937 when the Concordat came up for ratification, an Orthodox procession consisting of four Serbian bishops and fifty priests marched in protest through Belgrade. Thousands of people lined the streets and the police, who were under the orders of the Minister of the Interior, Father Koroshetz, a Catholic, were unable to break up the procession. It marched about a quarter of a mile along the road, until four lorry-loads of police caught up with it. They jumped out and charged using rubber truncheons, rifle-butts and, according to some eye-witnesses, bayonets. The Orthodox Bishop of Shabatz was knocked unconscious by a blow from a police truncheon on his heavy metal episcopal crown, and he had to be carried away. Ecclesiastical banners were destroyed, and four ambulances were required to deal with the casualties. Thousands of Serbs remained in the streets demonstrating against the Concordat.

Meanwhile in the Skupshtina itself the Minister of Justice, M. Subotitch, had opened the debate on the Concordat. When the disorders on the streets were reported by an Orthodox deputy who rushed in shouting, "The police are murdering our people!" a free fight developed between the members of the Government and the Orthodox opposition. The following day the Holy Synod of the Serbian Orthodox Church issued instructions for measures to be taken against all senators and deputies, whether priests or laymen, who had spoken in favour of the Concordat. Orthodox priests who did so would not be allowed to officiate in church, and would be brought before an ecclesiastical court, while measures tantamount to excommunication were threatened against laymen. The decision was read in all the churches, and black flags were flown over all Orthodox churches in Serbia for fifteen days. A week later, excommunication of some twenty-five deputies was pronounced in the churches, including the Prime Minister, the Speaker and nine Ministers, to the accompaniment by the congregations of cries of, "Down with the government!"; and after each name, the commination, "Let him be accursed!" In this way the Orthodox of Yugoslavia prevented the signature of a concordat. Relations between the Vatican and its Croatian faithful were not regularised until the Second World War and the arrival of the Fascist Dictator, Pavelitch.

The whole history of Papal relations with the Habsburg Secession States between the wars confirms that the Vatican fears in 1918 were well founded. The break-up of the Habsburg Empire brought a number of new and almost insoluble religious problems in Central Europe and the Balkans. While the fear that these new States might one day come under the hegemony of Russia was to be justified only too clearly after the Second World War.

11

Germany : From Weimar to National Socialism

THE MAIN SOURCE OF CATHOLIC STRENGTH IN GERMANY
extends along the valleys of the Rhine and Mosel, broadening out in the
south into the fertile plains and mountains of Bavaria. The climate of
these wine-growing regions, as well as their past, have made their
inhabitants more amiable and easy-going than other Germans.
Representing in 1922 a little over a third of the total population, they
comprised some of the most devout and intelligent Catholics in the
world. The character with which the great apostle, St. Boniface, stamped
this people in the eighth century can still be seen in the sincere
attachment of German Catholics to Rome, to which they look constantly in time of trouble. The Pope is venerated with an affection which
is often personal. At the height of Nazi power in 1942, Hitler ruled over
the largest Catholic community in the world. Together with the incorporated territories of Austria, Czechoslovakia, Poland and occupied
Russia, the number was approximately 110 million (cf. Italy and France,
forty million each, the U.S.A. with twenty-five million, Britain and her
dominions with twenty million). It is understandable, therefore, that
Germany should occupy a very high place among the countries whose
welfare concerned the Vatican.

The Centre or Catholic Party had been founded in the reign of Pius IX to defend Catholics at the time of Bismarck's *Kulturkampf* against them. The Pope had given it his blessing, and it had been remarkably successful. Faced with it, Bismarck had had to abandon his campaign in favour of a National Church, and it gradually became one of the most important political parties in the land. Its programme was based on the great social encyclical of Leo XIII, *Rerum Novarum*; and in the first decades of the twentieth century its trades unions were the most advanced in Europe. With its almost constant number of electors, and its almost equally constant strength in the Reichstag and the Prussian Landtag, the Centre Party soon occupied, as its name implies, a central position enabling it to ally itself with either wing as it saw fit. By the time of the Weimar Republic (1921), no government could exist which could not count on its active support or benevolent neutrality. Its power was due not only to this central position, but to its peculiar constitution which made it not merely a clearing ground for political thought, but also a recruiting ground for civil servants whose chief qualification had to be absence of political bias. The Centre Party alone could always provide this material, and it played a leading part in guiding Germany along the path of Conservative Republicanism in the twenties. The word "party", as indicating a body of men elected to achieve certain well-defined political ends, had little if any meaning when applied to the Centre. It represented no particular class or interest, but existed solely to further the affairs of Catholics, be they employers or employees, landlords or peasants. It was a parliament in miniature, comprising every shade of political thought. It contained feudal landlords as well as farmers; there were bishops and priests, a cross-section of the bourgeoisie, as well as Catholic trades union leaders, whose ideas about social progress were indistinguishable from those of the Socialists. All these men sat together in the Reichstag and voted in unison, not because they necessarily thought alike, but because they had a common goal, to promote the interests of Catholics.

Why did this party become so important after the First World War? Under the Weimar Republic, the Reich had three Catholic Chancellors; and half the Weimar Cabinets were Catholic. Practically all the officials in the Reichskanzlei were Catholics, as were most of those in the Prussian Judiciary. How did this change come about, particularly in view of the great Lutheran predominance in the governments before the war? The answer appears to be the connection in the public mind of the Lutheran religion with Prussian ideals and the Prussian system of government, which had been discredited through the loss of the war. Prussia had owed everything to military prowess; but in acquiring it, she had developed certain defects inseparable from the severe training that went with it. The prestige, for instance, of a uniform was such that Jerome K. Jerome could say that "a Prussian child whom a policeman has patted on the head becomes insufferably conceited". The regulation in minute details of the routine of daily life, the persistent attempt from above to mould and guide, to make the nation a perfect machine of efficiency, all this was implied in the word "Prussianism". The system was successful so long as it was exposed to no great strain. It failed when qualities were required which it had not sought to develop. Defeat in war was bound to involve it in moral defeat. What contributed largely to the collapse of the German people in 1918 was, in addition to hunger and military defeat, a sense of bewilderment that the Prussian system had failed precisely where it was supposed to be invincible; efficiency had been beaten on its own ground. It followed that they began to ask themselves if perhaps all had not been so well in the past as they had been taught.

The collapse of Prussianism injured the moral authority and prestige of the religion which was its faithful standard-bearer, Lutheranism — while it assisted the other religion which had represented opposite ideals, Catholicism. That Lutheranism should have placed all its resources at the disposal of the Prussian system is understandable; it was the official Church, and supported official institutions and ideals because it was in its interest to do so. Before 1914, from a thousand Lutheran pulpits in Prussia the pastors delivered their Sunday exhortations, emphasising how fortunate the Prussians were to be administered by the best and most efficient system in the world; how wise and far-sighted was their Emperor; and how nothing could conduce more to the happiness of the individual and the welfare of the State than blind obedience to his authority. Nor was the military side neglected. In their sermons, the pastors told the congregations that war was a fine thing; the terms "Christian" and "soldier" were almost synonymous.

With the loss of the war, this situation was bound to favour Catholicism; when the majority fails, the minority benefits. Catholicism had been the only force in Germany before the war which had not agreed with the ideals and aims of the majority. During the 1914 war, the Centre Party had advocated a peace of compromise by which, it was now realised, Germany would have received much more favourable terms than those dictated at Versailles. The result was that after the war, Catholics were prominent everywhere, and the Centre Party the most important in the land. A network of Catholic charitable organisations included schools, youth associations for both sexes, hospitals, asylums and trades unions. In countless cases, the children of Catholics received all their education from these institutions; and afterwards they were drafted into the appropriate Catholic adult professional or vocational guild where they mixed with fellow Catholics. From the cradle to the grave they lived within the shelter of the Church.

It was during the Weimar period that the Bavarian and Prussian Concordats were signed (1924 and 1928), both granting concessions to the Church in the field of education, the appointment of bishops, guaranteeing the property of religious bodies, and increased State funds for the Church. In those days, before worse dangers beset the Church, the old Protestant antipathy was still the strongest; and Protestant circles denounced these concessions to Rome. The German Evangelical Assembly announced in 1924, "We Germans must never forget that behind the great global danger of Moscow is hidden a greater one, Rome." The Protestants contended that the Vatican "through its creature the Centre Party" intended to create a large Catholic State in Central Europe, consisting of the Rhineland, Bavaria and Austria under a restored Habsburg or Wittelsbach monarchy, directed against Protestant Germany.[1] In 1926, a Protestant Academy was founded at Elbersfeld, at which an official from the Finance Ministry, Regierungsrat Koch, made a speech openly attacking the Vatican on this score. This accusation of "a Catholic Central European block" was hotly denied at the Vatican.[2] And it is some measure of Papal power in Germany that the Vatican, by a strong complaint to Stresemann, secured Koch's removal from office for "trying to disturb the confessional peace of the predominantly Catholic Rhineland".[3]

Another example of the power of the Vatican under Weimar concerned the Czech gymnast organisation, Sokol. In 1926 it organised an elaborate ceremony in Prague in honour of John Hus, "the Czech martyr" who was burned at Constance in the fifteenth century by the Inquisition; and it invited sporting organisations from other countries to participate. The Germans like many others accepted. Whereupon the

[1] F.O. 371/16749(50), confirmed by Sir R. Lindsay from Berlin to Sir A. Chamberlain, 16th February, 1927. "If the Centre Party continues to occupy its present predominant position then, (1) the Hohenzollerns are definitely done with, and if the Empire returns it will be in a Catholic form, presumably under the Wittelsbachs; (2) the Anschluss, which the Holy See welcomes, will come more and more to the fore."

[2] A.A. Allegemeine auswartige Politik, Vol. 1. Compare also von Bergen's report from Rome, of "Vatican irritation that German newspapers allege that the Secretary of State Gasparri is engaged in the creation of a Catholic block of States directed principally against Germany."   [3] Germania, 8th February, 1926.

Papal Nuncio in Berlin, Mgr. Pacelli, informed the German government that the Vatican considered the Czech government's invitation to a country populated by so many Catholics an insult to the Pope. "I am instructed," he wrote, "to inform you that such participation by Germany would be regarded as an unfriendly act." His words were immediately effective. The Government ordered the German Youth organisation not to attend the Hus celebrations.

Such was the power of the Centre Party in the twenties. But, as we have seen, Pius XI was engaged in withdrawing his support from clerical political parties all over Europe. In the late twenties he did this to such an extent in Germany, by discouraging any clerical influence in the political field, that when Hitler came to power he found in the Centre Party a still active but much weakened opponent.

In the early days of the National Socialist party, the Vatican regarded it rather as did certain Conservative circles in England, as a bulwark against Communism which by 1931, after the world economic crisis, was becoming particularly threatening in Germany. The Vatican was also reassured by Article 24 in Hitler's National Socialist manifesto: "We demand the freedom of all religious beliefs in the State, in so far as they do not endanger the existence of the State, and do not offend against the manners and morals of the German race. The party bases itself on Positive Christianity without binding itself dogmatically to any single confession. It is convinced that a lasting regeneration of our people can come only from within, on the principle — Common interest before Self-interest."

To the Vatican there seemed nothing wrong with this. The points about not "endangering the existence of the State" seemed reasonable enough; "the manners and morals of the German race" an amiable truism. The phrase "Positive Christianity" might appear somewhat impertinent; but "Common interest before Self-interest" was a Christian precept. The manifesto added that the "party will not interfere in questions which lie outside the scope of its political work". This too seemed reasonable. Moreover, had not the Nobel Prize Winner, Professor Johannes Stark, a member of the Nazi party, written a pamphlet *National Socialism and the Catholic Church*, in which he said, "According to the declarations of Adolf Hitler, the party refuses to countenance any behaviour which, from the point of view of the Church, may be considered heretical"?[4]

Nevertheless, one or two German prelates such as the Bishop of Mainz,

[4] W. Gerdemann and Heinrich Winifred, *Christenkreuz und Hakenkreuz* (Kat. Tat. Verlag, 1931).

who had had a closer view of the Nazis, had fewer illusions. In 1929, he criticised the reassuring Article 24 from the pulpit. Of the statement "we demand the freedom of all religious beliefs in so far as they do not endanger the existence of the State", he asked indignantly, "How should we Catholics endanger the existence of our own State?" Of the phrase, "And do not offend against the morals and manners of the German race", he asked, "What exactly are *German* morals and manners? We Christians believe in loving one's neighbour — while these people [the Nazis] show precious little sign of doing so." "And what on earth," he asked, "is *Positive* Christianity? We need no 'positive' in front of the word. The National Socialists," he said, "want a new Trinity of their own — of Blood, People and Soil [*Blut, Volk und Boden*]. This means nothing less than a German National Church. So I say to you, No, a Catholic cannot be a member of the National Socialist party." He instructed his clergy to refuse the sacraments to any members of the Nazi party and issued a statement condemning the Nazi Storm-troops because they produced dissension in a people already sufficiently torn by political strife. "We do not wish to be reminded of such dissension at the time of Divine Service," he said. "Therefore we will not allow any of these groups in uniform to attend Church service. Nor may they enter the church in drill formation, nor with flags, banners or emblems."[5]

This statement did not please the Vatican, and Mr. Oglivy-Forbes, the British Chargé d'Affaires wrote, "Cardinal Pacelli was at pains to point out to me that the Bishop of Mainz was acting on his own initiative." Nevertheless, just before the Nazi seizure of power, the Bishops of Berlin and Westphalia echoed the words of their colleague in Mainz, and condemned the Nazis in pastoral letters.[6] At New Year 1930, Cardinal Bertram of Breslau said, "The National Socialist movement is no longer purely political. It teaches a misshapen philosophy which must be combated with all firmness."[7] Much indignation was caused among the Nazis by his refusal of a religious funeral for a National Socialist deputy, Peter Gemeinder, a devout Catholic, who died while addressing a political meeting. The funeral was attended by Prince August William of Prussia; but no priest was present.[8]

[5] F.O. Annual Report for 1931 from Sir H. Rumbold to Sir J. Simon.

[6] *L'Avvenire d'Italia*, 11th March, 1931 reports that a group of German bishops have spoken out against the Nazis who "do not recognise the supremacy of the Pope, and place race above religion".

[7] A.A. *Beziehungen des heiligen Stuhls zu Deutschland*, Vol. 4.

[8] F.O. Annual Report for 1931 from Sir H. Rumbold to Sir J. Simon.

Before Hitler came to power, he sent off his chief lieutenant, Hermann Göring, to Rome for an audience with the Pope (9th May, 1931). In those days when Hitler was acting constitutionally, needing every vote for the elections, he was aware of the effect this could have on the thirty million Catholics in the Reich. The Vatican appeared to welcome the visitor; for the *Osservatore Romano* wrote sympathetically of Göring, that he had fought valiantly against Bolshevism and, as Police Chief of Prussia, had taken firm measures against corruption and immorality (this last piece of praise causing some mirth in Germany). The Nazi press announced that Göring had been most cordially received by the Pope; they had discussed the anti-Nazi attitude of certain German bishops, such as the Bishop of Mainz, but in a most friendly way.[9] Göring had assured His Holiness that the party would show the greatest regard for the Catholic religion, and was most anxious to get on to better terms with the Centre Party. Von Bergen, the German Ambassador at the Vatican, was reported in the Nazi press as also being present at this interview. But von Bergen, in his despatch to Berlin, says he was not; moreover, he says that Göring did not see the Pope, nor even Cardinal Pacelli. His interview was with Mgr. Pizzardo, the Under-Secretary of State. The Pope was clearly waiting to see if the Nazi party achieved power, before committing himself too openly. The German Catholic paper *Germania* discovered that Göring had not seen the Pope, and had some entertainment at the expense of the Nazi press. After the "audience", Göring was reported as having made the traditional visit to St. Peter's, where he was recognised by some young German tourists who happened to be in the piazza. The columns of Bernini's famous arcade resounded to the unfamiliar cries of "*Heil Hitler!*" and "*Hoch der gute alte Göring!*"

Hitler was well aware of the strength of Catholicism in Germany, and he had no intention yet of a direct confrontation with the Vatican. "Do not imagine," he said to his friend, Arthur Dintner, "that I shall commit Bismarck's mistake. He was a Protestant and did not know how to handle the Catholic Church. Providence has made me born Catholic; I know how to."[10] In the review *Das Geistchristentum*, Dintner reports other conversations with Hitler in those early days. "To achieve power," Hitler told him in 1925, "it is important not to fall out with the Catholic Church, which has great influence in Germany ... What I propose to do is to oppose the Centre by its frequent alliances with the Social

[9] *Vorwärts*, 9th May, 1931.
[10] Robert d'Harcourt, *Les Catholiques d'Allemagne*.

Democrats in order to retain its power is acting against the true interests of the Church. We must show the Catholics of Germany that they are in safer hands among the National Socialists than with the Centre Party." Dintner adds that Hitler also said at a secret meeting of his party leaders, "Once I obtain power the Vatican will have little to laugh at, I can tell you. But to get there, I can't do without it." The Catholic Church, says Dintner, was to be "the stirrup-holder for the coming Third Reich".[11]

In *Mein Kampf* Hitler says all this more or less explicitly: how he will castigate the Centre Party for the havoc they cause by exploiting religious sentiment for political ends. "They boast about their faith," he writes, "but they would sell it tomorrow for a political advantage. For another ten seats in Parliament, the Centre would sign an alliance with the Marxists ... for a ministerial portfolio, they would marry the Devil." He goes on to show that the Vatican by supporting the Centre was damaging its own cause. Could it not see that all these "shady associations" of the Centre would finally open the lock gates to a flood of atheist Marxism which would bear away with it not only the German nation, but the Church itself. National Socialism, he argued, was the only sure protector of the Church against Godless Marxism. If such propaganda influenced many Catholics dissatisfied with the supine behaviour of successive Weimar governments towards the Communists and Socialists, the favourable effect at the Vatican of his strictures on Communism can be imagined.

Hitler was born and bred a Catholic and he never left the Church officially. But he soon ceased to subscribe to its doctrines, and the only feature of it which he admired was its organisation, thanks to which it had lasted so long. It had done something, he said, which the Germans and Huns had never been able to do — replace what it had destroyed, the Roman Empire. Although the Catholic Church was a Jewish affair smuggled into Europe, its 2000 years of "organisational achievement" was Aryan. Jesus too, being a Galilean, was of Aryan stock, a remarkable man whose teachings had, in the course of centuries, been deformed out of all recognition in the interests of the Catholic Church. In his conversations with Rauschning[12] Hitler regards the Catholic Church as a powerful institution which has outlived its time and purpose. He had no intention of persecuting it openly, he said, after the manner of the Russian Communists, because this would only create martyrs. He planned instead gradually to withdraw its influence from

[11] Gerdemann and Winfried, *Christenkreuz und Hakenkreuz*.
[12] Hermann Rauschning, *Hitler Speaks* (London, 1939).

the German people, in particular from the young. His attack was in fact more insidious than the Russian attack, because the Church would have to resist without the stimulus given by the blood of martyrs (Tertullian's *sanguis martyrum semen Christianorum*). In the words of Professor Hugh Trevor-Roper, "Hitler wished to be a new and more successful Augustus whose Empire, being free from the fertile seeds of decay — racial impurity and Jewish Christianity — would last for a thousand years."[13]

What Hitler hated in the Catholic Church was its priesthood because, "while always talking about love and humanity, they are in fact interested in only one thing, power — power over men's souls, and hence over their lives." By flattery and wheedling and false humility, they always insinuated themselves into people's lives. The Catholic Church, he said, was like a scheming woman who at first contrives to give her husband the impression that she is helpless and guileless, only gradually to take over power, finally holding it so securely that the man has "to dance to any tune she plays".[14]

However, in his early days Hitler treated the Catholic priesthood with care. "I cannot give them the answer now [sic]," he said, "but everything they do is entered in my little book. The time will come, and I shall not worry about legal niceties." His remark later during the Spanish civil war is significant: "If there had not been a serious danger of Bolshevism over-running Europe, I would not have helped Franco. Because under the Spanish Republic the priests would have been exterminated."

Hitler intended to break the great power of the Catholic Church in Germany — for its internationalism was in diametrical opposition to his Nazi nationalism. He would not do this, however, by a direct assault leading to another *Kulturkampf*, with unforeseeable international complications. Time, he knew, was essential in dealing with the Vatican. He once admitted that in his youth he had thought of the Catholic Church "in terms of dynamite"; but he had soon revised that opinion. The Church had withstood "dynamite" remarkably well throughout history. The power of the Church, he saw, rested on something more powerful than dynamite, on education, bringing up the youth to be Catholics first and Germans second. He would reverse this process.

Hitler's speech on the 1st February, 1933, immediately after he became Chancellor, seemed to most Catholics even more reassuring than Article

[13] Hugh Trevor-Roper, *The Rise of Christian Europe* (Thames and Hudson, 1965).
[14] *Hitler's Table Talk*, 1941-4 (London, 1953).

24 of the National Socialist manifesto. He referred to Christianity as "the basis of our collective morals", and the family as "the kernel of our people", which the State would take under its protection. It would defend "these religious foundations on which the strength of our nation is based". He finished by invoking the help of God for the hard task which lay ahead.

Seven weeks later he said much the same in a second speech, adding however a veiled threat to the Centre Party which still held a considerable number of seats in the Reichstag.

> The government [he said] is determined to rid the land of this political and moral poisoning, to ensure the conditions for a real and deep inner religious faith. Personal advantages by compromises with atheistical bodies destroy the general religious-ethical basis of our life [another reference to the Centre alliance with the Socialists] . . . The government sees in both the confessions, Protestant and Catholic, the most important factors for supporting our people morally . . . the agreements existing between them and the *Länder* will be respected . . . but the government will not allow membership of a specific religion or race to release a man from his general legal obligations to the State . . . the national government will ensure that the Confessions exercise their influence in schools and educational matters. It sincerely desires the co-existence of Church and State . . . our common fight against Bolshevism will serve the interests of the German nation as much as those of the Church . . .

Again in a personal letter to Cardinal Bertram of Breslau on the 28th April, 1933, Hitler wrote:

> On various occasions your Eminence has referred to the situation of the Catholic Youth associations, hoping they will not lose anything under the new government. I can assure Your Eminence that, in so far as these associations have no hostile political intentions against the party, there is no question of this. The government does not want to conflict with the Church — on the contrary, it wishes for sincere collaboration, for the benefit of both Church and State. I may add that no State official will be relieved of his post on account of his religious beliefs, as long as he shows no hostile intentions towards the new government . . .

The first reactions in Rome were favourable. The Vatican naturally approved Hitler's unexpected humility in invoking God's help for the tasks ahead. His remarks about combating Bolshevism and upholding peace and disarmament — all this seemed to justify the view that, faced with the responsibilities and problems of government, he was becoming more reasonable.[15] Even Cardinal Faulhaber of Munich who had been (and was to be again) one of the principal opponents of the Nazis, was satisfied. In a pastoral letter the Cardinal congratulated the government on their campaign against atheism and Communism, and he even said that Catholics could now join the Nazi Party. The Vatican daily bulletin of international information, *La Corrispondenza* (13th March, 1933) referred, in the first flush of enthusiasm, to a need perhaps "to revise some of our attitudes towards National Socialism. One should not fail to recognise a certain nobility in the National Socialist movement."[16] Sir R. Clive, the British Minister to the Vatican, reports an interview with the Secretary of State, Pacelli, a few months later: "Against Herr Hitler His Eminence had nothing to say. He considered that Hitler was becoming more moderate. It is of the extreme elements in the party that His Eminence is nervous."[17]

The honeymoon between Church and State was short enough — as an incident in Karlsruhe on the 10th March, 1933, less than six weeks after Hitler's accession to power, revealed. Dr. Stumpf, a local deacon, wrote about the official lunch offered by the city to the Papal Nuncio in Germany, Mgr. Orsenigo.

On the 10th March, we heard rumours that the Baden State government had been forced to resign. We had invited the Nuncio to an official luncheon and had understood that the State President, who is a Catholic, would be present to receive the guest of honour. Great was our surprise when the State President arrived, but in protective custody, escorted by two S.A. men with arms! One of them posted himself in front of the dining-room door while we ate, while the other mounted guard over the front door. In this strained atmosphere, the ceremonial meal in honour of the Nuncio took place. I need not say what a painful impression this appeared to make on our guest — his host clearly under arrest,

[15] *A.A. Beziehungen des heiligen Stuhls zu Deutschland*, Vol. 4, von Bergen to Berlin, 8th February, 1933.

[16] Written by the director of the bulletin, Dottore Giulio Castelli.

[17] F.O. despatch from Sir R. Clive to Sir J. Simon, 13th July, 1933.

although seated at the head of the table! I think we owe him an apology.[18]

Peter Gehrmann, the private secretary to the Nuncio was also present, and he reports, "It appears that the State President was arrested at 12.30 p.m. the hour at which he had invited the Nuncio to lunch. He was allowed to attend the luncheon only because he insisted that, as official host, he must receive the eminent guest. He obtained permission, but only for an hour, and in custody. After that he was taken off to gaol."

Hitler had started eliminating known anti-Nazi high officials in the State governments. Had he or his zealous lieutenants known that the Pope's personal representative was coming to the luncheon that day, they would almost certainly have postponed the arrest. For Hitler was now planning his Concordat with Rome.

[18] *A.A. Beziehungen des heiligen Stuhls zu Deutschland*, Vol. 4, letter from Dr. Stumpf, 19th March, 1933.

12

The Concordat with Hitler, 1933

HITLER WANTED A CONCORDAT FOR TWO PRINCIPAL REASONS: firstly, for prestige, to make his upstart regime appear more respectable abroad; secondly, to obtain control over, if not to eliminate, the refractory Centre Party. The Centre had, we have seen, fallen into disrepute in Germany during the last days of the Weimar Republic, sharing its blame for the poverty and unemployment. But it had ninety-two deputies in the Reichstag, still a democratic body in which Hitler's party had gained a majority by constitutional methods. He now intended to pass his *Ermächtigunggesetz* which would give him full dictatorial powers — on the ground that otherwise he could not "clean up" the catastrophic unemployment situation inherited from Weimar. A number of the Centre deputies were priests and they, together with the Communists, were not afraid to raise their voices and could block this legislation. Hitler eliminated the Communists, as we now know, by trumped-up charges connected with the Reichstag fire. But the Centre Party was a much harder nut to crack, and he knew it could certainly vote against the *Ermächtigunggesetz*. He also knew that Pope Pius XI disapproved on principle of Catholic political parties, and had preferred Mussolini's

Fascists in Italy to the Catholic Popular Party, because Mussolini had made a number of concessions to the Church, with which he had finally signed a concordat. Hitler determined to do the same, offering concessions over religious education in return for the Pope's withdrawal of support from the Centre Party. Within two months of assuming power, he suggested that negotiations should be opened for a German concordat.

No Concordat with Germany had existed since the Reformation. Under Bismarck a *Reichskonkordat* had not been possible, because Article 5 of the Constitution (16th April, 1871) stated that the Reich government had no competence in matters relating to the Church, which was to be left to the individual States of the Federation. Prussia, Bavaria and Baden therefore dealt directly with the Vatican, with which by 1929 they had all made concordats. As these catered for some eighteen million of the twenty million German Catholics, the Church had not felt the need for a general Reich concordat. As late as 1932 this was still the view of the Vatican.[1] Yet by the summer of 1933, it had signed a concordat with Hitler's Germany. What accounted for this sudden change? Normally, the Vatican, thinking in terms of centuries, spins out concordat negotiations for years. Why then this urgency?

There appear to have been several reasons. One was almost certainly that the Vatican thought Hitler would prove to be, in religious matters, a second Mussolini, requiring a fair element of Church support in order to govern effectively. Another was the fear that if no agreement were reached with the new Germany, the Nazi government might favour a German National Church. Another was that the conditions offered by Nazi Germany were more favourable, at least on paper, than anything which could have been obtained under the Weimar governments (whose Protestant and Socialist elements would certainly have thwarted a concordat). Most important of all — it is now clear from the captured German diplomatic documents that Hitler let the Vatican know unofficially that if he could not obtain a concordat, he intended to close the confessional schools and abolish confessional youth movements. This would touch Pius XI on the quick for, if the Pope had shown that he was relatively indifferent to the fate of Catholic political parties,[2] he was deeply concerned, in this irreligious twentieth century, with religious instruction for the young, and with maintaining the Catholic Youth

---

[1] F.O. 371/16749, Sir R. Clive to Sir J. Simon, 22nd April, 1933.

[2] *A.A. Allegemeine Auswärtige Politik*, Vol. 1. When in the mid-twenties the Chairman of the Centre Party, Mgr. Kaas, together with two lay members, sent a telegram to the Pope on a purely political matter, only the two laymen received replies.

organisations. The Germans let the Vatican know that Hitler had no intention of destroying Catholicism; but that he was determined to give the wilder men of the Nazi Party a free hand until the Catholic Church withdrew their claim to special privileges and a special position in Germany. These claims could be regulated by a concordat. Once the Vatican admitted the inevitability of totalitarian State authority, it would find Hitler ready to meet it and protect it against Liberal attacks.

A more cynical explanation of the Vatican's need for a German concordat was given by M. Charles-Roux, then the French Ambassador to the Vatican (whose country of course saw only disadvantages for herself if Germany profited from a Concordat). Charles-Roux says that in the Yugoslav, Rumanian, Polish and Czechoslovak Concordats the Pope had been unyielding, driving hard bargains because he was not frightened of these countries, and knew he could maintain the position of the Church in them without making concessions. But he was frightened of Nazi Germany, and wanted to obtain what favourable terms he could before it was too late.[3] A similar reason was given by another Frenchman, a Jesuit, Yves de la Brière, a Professor of Common Law at the University of Paris. Writing well after the event in 1937 in the French Jesuit monthly, *Études*, he says, "The Pope and his negotiatiors at the time of the German Concordat foresaw, and feared, what is happening in Germany today ... He hoped that in the probable event of an extreme conflict between Church and State in Germany, the legal value of a concordat would give the claims and protests of the Church hierarchy a surer legal basis. We know now that this was the view of Cardinal Faulhaber in 1933 when, in spite of all misgivings, he recommended the signature of the Concordat."[4]

On the 22nd April, 1933, less than two months after Hitler came to power, the British Minister to the Vatican reported that the UnderSecretary of State, Mgr. Pizzardo, had told him, "The Holy See is not interested in the Centre Party. We are more concerned with the mass of Catholic voters in Germany than in the Catholic deputies who represent them in the Reichstag."[5] On the 13th July, 1933, while the Concordat negotiations were still in progress, this is confirmed in an interview the British Minister had with Cardinal Pacelli: "His Eminence said that the Vatican really viewed with indifference the dissolution of the Centre Party. They had been accused of supporting it and using influence to

[3] F.O. 371/16749(50), despatch from Sir R. Clive, 29th August, 1933.
[4] *Études*, 5th April, 1937.
[5] F.O. 371/16749, despatch from Sir R. Clive, 22nd April, 1933.

keep it in being. This was not the case."[6] Again on the 4th August, 1933, the British Minister reports, "In conversations I have had with Cardinal Pacelli and Mgr. Pizzardo, who both played an important part in the German Concordat, neither gave me the feeling of the slightest regret at the eclipse of the Centre, and its consequent loss of influence in German politics."[7] And von Bergen writes on the 23rd June, 1939: "Cardinal Pacelli told me that the fate of the Concordat depends upon the handling of the Germans' wish for the diminution of the political work by priests."[8]

To undertake the Concordat negotiations with Rome, Hitler selected Franz von Papen, his Vice-Chancellor, a Catholic and a man of considerable diplomatic experience. He was also something of an intriguer and owed his political advance to friendship with Oskar Hindenberg, the Field-Marshal's son. With him Papen had engaged in a series of cabals which had led to the appointment of Dr. Brüning as Chancellor in 1930, to the subsequent removal of Dr. Brüning as Chancellor, and the appointment of himself, Papen, as Chancellor in 1932. In his memoirs, Papen reports that on his arrival at the Vatican in June 1933, Pius XI "greeted me with paternal affection, expressing his pleasure that at the head of the German State was a man like Hitler, on whose banner the uncompromising struggle against Communism and Nihilism was inscribed".[9] Papen says that the atmosphere was so friendly that "within an unusually short space of time for the Vatican the main lines of an agreement had been laid down". The Concordat was signed on the 20th July, 1933, after only eight days of negotiations. The Nazis guaranteed the right of the Church to run its Catholic schools, which had been contested for a hundred years by German Protestants. Theology students were to be exempted from *Arbeitsdienst* (Labour Service). The Vatican could nominate university theological professorships. Most important of all for the Church, Article 31 ensured, "the uninhibited freedom of action for all Catholic religious, cultural and educational organisations, associations and federations". This embraced Catholic Action, "the apple of Pius XI's eye". In return, the Church conceded that priests should no longer take part in politics — which meant, in effect, the end of the Centre Party. Only over the definition

[6] Ibid.

[7] Ibid.

[8] *A.A. Abschluss von Konkordaten mit Deutschland und deutschen Länder (ausser Preussen)*, Vol. 9.

[9] F. von Papen, *Der Wahrheit eine Gasse* (Paul List Verlag, 1952).

of the Youth organisations — those controlled by the Church and those controlled by the State — was full agreement not reached. This was left to Herr Butmann of the German Ministry of the Interior and the German episcopate, who were to draw up a list of the respective organisations and their competences.

On the 23rd July, 1933, the British Minister again saw Cardinal Pacelli and asked if he might congratulate him on the outcome of the negotiations. Pacelli appeared very satisfied with the result. The recent changes in Germany had made it essential, he said, for the Church to regularise its relations juridically with the Reich. Under the new agreement the essential guarantees for religious education had been given. "I suggested," writes Sir Robert Clive, "that this was an improvement from the Church's point of view on the 1929 Concordat which His Eminence had negotiated with Prussia. Pacelli agreed and said that it had then been impossible to obtain anything better than an exchange of notes about religious education, owing to Protestant and Liberal opposition, and this he had always considered inadequate." However Cardinal Pacelli then appears to have sounded a less reassuring note. "At the same time," continues Sir Robert, "I had the impression that His Eminence regarded the Nazi regime not without anxiety, as he said more than once that the Church had every reason to be satisfied with the new Concordat, *provided the German government remained true to its undertaking.* About Herr Hitler he had little to say. He considered that he was becoming increasingly more moderate."

With the Centre Party as a political force emasculated, the way was now open for Hitler to pass his *Ermächtigunggesetz* with a comfortable majority in the Reichstag, giving him absolute power. Moreover, with the signing of the Concordat his State had become respectable. Within six months of its birth, the Third Reich had been given full approval by the highest spiritual power on earth.

Criticism of the Concordat came first from those countries which regarded Germany as a potential enemy, and which regretted her increased prestige. *Le Temps* wrote on the 5th July 1933:

It appears that the main feature of the Concordat is the transformation of all Catholic associations into purely spiritual and religious bodies, without political or economic existence. This is a triumph for the National Socialist government. It took Mussolini five years to achieve this; Germany has done it in a week. Catholicism in Germany has lost everything save its life. The Church has retreated out of fear, because it believes this is the only way to save Catholicism in Germany. The prospect of a German National Church has made the Vatican succumb. Fear of Bolshevism has also played a part.

Another French paper, *L'Ere Nouvelle*, wrote critically under the heading *"Le dernier Avatar du Vatican — de l'Universalisme au Nationalisme"* (14th September, 1933), "The contradiction of a system preaching universalism making an agreement with a highly nationalistic state has been repeated throughout Vatican history ... The Church never attacks existing institutions, even if they are bad. It prefers to wait for their collapse, hoping for the emergence of a higher morality. This is probably what it hopes will happen in the case of Nazi Germany. *Cu us regio e us religio.*"

The Poles were even more bitter. The semi-official *Kurjer Poranny* wrote on the 19th July, 1933 :

Once again we see the methods of the Vatican — intransigent with the passive and amenable, but accommodating with the high-handed and ruthless. In the last century it rewarded its persecutor, Bismarck, with the highest Papal decoration, the Order of Christ. Today, it shakes hands with the neo-pagans. We may contrast this Concordat with the one Stanislas Grabski brought back to Poland ten years ago, in negotiating which the Pope had been tough and unyielding — while to Hitler he is friendly and gracious. This Concordat promotes Hitler's unification of Germany. With it, Bavaria and Baden can no longer speak for themselves at the Vatican. The Centre Party, which most courageously resisted the Nazis, has been disowned by the Vatican.

Another critic was the ex-Chancellor Brüning. He told a friend that Hitler had boasted just before the signature of the Concordat, "I shall be one of the few men in history to have deceived the Vatican." Brüning added that 300 Protestant pastors in Germany had been about to join the Catholic Church on account of the stand it had taken against the Nazis, but had refrained when they heard of the Concordat.[10]

An eminent member of the Curia itself also criticised the Concordat. Cardinal Ceretti, who had previously been Papal Nuncio in Paris, said that all Concordats made by Pius XI were more or less worthless. Because they were made with States which were fundamentally hostile to

[10] F.O. 371/30898, Brüning to E. Munser of the François Xavier University, Nova Scotia, 3rd January, 1942.

eligion, the State would always neglect the clauses favourable to the Church; and the Church did not possess the physical power to enforce them. This dissident Cardinal was soon proved substantially correct. Within a matter of weeks difficulties of interpretation arose over the Catholic Youth organisations, and it became clear that it had been drawn up too hastily, with little regard for the meaning of words. The Nazi press began publishing the clauses as they interpreted them. Thus, in the official text Article 21 reads, "In all religious education care will be taken to develop awareness of the duty towards the Fatherland, according to the precepts of Christian faith and morals." In the Nazi press, this read, "In all religious education, the *Church admits the obligation* [author's italics] to develop awareness of the duty towards the Fatherland, according to the precepts of Christian faith and morals."[11] Cardinal Pacelli complained about this to von Bergen, asking if it was a purely press interpretation, or did it represent the view of the German government? After some delay von Bergen received a telegram from Berlin (7th August, 1933) stating that the press alone was responsible for this version. But this incident was only the first of many.

Barely had the Concordat been signed than the Nazi press began boasting about the advantages Germany had gained from it. On the 23rd July, 1933 the *Völkischer Beobachter* carried the headlines: "Ban on all confessional parties!" and "Ban on priests in politics!" The Concordat was also used for propaganda at elections. A photograph bordered with swastikas was distributed in Catholic parts of the country showing the Papal Nuncio, Mgr. Orsenigo, shaking Hitler's hand at a ceremony in Munich. Beneath it, the Nuncio's alleged words were, "Chancellor, I have long attempted to understand you. Today, I am glad to say I do." A bystander who overheard the exact words informed the Church authorities that the Nuncio had said, "I have wanted to make your acquaintance for a long time, and today at last I do."

It now appears — from the German diplomatic documents captured after the war — that there were two secret clauses in the Concordat, one concerning a common front against Russia, and the other dealing with the duties of conscripted priests in the German army.[12] Cardinal Pacelli told von Bergen in confidence at the time of the signature that he was particularly anxious that these should not be known by the press. His concern was understandable, because the second secret clause implied

---

[11] Wolf Agency. Also *Osservatore Romano*, 26th July, 1933, indicates the distortion.

[12] *A.A Abschluss von Konkordaten mit Deutschland*, Vol. 10, Pacelli's conversation with Botschaftrat Klee, 11th August, 1933.

Papal recognition of conscription in Germany (at this time, 1933, it wa‹ still forbidden by the Treaty of Versailles, which Hitler had not ye‹ denounced), and this would have caused very unfavourable reactions ir France and England. Von Bergen accordingly telegraphed Berlin sug‹ gesting that "a special courier should bring the documents from Berlin ir order to maintain secrecy about the additions".[13]

Another important secret item concerned German baptised Jews. Car‹ dinal Pacelli had suggested a clause recognising that they were Catholics with all the safeguards that this would imply. He was concerned that they might be dismissed from their employment because, in Nazi lan‹ guage, they were "a danger to the State". But on the ground that the question was "racial not religious", the German government objected to the inclusion of this clause. According to von Bergen the bargaining wa‹ hard, and it was only after the German government had given a *verba‹* promise to Cardinal Pacelli that baptised Jews would not be victimised, and would be regarded as Christians, that the Vatican yielded. (Even today most German baptised Jews do not know of this effort by Pacelli on their behalf.)[14]

It was not so much over the Concordat itself as over the "Regulations concerning its application" (*Ausführungsbestimmungen*) that difficulties arose. In the most important clauses the wording was equivocal. Articles 1 and 33 guaranteed the public practice of the Roman Catholic religion, and recognised the right of the Catholic Church to establish its own educational tenets. But it contained this proviso: "The above is to be regarded as within the limits of the law applicable to all citizens." "Within the limits" could be interpreted as meaning the limitation of teaching to purely ecclesiastical doctrine, as the German government interpreted it; or it could be extended to embrace Christian social and moral obligations, as the Vatican interpreted it. Articles 31 and 32 were even more controversial. The first stated that those Catholic organisations which, beyond their religious and charitable aims, had others, either social or professional, should enjoy the protection of the State *provided they were non-political*. The Catholic trades unions, to which the Church was particularly attached, were immediately affected by this Article.

Founded in 1848 by the Pope, the Catholic trades unions had exercised

[13] Ibid., 13th August, 1933. See also *Journal de Genève*, 13th August, 1933 for press indiscretions about secret clauses.

[14] Pacelli has been criticised for giving in, but critics should not forget that as late as September 1938 British and French statesmen were still prepared to accept verbal promises from Hitler.

great influence in Germany. During the Weimar period they formed the kernel of the Centre Party or, as a Nazi critic said, they were "the Storm-troops of the Catholic Church". The Catholic Workmen's Guild had centres all over the country, and its President exercised as much power as the bishops. When the Concordat was being negotiated, the German government suggested they should follow the example of Mussolini who had disbanded all the Catholic trades unions as such, their rump being incorporated into the Italian Catholic Action. The Vatican considered the cases were not similar — the Catholics in Germany were a minority, whereas Italy was an almost entirely Catholic country. In Italy, they could still retain some sort of entity, in Germany they would disappear entirely. After much discussion, the matter was referred to a committee of three German bishops who were to negotiate with Herr Butmann of the Ministry of the Interior.

Here too complete deadlock ensued; and on the 10th September, 1934, nearly a year later, Pacelli sent a long memorandum to Frick, the Minister of the Interior, dealing with this and other debatable points of the Concordat still *sub judice*, and stating where, in the view of the Vatican, spiritual matters ended and political ones began. He referred to the German bishops who had just visited the Pope with a list of violations of the Concordat which had already taken place — within three months of its signature. In Bavaria all the deputies of the Popular Party (the Catholic) had been arrested, and a number of priests imprisoned. Pastoral letters had been confiscated. Two of the letters sent by the Papal Nuncio in Berlin to the Vatican, one to the Pope and the other to Cardinal Pacelli, had been opened by the German currency control authorities. Cardinal Pacelli informed the German Ambassador that the Pope intended to make a formal protest. He said the German government had offended the Pope and, "one must always reckon with His Holiness's authoritarian character; he may react sharply on his own". Von Bergen cabled Berlin, "Not even the influential and realistic (*realpolitisch*) Pacelli can overcome the stubbornness and unpredictability of the Pope ... the Pope does not like an argument ... The continual complaints about infringement of the Concordat cause him deep concern. He fully understands, he says, that the State wishes to educate its youth as good German citizens. But in the matter of Catholic Youth education he, the Pope, will not abandon his rights."[15]

Cardinal Pacelli evidently persuaded the Pope to replace the protest note by a memorandum of complaints (which would be private, whereas

[15] *A.A. Abschluss von Konkordaten mit Deutschland,* Vol. 10.

a protest would automatically be public) because, in von Bergen's words, "open criticism before the world will hold up the negotiation still in progress for completing the details of the Concordat." Von Bergen's part in this was considerable, persuading Pacelli to persuade the Pope, quoting Article 2 of the Concordat by which the contracting parties agreed to "a friendly arrangement of all outstanding difficulties". He also interviewed the German bishops who had complained to the Pope and managed to pacify them, persuading them that they would do better in future to address their complaints not to the Pope, but to the proper quarters in Berlin.[16]

That Cardinal Pacelli still hoped for a modus vivendi with Germany was indicated by a conciliatory article in the semi-official Catholic paper, L'Avvenire d'Italia — inspired, according to von Bergen, by Pacelli himself. It compared the two Concordats, Italian and German, emphasising how successfully the former operated. "We can see," says the article, "the fruits of the Italian Concordat daily. Catholic Action continues its work in Italy unhindered, and the State finds that the Church, far from obstructing its efforts for internal unity, furthers them. If the German Concordat is interpreted in the same co-operative way, Germany can obtain the same excellent results."[17] This article may well have been written or inspired by Cardinal Pacelli, for he was primarily a diplomat; throughout his clerical career he had never been anything else. He believed that all problems could be solved by compromise. A born negotiator, he always contended, even years later, that the German Concordat "brought advantages, or at least prevented greater evils".

His contention seemed confirmed in a speech by Staatsminister Wagner in Munich on the 31st March, 1934, only nine months after the signature of the Concordat. Wagner said that if the Church had not signed a concordat with Germany, the National Socialist government would have abolished the Catholic Youth organisations altogether, and placed them in the same "anti-state" category as the Marxist groups. It is possible that Cardinal Pacelli, who knew Germany well, was aware of this during the negotiations. If the maintenance of Catholic education and of the Catholic Youth associations was, as we have seen often enough before, the principal aim of Papal diplomacy, then his phrase, "the Concordat prevented greater evils" seems justified.

[16] Ibid.
[17] Ibid., Vol. 9, despatch from von Bergen, 17th October, 1933.

Many years later, on the 2nd June, 1945, in his allocution to the Sacred College Pius XII said of the German Concordat:

The German episcopate considered that neither the Concordats up to then negotiated with individual German States [*Länder*], nor the Weimar Constitution gave adequate guarantees or assurance to the faithful of respect for their convictions, rights or liberty of action. In such conditions the guarantees could not be secured except through a settlement having the solemn form of a concordat with the central government of the Reich, I would add that since it was the German government which made the proposal, the responsibility for all the regrettable consequences would have fallen on the Holy See if it had refused the proposed Concordat. Although the Church had few illusions about National Socialism, it must be recognised that the Concordat in the years that followed brought some advantages, or at least prevented worse evils. In fact, in spite of all the violations to which it was subjected, it gave German Catholics a juridical basis for their defence, a stronghold behind which to shield themselves in their opposition to the ever-growing campaign of religious persecution.

13

For the Mind of Youth

In its essentials, the Concordat was an agreement between Nazi Germany and the Vatican by which, in return for the latter's withdrawal of support from the Centre Party, the National Socialists permitted Confessional schools, and guaranteed the independence of the Catholic Youth associations, "in so far as their activities are exclusively religious, cultural and educational". In making this bargain, the Vatican was well aware after its experience with Mussolini that a feature peculiar to twentieth-century dictatorships was their concern to reach the juvenile mind. Youth was to be courted by the State, trained, educated, organised and finally marshalled. Nevertheless, the Vatican hoped that, through a solemnly ratified treaty, that part of education so essential to the Catholic apostolic mission would be permitted. Articles 23 and 25 of the Concordat stated that "the maintenance of Catholic schools is guaranteed. In all communes in which parents so desire, elementary Catholic schools will be allowed... Orders and religious associations are authorised to found and direct such private schools in accordance with the general laws and conditions fixed by the State."

This was clear enough, and the Nazis had to permit these schools. But within a matter of months of the signature of the Concordat, they had evolved a technique for undermining the Catholic school's authority.

The method employed with parents who insisted that their children should attend Catholic schools was to send party officials to their houses, and make them state in writing why they wanted their children to attend these schools. Typical of these methods was the case of a Catholic parent, a railway employee, who was courageous enough to complain to his priest, so that the matter came to the attention of the Papal Nuncio in Berlin. He had sent his three daughters to the local convent school. One day he received this letter from the local Nazi party headquarters:

> To: Herr Ried (foreman)
> Railway Office
> Erbach am Donau)

National Socialist Party
District: Ehingen-Danube.
15th July, 1934.

Dear Sir,

I understand that you have recently decided to send your daughters to the Convent school. I must remind you that it is not in keeping with the dignity of a State official to allow his children to be educated by organisations which are hostile to the State. I must ask you to inform me as soon as possible if you are prepared to remove your children from this Catholic establishment. Otherwise, it will be necessary to inform the appropriate authorities.

> (signed) Blankenhorn.
> District Commissioner.

The Nuncio complained about this to the Minister of the Interior, who admitted that the District Commissioner should not have written in this way.[1]

Faced with this form of intimidation, Catholic parents formed local "Catholic Parents' Associations" to give themselves a certain sense of collective security. But the Nazi police generally managed to find some pretext for dissolving them. For instance, a meeting of the Parents' Association of Sevittennen (Bavaria) was forbidden because a priest had been invited to speak at it; this made it "political". On the priest being replaced by a layman, permission was again refused on the ground that the subject to be discussed, "Education in Reverence and Obedience",

[1] *A.A. Pol III Abschluss von Konkordaten mit Deutschland*, Vol. 16, the Nuncio's complaint to the Minister of the Interior, 24th August, 1934.

was not a suitable school subject.[2] It was not long before all the Catholic Parents' Associations had been proscribed because "it has been observed that at meetings speeches are systematically made". In his letter of complaint about this to the German Ambassador, von Bergen, Pacelli is almost sarcastic — "How can you have meetings without speeches?"[3]

Soon so many cases of this kind were being reported to the Vatican by the Nuncio and the German bishops, that Cardinal Pacelli drew up a letter of protest to the German government. It consisted of twenty-two closely typed pages of foolscap listing at least a hundred such incidents. "It is now clear," he wrote, "that a planned attack is in progress against the Catholic schools. Party members go from house to house intimidating parents into signing in favour of State schools. Moreover, teachers who do not speak openly in favour of State schools are relieved of their posts. They have to say that these schools are more suitable in their opinion for the modern 'peoples' community'. . ."

As the figures reveal, this kind of attack on the Confessional schools proved most effective. In 1933, sixty-five per cent of Munich parents sent their children to Catholic schools; by 1935, the figure had been reduced to thirty-five per cent; and by 1937 to three per cent. As a result of this, the government announced that convent teachers were now supernumerary and would be removed, a beginning being made with 600 teaching nuns who were told to find civilian employment. This was deplored in a Pastoral Letter by the German bishops on the 21st June, 1936: "For a thousand years these good women have conducted the education of German youth, and have brought up German girls to be good mothers, faithful spouses and maintained alive that ideal of pure and pious German womanhood sung in the Nibelungenlied."[4]

Against this coercion of parents, Cardinal Faulhaber of Munich issued a Pastoral Letter to be read in all the Catholic schools entreating the teachers not to be intimidated by the prospect of losing their employment. Cardinals Bertram of Breslau and Schulte of Cologne published a warning to parents that, if they signed the document in favour of their children attending State schools, they would be "answerable before God if the children lose their faith and become alien to Christian life. Parents

---

[2] Ibid., Vol. 17, Pacelli's letter to von Bergen complaining of breaches of the Concordat in educational matters, 20th March, 1935.

[3] Ibid.

[4] F.O. 371/19941, report on the Pastoral Letter, 21st June, 1936.

aware of this responsibility will therefore only give permission when they are sure that the teacher in question will exercise no anti-Christian influence on the children."[5]

The Nazi method of dealing with the many written complaints from the Nuncio, and from Cardinal Pacelli himself, was the simple one of not replying to them. Dr. Kerrl, the Minister for Church Affairs in Berlin, to whom the complaints were addressed, admits at one point that he has not answered them for a year because "in their tone and manner of expression these complaints by the Holy See do not display that element of esteem which a sovereign State — and especially the new German State — has a right to expect from those who have signed treaties with it. Nor are they apparently aware at the Vatican that they are no longer dealing with those Liberal, individualist [sic] States to which they have become so accustomed."[6]

Nevertheless, certain German circles, particularly in the Foreign Office, were dismayed by this behaviour towards the Vatican. Von Neurath, the Foreign Minister, wrote to Rudolf Hess, the Führer's Deputy, suggesting "a meeting of all concerned to find a solution to the tactically unfavourable situation in which, as a result of the inordinate delay in replying to the Vatican notes, we find ourselves. It puts us in an invidious position, as if we are unable to give a pertinent reply to their complaints." To this Hess replied that he considered it most unwise at the moment to discuss these matters with the Vatican because "this might impair the measures we are taking at the moment in regard to the schools".[7]

Meanwhile similar pressure was being brought on the teachers, and on the 10th December, 1936 Cardinal Pacelli complained to von Bergen about a declaration which Catholic teachers were being made to sign by the National Socialist Teachers' Association. These were the three alternatives, one of which had to be signed:

(1) I am not a member of any Confessional organisation and hereby recognise my duty to the National Socialist Teachers' Association to inform them should I become one.

[5] A.A. Pol III—Abschluss von Konkordaten mit Deutschland, Vol. 17.
[6] A.A. Pol III Konkordat mit Deutschland, 5/36–12/37. Dr. Kerrl had formerly been a clerk in the law courts. In 1925 he joined the Nazi party and, for lack of competition, soon found himself its "legal expert"; this appears to have been only short step to becoming its "religious expert".
[7] A.A. Pol III Konkordat mit Deutschland, 5/36–12/37, letter from von Neurath to Hess, 10th March, 1937.

(2) I am a member of the following Confessional associations ....
.... I will at the latest by the 1st December, 1936 have broken off
all religious relations with them; nor will I rejoin any of them
without informing the National Socialist Teachers' Association.

(3) I belong to the following Confessional groups .... and I
intend to maintain my connection with them.

This "pressure on the conscience", Cardinal Pacelli complained, was a
flagrant breach of the Concordat. On this occasion he did receive a reply,
a very curt one, from Martin Bormann in the office of the Führer's
Deputy: "The measures taken by the National Socialist Teachers'
Association in no way infringe the provisions of the Concordat — for the
entry of teachers into the National Socialist Teachers' Association is
entirely voluntary"! [8]

The attack on the Catholic Youth associations was equally insidious.
Baldur von Shirach, the leader of the Hitler Youth, simply gave an order
that all Youth organisations other than the Hitler Youth were henceforth
forbidden to take part in any form of organised sport. This was a shrewd
measure because the enthusiasms of the human male between the years of
eight and fifteen, when the growing body requires to flex its muscles, are
physical rather than mental. The growing boy will put up with Bible
classes, even learn something from them, if he knows that afterwards he
can play football, basketball, or jump about in lively team games. Now,
if he belonged to the Catholic Youth, all forms of sport — athletics,
hiking, skiing, gymnastics, even camping — were denied him. The
Catholic Youth was henceforth to confine itself strictly to spiritual
matters, which meant in practice Bible classes and religious services.

In a Pastoral Letter the German bishops complained, "The government's contention that sporting exercises for the youth are no concern of
the Church and religion is erroneous. Christian teaching aims at forming
the whole being, in which physical training also plays an essential part.
The body, too, is the work of the Creator, and is not to be divorced
from the soul. The Catholic sport groups must be maintained."[9] On
which the Hitler Youth leader commented sarcastically, "Catholic sport?
What is Catholic sport? Has anyone ever heard of Catholic, or even
Evangelical, sport? Do you know what a Catholic hurdle race is? Or an
Evangelical short-arm stretch?"[10]

[8] Ibid., Pacelli's complaint to von Bergen, 10th December, 1936.
[9] H. Roth, *Katholische Jugend in der Nazi Zeit* (Altenberg, 1959).
[10] Ibid.

The next step to weaken the Catholic Youth organisations was to forbid all youth movements — apart from the Hitler Youth — from wearing uniforms, together with the badges, shoulder straps, lanyards, etc., by which children, and particularly German children, set such store. They were also forbidden from marching in formation, from having their own bands, carrying flags, banners and pennants. This last measure proved harder to implement than the Nazis expected; they appear to have forgotten the mentality of their own countrymen. In Munich on the 23rd April, 1934 a clash took place between the Catholic Boy Scouts, who persisted in wearing their uniforms and the Hitler Youth, who tore off the Scouts' badges and seized their banners. Injuries were sustained on both sides, and a fourteen-year-old girl who got mixed up in the fray had her clothes torn off her back.[11]

A similar situation arose at Easter 1935, when 1700 of the Catholic Youth went on a pilgrimage to Rome. They hid in their suitcases their uniforms and insignia which, as soon as they were across the German frontier, they donned, and later appeared in full regalia before the Pope. The Nazi newspaper, *Westdeutscher Beobachter* (4th May, 1935), described them as "black ghosts who have returned in their uniforms to demonstrate before the Pope once again as members of the dissolved Centre Party". The German frontier officials, who were waiting for them on their return, made them pay duty on the rosaries, souvenirs and other devotional objects acquired in Rome, including the Don Bosco medals which the Pope had personally bestowed on each pilgrim. While they stood for hours being searched, they were addressed by police officials with such phrases as, "You'd have done better to have stayed in Italy. You're no longer German." One Customs official took a coloured photograph of the Pope from a pilgrim and threw it on the ground saying, "You've had the old boy's blessing, you don't want his bloody fissog too." Another said, "Now, skeddaddle off, in God's name. The Pope's blessed you fucking well." They then confiscated the uniforms, interpreting the word in its broadest sense. According to the Catholic paper, *Germania* (11th May, 1935), they confiscated shirts, trousers, underwear, knapsacks, water-bottles, musical instruments, cooking utensils, wallets, cameras, binoculars, banners, pennants, clasp-knives, etc.

When the Pope heard about this, he said to the next delegation of German pilgrims, "We sincerely hope that you devout pilgrims to Rome will be better received when you return than were those pious and worthy youths who came last time to receive the blessing of the Holy

[11] *A.A. Pol III Abschluss von Konkordaten mit Deutschland und deutschen Länder*, Vol. 15.

Father. We pronounce before the whole Catholic and civilised world their praise and honour. Alas, we cannot say the same of those Germans who shamed them when they returned to their native land."[12]

A curious example of how the Nazis attempted to reply to Papal complaints by accusing the Catholics of using their own violent methods is revealed in a police report from Karlsruhe on the 22nd July, 1935. It was given great prominence in the Nazi press as an example of "the hooliganism of the Catholic youth".

In the night of the 19th July, the Scharführer of the Hitler-jugend, Alfons Lainer, was on his way home through Weiher when he was attacked by a band of ten D.K.J. [the Catholic Youth], who beat him up so severely that he was left unconscious in a ditch. Only when a bicyclist appeared, did the assailants leave their prey and disappear into the night. From later evidence, and from a remark made during the attack, "You brown dog! We will show you the Catholic Youth can strike when it wants," it is clear that the attack was premeditated. One of the assailants has since been arrested.

This incident was used as an excuse for a complete prohibition of Catholic Youth activity throughout the State of Baden. The ecclesiastical authorities immediately made enquiries, the result of which was the following statement: "The Weiher affair proves to have been completely trumped up. Reliable witnesses state that about half an hour before the alleged attack, they met the Hitler Youth, Alfons Lainer, who was lurching about in the road in a state of drunkenness. He appears to have bumped into a cyclist who knocked him over. That passing bicycle then is 'the ten Catholic D.K.J. who beat him up so severely that he was left unconscious in a ditch'!" The Church appears to have won this little propaganda battle, because a few days later the Landspräsident of Baden announced that "as a result of further investigations in the Weiher affair, the ban on the Catholic Youth organisations in Baden is lifted".

The methods employed by the Nazis for proselytising Youth and divorcing them from the Catholic religion are described in another secret document, this time in the British archives; it came into the possession of the British Consul-General in Munich, Mr. D. St. Clair Gainer in 1934.[13] It contains the notes of a young German Catholic who had been converted to National Socialism and who, with a number of other

[12] *Osservatore Romano*, 6th and 7th May, 1935.
[13] F.O. despatch from Mr. Gainer, 16th November, 1934.

recruits, attended a three weeks' indoctrination course at a Youth Labour camp. Afterwards he was so revolted by what he heard and saw, that he reverted to his former religious beliefs.

At the outset, it was made clear to him that National Socialism was more than simply a political philosophy. The camp commandant told the newcomers that it was "a religion born of blood and race, a new religion arising from the Nordic spirit and Aryan soul"; and that, for all "religious questions", their mentor must be Rosenberg. There were no such things as "Freedom of conscience" or "Freedom of teaching and thought"; the State assumed complete responsibility for all teaching and thought. Paragraph 24 of the National Socialist manifesto about religious freedom in the State was "so much eye-wash"; only a fool could believe it. It was obvious to anyone of common sense that National Socialism and the Churches were deadly enemies. The Oriental-Jewish teaching called Christianity was responsible for the decline of the Nordic race and the rise of Bolshevism.

During the course, the youths were taught that at birth a man becomes a National Socialist, and at birth the State's rights over him begin. Parents were no more than representatives of the State and the State had a right to remove children from the care of offending parents. During lectures he took the following notes:

The Pope is half-Jewish and a Freemason. So is his Secretary [Pacelli].

You must utterly reject the teaching of the Oriental Christ [sic].

The Führer's statement that he believes in Positive Christianity is adapted for present circumstances. It is purely temporary.

We do not believe that man is here on earth to prepare himself humbly for after-life. If he fights on earth courageously for his country, he will find someone there — whether God with his beard, or someone else — who will reward him.

Confessional religions will be allowed in Germany only for a limited time. Otherwise, they will conflict with the National Socialist philosophy, as revealed in the writings of Rosenberg.

Muckermann is half-Jewish.[14] Half the Catholic theologians are Jews.

Either you accept the National-Socialist philosophy 100 per cent and then propagate it 100 per cent — or we don't need you.

[14] Muckermann was a well-known anti-Nazi Jesuit priest who had to emigrate soon after the Nazis took power.

Pope Pius XI

Cardinal Segura, Primate of Spain

Cardinal Gasparri, Secretary of State

Mgr. Seipel, Chancellor of Austria

Bishop von Galen of Münster

Charles Maurras

At the signing of the Italian Concordat. Cardinal Gasparri and Signor Mussolini in the centre; Count Dino Grandi to the right.

Signature of the Italian Concordat. Cardinal Gasparri seated, Signor Mussolini reading.

Pius XII reading a war-time message from President Roosevelt,
handed to him by Mr. Myron Taylor

The young man appears at this point to have felt that he did not need National Socialism, and he left before finishing the course. He was permitted to do so only after signing the following statement: "I took the course, but I cannot agree with National Socialism and do not wish to become a member of the party." Signature of this document meant, he knew, that he was forfeiting any chance of later obtaining State employment.

The aim of this indoctrination was, as the Second World War was to show, to produce good fighting material, particularly for the S.S. elite. The Christian virtues of gentleness, compassion and charity were to be derided; the exaltation of violence and military virtue was to replace such soft and degenerate mores. Just before the war of 1939, Hitler himself proudly proclaimed, "My S.S. is completely churchless — and yet they know their duty towards the German people better than any catechism-reading Catholic." Three years later, in the apocalyptic days on the Russian front, he could still boast, "I can throw seven S.S. divisions who are absolutely churchless into battle — and they will die with the greatest confidence in the future." Hitler never grasped that religion is something more than simply a means of relieving people of the fear of death.

14

Mit brennender Sorge

———

DURING THE FIRST FOUR YEARS OF NAZI RULE IN GERMANY, THE Vatican was still obsessed with the fear of Communism, not only as the principal, self-avowed enemy of all Churches, but as the most dangerous and disintegrating influence on order and stability in the world. By 1937 the Nazi treatment of religion was beginning to displace Communism in this role. During these years, relations of the Vatican with Germany grew more tense and embittered, the prospects of conciliation more remote, the repression of freedom of conscience and religion more active and relentless; while the glorification year after year of Rosenberg's pagan theories at the Nuremberg party rally testified to his growing influence in the party. Communism, on the other hand, had displayed unmistakable weaknesses and sustained a number of reverses. In Spain, which Lenin had foretold would be the second Communist republic in Europe, General Franco appeared the probable victor. In France, the Communists of the Popular Front had failed to accomplish the revolution they had advertised so confidently. They even now issued an appeal to Catholics to join with them in fighting "social injustice", a sure indication of weakness. In Russia itself, the Communist experiment had been greatly discredited by the merciless extermination of the leadership.

In the first years of power the Nazis had refrained from making open attacks on the Church, confining themselves largely to criticism of "political clericalism". But as they began to flex their muscles internationally, to build up armaments without any serious objection from the Western Powers, they became less fastidious.[1] Leaders like Göring, who in the early days had obsequiously paid his respects at the Vatican, now insulted the Church openly. In a public speech, he accused the Catholic priests of being "black moles, as venomous as the red moles" (Communists). At a public meeting, the Nazi leader Julius Streicher read out a number of love letters alleged to have been exchanged between Archbishop Gröber of Baden and a twenty-year-old Jewess.[2] The S.S. magazine, *Das Schwarze Korps*, published a caricature of Cardinal Pacelli wearing his ceremonial robes and embracing an unattractive fat Jewess.[3] Another Nazi magazine, *Die Sonne*, said the Pope's grandmother was a Dutch Jewess called Lipmann, which was why he employed the Rabbi Levy in the Vatican library.[4] The *Brunnen Verlag* under the title "*Sie werd'n lachen*" published a series of salacious anecdotes about Pope Alexander Borgia, relating them to the present Pontiff. In Königsberg, gangs of Nazi youths went around at night to the churches and priests' houses placarding the walls with posters — "Down with Rome! Down with the Confessionals! The black rats out of the cloisters! Our people are being destroyed by Jewish fraud and Papal corruption! The Catholic is a hypocrite and idler who can only pray."

This atmosphere of open contempt for the Church, and the paganism which was spreading among the youth of the country, was typified by one of Hauer's Faith Movement (*Glaubensbewegung*) meetings in Munich on May Day. It took place in the *Löwenbräukeller*, and opened with the hymn, "The autumn breaks over the stubble field". The speaker, Herr Bachöfer, referred to "this May Day, rich in the sense of blood and earth, [which] is holier to us than any Church holiday". He went on to accuse the Vatican of turning Munich into "a hotbed of Jesuit reaction", and a "branch office of the Pope". He said that Wilhelm Busch, the anti-clerical caricaturist, "is holier to us than all the Saints". "Can you

[1] In February 1934, Anthony Eden had an audience of Pius XI who said "he felt it impossible to believe that even if Germany meant war, she would be in a position to wage it for ten or fifteen years at least." *Facing the Dictators* (Cassell, 1962).

[2] F.O. 371/19938, 15th April, 1935. Streicher's statements were notoriously inaccurate. In an attack on English Jewry he accused Queen Victoria of "having ennobled the Jew Disraeli with the title Lord Gladstone".

[3] *A.A. Pol III Beziehungen des heiligen Stuhls zu Deutschland*, Vol. 2, telegram from von Bergen, 21st August, 1937.

[4] Ibid., Menshausen to Aschmann.

imagine," he jeered, "a healthy Hitler Youth with a rosary dangling over his uniform? Or one of Hitler's S.S. elite making a pilgrimage to Rome to kiss the Pope's big toe?" These insults were enthusiastically applauded, accompanied by such cries as, "To hell with Faulhaber! Down with Christianity!" In another Munich *Lokal*, the Bürgerbräukeller, Dr. Ludwig Engel, a renegade Jesuit, addressed a similar audience. He said the Jesuits were a menace to every state, that Ignatius Loyala was a half-breed of Moorish and negro blood, and his principal patron, Pope Paul III, a full-blooded Jew.[5]

Violence had been used against a Catholic leader as early as June 1934, in the "Night of the Long Knives" when Eric Klausener, the head of Catholic Action in Berlin, had been included among the "conspirators" who were summarily executed. But this was explained by the Nazis as being a purely political affair, totally unconnected with his religion (he had certainly often criticised them for their political philosophy). Be that as it may, by the end of 1936 physical violence was being used openly and blatantly against the Catholic Church. The real issue was not, as the Nazis contended, a struggle with "political Catholicism", but that the regime would tolerate the Church only if it adapted its religious and moral teaching to the materialist dogma of blood and race — that is, if it ceased to be Christian.

Dozens of examples were now reported by the clergy. At Traunstein in Upper Bavaria, S.S. men used small mortars to bombard the house of the Catholic priest, Father Stelze. At the *Marianische Studentkongregation* in Munich, a Catholic meeting was broken up by uniformed Hitler Youth who got into the gallery and threw fire-crackers into the audience. During the Corpus Christi procession in the Munich Cathedral, stink-bombs were used and the Holy Water contaminated with a black substance. The worst excesses took place in Bavaria against the charitable organisations of Catholic Action which was so dear to the Pope. Authority had been granted in Munich by the police for a house-to-house collection on behalf of Catholic Action. For several days before this, detailed accounts of the philanthropic work of the Catholic organisation prepared the public. But on the day, Hitler Youth paraded the streets shouting, "No money for the black swine!" and "Down with political Catholicism!" "Nun condemned to five years' penal servitude for immorality!" and "Foreign currency profiteers in Holy Orders!" By midday, blows were being exchanged with the Catholic collectors. On

[5] F.O. 371/19938 these incidents are reported by the Consul-General, St. Clair Gainer from Munich, 17th May, 1935.

the grounds of "maintaining public order", the police announced that the collection must be stopped. This was the signal for a general attack on the collectors and those who wished to contribute. Badges with the Catholic Action inscription "Do good to all your neighbours" were torn off, and those who resisted were arrested. Priests were spat upon and insulted, particularly by fanatical Nazi women.[6]

Until 1936, it was still possible for a priest to speak in the pulpit on behalf of the persecuted Jews without being physically molested. Now, when the Catholic Dompropst, Bernhardt Lichtenberg, referred in a sermon to "the Jews and other unfortunates in the concentration camps", he was arrested and sent to one of them. He had protested against an anonymous pamphlet which was being distributed in Berlin households, stating that "every German who for sentimental reasons supports the Jews, commits high treason". "Do not let yourselves be led astray by these unchristian words," said Lichtenberg from the pulpit. "But behave according to the command of Christ, 'Thou shalt love thy neighbour as thyself'."

To discredit the Vatican, the Nazis began in 1935 a practice which was to become fashionable with all twentieth-century dictatorships, of bringing clerics to trial for alleged currency offences. On the 15th May, 1935, Sister Catherine Wiedendorfer was found guilty at Moabite (Berlin) of having illegally exported capital to Belgium, and sentenced to five years' imprisonment. On the 29th May a Franciscan, Otto Goertler, received ten years for a similar offence. These cases were given great publicity in the Nazi press, and the *Völkischer Beobachter* talked of "the systematic robbing of the nation by criminals wearing soutanes". *Das Schwarze Korps*, which could always be relied on for bad taste, had a caricature of the Pope in front of a huge sack of gold, underneath the motto, "*Ein feste Burg ist unser Gott*".

On the 4th January, 1936, after the New Year reception at the Vatican for foreign diplomats, the Pope asked von Bergen to stay behind and talk to him for a moment. Von Bergen's despatch to his chief in Berlin, von Neurath, describes the icy interview:

His Holiness told me that he was greatly distressed by events in Germany and could no longer contain himself. Contrary to all that the German government said, it was trying to destroy the Catholic Church. A real persecution of Catholics was in progress. But the Church could face it, it would stand up to all storms — *against even the*

[6] F.O. 371/19938.

strongest personalities. The Church had experience. Bismarck had tried for a National Church — in vain. After fifteen months of struggle he had retreated before Leo XIII. But then it had been a question of theology, canonical law and liturgy. Now it was Christianity itself which was threatened. Also, Bismarck always allowed German public opinion to know what the Pope thought of his policies. But Hitler did not. Not a word of Vatican opinion was printed in the German press today. I intervened to say that surely the French had persecuted the Church in this century — and yet France was still well regarded at the Vatican. At this remark His Holiness flew into a rage, saying he refused to speak with me of individual countries except my own. Then he repeated three times, speaking slowly and deliberately, that he no longer believed the German words that Germany was saving the world from Bolshevism ... I then went to see the Secretary of State, Cardinal Pacelli, and told him what His Holiness had said. Pacelli appeared surprised and distressed. He obviously could not say anything against his Chief, but I could see he was far from pleased at the Pope's outburst ... Personally, [finished the German Ambassador] I think we should not take this too seriously. Mussolini told me he had had much the same trouble with the Pope. And his advice to me was, "Let him talk, no point in arguing with the old man."[7]

To this von Neurath replied that he agreed the Pope's outburst should not be over-estimated as long as it remained private, and was not announced publicly.[8] Unfortunately for him however a German emigré Catholic paper, *Der deutsche Weg* which appeared in Holland, somehow managed to get hold of an account of this audience which it published, adding that the Pope was overheard "by his personnel" to have said to von Bergen, "If you want a *Kulturkampf* again, you can have it." This emigré paper was, the Nazis alleged, edited by the German Jesuit, Father Friedrich Muckermann; and they immediately instructed von Bergen to ask the Vatican to bring pressure to bear on the Jesuit not to inflame passions in this way. Cardinal Pacelli refused on the ground that it was not Vatican policy to influence the press of a foreign country.

The Pope had meanwhile instructed his Nuncio in Berlin, Mgr. Orsenigo, to make an official complaint about the various breaches of

[7] *A.A. Pol II Beziehungen des Vatikans zu Deutschland*, Vol. 5, despatch from von Bergen, 4th January, 1936.
[8] Ibid., von Neurath's reply, 20th January, 1936.

the Concordat. But the Nuncio found it impossible to make contact with anyone in authority.

The Nuncio told me [wrote the British Ambassador in Berlin] that the German government simply declines to answer his complaints. He had suggested negotiations, but the Germans prevaricate. He has told the German Ministry for Foreign Affairs that, if and when the Minister for Church Affairs consents to discuss the question he, the Nuncio, will insist on the presence of a member of their Ministry. At least, said the Nuncio, some of the diplomats are civilised people, who may be presumed to respect Germany's signature to the Concordat.[9]

The Pope did not intend to confine himself to words. When one of the leading Nazis, Frank, the Minister of Justice, visited Rome and requested an audience, it was refused. Von Bergen reports that Cardinal Pacelli tried to persuade the Pope to receive Frank, but that the Pope was adamant.

Pacelli told me [writes von Bergen] that His Holiness is filled with personal ill-humour (*Misstimmung*) over Germany. He refused the audience not on personal grounds, but because the Minister was a prominent member of a government which makes no attempt to protect a foreign sovereign from public insults, and permits the lie to be published in the German press that the representative of Christ on earth has allied himself with Bolshevism, the anti-Christ, against National Socialism. The Pope also feels particularly wounded by the repeated assertion that he is of Jewish origin. He has nothing against the Jews, but a great deal against false statements of fact.[10]

From this it may appear that Cardinal Pacelli did not play a very estimable role — attempting to modify the anger of the Pope, and to conciliate the Nazis. But as we have seen, Pacelli was primarily a diplomat, who believed that all problems could be solved by conciliation and compromise. That he was well aware of the true situation is revealed in his letter to Cardinal Schulte of Cologne. Here he has no illusions about the Nazis and their aims, referring to them as "false prophets with the pride of Lucifer", "bearers of a new Faith and a new Evangile". He

---

[9] F.O. 371/20742, Sir E. Phipps to Mr. Eden, 24th February, 1937.
[10] *A.A. Pol II Beziehungen des Vatikans zu Deutschland*, Vol. 5, von Bergen to Berlin, 6th April, 1936.

rites of "impious hands laid upon the Church", and of "the perfidious
ttempt to establish a mendacious antimony between faithfulness to the
Church and faithfulness to the Fatherland".[11]

The charge of weakness could certainly not be levelled against
Cardinal Faulhaber of Munich. On the 14th February, 1937, he preached
a sermon in St. Michael's Church in which he condemned the State's
confiscation of Pastoral Letters, the dismissal of nuns and Catholic
teachers from schools, the banning of the Corpus Christi procession, and
the flood of calumniation against His Holiness and the dignitaries of the
Church". He also condemned the political capital made out of the
currency trials. In retaliation, a posse of S.S. men forced their way into
his church when it was empty and placed electrical bugging devices in
the pulpit. When some priests, hearing the noise, tried to prevent them,
they were so severely mauled that several had to be taken to hospital.
The S.S. men left singing a profane song, each verse of which ended with
the words, "To hell with the Blacks!"

Nor could the clerical rank and file in Germany be accused of
weakness. Being German, they knew the language the Nazis understood
best. Frick, the Minister of the Interior, complained to the Nuncio that
Catholic priests were "insulting the State in the coarsest manner". For
example, Pfarrer Detzel of Schrobenhausen had said in the pulpit, "Let
those stinking S.S. bastards come at me, two thousand of them if you
like, and I'll bash in all their skulls so that their brains squirt out. It'll
make enough soup for a week." When the priest Schumbert of Mainz-
Moneberg heard that three Nazi Brown Shirts had been wounded in a
street brawl, he said in a lesson to school-children, "A pity they weren't
killed! Then there'd be three less. The Brown Shirt is supposed to be a
shirt of Honour, isn't it? Yes, brown's the word. Like something else
that's brown — and stinks!" Kaplan Klinghammer of Essen in a Lent
sermon referred to a recent speech by Göring as "a heap of shit"; while
Vikar Stocker of Bochum announced in the pulpit that Göring was a
homosexual and a morphino-maniac. He also referred to Röhm's
homosexuality and to "Hitler's love of him". He said that Goebbels, who
claimed to be anti-Semitic, had kissed the Jewish Italian Air Marshal,
Balbo. The priest Detzel said, "If I'd been Pacelli having to sign the
Concordat with this bunch, I'd have given His Holiness one up the arse
for making me do it." Quoting all these cases, and many others,
textually, Frick demanded that these priests be defrocked, or at least
removed from their clerical offices. The complaint reached Pacelli, who

[11] Robert d'Harcourt, *Les Catholiques d'Allemagne.*

had sorrowfully to admit in a reply to Berlin that the German priest were at fault for using such uncanonical language.

By 1937 things had become so bad that there was talk of an open breach and public denunciation by the Pope of the German government. Mr Osborne had reported as early as the spring of 1936 that the Vatican might publish a White Book on the German violations of the Concordat. He had it on good authority however, he said, that the general of the Jesuits Father Ledochovski, who had the ear of the Holy Father more than any other Vatican dignitary, had persuaded him that the Nazis, with all their faults, were still the principal bulwark against Communism. And Mr Osborne thought the White Book might be postponed.[12] It seems now, from the available diplomatic documents, that what persuaded the Pope to pronounce against Germany before the whole world was a curious by-product of the Spanish civil war.

In the summer of 1936 this war seemed to offer the Vatican a last chance of agreement with Germany, on the basis of forming a common front against Communism, which was assumed to be the inspiration of the Spanish Republican government. In this last hope, therefore, of some sort of conciliation, feelers were put out by the Vatican on two occasions — in the German bishops' Fulda Pastoral Letter of August 1936, and in the Christmas Pastoral Letter of the 3rd January, 1937. The two documents made a last offer of support for Germany in her efforts on behalf of Franco's Nationalists, but on the condition that the present state of Church affairs in Germany was radically improved. The bishops' words in the Fulda document are revealing: "As always when the call of the Fatherland is sounded, we German Catholics are prepared to place ourselves at the disposition of the Führer in his campaign against a creed which threatens the entire universe." The bishops add, nevertheless, that this creed must be combated on the basis of Christianity, for "to claim to be destroying materialism while remaining materialist oneself is vanity and folly".

This offer of help was brusquely rejected. The Nazis replied that it came strangely from a man who had been saved from drowning to offer himself as an expert in life-saving. By preventing the spread of Communism in Europe, it was Germany who had saved the Church, not the reverse. It was thanks to Hitler that the churches of Western Europe were not piles of smoking cinders, as they were in Spain. "You ask us to believe we need you," said the Nazis. "On the contrary, it is you who need us. We can do without your *oremus*. You cannot do without our arms." *Das Schwarze Korps* asked, "What in fact do we see about the Catholics in Spain? The

[12] F.O. 371/19940, Mr. Osborne to Mr. Eden, 5th March, 1936.

moment the uprising took place Gil Robles, reputedly the leader of Spanish political Catholicism, took to his heels and emigrated. The men who will make Moscow withdraw are those standing at the barricades — not those counting their beads behind monastery walls." For good measure, Rosenberg, the party theorist, announced that, far from combatting Communism, the Catholic Church was the finest nourishing ground for Communism in Europe, as had been seen in the last years of the Weimar Republic; Moscow was "the daughter of Rome". This was the final blow. In offering collaboration against Spanish Bolshevism, the Church had played its last card for conciliation, and had in return received nothing but insults. The Pope now decided to speak out before the whole world. The famous encyclical *Mit brennender Sorge* was written.

It seems that *Mit brennender Sorge* was composed in January 1937, and that its inspiration came from a group of German bishops who happened to be in Rome for an *ad limina* visit (Cardinals Bertram, Schulte, Faulhaber, and Bishops von Galen and von Preysing). They visited the Pope, who was ailing and in bed, to report on the latest anti-clerical excesses in Germany; and afterwards Cardinal Pacelli asked Cardinal Faulhaber to draw up the main lines of an encyclical condemning the Nazi persecution of the Church. Faulhaber set to work that night — for security reasons without a stenographer — and by dawn of the 21st January, 1937, he had finished it, in his own hand, with the title *Mit grosser Sorge*. Modestly he told Pacelli that he thought it adequate for a pastoral letter, but not for a Papal pronouncement of such importance. Pacelli, however, was most satisfied and, after one or two modifications (the title changed to *Mit brennender Sorge*) it was printed with the sub-title *Rundschreiben über die Lage der katholischen Kirche im deutschen Reich*. The whole incident reveals the close relations existing between the Pope and the German episcopate.[13]

Such is the account from Vatican sources. Von Bergen, however, reports from one of his many *Vertrauensmänner* that the encyclical was composed in Castelgandolfo, but that once again its publication was temporarily postponed, largely due to the influence of Cardinal Pacelli, in the hope that, even at this late hour, the situation in Germany might improve. "But the Pope feels," warned von Bergen, "that if he condemns the persecution of the Church in Russia and Mexico, he must do the same where similar events are taking place."[14] In spite of this favourable

[13] Angelo Martini, "Il Cardinale Faulhaber e l'Enciclica 'Mit brennender Sorge' ", *Archivum Historiae Pontificae*, 2, 1964.

[14] *A.A. Pol III Politische Beziehungen des heiligen Stuhls zu Deutschland*, Vol. 2.

reference to Cardinal Pacelli, the Germans believed that he had had a large part in its composition because it was written in the language he had mastered, German (instead of the customary Latin).

By the beginning of March 1937 all doubts about the wisdom of issuing it were dispelled, and instructions were issued for it to be read simultaneously on Palm Sunday from every pulpit in Germany. To prevent possible confiscation before the day, the greatest security measures were taken. Normally, Catholic tracts in Germany were printed at the presses of *Germania*, the Catholic newspaper; but in the week before publication, the encyclical *Mit brennender Sorge* was sent out clandestinely to hundreds of towns and villages where it was printed locally, and then distributed to the dioceses. This was a wise precaution because the Nazis seem to have suspected that something was afoot, and during the first week of March they suddenly descended on the *Germania* offices and searched them from top to bottom; but they found nothing. Nor were the lay Catholics who had been entrusted with the delivery of the encyclical to the churches taking any chances. Rather than confide it to the post or public transport, they sent it out by their own men on an army of motor-cycles, to be distributed all over the country. To give it full force, the bishops read it from the pulpit themselves and did not, as was customary, leave it to their subordinates.

Mit brennender Sorge did not prevaricate. Although it began mildly enough with an account of the broad aims of the Church, it went on to become one of the greatest condemnations of a national regime ever pronounced by the Vatican. Its vigorous language is in sharp contrast to the involved style in which encyclicals were normally written. The education question was fully and critically examined, and a long section devoted to disproving the Nazi theory of Blood and Soil (*Blut und Boden*) and the Nazi claim that faith in Germany was equivalent to faith in God. There were scathing references to Rosenberg's *Myth of the Twentieth Century* and its neo-paganism. The pressure exercised by the Nazi party on Catholic officials to betray their faith was lambasted as "base, illegal and inhuman". The document spoke of "a condition of spiritual oppression in Germany such as has never been seen before", of "the open fight against the Confessional schools and the suppression of liberty of choice for those who desire a Catholic education". "With pressure veiled and open," it went on, "with intimidation, with promises of economic, professional, civil and other advantages, the attachment of Catholics to the Faith, particularly those in government employment, is exposed to a violence as illegal as it is inhuman." "The calvary of the Church": "The war of annihilation against the Catholic Faith"; "The cult of idols". The fulminations thundered down from the pulpits to the delighted congregations. Nor was the Führer himself spared, for his "aspirations to divinity", "placing himself on the same level as Christ"; "a mad prophet possessed of repulsive arrogance" (*widerliche Hochmut*).

On the 25th March the German government, having got over its initial surprise, issued an official comment, adopting at first a tone "more in sorrow than in anger", making light of the whole affair. It maintained that the Concordat was merely a framework, that the present differences of opinion about its interpretation concerned the executive regulations to which the Vatican had refused its approval in 1934, and which were still the subject of diplomatic negotiations. In reply to the accusation that the Catholic schools were not permitted liberty of action, the Nazi government alleged that the Church, through these schools, had brought powerful influence to bear against the interests of the National Socialist State which, it alleged, "had met continuous opposition from Catholicism in undisguised collaboration with foreign agencies". In his May Day speech, Hitler referred to the trials of the priests for currency trafficking, and said that the Church should not criticise the morals of the State when it had more than sufficient grounds to be concerned with its own.[15] Von Bergen was instructed to make the most energetic representations at the Vatican against "this attempt to destroy the unity of the German people". This he did to the Secretary of State, Pacelli, who, on this occasion, remained as unbending as his master. He supported every word in the encyclical stating that, as the normal diplomatic channels had been exhausted, this form of public protest was all that remained.[16]

The true extent of the Nazi fury at this encyclical was shown by the immediate measures taken in Germany to counter further propagation of the document. Not a word of it was printed in the newspapers, and the following day the Secret Police visited the diocesan offices and confiscated every copy they could lay their hands on. All presses which had printed it were closed and sealed. The bishops' diocesan magazines (*Amtsblätter*) were proscribed; and paper for church pamphlets or secretarial work was severely restricted. A host of other measures, such as diminishing the State grants to theology students and needy priests (agreed in the Concordat) were introduced. And then a number of futile,

[15] F.O. 371/21692 Annual Report for 1937 from Sir N. Henderson to Mr. N. Chamberlain, 10th January, 1938.
[16] *A.A. Pol III Politische Beziehungen des heiligen Stuhls zu Deutschland*, Vol. 2, von Bergen to Berlin.

vindictive measures which did little harm to the Church — such a
prohibiting Catholic flags at religious ceremonies, or rechristening
towns and villages with religious names, Heiligenstadt, Mariendorf
Gottesberg, etc.[17]

The encyclical was well received abroad. The German Ambassador in
Budapest reported on the 9th April, 1937 that not a single Hungarian
paper had taken the side of Germany, all of them maintaining that
Germany was entirely responsible for the conflict with the Vatican. And
not only Catholic Hungarians had shown these anti-German feelings
but their Protestant cousins as well.[18] The German Minister in
Switzerland reported on the 30th September, 1937 that the attitude of
the Swiss Catholics towards Germany was decided entirely by what the
Vatican said; and the encyclical *Mit brennender Sorge* was, for them
addressed not only to German Catholics but to the entire Catholic
world.[19] From Belgium, the German Consul in Antwerp reported that
at a Catholic meeting to discuss the encyclical, the speaker announced
that the Catholic Church was less in danger from Communism, which
was "at least open in its attack" than from the "secret, creeping poison
of National Socialism".[20] From Chile the German Ambassador reported
that the encyclical "has had a great effect in turning the people against
Germany".[21] The most important effect however was in the United
States. On the 24th December, 1937, the German Ambassador in
Washington reported that thanks to the anti-Catholic campaign
Germany was losing the support, which had hitherto been very active
when the National Socialist anti-Communist policy was announced, of
twenty-five million Catholics who "stand united and determined
behind their Church".[22]

From these representative samples of world opinion, it might be
supposed that the Nazis would have learnt the old lesson, *Qui mange d'*
Pape en meurt. But so obsessed were they with the vast military machine
they had built over the last four years that they only became more
overweening, determined to teach the Papacy a lesson. For the moment
with the time not yet ripe for war, there were only two ways of doing

[17] *Osservatore Romano*, 10th September, 1937.
[18] *A.A. Pol III Politische Beziehungen des heiligen Stuhls zu Deutschland*, Vol. 2, from
Budapest.
[19] Ibid., report from Consul, 30th September, 1937.
[20] Ibid., Vol. 1, 30th September, 1937.
[21] Ibid., Vol. 5.
[22] Ibid., Vol. 5.

this — one purely symbolic, the other to take revenge on the unfortunate Catholic clergy in their own land. The first concerned the long heralded State visit of Hitler to Italy in return for Mussolini's earlier one to Germany. On these occasions protocol demands that a Head of State visiting the Quirinal shall also make a formal call at the Vatican. This Hitler ostentatiously refused to do. He spent the four days in the company of Mussolini, visiting the King, attending military parades, inspecting battleships; but he studiously avoided asking for a Papal audience. The contention that Pius XI would have refused to grant Hitler an audience if it had been requested is not supported by precedent. The Pope never refuses a Head of State, which would be tantamount to refusing the nation. The German Ambassador at the Quirinal, von Mackensen, deeply shocked at his ruler's behaviour, said the Pope would even receive Stalin if he were Head of State and requested an audience when in Rome. In protocol terms, Hitler's gesture was a gross insult.

The Pope was not slow to react. Informed that Hitler would not ask for a Papal audience, he ostentatiously withdrew during the German visit to Castelgandolfo, in May (a procedure adopted normally only in the heat of August and September); and on learning that certain members of Hitler's suite wished to visit the Vatican museums, directed that they were to be closed during the German visit. He stated in an allocution to pilgrims that it was neither seemly nor timely to display in Rome on the day of the Holy Cross (3rd May) the emblem of "another Cross which is not the Cross of Christ" (for huge *Hakenkreuzs* were displayed all over the city, even in the via della Conciliazione itself). The *Osservatore Romano* published no details of Hitler's visit, but found the occasion propitious to print a number of extracts from works by German professors comparing the relative merits of the Nordic and Mediterranean races, greatly to the disadvantage of the latter, which they depicted as dirty, voluble, shallow, sensual, cowardly and lazy.

The second, more concrete way of retaliating for *Mit brennender Sorge* was by pillorying the Catholic clergy in Germany. To the Statthalter of Baden, Wagner, Hitler said, "I shall open such a campaign of propaganda against them in press, radio and cinema that they won't know what's hit them. I'll show the people all the abominations of their history — how the priests really live, in sin and debauchery." But he was also careful to ensure that in so doing he did not make them martyrs; it was still too early for that. To the Statthalter he added these significant instructions, "Let us have no martyrs among the Catholic priests. It is more practical to show that they are criminals."[23] In this way began the notorious "morality" trials of the late thirties.

Attacks had been made on priests' morals before, but they were nothing compared with the new accusations and mass trials. At Koblenz 170 Franciscans were arrested and tried for "corrupting the youth and turning the monastery into a male brothel". That the trial was conducted *in camera*, and that most of the witnesses were children, raised doubts as to its equity. The *Völkischer Beobachter* wrote about "orgies which the pen refuses to describe"; and the *Schwarze Korps* showed a cartoon of small boys being beckoned by a lascivious-looking monk, with the caption, "Let the little children come unto me!" Goebbels' paper *Angriff* published a series of indignant articles about monastery schools which had become "incubators of homosexuality", and Goebbels boasted sanctimoniously of how the National Socialists had punished *their* homosexuals like Röhm and Heines. *Das Schwarze Korps* alleged that even at the altar rail, priests practised their disgusting tricks on old men and crippled children. A Hitler Youth film showed priests dancing in a brothel. Over the Schulle case of incest alleged to have been committed by a young ecclesiastic, the Nazis shed many crocodile tears, and Goebbels worked himself up into a fit of righteous indignation. In a speech on the 28th May, 1937 he said, "Today I speak as the father of a family whose four children are the most precious wealth I possess — of a father who therefore fully understands how parents are shocked in their love for the bodies and souls of their children, of parents who see their most precious treasure delivered to the bestiality of the polluters of youth. I speak in the name of millions of German fathers..."[24] And the *Völkischer Beobachter* echoed him on the 30th April, 1937: "What parents conscious of their responsibility can still entrust their children to an organisation which possesses more than a thousand sexual criminals?" The *Trier Nationalblatt* even went so far as to sully the reputation of the Pope himself. When Father Werner was accused of sodomy, he managed to flee the country to Italy; and the paper wrote, "He has been recalled to Rome to serve the Pope."[25]

The great publicity accompanying these immorality trials was intended of course to counter the effect of *Mit brennender Sorge* in the

[23] A.A. *Pol III Beziehungen des heiligen Stuhls zu Deutschland*, Vol. 5, 16th January, 1938.

[24] Seven years later Goebbels murdered his four children.

[25] A.A. *Pol III Strafverfahren gegan katholischen Geistlicher und Ordens-angehöriger wegen Sittlichkeitvergehen*, 2/6/36–31/7/37.

eyes of the world; and German diplomats abroad were fed with quantities of inflammatory material for distribution. This did not always have the desired effect. The German Consul in Caracas complained that the material he was receiving contained nothing but cases of homosexuality. "Owing to the unpleasant incidents at the court of Wilhelm II," he wrote, "not to mention the more recent sexual habits of Röhm and his friends, homosexuality has come to be known in Colombia as 'the German vice' — and these cases against German priests only add to this unfortunate impression. Could we not therefore have a few *heterosexual* incidents?" His request was soon gratified by a number of photographs showing priests in compromising attitudes with half-naked women (the method being, according to the Catholic paper, *Der deutsche Weg*, to entice a priest on some pretext into a private house, where a naked woman would suddenly throw herself on his neck while a flashlight photo was taken).[26]

The old Pope, for his part, did not give way. In his addresses he now referred to Russia and Germany in the same breath; and in a series of speeches during 1938 he never ceased attacking Nazi Germany. He told one congress of bishops that he still tried to maintain good relations with Italy, but warned Italian Catholics not to put their trust in Germany (he was here doubtless referring to the recently signed "Pact of Steel" between the two countries). In his Christmas address to the College of Cardinals on the 28th December, 1938, only two months before his death, he said:

Let us call things by their true name. I tell you, in Germany today a full religious persecution is in progress. A persecution which does not shrink from using every weapon, lies, threats, false information, and in the last resort physical force ... A lying campaign is being carried on in Germany against the Catholic hierarchy, the Catholic religion and God's Holy Church ... the protest we make before the whole civilised world cannot be clearer or more unequivocal ... Their excuse is that the Church is political. The same accusation was made against Jesus Christ when he stood before Pontius Pilate, who asked him if he had come to overthrow the established order. To which Christ replied, "My kingdom is not of this world. If it were my

[26] In September 1944, when the Allied armies were pressing on towards the Reich, all documents concerning these morality trials were destroyed by order of the S.S. (see letter from Brother Willigis of the Franciscans to Herr V. Engelhardt, 17th February, 1961).

army would come to my help." That is the answer we give these modern persecutors.[27]

During this period of extreme tension between Church and State in Germany, the unfortunate von Bergen had to act as intermediary, conveying the insulting messages of his government to Cardinal Pacelli. That he tried to palliate them is indicated by the sharp reproof he received at the end of 1938 from Dr. Kerrl, the German Minister for Church Affairs: "To my regret, I must state that the National Socialist German State does not appear to be represented at the Vatican with that degree of firmness, enthusiasm and awareness of our aims which is demanded when dealing with this Pope."[28]

In the spring of 1938 when the Sudeten crisis developed, the Vatican stated that, although the Sudeten Germans undoubtedly wanted union with the Reich, German intervention in the domestic affairs of Czechoslovakia was inadmissible. It did not view Lord Runciman's efforts to satisfy the Sudeten Germans with much favour. Mgr. Pizzardo told the British Minister that the Czechs were an obstinate people, of whom the Vatican had recently had considerable experience, and he believed they would fight. On the 22nd August, 1938, the Pope addressed the Missionary College near Rome on the evils of nationalism. A moderate nationalism, he said, was permissible, but "beware of exaggerated nationalism as of a curse". This was a clear enough reference to Germany.

Mr. Chamberlain's flight to Hitler at Berchtesgaden made a very favourable impression. The *Osservatore Romano* wrote that to resort to force after such a gesture of peace would be monstrous. On the evening of the 28th September, with the crisis at its peak, the Pope broadcast an appeal to the whole Catholic world to join him in prayer for the preservation of peace, offering his own life to God as a sacrifice. After the Munich settlement, the *Osservatore Romano* wrote that the Prime Minister of England had been revealed as a statesman of the first rank, and that the world would now know to whom it owed its salvation.

[27] Bundesarchiv, Koblenz, Reichskanzlei file R4311/15040, report of the Pope's Christmas address.

[28] *A.A. Pol III Beziehungen des heiligen Stuhls zu Deutschland*, Vol. 4. On the 19th October, 1938 Kerrl tried to retire von Bergen on the grounds that an Ambassador was no longer really necessary at the Vatican. But the German Foreign Office argued successfully that it was an important post, and that von Bergen, who had been there since 1921, was still the man best qualified to fill it.

15

The Achievement of Pius XI

———

THE DEATH OF PIUS XI AT THE AGE OF EIGHTY-ONE ENDED A Pontificate memorable not only for his vigorous, unbending personality, but for the violent attacks on his Church in the aftermath of the Great War, a period of spiritual, intellectual and political upheaval unknown since the French Revolution. A comment on the Monk of Padua in the early eighteenth century is applicable to the life of Achille Ratti — "Here is Faith intrepid and a terrible immolation". Certainly Pius XI showed intrepid faith in the face of great hostility; while the fate of his Catholic priesthood and laity in Russia, Mexico, Germany and Spain justified the words, "a terrible immolation". During the last years of his life, he had to meet the attacks on the one hand of the Communists vowed to eradicate religion, and on the other of the German National Socialists, intent on substituting their own brand of racial opiate. In an obituary letter to Mr. Osborne, Lord Halifax, the British Foreign Secretary, refers to "the courageous stand which this old, frail but determined man has made in the last years against the attack of the new paganism. It has won him real respect abroad in all circles where any freedom of thought remains" (20th February, 1939).

During a Pontificate of seventeen years his principal aim was, in the face of modern technical advance which appeared to be absorbing all man's energies, to encourage a return to spiritual values and Christian living. For this purpose he created what he believed was his greatest achievement, the apolitical Catholic Action, a lay association for the diffusion of Catholic principles among all classes of society. It was, he believed, the only system capable of combating what he called "the dizzying swirl of modern life".

Three great political systems flourished during his reign, Fascism, Liberal Capitalism and Communism. The one for which he had the most sympathy (or it would be fairer to say, the least antipathy) was Fascism. If the Fascist States had left the Church sufficient control over education to ensure that Youth could be brought up on Christian principles, co-operation might have been possible. Although the two creeds were in certain respects fundamentally opposed, particularly as regards the apotheosis of the State, co-operation of a kind did exist in Italy for nearly a decade. An authoritarian form of government cannot be wholly repugnant to a Pontiff who is himself an autocrat. "The Church," wrote the Catholic paper, *L'Avvenire d'Italia*, "is not a more or less parliamentary democracy whose policies are determined by a majority. It is a divine institution in which the Pontiff directs the flock of the Faithful."[1] This might almost be taken for a definition of *Führerprinzip*; but there were irreconcilable differences. The Pope's condemnation of Fascism was, in the last resort, that "it makes of man a means, and the State an end"; whereas the Catholic conception is that man forms part of the State only as a member of another, more important body, the family.

As regards the second political system of his time, Capitalism, Pius XI approved of property because it makes a man free. Thus, a peasant with his own cottage and plot of land is freer than a more highly paid salaried worker. What he condemned in the Capitalist system was its rapaciousness and insatiable appetite — "the ruin of souls" he says in one of his encyclicals, "brought about by the unquenchable thirst for temporal possessions". In 1929 the Anglo-Saxons, with their notion that success in business is a sign of divine favour, had brought untold misery on the world. Capitalism shared with Communism its "satanic optimism which presupposes the negation of such things as sin", its faith in science, the cult of political economy, the fetishism of production, "the religion of progress". All these beliefs must inevitably diminish human dignity.

In this parallel with Communism the Pope was perhaps a little hard on the Liberal Democracies. His condemnation of the undignified scramble

[1] It was this authoritarian attitude which was severely criticised at the Vatican II Council after the war (1962); far more latitude was given to local bishops.

for wealth which had led to the disaster of 1929 seems to have blinded him to the humanitarian motives and measures by which certain Western capitalist States had improved social conditions for the poor. He did not appreciate, for instance, the extent to which a country like England had, by factory and insurance legislation, combated the evils of *laissez-faire* individualism and, by recognising the rights of association and strike, enabled the workers to improve their condition. Nor did he recognise that representative parliamentary government is the surest guarantee today against the abuses of dictators whose power, in a technical age, can be almost limitless. He would never admit that in the modern world the immediate and wholesale application of Christian principles to everyday life is not always possible, or that these principles often prove less effective than more mundane and concrete safeguards. In the trials to come, Christian Europe was to be saved less by the words of the Pope than by the energy and courage of the Liberal Democracies, who first opposed and defeated pagan Germany, and then barred the way to godless Russia.

Pius XI has often been criticised for his failure to support the Catholic Centre Party in Germany, and the Catholic Popular Party in Italy. And history may well record that his greatest error was to reverse the policy of his predecessor, Benedict XV, who had preferred to put his trust in these Catholic political parties rather than in the good faith of countries with whom the Church made Concordats. The whole foreign policy of Pius XI was based on the many Concordats he made, eighteen in all, a record for any Papal reign. By suppressing the Catholic parties, Pius XI was left only with the Concordats; and in the words of the Italian statesman, Count Sforza, "Concordats are worth precisely what so many other treaties and international agreements in the present 'dynamic' Europe are worth."[2]

Pius XI will be remembered particularly for his attitude towards the education of the higher clergy. He stipulated that all candidates for high preferment must come to Rome. Without a course of studies in Rome lasting at least a year there could be no advance. To this end he summoned all the best professors from Germany, France, Belgium, etc., and they taught a variety of subjects, from archaeology and orientology to missionology and ecclesiastical music.

Pius XI's last year was embittered by the adoption in Italy of the German racial and anti-Semitic laws, the Italian legislation forbidding marriages between Jews and Aryans. This was a great grief to the old and

[2] His letter to the *Manchester Guardian*, 16th January, 1938.

ailing Pope, who frequently and openly condemned the "gross and grave error of racialism" as anti-Catholic; for the word Catholic means Universal, and in the eyes of the Church there is no distinction between the races of the great human family. He addressed autograph letters on the subject to the King and Mussolini before the law was passed; and when the offending Article was not deleted, he lodged a formal protest with the Italian State. This brought him recognition and praise all over the world. Even the English *Church Times*, a journal disinclined to see virtue in Rome, described his statements against anti-Semitism as of "the greatest historical and moral importance" (5th August, 1938).

As for Germany, he had delivered in 1937 his great philippic against National Socialism persecuting the Church, *Mit brennender Sorge*. If this encyclical obtained the desired effect among the Faithful, it produced quite another in Nazi circles. Far from decreasing, in the next three years the persecution of religion increased, with results which were even more disastrous for Catholics who suffered both in their persons and their property; and for the Church, whose pastoral and apostolic activity was subjected to even more rigorous restrictions. In the Bishoprics of Cologne, Trier and Aachen, the most confidential dossiers concerning pastoral activities were seized. And in September 1937 — only four months after *Mit brennender Sorge* — at the Nuremberg Party Conference (attended for the first time by the Ambassadors of France and England) the "National Prize" was awarded to Rosenberg whose *Myth of the Twentieth Century* thereby became the official catechism of the new Teutonic religion.

Disinclined to delegate authority and no respecter of persons, reserved in manner and of great personal dignity, Pius XI discharged the many duties of his great office with unflagging energy. He was engrossed down to the smallest detail in his work, which he often transacted without consulting the Curia. His experience of diplomacy, acquired after a year and a half in Poland in 1920, was limited. He never acquired — in the memorable words of Professor Binchy — "that prudent scepticism about the value of statesmen's assurances which comes from long experience of their ways. On the contrary, he was always willing to credit them with his own limpid honesty and when, as frequently happened, he was deceived, his reaction was correspondingly violent."

His autocratic temperament tended to discourage independence of thought and initiative in his subordinates. "There is no doubt," wrote Sir Charles Wingfield, "that His Holiness discourages advice or suggestions from others — to the extent that his own Secretary of State is said to be often unwilling to make representations which would be likely to annoy him."[3] His greatest weakness lay in this tendency to select worthy mediocrities, whose loyalty and industry were undoubted, but whose ability was questionable. Prelates at the Vatican were probably never so respectable as under Pius XI — and probably never so dull. Coming from the peasantry himself, he had a suspicion of anyone who was, to use his own word, "over-elegant", his euphemism for "urbane", or what the French call *homme du monde*. Mr. Hugh Montgomery describes how on one occasion in 1935 there was some question of Cardinal Pacelli resigning as Secretary of State. The man to replace him, says Mr. Montgomery, was clearly the highly civilised Mgr. Tedeschini. "But there is little chance of this," writes Mr. Montgomery, "for the group around Mgr. Pizzardo, the Under-Secretary of State, will effectively prevent it. For them Tedeschini is 'too much of a gentleman'", and "they come from the '*piccola, piccola borghesia*'". He adds that Pizzardo unfortunately has great influence with the Pope, "more than has Pacelli". So small-minded was this "Pizzardo group" that they were shocked when, after Tedeschini had a slight motor accident, it transpired that two ladies had been in the car with him! — although both were "elderly and respectable".[4]

Pius XI's wide interests and inexhaustible energy found many secondary outlets. He never forgot his youthful pursuit, Alpinism, and often contributed anonymous articles to journals on the subject. He took great interest in the Vatican radio station and the technique of the wireless allocution, and kept himself well informed about other scientific developments, aviation, radiography, etc. A librarian by profession, he also made many valuable additions to the department he first worked in at the Vatican. But his construction of the new galleries and buildings in the Vatican City, and the restoration in the grounds of his summer residence at Castelgandolfo, suggest that his taste was not equal to his intellectual energy. He insisted on employing an architect from his native Milan whose decoration was pretentious, more suited to the industrial city of his birth than to the standards and traditions of Rome. This aesthetic insensibility was a continual cause of complaint by the Romans against the Milanese Pope.

In the winter of 1937, a combination of cardiac weakness, arteriosclerosis and asthma brought him near to death. Until then, he had never

---

[3] F.O. 371/19538, Sir C. Wingfield to Sir J. Simon, 3rd January, 1935.

[4] F.O. 371/20410, report from Mr. H. Montgomery, 28th November, 1935.

even been examined by a doctor. He suffered greatly and declared that the suffering was a new and necessary experience. Until the day of his death, the lucidity of his mind, the richness of his memory and the vigour of his spirit remained unimpaired. After the first attack, he made an extraordinary recovery, which he publicly attributed to the intervention of Saint Teresa of Lisieux, whom he had himself canonised. After spending six months at Castelgandolfo in 1938, he returned to Rome in comparatively good health. But the treacherous Roman winter accelerated his decline. As always, he defied the doctors and declined to submit to an invalid life, saying he would work for the Church until he died, and that he asked nothing better than to die at his desk. In November 1938, he had a further heart attack, but made another remarkable recovery. In the first week of February 1939, he caught cold by sitting up working all night on a speech he was to deliver to the Italian episcopate on the tenth anniversary of the Concordat.

This speech was to be followed the next day by a solemn Mass in St. Peter's, in joint celebration of the anniversaries of the Concordat and of his Coronation. Speculation as to whether, in view of the uneasy relations existing with the Italian State, the latter would take part were set at rest by the announcement that the Royal Family would be represented by the Prince of Piedmont, and the Italian government by Count Ciano. The Pope considered this speech of the greatest importance, for he intended it to include a detailed criticism of Fascist faithlessness. To his doctor he said, "Try at all costs, Milani, to keep me alive till Saturday." In view of his considerable powers of recuperation it was hoped until a few hours before his death that he would not be disappointed. But he had drained his diminished sources of strength, and this time death would not be cheated.[5]

Since this was written, allegations have appeared in the French and Italian press (1972) that Pius XI in his last illness was assassinated, at the orders of Mussolini who had learned of the contents of the Pope's coming speech. They are based on "revelations" said to be contained in

[5] The announcement of his death was drawn up in Latin in the usual document by three Cardinals and transmitted to foreign Heads of State all over the world. Hitler, who had no Latin, is reported on receiving the document to have said, "I will know exactly what to do with *that*!" while the Nazi paper *Der Angriff* in its obituary notice called Pius XI "a political adventurer". A curious feature of the Nazis' psychology, incidentally, was their habit of describing their adversaries as what they were themselves. When Roosevelt died in 1945 Hitler called him "the greatest war criminal of all time".

the memoirs of the late Cardinal Tisserant, which reveal that a certain Dr. Petacci (the father of Mussolini's mistress) somehow reached the Pope's sick bed, where he administered the fatal injection. Arguments for and against this thesis continue to be bandied about, and will doubtless be repeated when Cardinal Tisserant's memoirs are published. All we can say here is that neither the German Ambassador to the Vatican, von Bergen, nor his British colleague, Mr. D'Arcy Osborne, make any reference in their despatches at the time to any rumours of "assassination"; and they had a very good reason for following the Pope's last illness with the closest attention. As will be seen in the next chapter, this reason was less concern for the aged and dying man than the question of his succession. With a European war now almost certain (February 1939), both sides, the Western democracies and the totalitarian States, were much concerned with who would sit on the throne of St. Peter ruling over the souls of some 300 million people throughout the world. If Mr. Osborne had even suspected that the Fascist States were already engaged in assassination, he would surely have reported it.

16

The New Pope, Pius XII: and the Outbreak of War, 1939

PIUS XI HAD HOPED THAT HIS SUCCESSOR WOULD BE THE Cardinal Secretary of State, Eugenio Pacelli. On the 22nd February, 1939, a week before he died, he told Mgr. Tardini that it was to prepare Pacelli for the Papacy that he had sent him abroad so often, as far afield as the Americas. In his book *Memoirs of Pius XII*, Tardini writes, "Pius XI looked me straight in the face with his keen eyes and said, 'He will make a fine Pope!' He did not say 'he would make' or 'he could make', but 'he *will* make' a fine Pope." Officially, the Pope has no voice in the selection of his successor, but at this time of international tension his wishes would undoubtedly have influenced the Curia.

If ever a man was destined through heredity and upbringing for high office in the Church, it was Eugenio Pacelli. His grandfather, Marcantonio, had held a clerkship in the Interior Ministry for the Papal States, and had taken part in launching the *Osservatore Romano*. His father, Filippo, was a Consistorial lawyer who prepared cases for beatification. His brother, Francesco, was the Vatican lawyer who negotiated the Concordat of 1929 with Mussolini. Both his sisters married Vatican officials. But this family which had served the Popes for nearly a hundred years was not, as is often supposed, of ancient Roman lineage. They came from Aquapendente in Lazio from where the grandfather, seeking preferment in the 1840s, had emigrated to the capital. Whether their name derives from *pax coeli* (as popular etymology has it) or not, its most distinguished member embodied that expression.[1] His family relate that when Eugenio was six, he constructed a small altar in his bedroom, which he decorated with flowers, candles and pictures of the saints. On his way to school he would always stop for a few moments at a small wayside shrine for prayer. In the photographs of him as a boy among his school companions, his gaze is already deep, serious, strangely detached. It was this natural piety which, throughout his life, most impressed those who met him. The French writer Henri Bordeaux wrote, "He has the sublime greatness of a mortified, almost translucent body, which seems destined to serve only as a cover for a soul." Mr. Ivon Kirkpatrick, sometime British Chargé d'Affaires at the Vatican, commented, "It does not require a long conversation with Cardinal Pacelli to realise that even in politics he believes in the efficacy of prayer and in the reality of divine intervention . . . and he has surrounded himself with men of a deeply religious character, who survey the world through what appears to be the glass of medieval mysticism."[2] Pacelli's later photographs continually reveal him in this light — the long, pale face with the deep-set eye-sockets, the aquiline nose, the hands joined as if in some liturgical ceremony. One of his biographers, Carlo Falconi, observing that Popes always eat their meals alone, says that Pacelli invariably ended his lunch with three stewed plums.[3] Mr. John Guest, who had a Papal audience at the end of the war, says that what impressed him most about Pius XII was his strange hygienic smell, "the odour of sanctity".[4]

From this it might appear that Eugenio Pacelli lacked charm. But Mr. Osborne, the British Minister, relates during the war, when he frequently had to convey to the Pope his Government's complaints, "It is impossible not to be disarmed by the Pope's simplicity, friendliness and sincerity, and by his devastating combination of saintliness and charm. One talks so easily to him; he listens so readily, responds so frankly, and smiles so enchantingly and easily, that one's carefully prepared attitude of dignified disapproval simply evaporates."[5]

[1] The family arms are a dove on a rock, an olive branch in its beak—the device *opus justiciae pax*. It was a fearful irony that he should be Pope during the greatest of all wars.

[2] F.O. 371/17759, 20th March, 1933.

[3] Carlo Falconi, *I Papi del Ventesimo Secole*.

[4] John Guest, *Broken Images*.

[5] F.O. 371/30174, Mr. Osborne to Mr. Nicols, 13th June, 1941.

Here was a man destined, it seemed, for the priesthood in its most divine and supernatural form; and he often said later in life that he would have preferred to have lived as a pastor of souls, either as a simple parish priest or, had promotion come, as a bishop concerned with the moral and social problems of his diocese. But it was not to be. He had other, more practical, gifts which, when he was ordained, were quickly recognised by his superiors, and he was seconded to the Congregation for Extraordinary Affairs, the Vatican Foreign Office. When Gasparri, the Secretary of State, invited him to enter this department, Pacelli objected that he only wanted to be a parish priest, "the shepherd of souls". "I will teach you then," said Gasparri, "to be the shepherd's dog."

He was soon entrusted with the difficult mission of dealing with France, which was still anti-clerical and estranged from the Vatican. So successful was he here that during the First World War he was sent to the Kaiser to explore the possibilities of a compromise peace. Although he failed, this experience in dealing with Germans was to be of great value in the years immediately after the war when he was made Nuncio, first in Munich from 1919 to 1926, and then in Berlin until 1929. It was in Munich in 1919 that he made his first acquaintance with Communism during the Spartacists' rising, when they invaded his Nunciature and threatened him with revolvers. He stood his ground and ordered them to leave — which they did, overawed, it is said, by his spiritual presence. He later described the episode to the correspondent of *Le Matin*: "I was one of the first non-Germans to witness the Bolshevist regime in Munich. They were headed by Russians, and forced their way into my Nunciature where they threatened me. I learnt then of the fearful way in which they massacred hostages."[6] This experience left a mark, and until the end of his life he told friends that he still dreamt of it.

In spite of Pacelli's early desire for a purely pastoral role, he was to become by the force of circumstances the greatest of the twentieth-century Papal diplomats. Pius XI sent him all over the world as his personal legate. No recent Secretary of State in office had even crossed the Alps and left Italy; but Pacelli, when Secretary of State, crossed the Atlantic to both the Americas. As Papal Legate he spoke to the Eucharistic Conference in Buenos Aires in 1934. He visited Uruguay. He addressed the Parliament in Brazil. In 1936 he travelled all over the U.S.A. by aeroplane; and in Washington he met President Roosevelt, promoting relations with a country which had not been represented at the Vatican since 1870. He represented the Pope at the coronation of

[6] J. Nobécourt, *Le Vicaire et l'Histoire* (Editions de Seuil, 1964), p. 136.

George VI in 1937. He made a long speech in German at the Ecumenical Congress in Budapest in 1938. At the Lourdes celebrations, he established better relations with the Free-thinking French politicians of the Third Republic. It is not surprising therefore that such a man should believe that all international problems can be solved by negotiation; and he was to remain all his life essentially a diplomat. In the words of Peter Nichols in his *The Politics of the Vatican*, "Pius XII had a delicate awareness of all the issues comprising a particular policy. This aptitude made his mind an accurate reflexion of the varied, and sometimes contradictory, considerations which a Pope must take into account even when faced with a situation which appears to require a simple denunciation."

A curious sidelight on his character is thrown by his habit of making speeches — on almost every conceivable subject. Although nervous of crowds, he never tired of addressing them. The *Index of Speeches by Pius XII*[7] contains an astonishing range of subjects — the press, mineral separation, sport, nuclear physics, medicine, footwear through the ages, cinema techniques, psycho-analysis, slaughter-houses, the tourist industry, railway and postal services. Cardinal Tardini once saw a large pile of books on the Pope's desk; he showed curiosity and the Pope said, "They're all about gas." It was true. The next day Pius XII addressed the International Conference of the Gas Industry.[8] In these hundreds of sermons and allocutions he developed his own special brand of baroque oratory which was often far above the heads of his listeners.

Pius XII was one of those unfortunate people who are unable to relax and enjoy leisure or natural surroundings. His *villegiatura* at Castelgandolfo bored him profoundly, and he was always looking forward to his return to Rome. Even here, on his daily walks in the Vatican garden, he was always studying one of his speeches and he rarely lifted his eyes from the documents held close before him, to look at the flowers and trees of his garden, or the view over Rome.

Opinions about his mental capacity vary. The French Ambassador, Vladimir d'Ormesson, contended that his piety was only equalled by his wide culture and sharp intelligence. Cardinal Tardini says much the same, "His discourses and messages — as though they were a monument erected to himself — will remain through the centuries as witness of his lofty wisdom, human and divine, to the undying glory of the incomparable teacher."[9] On the other hand, the Spanish Ambassador said in 1937

[7] Published by Poliglotta Vaticana, 1956.
[8] Domenico Tardini, *Memoirs of Pius XII* (Newman Press, 1961).
[9] Ibid.

to Weizsäcker of the German Foreign Office, "Pacelli presents no real counterweight to Pius XI, because he is completely devoid of will and character. He hasn't even got a particularly good mind."[10] Mr. Hugh Montgomery, sometime British Chargé d'Affaires at the Vatican described him as "a good man, a pious man, not devoid of intelligence, but essentially there to obey".[11] And Tardini, his official apologist, also wrote, "By nature gentle and almost shy, he was not born with the temperament of a fighter. This is what distinguished him from his great predecessor."

Pius XII has often been criticised for being "pro-German", even "pro-Nazi" — because, presumably, having spent twelve years in Germany after 1917 as Nuncio, he had learnt the language and often expressed his affection for the people he had come to know. But this is very different from being "pro-Nazi". He disliked the Nazis intensely, abominated them even, but knew that the Papacy must maintain relations with them on behalf of the thirty million Catholics in the Reich. That he had no illusions about them is clear from his remark to Mr. Osborne concerning the German denunciation of the treaty of Locarno — "He expressed his unhappy conviction that no signature of the present German government is worth the paper it is written on."[12] And at the time of the German remilitarisation of the Rhineland he said to the French Ambassador, "If you had acted with 200,000 troops, you would have done an immense service to the world."[13]

The election of the new Pope in March 1939 was preceded by much diplomatic activity on behalf of the various candidates. War between the totalitarian and democratic countries now seemed inevitable; and both hoped for a Pope whose influence over the 300 million Catholics in the world would operate in their favour. "It is a matter of supreme importance," commented Sir Robert Vansittart of the Foreign Office, "that the right man — and not one of Totalitarian straw — is elected."[14]

At the outset, the Italian government was opposed to Pacelli's candidature. An article in the February number of the Fascist *Relazioni*

[10] *A.A. Beziehungen des Vatikans zu Spanien, 1937.*

[11] F.O. 371/17759.

[12] F.O. 371/21164, Mr. Osborne's conversation with Cardinal Pacelli.

[13] F. Charles-Roux, *Huit ans au Vatican.*

[14] F.O. 371/23789, minute, March 1939.

Internazionali stated that there was "general anxiety among the Cardinals that the new Pontificate should preserve that secular prudence and peculiar sensibility which, without deviating from any principles, indeed solemnly affirming them, will permit the particular exigencies and political reactions of time and place to be taken into account". This cryptic and vaguely admonitory statement implied that the new Pontiff would be well advised not to continue Pius XI's practice of criticising and obstructing the racial and religious policies of Italy and Germany — policies with which Pacelli had been closely associated. The new Pope, the paper declared, must be "a *homo novus* before (*nei confronti di*) all Powers", a man who "in his previous activities has not experienced situations or occasions for endorsing or opposing any political factor". In the last paragraph, the author of the article hoped that under the new Pope the College of Cardinals would once again "make its influence and counsels felt in the government of the Church" — a reference presumably to the alleged arbitrary methods of Pius XI. The Fascists' candidate was Cardinal della Costa of Florence who was much noted for his piety and unworldliness (described by Mr. Osborne as "a man of rigid and forbidding austerity which precludes any human contact"); he would be more amenable to their influence.

The Germans took much the same line as their Axis allies. That they did not approve of Pacelli's candidature seemed indicated in the address by the German Ambassador, von Bergen, which, as doyen of the Diplomatic Corps, he gave to the College of Cardinals on the death of Pius XI. It contained, in the words of Mr. Osborne, "a veiled warning against the election of Pacelli".[15] "We are present," said von Bergen, "at the elaboration of a new world, raising itself on the ruins of a past which no longer has any raison d'être." In this "new world" the Papacy had an essential role to play. Shorn of its diplomatic phraseology, what von Bergen said, or had been instructed to say, was that the Cardinals should choose a Pope who would support "the new world" (of the Dictators), not the old world (of the democracies). That von Bergen had his orders seems to be indicated by his failure, or refusal, on this occasion to consult his *chers collègues* of the Diplomatic Corps in the customary manner about the contents of the speech he was to make on behalf of them all. Nor did he deliver it in the customary diplomatic language, French, but in Italian, a language of the Axis. It is unlikely, too, that von Bergen would have made insinuations on his own against

[15] F.O. 371/23789, 17th February, 1939.

Cardinal Pacelli, for whom he had always expressed the greatest regard and admiration.[16]

The Nazi press was openly hostile to Pacelli. *Der Angriff* warned against "a political Pope", contending that "the policy of Cardinal Pacelli will lead a crusade against the totalitarian States". (In extreme Nazi circles, however, it was declared that in the modern world the personality of the Pope mattered not a jot. The influence of the Catholic Church on the youth of Germany, they boasted, was now practically non-existent.)

The British were in favour of Pacelli, but they made no effort, as did the Italians and Germans, to influence the election. Cardinal Hinsley of Westminster lunched at Mr. Osborne's residence in Rome just before the Conclave, and told the British Minister that he had been in two minds about accepting his invitation, "lest I should disturb the spirit of impartiality and receptivity to divine guidance with which I shall enter the Conclave" (i.e. Mr. Osborne might, over a good lunch, have tried to put in a word for Pacelli). Pacelli was undoubtedly well regarded in England. *The Times* wrote of the excellent impression he had made at the coronation of George VI. The *Manchester Guardian* wrote, "Pacelli is a man big enough and strong enough to refuse to be dragged at the tail of any party . . . he will remain above them all." Even the *Daily Worker* had quite a dignified little article about him.

It was the same in America and the other democracies. The *New York Times* wrote, "Pius XII — not the Pope the totalitarians desired. This ally of Western democracy will uphold the claims of human personality and brotherhood against a sea of enemies." While in France *Le Populaire*, the organ of the Socialist Party, announced Pacelli's election with the headline, "Set-back to Mussolini!"

A more balanced German judgment was expressed in a confidential memorandum from the Wilhelmstrasse. Graf du Moulin the *Referent* for Vatican affairs wrote:

At first sight he seems pro-German. His excellent knowledge of our language is significant, and he has frequently expressed at our Embassy his desire for friendly relations. He has always advocated good relations between the Church and Italian Fascism; and during the Abyssinian war, he supported and furthered the patriotic attitude of the Italian clergy . . . But his championship of an orthodox Church policy has

[16] His *chers collègues* were extremely annoyed by this, and they instructed the ruvian Ambassador (the next in seniority) to inform von Bergen of their annoyance.

frequently led him into basic differences with National Socialism. He must also be reproached with co-operating in the power politics of Pius XI, particularly with the late Pope's outspoken and hostile allocutions. He also took over a year to recognise Franco during the Spanish civil war ... In recent times he has been much criticised for insufficient opposition to Pius XI's power politics.[17]

An oddly discordant note among the eulogies in the democracies was struck by the Weimar ex-Chancellor, Dr. Brüning who had known Pacelli well in Berlin in those far-off days. He had now found asylum in the West; and Vansittart of the Foreign Office reported, "This devout German Catholic considers there is much naivety in Pacelli's make-up, particularly in that he believes in temporising with the present regimes in Germany and Italy."

This, in fact, was the general criticism that was shortly to be levelled against the new Pope. Within three days of his coronation he had called a conference of the German Cardinals, who were all in Rome for the Conclave, with a view to a new approach to the German problem, hoping even at this eleventh hour for a modus vivendi. Immediately after his election he had announced that he intended to reserve the handling of the German question for himself.[18] The minutes of this conference, which are published in the Vatican White Book, *Actes et Documents du Saint Siège relatif à la seconde guerre mondiale* (Vol. 2. *Lettres aux Eveques Allemands*) reveal clearly what was in his mind.[19] To the assembled Germans — Cardinals Bertram of Breslau, Schulte of Cologne, Faulhaber of Munich and Innitzer of Vienna — he recalled that on a previous occasion when a new Pope had ascended the throne of St. Peter, a new start had been made in relations with Germany. He was referring to Leo XIII who, succeeding Pius IX in 1878, had addressed a conciliatory message to Bismarck, with the result that the notorious *Kulturkampf* against the Church was gradually abated. There was, he emphasised, no question of any essential change in the attitude of the Church; it was a case of "attempting another form of tactics in the hope of arriving at a practical result". He proposed for a start to write a personal letter to Hitler announcing his accession. The minute

[17] *A.A. Büro des Staatssekretärs*, April, 1939.

[18] To counterbalance, as it were, this special interest in German affairs, h appointed as his Secretary of State Cardinal Maglione who was an expert in Frenc affairs, having long been Nuncio in Paris.

[19] See also A. Martini, "Pio XII e Hitler", *Civiltà Cattolica*, I, 1965.

of the conference, which were fortunately taken down by a stenographer, throw an interesting light on Pacelli's character and methods:

Holy Father: In 1878 Leo XIII at the beginning of his Pontificate sent a message of peace to Germany. In my modest person, I should like to do something of the same sort (here he read the draft of the letter in Latin to Hitler). Is that all right? Does it need altering? Or amplifying? I should be most grateful for Your Eminences' advice.

Cardinal Bertram: I don't see there's anything to add.

Cardinal Faulhaber: No definite wish can be expressed in a letter of this kind. Only a blessing. But there's one point. Must it be in Latin? The Führer's very touchy about non-German languages. He won't want to call in the theologians to explain it.

Cardinal Schulte: As far as its contents are concerned — excellent.

Holy Father: It can be sent in German. If it's treated as a purely protocolar affair, the implication about the bad state of affairs for the Church may be missed. And we are concerned above all with what is best for the Church in Germany. For me that is the most important question. Perhaps it could be done in both Latin and German.

Cardinal Faulhaber: Better to send it in German.

(It was finally decided to send it in German as well.) Then the following problem arose:

Holy Father: Do we address him as "Illustrious" or "Most Illustrious"? (*Hochzuehrender* or *Hochzuverehrender*)

Cardinal Schulte: *Most* Illustrious! That's really going too far. He hasn't earned that.

Cardinal Innitzer: Should you use the plural in addressing him?

Other Cardinals: That is normal usage.

Cardinal Innitzer: I mean in the salutation. Do you address him as *Sie*, or *Du*?

Cardinal Bertram: A Third Reich regulation dispenses with titles. I should say *Sie*.

Holy Father: In Italian you now say *Tu* or *Voi*. Personally, I say *Lei*. But I suppose it's different in Germany, now.

Cardinal Bertram: I should say *Sie*. Otherwise it's good.

Holy Father: All in order then?

Cardinal Bertram: You haven't referred to him as *Dilecte Fili* (Beloved

Son). Quite right! He wouldn't appreciate that. (Joking) He'd like the Holy Father to cry "Heil! Heil!"

Cardinal Innitzer: In the school the priests have to say "Heil Hitler!" — and "Jesus Christ — thy Kingdom come!"

Cardinal Bertram: I told the children — "Heil Hitler!" — that's for the worldly realm. And "Jesus Christ — thy Kingdom come!" — that's the link between Earth and Heaven.

It was agreed that the usual form of greeting *Dilecte Fili* (Beloved Son) would hardly be appropriate in Hitler's case; and the final text read:

To the Illustrious Herr Adolf Hitler, Führer and Chancellor of the German Reich! Here at the beginning of Our Pontificate We wish to assure you that We remain devoted to the spiritual welfare of the German people entrusted to your leadership (*Obsorge*). For them We implore God the Almighty to grant them that true felicity which springs from religion. We recall with great pleasure the many years We spent in Germany as Apostolic Nuncio, when We did all in Our power to establish harmonious relations between Church and State. Now that the responsibilities of Our pastoral function have increased Our opportunities, how much more ardently do We pray to reach that goal. May the prosperity of the German people and their progress in every domain come, with God's help, to fruition!

Given this day, 6th March, 1939 in Rome at St. Peter's in the first year of Our Pontificate.

After agreeing on the final form of this letter, the Pope said to the German Cardinals, "So we have taken the risk of trying again. Now we will see. If they want a fight, we are not afraid. But the world shall see that we have tried everything to live in peace with Germany." This was followed by some question among the Cardinals about breaking off relations if Hitler failed to respond. Should the Nuncio in Berlin be recalled?

Holy Father: Yes, Pius XI was so indignant about what was happening in Germany that he once said to me, "How can the Holy See continue to keep a Nuncio there? It conflicts with our honour!" The Holy Father feared that the world would not understand how we could continue diplomatic relations with a regime which treated the

Church in such a manner. So I replied to him, "Your Holiness, what good would that do us? If we withdrew the Nuncio how can we maintain contact with the German bishops." The Holy Father understood and became quieter. No, it is best as it is. If the German government cares to break off relations, well and good. But we would not be very clever if we broke them off.

Cardinal Bertram: Yes, it must not appear that the Holy See breaks them off.

Holy Father: Certain Cardinals have approached me and asked why I still grant audiences to the German Ambassador after all this. How, they say, has he the face to ask for an audience? My reply is, "What else can I do? I must treat him in a friendly manner. There is no other course. To break off negotiations is easy. But to build them up again — God alone knows what concessions we would have to make! You can be sure the regime would not take them up again without concessions on our part."[20]

The conference then closed with a word about the *beneficial* effect of the persecution in Germany.

Cardinal Schulte: The general interest in Church affairs is far more lively than before.

Holy Father: Such is the effect of persecution.

Cardinal Schulte: The churches are full to overflowing.

Cardinal Innitzer: The same in Austria.

Holy Father: Well then, we must not lose courage.

Cardinal Bertram: It is a great task, to give the priests courage. *Christus Vincit!* I often say to the priests, "The times in which we live

[20] The official reasons for not withdrawing the Nuncio from Berlin were later given by Pius XII before the Cardinals of the Congregation of Extraordinary Affairs on the 20th June, 1939. (a) To break off negotiations in this way would be a considerable service to the Nazi government which would thus be freed from the remaining constraints exercised by the Concordat. (b) The Nuncio may be a diplomat, but he also has an ecclesiastical mission which can be of great advantage to the Church. (c) Experience had shown, as in Mexico, that had a Nuncio been there during the persecution, the Church would have been in a much stronger position. So why withdraw him when he is firmly installed in a country which is in the process of becoming another Mexico? (d) The German bishops do not want the Nuncio withdrawn; if this were done, they would not be able to communicate so freely with the Vatican. (e) It was only with great difficulty in 1920 that the Vatican succeeded in installing a Nuncio in Berlin. If he were withdrawn by the Church, it would be unlikely that a Nunciature could ever be installed again.

are not the worst. The worst are those of indifference (*Glaubensgleichgultigkeit*). Hitler made no reply to their letter.

In the six months which elapsed between his coronation and the outbreak of the Second World War, the new Pope made further strenuous efforts to keep the peace of Europe. On the 21st April, 1939, he sent Father Tacchi-Venturi[21] to Mussolini to tell him that the Pope, now fearing the worst, wanted to call a five Power conference, of Great Britain, France, Germany, Italy and Poland to discuss how war could be avoided. (It was significant that he did not include the other great Power which would be ultimately affected by a German-Polish war — the Soviet Union.) Mussolini was guarded in his reply, but seemed on the whole to welcome the idea. The Pope accordingly sent telegrams to the Powers, adding in the message to Poland that he hoped Colonel Beck in his coming speech about Danzig would show moderation and reserve.

The response to this invitation was not encouraging. Britain and France, while appreciating the Pope's good will, seemed concerned that an international conference at this point would only repeat the fiasco and humiliation of Munich. The German reply was even more negative. When the Nuncio in Berlin requested an urgent meeting with Hitler, he was told he was in Berchtesgaden; however a plane was put at his disposal. Hitler received him politely, thanked the Pope for his solicitude and spent the rest of the time fulminating against Great Britain. All he agreed to do was to discuss the proposal with Mussolini.[22] Poland, too which might have been the most interested in avoiding war, replied in evasive terms, reassured apparently by the British-French guarantee that she could take on the Wehrmacht.

The Pope was not discouraged, and he now instructed the Nuncio in Berlin to approach Ribbentrop and impress on him the danger to Germany of a conflict with the West in which the United States might become involved. Ribbentrop replied in his usual undiplomatic manner that if Poland were unwise enough to cause a war she would be crushed instantly. "In a war against a people like ours," he said, "with eighty-five million inhabitants armed to the teeth, Poland will fight for only a few days. She will be crushed with the speed of lightning, for she will be attacked from ten different sides at once." Of this rodomontade, the

[21] Father Tacchi-Venturi, it will be recalled, was used at the time of the Italian Concordat negotiations as middle-man with Mussolini.

[22] Documents of German foreign policy (D. IV), memorandum by Walter Hewel, 10th May, 1939.

Vatican White Book (Vol. 1) says ingenuously, "When receiving these replies the Pope and his advisers had reason to be worried by the turn of events in Germany and elsewhere."[23]

The chief result of all this was that the Secretary of State, Mgr. Maglione, received the French Ambassador, Charles-Roux, and invited him to persuade Poland to show a more conciliatory attitude towards Germany. At the same time another attempt was made with Mussolini, who was thought to be the only man who could restrain Hitler, as he had at Munich. Tacchi-Venturi again obtained an audience; but unfortunately since his first meeting at the beginning of the month, Mussolini had signed the "Pact of Steel" with Hitler (May 22nd, 1939), and his reception was frigid. Mussolini listened to Tacchi-Venturi without uttering a word. "Does your Excellency then consider that war is inevitable?" asked Tacchi-Venturi. "Certainly," was the reply. "But what if Russia concludes an alliance with France and Britain?" "That does not matter," said Mussolini. "What Russia does makes no difference."[24]

Although this gave the impression that Mussolini was prepared for war, the Vatican received a contrary view from Marshal Caviglia, the Italian Chief of Staff. He told Cardinal Maglione that Italy was not ready, that the only army which was really prepared was the French, and that Mussolini would be mad if he went to war. This more cheering news was confirmed on the 13th June when Borgongini-Duca, the Nuncio at the Quirinal, met Ciano who said that there was no danger for the next six months, because Germany had no intention of attacking Poland. Within six months everything could be settled by diplomacy and peace would be assured. The only danger was, said Ciano, that Poland might do something silly to provoke Hitler; but he added Poland would certainly listen to the Pope, who should now try to persuade Poland to act with restraint.

Fortified with this more encouraging news, the Pope now turned to Poland and instructed his Nuncio in Warsaw, Mgr. Cortesi, to inform the Polish government that from reliable information the Vatican believed Germany had no intention of attacking Poland, and that moderation was essential. On the 30th June, the Nuncio in the Quirinal informed Count Ciano that the Vatican had approached Poland in this sense. He hoped that in return the Italian government would play the same restraining role with Hitler. Ciano's reply was most reassuring. He said that when he had recently been in Berlin, Hitler had told him personally that the situation was now less inflammable, and that Germany needed a long period of

[23] *Actes et Documents du Saint Siège relatifs à la Seconde Guerre Mondiale*, Vol. 1, p. 18.
[24] Ibid.

peace. "In any case," said Ciano, "Germany will not make a move without our consent. And neither Mussolini nor I want war."

In spite of this, in the next two months the situation continued to deteriorate as the Danzig Question was brought forward by Hitler, and the city began to fill with German "tourists", while German troops concentrated on the frontier. The French Ambassador now wrote to the Vatican Secretariat of State suggesting that the time had come for the Pope to abandon his habitual reserve. Hitler was repeating the methods used against Czechoslovakia, and M. Charles-Roux wanted an outright condemnation. "Matters have reached the point," he said, "when to preserve the peace the Holy Father, whose efforts to preserve it have been so untiring, should now state with the authority which He alone disposes that a country whose huge territorial annexations have only increased its insatiable appetite is entirely responsible for the present dangerous situation."

The Pope did not respond to this suggestion; so on the 24th August, after the signature of the Russo-German pact, Charles-Roux came again to the Vatican to say that his government now believed that within a matter of days Germany would attack Poland. He again implored the Pope to condemn in advance this aggression against a Catholic country, and thereby perhaps prevent it. Again the Pope preferred to avoid condemnation, believing that this might only encourage the aggression. Nevertheless, he decided to make a broadcast that night, to be translated into foreign languages. It was his last appeal for peace and it contained his most famous cliché, "Nothing is lost by peace; everything may be lost by war."[25]

Let the force of reason prevail over the violence of arms, [he said] for the triumph of justice. Conquests not founded on justice cannot be blessed by God. Politics emancipated from morality betray those who so act. May the strong and powerful hearken to us, and use their power not for destruction but for construction, for the protection of peace, order and the welfare of nations. We beseech you by the Blood of Christ, whose strength is Our support, conscious that all men of good will, all who thirst for justice, all those who suffer, are with us.

These fine words had no effect, and once again the Jesuit, Tacchi-

[25] It appears that this cliché was invented by Mgr. Montini (later Paul VI), then a *sostituto* at the Secretariat of State. See Burkhardt Schneider, "Der Friedensappel Pius XII von 24 August 1939", *Archivum Historiae Pontificae*, 6, 1968.

Venturi, was sent to Mussolini, on the 29th August, 1939. Mussolini recommended that, to avoid war, Poland should not oppose the return of Danzig to the Reich, and resume talks with Germany on the question of the corridor. He suggested that the Pope should put this proposal to the Polish government.

The effect this last-minute proposal had on the Polish government is described by Colonel Beck in his memoirs: "The initiative of the Holy See was unfortunate. In the last days of August 1939 the Pope approached us suggesting that the cession of Danzig would save the peace. I replied that the publication of this proposal would offend the most sensitive feelings of the Catholic majority of citizens in our country."[26] This is confirmed much later by von Bergen. He says that up to the last minute the Pope recommended the Poles to accept the German demands, particularly in regard to Danzig.[27]

So ended ended Pius XII's attempts at keeping the peace. The British Minister, Mr. Osborne, reported, "We are in a position to state that His Holiness, up to the last moment, has unceasingly tried to prevent hostilities, not only through the initiatives already known to the public, but also through more confidential steps."

[26] Joseph Beck, *Dernier Rapport, Politique Polonaise*, 1926–1939 (Edition de la Baconniére, 1951).

[27] *A.A. Büro des Staatssekretärs*, Vol. 3, von Bergen, 21st February, 1942.

17

The German Spring Tide

THE 1939 WAR, LIKE THAT OF 1914, WAS WAGED FUNDAMENTALLY between the Western democracies on the one side, and the Central Powers on the other. Even the *mise-en-scène* was the same. In September 1939, as in August 1914, the British Expeditionary Force found itself in Flanders digging trenches near Vimy Ridge. Ahead lay the second instalment of another Punic war. For the Vatican, however, there could be no such comparison. In the 1914 war, its sympathies had lain with His Apostolic Majesty in Vienna — not from any particular belief in the justice of the Habsburg cause, but because the Vatican considered that the victory of a Catholic Austria, and partly Catholic Germany, would be better for the Church than that of anti-clerical France, Protestant England and Orthodox Russia. In 1915 Prince Ghika, the Foreign Minister of Rumania (which was then neutral) told a friend that the Pope, Benedict XV, had spoken to him most critically of the Western Allies, blaming them for the continuance of the war. The Pope sympathised, he said, with the Central Powers as representatives of order, discipline and the religious spirit.[1] Cardinal Gasparri, Prince Ghika said, was planning with President Wilson to

---
[1] F.O. 371/7671, Count de Salis's report on the Vatican, 1915–1922.

stop the war by prohibiting the despatch of arms to the Western allies; and Gasparri had said that the German submarine blockade was justifiable in international law.[2] It was clear in 1914 where the sympathies of the Vatican lay.

By 1939, in the twenty-five years that had elapsed, the Vatican's relations with the warring nations had changed completely. France had made her peace with Rome and restored diplomatic relations. Relations with England had never been better (largely due to British tolerance towards the Catholic minorities scattered throughout the Empire). The steady growth of the Catholic population in the United States, and the increasing financial support given by that country to the Church, also promoted a favourable disposition towards the West. On the other hand, the Central Powers now consisted exclusively of pagan Nazi Germany, which had invaded and oppressed Catholic Austria and now, aided by atheist Russia, was about to dismember Catholic Poland. On the 1st September, 1939 there could again be no question where the Papal sympathies lay.

And yet in their conduct during the two world wars the two Popes behaved in precisely the same way, to maintain their neutrality. In his various war-time messages between 1914 and 1918, Benedict XV refused to call the belligerent States by name; he always spoke of facts, never of countries or individual statesmen. If reprehensible acts were committed, however, he was the first to condemn them. Thus, concerning the German occupation of Belgium, he said in a public audience on the 4th December, 1916, "We see minority nations, even those invested with high dignity, shamefully outraged and a number of peaceful citizens taken from their homes and deported to distant regions." The condemnation was clear, but not specific. For had Germany been specified — it was pointed out at the Vatican — reference would also have had to be made to the Russian armies, whose conduct of the war in East Prussia and Galicia appeared closely to resemble that of the German in Belgium. Moreover, before being the object of a specific Papal condemnation, the truth about both cases would have to be ascertained in detail by an impartial enquiry which, in the awful circumstances of war, the Vatican with its limited resources could not possibly carry out.

Instead of condemning, therefore, Benedict XV expended his

2 Ibid.

efforts on an intense humanitarian and charitable activity in every country affected by the war; and he used all his efforts to prevent it spreading, against the entry of Italy in 1915, and of the U.S.A. in 1917. In all these respects Pius XII followed his predecessor most faithfully in the Second World War. His attitude in 1939 was well summed up in a telegram from Woermann of the Wilhelmstrasse to von Bergen, "I have learnt from a trustworthy source that France and England have requested the Pope to condemn Germany as an aggressor against Poland. The Pope has refused to do so on the ground, it is said, that the Vatican always avoids direct intervention in international conflicts. It seems more likely, however, that the Pope does not wish to damage the situation of the Catholics in Germany, or his peace efforts and relations with Italy."[3]

In fact the Pope did pronounce on the invasion of Poland, but in the approved periphrastic manner of the Vatican. In the encyclical *Summi Pontificatus* on the 27th October, 1939 he said, "The blood of countless human beings, including many civilians, cries out in agony, a race as beloved by Us as the Polish, whose steadfast Faith in the service of Christian civilisation is written in ineffaceable letters in the Book of History, giving them the right to invoke the brotherly sympathy of the entire world." He went on to denounce the deification of the State at the expense of the individual and the family; the unilateral denunciation of treaties; and the recourse to arms. Although this language seemed inadequate to the statesmen of the West, it was not lost on the Germans. Heydrich, Head of the German security department, immediately forbade the publication of the encyclical in Germany, commenting that its effect on world opinion would be most damaging to Germany.[4]

Nevertheless, the Poles were far from satisfied with an address he gave to some Polish pilgrims at about this time, in which he again made no reference to Germany. Accordingly, on the 25th December, 1939, Cardinal Hlond, the Primate of Poland, who had escaped to the West, submitted to the Vatican a detailed report on the brutal oppression in German-occupied Poland. According to Mgr. Montini, the *sostituto* at the Secretariat of State, the Pope, having read this, gave the following directive: "*Ex audienta sanctissimi*. This information to be handed to the Vatican Radio for

[3] A.A. *Büro des Staatssekretärs*, 6th September, 1939.
[4] Bundesarchiv, Koblenz, Reichskanzlei file R4311/15046, letter from Heydrich to Lammers, 10th November, 1939.

German emissions."[5] The Vatican Radio accordingly broadcast the report, and the emission was picked up on the 21st January, 1940 by several foreign stations and reported widely in the press of England, France, Switzerland, the U.S.A. and Italy. The speaker drew a fearful picture of conditions in Poland where the Poles were "living in a state of terror and brutalisation which can only be compared with that imposed on Spain in 1936 by the Communists". The *Manchester Guardian* in its editorial of 24th January, 1940 wrote, "Tortured Poland has found a powerful advocate in Rome... The Vatican Radio emission is a warning to all who care for civilisation that Europe is in mortal danger."

The Germans were not slow to react, and von Bergen was instructed to make the strongest possible protest. He was received by Mgr. Montini who made the usual excuse that the Vatican Radio was not under the Secretary of State but was run by the Jesuits.[6] Well trained by his master in the arts of diplomacy, Mgr. Montini assured the German Ambassador that nothing could be further from the truth than that the Vatican was anti-German. He repeated the old refrain that Pius XII, having lived for so long in Germany, was much attached to that great country and appreciated the sterling qualities of its people. But for that very reason, His Holiness regretted all the more that the information he was receiving from Poland was so unsatisfactory. He had been waiting a long time for a sign of good-will from the German government. As for Poland, in the months before the war, the Pope had always recommended moderation and willingness to negotiate with Germany. He had even told the Nuncio in Warsaw, Mgr. Cortesi, to say to the Poles in connection with the German claims on Danzig, "It is better to undergo pain today than to lose your life tomorrow" — a sure sign that the Pope had regarded the German claims with a reasonable eye. Certainly the Pope did not want Germany to be defeated, because this would open the way to atheistic Communism in Europe.[7]

Von Bergen then turned to the *Osservatore Romano* and its "Francophile editor", Count della Torre, who was he said writing articles about the Germans in Poland "as if he were writing for a

[5] *Actes et Documents du Saint Siège*, Vol. 3, No. 102, 19th January, 1940.
[6] *A.A. Pol III Büro des Staatssekretärs*, Vol. 1, 29th January, 1940.
[7] *A.A. Pol III Beziehungen des heiligen Stuhls zu Polen*, Vol. 1, 23rd December, 1939.

Polish paper". "In spite of all directions from above about maintaining a neutral line," said von Bergen, "his Francophile attitude is always breaking through." The Germans had tried to furnish della Torre with material and photographs about Polish atrocities committed against the German minority in Danzig; but della Torre had refused to print them, on the ground that if he did so he would have to open his columns to Allied propaganda.

Montini then went over to the attack himself. He said the Pope had been deeply offended by the German government's refusal to allow the Church to undertake charitable and relief work among the Catholics in occupied Poland.[8] Reporting this back to Berlin, von Bergen adds, "If we continue to exclude the Vatican charitable organisations from Poland now the military campaign is over, we shall lose all influence in Rome to our enemies." He recommended that the Nazi government should handle Pius XII more tactfully, and realise how fortunate they were in having him as Pope, and not his predecessor. Pius XI, he said, would have behaved quite differently over the Polish war. In the Wilhelmstrasse, Weizsäcker agreed with him: "It would be so simple and cheap to appease the Catholic Church by giving it a little," he wrote on the 19th January, 1940.

But in spite of their efforts, von Bergen and Weizsäcker could make little impression on the Nazi leaders who, intoxicated with their lightning success in Poland, were now treating the Polish Church worse than they treated their own. The Vatican short-wave transmitter reported how priests were imprisoned without trial in Poland, Church property seized; how the Church of Mary Magdalene in Cracow, one of the most beautiful in Poland, had been turned into a concert hall; a police school had been installed in the bishop's seminary, etc. It also announced to the world that certain Polish youths and maidens were being forcibly sterilised to stamp out the race.

Again and again in the German files we come upon such memoranda as, "The Nuncio asked me today whether we had further reasons to complain about the Vatican Radio. As far as the recent past is concerned, I answered in the negative" (Weizsäcker on the 26th June, 1941); or "The Nuncio asked me today whether the

[8] Ibid. Martin Bormann wrote on the 26th December, 1939 that it was refused on the grounds that the 1933 Concordat with the Reich did not refer to Poland; and as Poland no longer existed, the Polish Concordat of 1934 no longer existed.

Vatican Radio had left any more unpleasant impressions." It was an odd situation — the Jesuits, so long the bogey-men of Catholicism in English eyes, now seemed to be England's staunchest supporters.

If the Pope hoped that Germany would not be destroyed by the Western Powers while Soviet Russia was still in existence, he had no sympathy for the Nazi regime. This is revealed by his connection with the "Generals' plot" of early 1940. In January 1940 Dr. Josef Müller, a German Catholic who had known the Pope well in his Munich days, was deputed by a clique of German generals to approach him and try to establish communication through the Vatican with the British government. They were planning a *coup d'état* to remove Hitler, and wanted to warn the Western Allies to make no military move in the west before it took place.

The first intimation of this in the British documents is a personal letter from Mr. Osborne to Lord Halifax, the Foreign Secretary, on 12th January, 1940. That morning, the Pope had told him he had information that if the German General Staff could be assured of a peace with the West which would be neither "another Compiègne nor Wilsonian in nature", they would overthrow the Nazi regime and replace it by a "government capable of negotiating" (*eine verhandlungsfähige Regierung*). The Pope added that his "conscience would not have been easy" if he had not informed the British representative of this; but Mr. Osborne must understand he had no hand in it himself and was merely acting as an intermediary, passing on a message. He had told no one else about it, and he asked Mr. Osborne to regard it as absolutely confidential. Osborne finished his letter to Lord Halifax with the words, "Whether this German communication is in good faith or not, I think it is clear that the Pope's humanitarian feelings are being played upon."

Mr. Osborne was again summoned to a Papal audience on the 7th February, 1940, this time in a most surreptitious manner. He was told to arrive unannounced, at any time he liked, and to wear informal dress ("all very E. Phillips Oppenheim" he wrote to Lord Halifax). The Pope had a sheaf of German notes in his hand, from which he read that the German General Staff intended to arrest Hitler and try him. They proposed to start their action not in Berlin, which was full of S.S. detachments, but in the country. They would rule to begin with through a military dictatorship; but this would be temporary, soon replaced by a government which the

Pope described as "Conservative and Democratic", which would restore the old 1939 frontiers. The German generals were anxious to negotiate peace at the earliest possible moment, but under "reasonable, acceptable conditions". "This last, rather important part of the typescript," wrote Mr. Osborne, "seemed somewhat obscure to His Holiness, and it is not clear whether any sort of preliminary negotiations are contemplated before the *coup d'état* takes place."

All this was duly communicated to the British government, which received the proposals coolly. Vansittart commented, "I'm not a great believer in the German generals. There is always too much 'jam tomorrow' about them. Their plan would provide the means for Germany to get away with the Hitler loot without any of the assurances we demand against ulterior aggression." Mr. Osborne was instructed to inform the Pope that England would promise the German generals nothing, nor discuss the matter, until Hitler and his gang had been eliminated.

In the nine months of the "Phoney War", before the German attack in the West, this episode with the German generals was not the only attempt by the Vatican at mediation. On three more occasions, Mr. Osborne was approached with offers. In general, these offers were coolly received by the Allies, for peace at this point would have left Germany in a stronger position than before — a situation which the Pope did not appear to appreciate. Vansittart feared a peace initiative "engineered through the naivety of the Pope and the new American arrival" (he was referring to President Roosevelt's personal envoy, Mr. Myron Taylor, who had just arrived at the Vatican with his peace plans). "The Germans," wrote Vansittart, "have already begun to play the Pope up by hinting at an improvement of the lot of the Catholics in Germany. The Pope is an innocent man, and he might bite at this allusive bait. Moreover, he is by profession a man of peace, and might easily succumb."

Mr. Osborne's position at the Vatican during these peace initiatives was not easy because he, or rather his government, refused to respond to them. On one occasion he was taken to task by the *Osservatore Romano* which contrasted the Pope's efforts for peace with England's unhelpful attitude. In a fulsome article on the 8th February, 1940 the paper wrote, "After the death of Pius XI on a mild March morning which already had all the softness of spring, the new Pontiff, Pius XII, with his slender and almost superhuman figure, appeared on the Loggia balcony to give his blessing to the City and the World. A new breath of hope passed over fearful humanity, and the dove appeared to fly once more over the globe bearing the olive branch."

This sounded like the language of the Pontiff himself; but he now seemed, as his peace attempts foundered one by one, to have given up the task as hopeless. In his Christmas 1939 broadcast he said almost despairingly, "We have done Our utmost to establish that concord which has been disturbed for so long, and which now appears to be finally shattered. The clash of arms has silenced Our voice . . . but if it is not heard on earth, it will surely be heard by the Father of Pity in heaven." He now seemed to be waiting for the conflagration to burn itself out.

It was not easy for the British government to resist the Papal "Peace Offensives", as they came to be called at the Foreign Office. Everyone except England seemed to want peace. The Low Countries neutrals, fearing they might be dragged in, wanted peace at any price. Rumania and Hungary wanted peace because they thought it would save them from the Soviets. Italy wanted "Peace with Justice", whatever that meant. Franco wanted peace as distinct from war. The Pope wanted peace, so that the world could form a united front against Bolshevism. Germany wanted peace, because it would leave her in full possession of what she had engulfed. The only government which did not want peace was that of probably the most pacific and war-abominating nation in the world.

Add to this that in April 1940, President Roosevelt sent his own personal envoy to the Pope to encourage him in these peacemaking efforts, and to discourage Mussolini from entering the war. This envoy, Mr. Myron Taylor, was a business man with little experience of international affairs; and he asked the Pope to threaten Mussolini with excommunication if he went to war on behalf of Hitler. The Western Allies regarded this as sheer lunacy, as excommunication would almost certainly make many patriotic Italians more nationalistic. The Pope however welcomed this American initiative. He was particularly pleased that in a letter Mr. Taylor brought him, President Roosevelt addressed him as "my old friend and good friend". "His Holiness," wrote Mr. Osborne, "has on two occasions blissfully informed me that the President signs letters to him 'your good old friend'. There is no doubt that the Pope is a victim of the President's notorious charm and political adroitness."

Mr. Taylor was accordingly granted a privileged position at the Vatican, a fact which he was quick to appreciate, and he adopted a vice-regal conception of his diplomatic role. He alone had a regular weekly audience with the Pope — whereas to all the other diplomats this was accorded much less frequently. When he visited his villa in Florence, he secured a private plane to convey himself, his wife and servants there and back.

Mr. Taylor also suggested to the Pope that Mussolini might be bought off from going to war by two other measures — a large bribe, and the "internationalisation" of Gibraltar. This last suggestion, in the middle of a war, was described by Vansittart at the Foreign Office, when it reached him, as "quite fantastic and quite out of the question". The only result of this American visit to the Pope in 1940 was to sour Anglo-American relations.

When in May 1940 Hitler invaded the Low Countries, their rulers sent telegrams to the Pope asking for his support. "I beg leave to implore Your Holiness," wrote the King of the Belgians, "to lend your high moral authority to the cause which with unbreakable will we shall uphold." To this the Pope immediately replied, "While for the second time, against Right and its will, the Belgian people see their territory exposed to the cruelties of war, We, full of emotion, send Your Majesty and the whole beloved nation, the assurance of Our paternal love. In praying to Almighty God that this heavy burden will be removed in favour of the re-establishment of the full liberty and independence of Belgium, We give with all Our heart to Your Majesty and Your Majesty's people Our Apostolic Benediction." Similar telegrams were sent to the Queen of Holland and the Grand Duchess of Luxemburg.

As with the Papal reaction to the Polish invasion, the Western Allies considered these pronouncements inadequate. The French Ambassador, M. Charles-Roux, told Mgr. Tardini on the 13th May, 1940 that it was one thing to express sympathy with the victims of aggression, but quite another to condemn the aggressor. He asked for an official condemnation of Germany. Mgr. Tardini replied that "for those wishing to read the Pope's telegrams properly, they contain all the French Ambassador requires".[9]

Once again, the question of how far the Pope should go in

[9] *Actes et Documents du Saint Siège*, Vol. 1, p. 75.

condemning nations whose actions he reprobates, and in naming them, was put to the Secretariat of State. In private, the Pope told Mgr. Montini, "We would like to utter words of fire against such actions; and the only thing restraining Us from speaking is the fear of making the plight of the victims worse."[10] If the Western Allies thought he had not gone far enough in these telegrams, Mussolini considered he had gone too far. His principal ideological lieutenant, Farinacci, wrote in the *Regime Fascista* on the 25th August, 1940, "With these telegrams the Pope incites the Catholic King of the Belgians to cause the blood of his people to flow, in order to help the Jews, the Freemasons and the bankers of the city of London."[11] Less asinine but equally vehement, Mussolini's Ambassador at the Vatican, Signor Alfieri, made the official Fascist complaint. His audience with the Pope on the 13th May, 1940 is described graphically in Mgr. Montini's notes:

The Italian Ambassador said that the messages addressed by the Holy Father to the sovereigns of Belgium, Holland and Luxemburg were a cause of serious displeasure to the Head of the Italian government, who saw in them a move against his policies. The Holy Father explained that this evaluation was completely wrong, the more so as it was impossible to find in these messages an offensive word against Germany — while it would have been his duty to affirm the same principles and to make the same statements if the violation of the neutrality of those countries had been committed by the Allies. The Italian Ambassador let it be understood that a great state of tension and nervousness reigned in Fascist circles, and he did not even exclude the possibility of serious things happening. The Holy Father understood what this meant and showed himself very tranquil and serene. He said he would not be in the least afraid of falling into hostile hands or going to a concentration camp. "We were not intimidated," he said, "by pistols pointed at Us once, and we will be even less frightened next time." [He was referring to the Spartacist incident in Munich in 1919.] "The Pope," said Pius XII, "cannot on certain occasions remain silent." How could he remain the disinterested spectator of such heinous acts while the entire world was waiting for his word? The

10 Ibid., No. 313.
11 Ibid., Vol. 4, p. 34.

Italian government could not insist that the Pope remained silent just because it suited the government. What sort of freedom would the Pope then enjoy? And why, said His Holiness, be offended by his words when everyone knew how justified they were? The Italian government had known that Germany intended to invade these countries. They were aware of it since January. How could they complain when the Pope addressed words of comfort and hope to Sovereigns who had good relations with the Holy See? "Beware," ended His Holiness, "all of us will be subject to God's judgment. None will escape. No temporal success on earth can exempt us from this fearful judgment."[12]

This report by Mgr. Montini is confirmed in the German files, by a conversation Signor Alfieri had that evening with von Mackensen, the German Ambassador to the Quirinal. Alfieri told him that the Pope had said he had given much thought to the telegrams he sent to the Low Countries, and that he had been most careful to avoid any political word such as "invasion" which might give the impression that he was adopting a political attitude.[13] Critics of the Delphic nature of so many Vatican pronouncements may well ask how can the Pope, while telling Alfieri that he cannot remain silent when confronted with "heinous acts", refuse to call an invasion an invasion.

That the Vatican had, in these days when one German victory succeeded another, given up hope in the Western Powers is understandable. There now seemed no prospect in the foreseeable future of a collapse of the Nazi regime. The Church would have to accommodate itself for a long time to come with the existing situation. After the successful German attack in the west, the *Osservatore Romano* which, on account of the Francophile attitude of its editor, Count della Torre, had increased its circulation enormously since September 1939, began to appear in an expurgated form, evidently on instructions from above. Osborne reported as early as the 21st May, 1940, "The *Osservatore Romano* no longer publishes its admirable leading articles, nor does it contain any comment on military or political events, as hitherto. Its columns are now devoted almost entirely to information of a religious nature. It

[12] Ibid., Vol. 1, No. 313.
[13] *A.A. Pol III Büro des Staatssekretärs*, Vol. 2, 13th May, 1940.

is a tragedy not only for Catholics but for the world in general that the German government and the Fascist extremists should have succeeded in suppressing the only source of impartial and reliable information available to Italians."[14] While von Bergen reported smugly, "The Vatican has instructed the *Osservatore Romano* to confine itself to military communiqués, and the editor hasn't set foot outside the Vatican City for days."[15]

This despairing attitude of the Vatican is reflected in the conduct of the Nuncio in Berlin, Mgr. Orsenigo. On the 10th June, 1940, when the German armies were approaching Paris, Orsenigo saw the Under-Secretary at the Wilhelmstrasse, Woermann, who reported that the Nuncio had expressed his satisfaction at the German advances. "He added jocularly," says Woermann, "that he hoped when we march into Paris, we will do so through Versailles. He also seemed actually to look forward to Italy's entry into the war."[16] Later, on the 26th July, 1940, Mgr. Orsenigo saw Weizsäcker of the German Foreign Office, who commented, "The Nuncio finds the English reaction to our peace offer inexplicable. He praised the unambiguous speech of the Führer and said there is no more to be done. For a marriage the consent of two parties is required" (*Zur Eheschliessung gehören zwei*).[17]

The despairing attitude of the Vatican before the German successes was, characteristically, not manifest in the Vatican Radio which was controlled by the Jesuits, and which still criticised the Germans severely. Mr. A. W. G. Randall, who was in charge of Vatican affairs at the Foreign Office, wrote on the 21st July, 1941, "The Vatican wireless has been of the greatest service to our propaganda and we have exploited it to the full. No other neutral power would have persisted so long in furnishing us with such useful material."[18]

As the German armies penetrated deeper into France, the question of Italy's entry into the war became the principal concern of the Vatican. In early 1939 the Pope had addressed a series of requests to Mussolini entreating him to remain neutral if war came. They had all been rebuffed. Now he tried again. The French were pressing

[14] F.O. 371/24935.
[15] *A.A. Büro des Staatssekretärs*, Vol. 2.
[16] Ibid.
[17] Ibid.
[18] F.O. 371/30177, minute by Mr. Randall.

for him to use his influence to keep Italy out at this crucial moment; and on the 25th May, 1940 Cardinal Maglione wrote to Cardinal Suhard, the Primate of France, "The Holy Father has done all in his power with regard to Italy, in the sense you desire. Unfortunately however he cannot be too sanguine about it."

On the 25th May, 1940 the Pope saw the French Ambassador to the Quirinal, M. François-Poncet, who relates in his *Au Palais Farnese, Souvenirs d'une Ambassade*, "Later when it was obvious that Mussolini was preparing to enter the war and deal France a final blow, I had a further audience of the Holy Father. I asked him if there was any chance, any means, of restraining the Duce, whether the Pope could intervene and dissuade him from this shameful act. Pius XII did not conceal from me that he had used up all his credit, that the Duce refused to listen to him and no longer read his letters..." On the same day the Pope discussed the question with Mr. Osborne, contemplating, he said, a new approach to Mussolini, suggesting that France might make concessions if Italy would keep out of the war. Could he say the same for Great Britain? Osborne was "rather reserved", and the British government confirmed his reserve a few days later. England had had enough of concessions to the Dictators. But the question of France, or indeed Great Britain, making concessions to Italy was no longer relevant. On the 10th June, 1940, Mussolini declared war on those two countries.

In the first days after Italy's entry, the attitudes adopted by the Vatican and the Italian episcopate recalled their curiously ambivalent behaviour during the Abyssinian war. The Pope and the Vatican remained silent; while the Italian bishops and most of the clergy became vocal. Two weeks after Italy's declaration of war, von Bergen reported that the Italian press was almost daily printing Pastoral Letters from the bishops expressing their patriotism. Thirty Italian bishops sent a telegram to the Duce exulting that after the inevitable victory of Italian arms, the Italian flag would fly "over the grave of St. Peter".[19] The Rector of the Catholic University in Milan, Gemelli, identified Catholicism with Mussolini's *Credere, Obbedire, Combattere*. "Let us obey the Duce. In God's eyes nothing is nobler in time of war than sacrifice." Other bishops announced

[19] *A.A. Beziehungen des heiligen Stuhls zu Italien*, despatch from von Bergen on the attitude of the Italian bishops, 24th June, 1940.

that "obedience to the State in war-time is ordained by God as a religious duty." The President of the Catholic Youth spoke of "the glorious martial tradition of our Youth which has proved itself in the past, and will do so again".

Although the Vatican remained silent, the Pope was still thinking in terms of peace. On the 28th June, 1940, Cardinal Maglione summoned von Bergen and told him the Pope was sending an appeal to Germany, Italy and England to make peace. But before doing so he wanted to know, confidentially, what would be the reaction of the German government. Three days later Mr. Osborne (who had been forced by the Italian declaration of war to take refuge in the Vatican) reported, "The success of the threatened invasion of Great Britain is, I fear, taken for granted by His Holiness. For this reason, he hopes that England will accept the peace offer made by Hitler in his Reichstag speech."

A telegram to the Apostolic Delegate in London was drawn up by Cardinal Maglione and the Pope corrected it himself. It read:

Persons in authority, supporters of a just peace, have expressed the wish that the Holy See should approach the British government suggesting that it should not discard the offer of peace made by the German Chancellor without examining it carefully, but should rather ask the German government to specify a concrete basis for eventual negotiations . . . The Holy see instructs you if you consider it opportune to take appropriate steps with the British Government, acting confidentially and with due tact, on behalf of the Holy Father, who fervently prays and works for peace.[20]

The reply came on the morning of the 29th July, 1940. The British Government saw in Hitler's speech not an offer of peace, but another dishonest manoeuvre. It was, said the British, full of lies and threats, and offered no guarantees for the occupied nations. Both the Pope and his Secretary of State expressed their regret to Mr. Osborne about this British reply, that Lord Halifax had not invited Hitler to state his peace conditions more clearly. They urged His Majesty's government not to accept so lightheartedly responsibility for the continuation of the war. They considered that England should have gone much further to avoid the onus of responsibility.

With Italy's entry into the war, the high position and prestige

[20] *Actes et Documents du Saint Siège*, Vol. 1, No. 370.

enjoyed by the Papacy throughout the world declined. The voice of the Vatican which, under Pius XI, had fearlessly pronounced the moral verdict of Christian civilisation against Nazism was discreetly lowered, though not stilled, and its words and sentiments were still more discreetly adjusted to the exigencies of an anxious neutrality. Criticism of this was significantly expressed by a senior member of the Curia itself, the French Cardinal Tisserant. "I fear that History may reproach the Holy See for having followed a political line of commodity, for its own exclusive advantage — and very little else. And this is extremely sad — particularly for one who has lived in the reign of Pius XI."[21]

Pope Pius XII, sensitive and impressionable and naturally inclined to caution and compromise, bowed to what he conceived to be both duty and necessity and entered on the path followed by Benedict XV in the First World War. The physical and political position of his State as a neutral enclave in a belligerent country was a delicate one, and the growth of German influence in Rome made his position even more difficult. It is also fair to add that he had another reason for preserving an unimpeachable neutrality — he hoped to play a leading role in the peacemaking. Having been unable to avert war, and being unable for the moment to restore peace, he took consolation in his unceasing attempts to do all in his power to alleviate the sufferings of refugees, prisoners of war and interned civilians; and he opened a bureau to deal with these questions.

The two Dictators were now at the height of their power, and the Germans no longer even bothered to make a show of respecting religion. A despatch by the Nuncio dated Berlin 2nd July, 1940 lists the ever-increasing measures taken against the Church.[22] Although some may appear minor, they reveal as a whole a deliberately gradual undermining of Catholic authority in the Church's own organisations. In the Convent of the Sisters of St. Paul near Salzburg, a civilian administrative commissioner was appointed; the Sisters of the Sacred Heart were expelled from their house in Berlin-Grünewald; the work of the Kolping Association was suspended; at Hildesheim a clerical printing-works which had published a paper on peace was sequestrated as "defeatist"; in Hamburg the Society of St. Raphael for emigrants was suppressed; funds destined for the Catholics in the Warthegau by the Catholic Association of Munich were confiscated and the Abbey of

---

[21] Letter to Cardinal Suhard of Paris, 1st June, 1940.
[22] *Actes et Documents du Saint Siège*, Vol. 5, No. 1, 2nd July, 1941: also Vol. 2, pp. 27–8.

the Benedictines in the Graz diocese forcibly occupied. The Pope's message of 29th June, 1940 was ignored by the German press and radio and "Catholic periodicals have now almost completely disappeared." In August Orsenigo reported a further closing of half a dozen convents and monasteries, and the suppression of the religious Youth magazines, *Die Wacht, Am Scheideweg, Der Jungführer, Der Jugendseelsorger*; while Catholic charitable organisations were replaced by a party organisation, described as "for the public welfare" (*Nationalsozialistische Volkswohlfahrt*).

The Nuncio in Berlin has often been accused of being pro-German, and what he is reputed to have said to Woermann about the fall of Paris has been mentioned. Nevertheless the Nazis now treated him in a most contemptuous manner. He had asked, as is normal in war-time, for permission to visit the prisoner-of-war camps and minister to the religious needs of the hundreds of thousands of Polish and French Catholic prisoners. This was refused on the ground that he would have a series of private and "probably treacherous" conversations with the inmates. His servant was arrested in Berlin by the Gestapo on the charge of hiding arms in the Nunciature. When Mgr. Orsenigo sent this unfortunate man food, clothing and a change of linen, the last two items were returned without a word of explanation (he had been executed). In Paris, the house of Cardinal Baudrillart, and that of Cardinal Liénart in Lille were also searched for arms, and all the private correspondence of Cardinal Suhard, the Primate, with the Vatican was intercepted and examined. A number of French monasteries were searched, as were the offices of the Catholic Action in Paris.

Most overbearing of all was Ribbentrop, with whom the Vatican had of course to deal in all diplomatic matters. To his Ambassador, von Bergen, he wrote ebulliently on the 15th February, 1941, "I hear from confidential sources that the Pope in conversation with top Roman aristocratic circles has said that everyone must accustom themselves to the certitude of a German victory. I would like a report on this."[23] In his reply, von Bergen poured a little water into his Foreign Minister's wine (including incidentally a remarkably accurate description of Vatican methods):

This Embassy is frequently the recipient of allegedly important pronouncements by His Holiness extracted in conversations at official

[23] *A.A. Pol III Büro des Staatssekretärs*, Vol. 2, 15th February, 1941.

receptions (as for example the one Your Excellency refers to concerning the Roman aristocracy); or in the course of private Papal audiences, of which confirmation is impossible; or from impromptu, often naive, questions, especially by female visitors. Where the source of information can be investigated and checked, this Embassy has generally found that the alleged remark by His Holiness, or the Vatican dignitary in question, has been taken from its context and given a more imaginative than objective interpretation. Frankly, I feel it was most unlikely that His Holiness made a simple statement of this kind — not necessarily because he doubts that we shall win the war, or hopes we shall not win it, but because as I know from experience he is always scrupulously careful (*geradezu ängstlich*) never to pronounce on the possible outcome of a war. What *is* probable is that in reply to the question of some visitor about the military situation, or the possibility of German aid to Italy, he pronounced words of general encouragement which were repeated, and distorted, in the sense stated by your informant.

Undoubtedly, the great German military and diplomatic successes have not failed to impress His Holiness. But we should not forget that recent Italian reverses have caused certain apprehensions at the Vatican [here, he was referring presumably to North Africa]. We know of course that the Pope, although he must appear above nationalities, feels himself in the last resort an Italian; and for this reason would not wish an Axis defeat. He is also undoubtedly nearer to the Germans than to any other foreign nation, and for our great qualities he always expresses undisguised admiration. Any resentment he ever expresses against Germany is of a purely religious and "church-political" nature. To stamp him therefore as many people do, even Germans, as "Francophile" is completely erroneous. Yet with all his sympathy for the Axis powers, the Pope sees a very real danger in the total destruction of England and France, or in a too long war, with the probability of Bolshevist penetration into Europe. His present aim therefore is, as always, to do what he can to shorten the war, playing in the wings, as it were, at the right moment the role of mediator. In view of this fundamental attitude always adopted by the Vatican, it is clear that off-the-cuff pronouncements in favour of one side or the other would seriously prejudice his role as a peacemaker.[24]

[24] Ibid., 16th February, 1941.

The Pope's statement about peace in the spring of 1941 exemplified this (reported in the *Osservatore Romano*, 13th March, 1941). His condemnation of all that Nazism stood for was clear, but implicit and sybilline. With Nazism still amok in the world, the speech reads like a counsel of perfection, beyond human aspirations and divorced from all practical possibilities, contemplating some kind of ideal Christian commonwealth of contented nations. During these years of Axis ascendancy, within his self-imposed political vacuum, the Pope's only outlet for expression lay in indulging his oratorical virtuosity and he had never been entirely free from the human vanity of the artist. For instance, when Mr. Osborne suggested that he should say something against the German bombing of cities, the Pope uttered this oratorical gem, "There are whirlwinds which in the light of day, as in the dark of night, scatter fire, terror, destruction and slaughter on helpless folk." Always susceptible to flattery about his eloquence (a flattery not neglected by his immediate entourage), any suggestion that its baroque character might diminish the force and clarity of his teaching wounded him deeply.

In these days of Axis supremacy the Pope had to play the host to over a hundred Allied diplomats accredited to the Vatican who, with their families and staffs, could not remain on enemy territory. In the Italian Concordat a section deals with the diplomatic relations of the Vatican and nations at war with Italy. Although the Vatican had full sovereignty over its own territory, it appears to have accepted certain limitations of this right in war-time. For instance the French Ambassador, Count Vladimir d'Ormesson, received a Papal reprimand when, after attending Mass in St. Peter's, he walked back to his quarters across the piazza in front of the basilica — that is across Vatican territory. But enemy diplomats were evidently not allowed even to be visible to "Fascist Italy". By March 1941, the Vatican State had a population of 970, including about a hundred diplomats and their families. For four years they were to be confined in the most exiguous of quarters, in the "Palazzino" (formerly a guest-house for foreign pilgrims) cheek by jowl with their *chers collègues*, many of whom after four years of such intimacy were no longer *chers*.

During 1942 and 1943 as the South American republics found it expedient to declare war on the Axis, the Pope became host to more and more diplomats — the Brazilian, Peruvian and Bolivian Ambassadors, the Minister of Venezuela, and the Chargés d'Affaires of

Colombia, Cuba, Ecuador and Uruguay. These new guests caused some concern owing to their lighthearted interpretation of the restrictions of their incarceration, and their vigorous insistence on their rights as guests. They were highly incensed, for instance, at the rules imposed in 1943 by the Italian government which, in the words of Farinacci, now regarded the Vatican as "a nest of spies". Having little work, plenty of money, large families and the gregarious, pleasure-loving instincts of Latin-Americans, they did not take kindly to the restrictions on their movements. They were accustomed, through their chauffeurs, to supplementing the Vatican City rations by purchasing outside in Rome, to send their cars to fetch their friends, to visit them, and in all possible ways to relieve the tedium of their confinement. These movements were now much restricted.

Article 12 of the Italian Concordat states that Italy will not interfere with postal and telegraphic traffic between the Vatican and foreign States which may be at war with Italy. Foreign diplomats were therefore allowed to use the Vatican courier, and transmit once a week to their governments over the Vatican short-wave transmitter a specified number of words. All correspondence had to pass the Vatican censorship, and telegrams were sent in the Vatican code. France had the largest staff, of seventeen diplomatic personnel; Poland came next with fifteen; the U.S.A. had seven; England, under the direction of Mr. Osborne, had five. The condition attached to using the telegraphic facilities was that no reporting on Italian affairs (as distinct from Vatican affairs) was allowed; and on one occasion in December 1941, when the British Minister for Economic Affairs asked Mr. Osborne for such information, Mr. Osborne had to refuse.[25]

The tedium of not being able to leave the confines of what was virtually a large garden was felt most by the wives and female staff, who complained that even in the heat of a Roman summer thay had, by Vatican regulation, to wear stockings. For some peculiar reason also connected with their sex, they were not allowed to ride bicycles in the grounds. Out of sheer desperation, they founded a bridge club which, as the war continued and more countries declared war on the Axis, became a Babel of tongues, with members from Cuba, Uruguay, Peru, Bolivia, Colombia, Venezuela as well as the Europeans. The Polish Ambassador, Casimir Pappé, an ex-professor from Vilna University, spent the four years writing a book, and he buried himself more or less permanently in the Vatican library. The French

[25] F.O. 371/29931, despatch from Mr. Osborne, 1st December, 1941.

Ambassador indulged his hobby of taking cinematographic films; while Mr. Osborne passed his spare time fishing in a small pond in the Vatican garden, and organising an exhibition of 600 photographs of his dogs. The great day for everybody was Sunday, when the latest American film arrived with the Lisbon courier.

The unsatisfactory situation of the Vatican when Italy is at war, the anomalies of Article 16 of the Concordat, were now fully revealed. Although a sovereign State, it was no more than an enclave in the heart of a Great Power, upon which it was completely dependent for all the material needs of life. The Italian State had only to cut off the water supply, and existence for the 970 human beings living within its walls would become intolerable.

18

The Turn of the Tide

UNTIL THE SECOND WORLD WAR IT WAS A GENERALLY accepted European axiom that wars of religion had ended in 1648 with the peace of Westphalia. The previous century had been full of them — eight civil wars in France, a revolt in the Netherlands, Philip II's attempt to invade England and restore the Catholic Faith, the Reformation with its many bloody secessions from the Church . . . Although elements of economic and strategical motives might be discerned in these wars, they were primarily spiritual struggles, in which men shed their blood for their faith. In 1941, the religious element returned, at least in so far as Communist Russia was concerned.

The Vatican has always made a distinction between the two systems, Communism and Socialism. Although to many people they appear blood relations, they are to the Church very different. The Catholic Church regards Socialism as an economic-syndicalist movement with no spiritual side, offering no answer to the riddle of life. Because Socialism does not pronounce on transcendental matters, it presents little danger and will wither away as economic conditions alter. Communism, on the other hand, with its militant atheism is not simply a mixture of economic and social reforms, but a new religion in the most embracing sense, with the conquering and converting force of another Islam.

When, therefore, in June 1941 the Soviet Union was attacked by Germany, to many good Catholics the war took on something of the nature of a crusade. They recalled Pius XI's encyclical *Divini Redemptoris* against atheistic Communism, "Communism is intrinsically evil, and no one wishing to save Christian civilisation can collaborate with it in any conceivable enterprise."[1] Mr. Osborne telegraphed on the 5th July, 1941 that the Pope himself had informed him that in many countries, particularly in Italy, Spain and South America, the war against Russia was being regarded as a religious crusade.[2] The Italian Ambassador to the Vatican, Attolico, suggested to Mgr. Tardini that the Pope should make a declaration on these lines in favour of the German and Italian troops now fighting "the crusade" in Russia. This would give a great boost to Italian morale. Mussolini, he said, had persuaded Hitler to emphasise in his propaganda to the world the "crusade" or anti-Bolshevik nature of the campaign.[3] To this Mgr. Tardini replied that the attitude of the Vatican towards Communism required no further clarification. The Vatican had already condemned Bolshevism with all its errors. There was nothing to add or retract. To pronounce on it again in the present situation would be to add a political to a moral condemnation. The Holy Father had spoken clearly *tempore non suspecto*. On the contrary, said Mgr. Tardini pertinently, those who had in the past made pacts of friendship with Soviet Russia might explain their new attitude. Those who until yesterday had contended that an alliance with Russia was beneficial to European welfare now declared a crusade against that country! They were the ones who should make a pronouncement — not the Vatican! The Vatican had not changed its attitude towards Communism one iota. "For my part," replied Tardini to Mussolini's Ambassador, "I should be only too pleased to see Communism disappear from the face of the earth. It is the Church's worst enemy. But it is not the only one. Nazism has conducted, and still conducts, a violent persecution of the Church. As a result, the Church can hardly regard the Hakenkreuz as . . . the symbol of a Crusade!"[4]

[1] The original is "Il communismo è intrinsicamente perverso e non si puo admettere in nessun campo la collaborazione con lui da parte di chiunque voglia salvare la civilizzazione cristiana."

[2] F.O. 371/29486.

[3] *Actes et Documents du Saint Siège*, Vol. 5, p. 9.

[4] Ibid., No. 62, notes of Mgr. Tardini. Much later, on the 25th February, 1946, to the Sacred College and the Diplomatic Corps, Pius XII confirmed this. "We took special care," he said, "notwithstanding certain tendentious pressures, not to let fall from Our lips, or from Our pen, one single word of encouragement for the war against Russia in 1941."

But Attolico continued to press his suit. It was not so much, he said, a question of preaching a crusade, as to reaffirm Catholic principles in the confrontation with Bolshevism. When Mgr. Tardini repeated that he could not contemplate the errors and horrors of Communism without also remembering "the aberrations and persecutions of Nazism", Attolico referred to his own experiences as Italian envoy in both Berlin and Moscow: "The situations cannot be compared," he argued. "In Russia it is worse, because the cult of religion is forbidden. Whereas in Germany it is free."

"To this I replied," says Mgr. Tardini, "that this might well be the situation at the moment, but it was clear from present information that Germany undoubtedly intended one day, perhaps in a not too far distant future, to go further. For this very reason today, instead of talking about a crusade, it would be better to quote the old proverb, "It is a case of one devil chasing out the other'." That was as far as Attolico could get with the obstinate Secretary of the Congregation for Extraordinary Affairs; and he left with the despairing comment, "The silence of the Holy See has been a thorn in the heart of Mussolini."[5]

Strangely, the Germans more than the Italians seemed to have understood this attitude. In a despatch to Berlin Menshausen, the German Botschaftsrat under von Bergen, wrote, "If His Holiness were now to speak up against Communism in Russia, the system against which he has so often expressed himself in principle, he would also have to take up a position against what he calls 'the anti-clerical measures and anti-Christian tendencies in Germany'."[6] Indeed, says Menshausen two weeks later, the Pope had intended speaking publicly against the Nazi persecution of the Church, "but then came the Russian war, and he kept quiet again — so as not to embarrass us".[7]

Nevertheless the Vatican, although true to its principle of not condemning nations by name in war-time, and refusing to say any more about the German invasion than it had about that of the Low Countries, undoubtedly approved the German invasion of Russia. If Russia had succeeded in keeping out of the war while Germany and England destroyed one another, into the resulting vacuum would have stepped rampant Communism. In a wireless speech on the

[5] *Actes et Documents du Saint Siège*, Vol. 5, No. 151, 27th November, 1941.
[6] A.A. *Büro des Staatssekretärs*, despatch from von Bergen, 23rd August, 1941.
[7] Ibid., 12th September, 1941.

29th June, 1941, Pius XII included a passage which gave considerable satisfaction to the Axis Powers: "Certainly in the midst of surrounding darkness and storm, signs of light appear which lift up our hearts with great and holy expectations — these are those magnanimous acts of valour which now defend the foundations of Christian culture, as well as the confident hope in victory."[8] While the Italian episcopate went even further. Archbishop Constantini, head of the Congregation for the Propagation of the Faith, said in the basilica at Concordia, "Yesterday on the soil of Spain, today in the Bolshevist land itself, in that immeasurable land in which Satan appears to have found his representatives on earth, brave soldiers, many from our own land, are fighting the greatest of all fights. With all our heart we pray that this struggle may bring us final victory and the destruction of a system based on negation and subversion."[9] Constantini concluded by blessing the Italian soldiers who "at this decisive hour defend our ideals of Freedom against the Red Barbarism".

To men in the Vatican like Mgr. Tardini, who had so pertinently pointed out that the Vatican had remained absolutely consistent in its policy towards Communism, while Nazi Germany had not, the new situation and set of alliances was not without a certain piquancy. Communism which had for twenty years never ceased reviling "the Western plutocracies and war-mongers" was now allied with them; and in July 1941 Stalin, in order to make his Godless regime appear more respectable in the eyes of the Christian world, did a political somersault. Up to and during the 1939-40 war, when the Soviets were invading eastern Poland, the Baltic States, parts of Finland and Rumania, he had continued with his old atheist policy. The Union of the Godless under Jaroslavski had extended its activities to these conquered lands; 4000 clerics of various confessions were deported from eastern Poland alone before mid-1940, and replaced by 25,000 anti-religious agitators (*Agitprop*). But now all this was changed overnight. One of Stalin's first acts after the German invasion in June 1941 was to announce the death of Jaroslavski (not, it later transpired, from natural causes). Stalin even told the Polish-American priest, Stanislas Orlemanski, that he would like to "collaborate with the Pope against the coercion and persecution of the Catholic Church in Germany", adding that he was "a champion of Freedom of

[8] *A.A. Pol III Büro des Staatssekretärs*, Vol. 3, report from Menshausen, 12th September, 1941.
[9] Ibid.

Conscience and religion".[10] A Soviet Department of Church affairs was set up in Moscow under Ivan Poljanski, its function being "to organise friendly relations between the Government and the Confessions". At this fearful moment, with the Germans at the gates of Moscow, the Soviets searched for support from every conceivable quarter. Their military authorities now permitted the Polish forces under General Anders to have their own army chaplains; and some fifty Polish Catholic chaplains who had disappeared into concentration camps in September 1939 were released for this purpose. In Moscow, the French church was reopened and placed at the disposal of the Polish Catholic community.

All this had an immediate effect in certain quarters in the West. In October 1941, President Roosevelt announced joyfully, "It is now hoped that an entering wedge for the practise of complete freedom of religion is definitely on the way in Russia." English Protestant clergymen who went to Russia in 1942 were of the same opinion. According to the Rev. F. Hoare who accompanied the Archbishop of York to Moscow in 1942, the number of churches in Moscow now open was greater than in 1941.[11] The churches were now allowed, he reported, to distribute Pastoral Letters and pamphlets, of which some 10,000 were in circulation. On the return from this visit, the Archbishop of York declared, "There is nothing fundamentally irreconcilable between Christianity and Communism — whereas between it and 'Racial Fascism' there are vast gulfs which can never be bridged." There was now, he said, complete religious freedom in Russia, and all anti-religious propaganda had ceased. The Bishop of Chelmsford, who was President of the British-Soviet society, considered "the suppression of all anti-Bolshevik movements a task of life importance".[12]

The Vatican remained singularly unimpressed by these pro-Russian transports in the West. Mgr. Tardini observed drily that, whatever might be said or done in Moscow now, the ultimate authority for Communism rested on the writings of Marx, Engels and Lenin; and the words of these men about religion were absolutely clear and unequivocal. They

[10] *A.A. Abteilung Inland*, pak. 16, Vol. 3, 12th May, 1944. Of such volte-faces Stalin had previous experience. Less than two years before he had signed a treaty of friendship with Nazi Germany which had for years — in his own words — "been pouring pails of manure over my head".

[11] *A.A. Informationsberichte über die politischen Kirchen*, June 1944, Kipa No. 83, 17th February, 1944.

[12] Ibid., for pronouncements of British bishops.

repudiated it utterly and said they intended to destroy it. And their words had been supported by their deeds. In twenty years of Soviet rule, some 24,000 churches and convents had been destroyed or converted into social clubs, cinemas and warehouses. Thousands of priests had been murdered. To Roosevelt's contention that Stalin's dissolution of the Third International indicated a change of heart, Mgr. Tardini replied that he attached not the slightest importance to any undertaking given by the Russian Dictator. Stalin's word, he said, was of no more value than Hitler's or Mussolini's. The most the abolition of the Third International could mean was that Communist propaganda would, for the time being, go underground and be carried on in greater secrecy. Mgr. Tardini was equally scornful of the material sent to the Vatican by the British Foreign Office to present the new Russian ally in a favourable light. One document contained a part of Stalin's speech of the 6th November, 1941. In this he made what must seem to us today (1972) a remark of unparalleled hypocrisy,

We have not, and could not have, such war aims as the imposition of our will and system of government upon the Slavonic and other subjugated peoples of Europe who expect our help. Our object is to assist these people in their war of liberation against Hitlerite tyranny, and thereafter to leave it to them to organise themselves as they like in their own countries. Our cry is — No intervention of any kind in the internal affairs of other peoples! The equality of nations! The inviolability of territory!

When Mr. Osborne showed Cardinal Maglione these fine words, and said the British government believed that after the Allied victory Russia would be too fully occupied with developing Siberia and the East to think of controlling other countries, the Secretary of State displayed "polite but marked scepticism".[13]

In England, the Catholic answer to the Muscovite Anglican bishops was given by the Rev. J. C. Heenan who had also been recently in Russia.[14] The Anglican clergymen had described, he said, the large congregations in the churches. But in a city like Moscow with a large population, where there were very few churches, those that were open would naturally appear full. He also believed that these congregations

[13] F.O. 371/37538, despatch from Mr. Osborne, 12th February, 1943.
[14] *A.A. Informationsberichte über die politischen Kirchen* (secret report for R.S.H.A. chief) No. 82, 16th Feb. 1944. Today Cardinal Heenan, Archbishop of Westminster.

had been "rigged" for the distinguished visitors. In 1919, he said, the population of Moscow had been two million and there were 560 churches. Today, it had a population of four million, and there were twenty-two churches. Not until the Russian leaders had given proof of returning sincerely to the supernatural past of their mystical land would there be any real change for the better. His final comment on the Anglican bishops was, "Those who, in full knowledge of this fact, still insist there is no religious persecution in Russia are enemies of Christ's Church." The Catholic Archbishop of Westminster, Cardinal Hinsley, went even further. On the 19th October, 1941 he said, "A beast of prey remains a beast of prey. National Socialism has not changed in essence at all, simply because it has attacked the Russian people."

The Russian entry into the war had repercussions far outside Europe, in particular in the U.S.A., which was still neutral. The decision of President Roosevelt to support Russia by sending her arms met immediate Catholic opposition. Here, too, the Catholics recalled the words of the encyclical *Divini Redemptoris* against atheistic Communism. The Apostolic Delegate in Washington, Mgr. Cicognani, commented that "a dogmatic authority is given to this interpretation, and most American Catholics conclude that Pontifical instructions conflict with the policy of the U.S. government".[15] While Lord Halifax reported from Washington that a poll of the Catholic clergy throughout the country by the Catholic Layman's Committee revealed that ninety per cent opposed U.S. aid to Russia.[16]

To change Catholic opinion in America, or at least to persuade American Catholics to accept his foreign policy, President Roosevelt realised that he must enlist the support of Rome. Here his meeting with Pius XII five years before, and the establishment of personal relations between the two men, proved of considerable value. He sent Mr. Myron Taylor with a personal letter to the Pope on the 9th September, 1941. His aim was to persuade the Pope to modify the passage in the encyclical *Divini Redemptoris* which condemned collaboration with Communism "in any conceivable enterprise". In certain circumstances, he contended, collaboration was justified. His letter explained why:

I believe that the Russian Dictatorship is less dangerous to the safety of other nations than is the German. The only weapon which the Russian Dictatorship uses outside its own borders is Communist propaganda which I, of course, recognise has in the past been utilised for the

[15] *Actes et Documents du Saint Siège*, Vol. 5, No. 56, 1st September, 1941.
[16] F.O. 371/26146, despatch of 31st October, 1941.

purpose of breaking down the form of government in other countries, religious belief, etc. Germany, however, not only has utilised, but is utilising, this kind of propaganda as well, and has also undertaken the employment of every form of military aggression outside of its borders for the purpose of world conquest by force of arms and propaganda. I believe that the survival of Russia is less dangerous to religion, to the Church as such, and to humanity in general, than would be the survival of the German form of dictatorship.[17]

He added that the United States government, although remaining neutral, intended to give moral and material support to the two nations now fighting Nazi Germany — Britain and Russia. And he suggested that the Pope should associate himself with the signatories of the Atlantic Charter which, while laying down the conditions for a just peace, also included a clause about religious liberty.

The Pope replied to Mr. Taylor through his Secretary of State, Mgr. Maglione, that in the encyclical *Summi Pontificatus*, as well as in the Christmas allocutions of 1939 and 1940, he had clearly announced the conditions for a just peace and had demanded for all peoples the right to independence, liberty of speech, religion etc., as required in the Atlantic Charter. He was prepared to repeat this if necessary, but he "would not join his voice with that of any individual statesmen"— for that would lay him open to the charge of abandoning his neutrality.

Regarding the relative malignity of Communism and Nazism, the Vatican admitted that Communism might be less dangerous than Nazism, militarily; but the German Nazis had not eliminated the cult of religion, as had the Communists. The question which concerned the Church was — which was the more dangerous to religion? Both systems, His Holiness admitted, were pernicious, both materialist, both oppressors of the most elementary human rights, both enemies of the Vatican. But, said Maglione to Mr. Taylor, if the Russians won the war, the victory would not belong to the Russian people, with whom they had no complaint, but to atheistic Communism. Then Maglione came to the most important part. The Vatican hoped that in the war being waged in Russia, Communism would be defeated, and Nazism weakened — so that afterwards it, too, could be destroyed.[18] This very important part of

---

[17] *Actes et Documents du Saint Siège*, Vol. 5, No. 59, 3rd September, 1941.

[18] Ibid., No. 78, notes of Mgr. Tardini. His actual words are worth quoting – "Per parte mia spero che dalla guerra che ora si combatte in Russia, il communism esca gia sconfitto e annientato e il nazismo esca debilitato e . . . da sconfiggere."

the Vatican answer describes precisely what the Church hoped for — first, destruction of Soviet Russia by Nazi Germany; second, the destruction of a weakened Nazi Germany by the Western Powers. The Vatican believed that this was basically the thought of President Roosevelt; if he wished to eliminate dictatorships, he must logically eliminate Stalin's too.

Nevertheless, His Holiness would relieve American Catholics of their scruples about military aid to Russia — but not by a Papal pronouncement. He would instruct the Apostolic Delegate in Washington to arrange that a member of the American episcopate should publicly interpret the encyclical *Divini Redemptoris* in the sense desired by President Roosevelt, namely that war with Nazi Germany altered the Papal attitude to Russia in certain respects. For this announcement Mgr. McNicholas, the Archbishop of Cincinatti, was selected; he was known for his reserve and political neutrality, and he could not be accused of having succumbed to governmental pressure. In a pastoral letter, Mgr. McNicholas accordingly examined the passage in question of *Divini Redemptoris* placing it in its true context and concluding that it could not be applied at the moment. Certain fire-eating bishops such as the Archbishop of Dubuque continued to issue anti-Soviet statements — "it is high time to finish making a distinction between the Red Army and the Soviet State. The Soviet army is admittedly fighting heroically. But it *is* the Soviet State, as long as it is at the behest of a Godless tyrant." But the other anti-Soviet prelates, such as Mgr. Shaughnessy of Seattle and Mgr. Beckmann, who were about to give a broadcast on "Religion, the U.S.A. and Russia", attacking the latter violently, agreed to follow the Vatican ruling. The broadcasts were cancelled.

The Vatican White Book, *Actes et Documents du Saint Siège*, concludes its section on this controversy by admitting that here the Pope yielded to Roosevelt — "He caused His Secretary of State and the American episcopate to agree with Roosevelt that Hitler was the most dangerous enemy, who must be defeated militarily, even if this involved cooperation with Soviet Russia."[19] British sources somewhat later confirm this change of attitude. A report from the Embassy in Madrid relates that the Spanish Ambassador to the Vatican said, after an audience with the Pope, that His Holiness had informed him that he now regarded Nazism, and not Communism, as the greatest menace to civilisation and the Catholic Church.[20]

*　　*　　*

[19] Ibid., pp. 25–6.
[20] F.O. 371/37538, despatch from Mr. J. Bowker, 10th May, 1943.

In spite of the personal relationship between Pope and President, there was a further reason why relations between the Vatican and America were, in 1941, less cordial than they might have been. Many Americans, both Catholic and Protestant, considered that the Pope had not protested sufficiently against the German aggressions and atrocities in the occupied lands, which were now being reported in such proportions that they could no longer simply be dismissed as Allied propaganda (of which the Allies had proved themselves masters in the First World War). On the 16th July, 1941, Ribbentrop's office sent the following report to von Bergen:

Considerable differences appear to have arisen between the Holy See and the Archbishop of New York, Cardinal Spellman who, in a letter to the Secretary of State, Maglione, has stated that the prestige of the Pope has declined sharply in America owing to the Pope's unclear pronouncements. On account of pro-Axis statements by Italian bishops, Spellman adds, American Catholics no longer have the same confidence in the Pope's impartiality, because he is behaving first and foremost as an Italian, who probably sympathises with Mussolini's imperial ambitions. We understand that this letter was so offensive that the Secretary of State would not show it to the Pope.[21]

Another German document relates that Mr. Tittmann, the assistant to Mr. Taylor, complained to the Secretariat of State that the Vatican was too lenient with the Dictators. Tittmann is reported to have used this opportunity to "point out something completely unknown to the general public". Before the war important contributions to Vatican funds had come from France, Austria, Spain, Belgium, the Netherlands. These had now stopped, and since the war the Vatican had been receiving foreign contributions from one source only, the U.S.A., large sums. This was described as money collected by American Catholics, the Knights of Columbus, and so on. In reality it was drawn from secret State funds at Roosevelt's disposal. Tittmann, says the German report, in complaining about American Catholics' dissatisfaction with the Pope's silence, "harped on these American funds like a banker calling a debtor to account".[22]

---

[21] A.A. Pol III Büro des Staatssekretärs, Vol. 3, from the Verbindungsmann der deutschen Inf. Stelle III in Prague, 16th July, 1941. This information emanating from Ribbentrop's office must be regarded as not as reliable as von Bergen's despatches.

[22] A.A. Pol I Amt Ausland, Abw. III, 12th July, 1941.

Evidence of further Vatican–U.S.A. friction was confirmed by von Bergen some months later just after the Japanese attack on Pearl Harbor which brought America into the War. To Berlin he telegraphed, "In responsible Vatican circles there is much criticism of Roosevelt. It is said that not only did he not try to prevent the war spreading, but he had manoeuvred his own country into it. His actions are regarded as all the more reprehensible because in his negotiations with the Vatican in 1939 and 1940 — by sending his special envoy, Taylor — he had spoken only of trying to prevent the war spreading and to promote peace in every possible way."[23] On the 15th December, 1941 von Bergen cabled again, "Criticism of Roosevelt is becoming sharper at the Vatican . . . authoritative sources there say that he has lacked sincerity from the outset and is playing a double game."[24]

A revealing sidelight on Vatican–U.S.A. relations at this time is also thrown by Saul Friedlander in his *Pius XII and the Third Reich*. He says that at the Rio de Janeiro Conference in January 1942, the Americans did all they could to make the South American nations break off relations with the Axis Powers; but that the Vatican effectively thwarted these efforts. On this subject Bergen cabled Berlin on the 21st March, 1942, "I have secret information that the Holy See has used its diplomatic representatives to lobby the countries taking part in the Rio de Janeiro Conference with the object of keeping them neutral."

In the early days after America's entry into the war, both the Vatican and the Axis Powers seem to have thought that America was so incompetent militarily that she could not possibly present any serious danger to the Axis for a long time. Bergen describes how the Director of the Vatican Economy Service, a certain Galeazzi, returned from a visit to the United States with a tale of extraordinary lack of preparation for war. The continual strikes in most of the main industries would, he said, completely sabotage Roosevelt's war plans. He contrasted the self-discipline of the English at war with the lack of that quality, or indeed any discipline at all, in America.[25]

However this estimate of American military incapacity was soon to be sharply revised. The German colony in Rome were still belittling American military prowess and pouring scorn on the President's envoy, "the Non-conformist business man Myron Taylor", until the 20th

[23] *A.A. Pol III Büro des Staatssekretärs*, Vol. 3, telegram from von Bergen, 11th December, 1941.
[24] Ibid., telegram from von Bergen, 15th December, 1941.
[25] Ibid., despatch from von Bergen, 15th December, 1941.

September, 1942, when they received a rude awakening. Until that date von Bergen as a patriotic German, even if far from being a Nazi, could look back on his work at the Vatican with, on the whole, satisfaction. By a mixture of diplomatic urbanity and the occasional veiled threat, he had kept the Vatican on at least formally polite terms with his truculent masters. In spite of the Nazi persecution of the Churches, the Pope still sent cordial birthday greetings to Hitler, gave Ribbentrop presents, received high-ranking Nazi bosses, etc. Nazi Germany, palpably the greatest aggressor in history, which had over-run a dozen countries in as many months was, at least overtly, equated at the Vatican, it seemed, with Germany's enemies, unwarlike Britain and palsied France; they were all treated as errant nations which had somehow strayed from the straight and narrow paths of peace. This was some achievement by the German diplomatic mission.

But now the situation changed abruptly. The occasion, the 20th September, 1942, did not seem on the face of it of any particular importance — another visit to the Vatican by Mr. Myron Taylor, with another personal message from President Roosevelt. There was some jocularity among the Germans in Rome about his drive in a closed car flanked by an Italian police escort from the airport to the Vatican. Further jokes were made when it was learned that the Pope, who normally received Mr. Roosevelt's envoy punctually, had kept him waiting some time in the ante-room. The fact, too, that the Secretary of State, Maglione, was away from Rome and made no attempt to return, added to the general impression. It seemed, however, rather odd that after the first audience with the Pope, which was quite long, Mr. Taylor had another of equal length the next day, and another the day after. He then had a long interview with the Secretary of State, who had returned post-haste to Rome. Mr. Taylor had also apparently demanded to see — and had seen immediately — certain other high Vatican dignitaries. Then slowly — through von Mackensen, the German Ambassador at the Quirinal — the horrible truth began to come through to Berlin.[26]

Mr. Taylor had brought something more than a mere good-will message from President Roosevelt. He had told the Pope that a compromise peace, if it had originally seemed desirable to the American President, was not so any longer. America had had enough. President Roosevelt had done what he could to dissuade the Axis Powers from their reckless actions, and they had only insulted him. Now they were going to pay for it. The President and America's allies had recently covenanted to eradicate Nazism and

[26] *A.A. Pol III Büro des Staatssekretärs*, Vol. 4, 20th September, 1942.

Fascism from the soil of Europe and the earth, to pluck it out "root and branch". They were to be exterminated, and the Allies did not mind how much time or money they spent in the process.[27] He also informed His Holiness that America and Great Britain had a close alliance and excellent relations with Soviet Russia. It was their intention when the war was won, that Russia should play its part in ordering the new world. The principles of Communism, he said, were now spread over a large part of the globe, and many millions of people believed in them. When the Pope objected (so ran the German report) to Mr. Taylor — how could powers calling themselves Christian have "excellent relations" with an avowedly atheistic State as Soviet Russia? — Mr. Taylor told him that President Roosevelt considered that Soviet Russia had changed its character.

It is not difficult to imagine the effect this must have had on the Pope and his entourage — at first of incredulity and then, as the weeks passed and news of the first Axis reverses began to come in, and the Allied Unconditional Surrender conditions were announced at Casablanca (27th January, 1943), realisation that the Soviet Union, far from being annihilated, might emerge from the war not only intact but enlarged. The haunting fear of the Popes in the twenties and thirties that another world war might, by some inner law of its own, be deformed and slide from a national to a social level, and thence to a revolutionary level, seemed justified. The Pope's great dream that as a new Innocent XI he might unify the nations of the Christian West against the Infidel and save Vienna, Budapest and Warsaw as Innocent had saved those cities from the Turks — but this time from the Bolshevists — was over. The 20th September, 1942, when Myron Taylor brought him this message, may well be described as the turning-point of the war, at least as far as the Vatican was concerned. That it was hardly welcome news is revealed by Mgr. Tardini's comment in his notes about the conversation with Mr. Taylor, "The Americans are preparing to reorganise Europe as they think fit. And none of them, or almost none, understand the European situation; this desire on their part may cause enormous damage to Europe."[28]

The texts of President Roosevelt's messages which Mr. Taylor brought have recently been published by the Vatican (1969) in *Actes et Documents du Saint Siège relatifs à la Seconde Guerre Mondiale* (Vol. 5. Nos: 472 and

[27] *Actes et Documents du Saint Siège*, Vol. 5, No. 431. "Peace with the Axis will not be envisaged by the government of the U.S.A. before Hitlerism has been completely obliterated."

[28] Ibid., No. 480.

374). A few excerpts will convey the vehemence as well as the dignity of the President's language.

It is of great importance that, at this juncture when the Allied Powers are passing to the offensive in the conduct of the war, the attitude of the United States government with respect to the present world struggle should be restated to the Holy See . . . A peace-loving people, we exhausted every honourable means to remain at peace; in the midst of peace negotiations we were foully attacked by Germany's partner in the Orient. Like Austria, Czechoslovakia, Poland and the rest, we were made the victims of Axis aggression at the very moment when their diplomats were talking peace. How then could we have confidence in the word of any Axis Power? In the conviction that anything less than complete victory would endanger the principles we fight for and our very existence as a nation, the United States of America will prosecute this war until the Axis collapses. We shall not again allow ourselves to be imperilled from behind while we are talking peace with criminal aggressors. Our confidence in complete victory is based upon the most objective foundation. There is nothing of emotional optimism or wishful thinking in it. We are prepared for a long war. We foresaw early reverses. But in the end, we know that no nation or combination of nations can stand against us in the field . . . The entire industry of the world's greatest industrial nation is now directed to one objective — to manufacture, by mass production methods in which we excel, the implements of war. We have only begun and yet we have already surpassed the arms output of Germany at her peak. The world has never seen such an avalanche of war weapons, manned by skilled mechanics and stout-hearted freemen, as we shall loose in 1943 and 1944 against the Axis. In some sectors we have already taken the offensive, months ahead of our original plans. That offensive will rise in irresistible crescendo, more and more rapidly, more and more powerfully, until totalitarianism, with its menace to religion and freedom, is finally and utterly crushed.

The Axis knows this, knows that its ill-gotten gains cannot be held by continuing the war. What they won through treacherous war, they may not try to retain by a treacherous peace. We have reason to believe that they are casting about for someone to make a peace proposal which will enable them to escape the inexorable results of defeat in the field. This is no time for a recourse to diplomacy. Having made every effort to avoid this war, we shall not now be weakened by

Axis cunning when we have taken the field. We consider that Axis-inspired proposals of "peace" would be nothing less than a blow aimed at us. There is reason to believe that our Axis enemies will attempt, through devious channels, to urge the Holy See to endorse in the near future proposals for peace without victory. In the present position of the belligerents, we can readily understand how strong a pressure the Axis Powers may bring to bear upon the Vatican. We therefore feel it a duty to support the Holy See in resisting any undue pressure from this source.

These admonitory references to Axis peace proposals must have been carefully premeditated, because five months before this the Axis Powers had put out peace feelers to the Vatican through the Apostolic delegate in Ankara, Mgr. Roncalli and Roosevelt must have had wind of it. By the spring of 1942, it must have become clear even to Hitler that his hitherto unfailing time-table of military success would require considerable revision. Russia, far from being knocked out by November 1941 as planned, was now launching a series of energetic counter-offensives. A compromise peace which left Germany most of her acquisitions was the best option.

In April 1942 the German Ambassador in Ankara, von Papen, had approached Mgr. Roncalli and reminded him of the famous five points of Pius XII's speech in late 1939 for a just peace; he suggested that the Vatican might take them up again and make soundings among the Allied governments. In his despatch reporting this Mgr. Roncalli refers to the suggestion of "the grandiose and holy task which Providence has reserved to the Holy Father in the preparation of world peace".[29] Von Papen, he said, returned to the subject several times, "with an accent of lively solicitude, if not anxiety"; and Roncalli says he began to wonder if von Papen might not be expressing the views of his master — particularly as he knew that von Papen was the only German Ambassador whom Hitler received alone, without the presence of his Foreign Minister.

A week later Mgr. Roncalli announced that a certain Baron von Lersner, who frequently stayed at the German Embassy in Ankara, and was said to have close contacts with the German High Command as well as with the magnates of German industry, was going to Rome, ostensibly to sign a commercial agreement with Italy, but in reality *exit seminare semen suum*. Von Papen had told Roncalli that Baron von

[29] Ibid., No. 345, 16th April, 1942.

Lersner would like to meet certain high officials at the Vatican; perhaps, he had suggested, he might be received by the Pope. Roncalli gave him a letter of introduction. (He later wondered if he should have done this, and wrote to Mgr. Montini, "Your Excellency will understand me, may admonish me but will excuse me if you do not think it right to put this suggestion to Cardinal Maglione".[30]

On the 22nd May, von Lersner arrived in Rome, where he let it be known discreetly that he was visiting the Vatican to admire the famous gardens. From the gardens he was equally discreetly conducted to the Cardinal Secretary of State, Maglione. Here, claiming to speak only for himself, he said that the German generals were convinced that victory would not bring a proper peace, that Turkey would willingly offer herself as mediator; but that in his opinion, and in view of the Pope's five peace points announced in 1939, the Vatican was better suited to the role. He then repeated almost verbatim to Maglione what von Papen had said to Roncalli: "The Holy See should sound the various Powers, and then in October 1942 proposals might be made to the Axis."[31]

To this Maglione replied that the present moment did not appear very timely; and he took advantage of what he saw was the first sign of Axis military weakness to change the subject, saying that what he particularly regretted about the present state of affairs in Germany was that a real persecution of Christianity was in progress (at which the Baron observed glumly, "Je suis parfaitement d'accord avec vous"). Baron Lersner also had an interview with Mgr. Montini, to whom he made the same propositions, adding that the war could still last a long time, the power of the totalitarian States being such that they could fight much longer than in 1918.[32]

These "personal peace proposals" were, Mgr. Tardini was convinced, those of the German government — particularly as the Italian Ambassador arrived at the Vatican almost on the heels of Baron von Lersner and announced "We know that Mgr. Roncalli has had an interview with von Papen in Ankara. Does Your Eminence not realise that behind von Papen stands the German government?"[33] Now how, continues Tardini in his notes, could the Italian government have known about the Ankara conversations, except through the German

[30] Ibid., No. 353, 23rd April, 1942.
[31] Ibid., No. 371, notes of Mgr. Tardini, 22nd May, 1942.
[32] Ibid., No. 372, notes of Mgr. Montini, 22nd May, 1942.
[33] Ibid., No. 371, notes of Mgr. Tardini, 22nd May, 1942.

government itself? In any case, he realised that to say victory would not bring peace simply meant that the Germans now knew that they could not win the war. They evidently hoped, however, to have some sort of military success by October, and to use it in the bargaining.[34]

The United States government must undoubtedly have had wind of all this, as the unequivocal warnings about Axis peace proposals in the President's letter of the 19th September, 1942 to the Pope clearly indicate.

There can be no doubt that, as far as the Allies were concerned, President Roosevelt's letters of the 19th September, 1942 had a most salutary effect in the Vatican. The Secretariat of State now knew how — short of a miracle or some Axis "secret weapon" — the war was going to end, and they could make their plans accordingly. Whether the "Unconditional Surrender" formula was right or not does not concern this study. What is certain is that it had an immediate effect on Papal policy. Within a matter of days after the Presidential message, the Pope had begun to take a more definite line.

Von Bergen knew it too because on the 12th October, 1942, less than three weeks after the Myron Taylor visit, he reports he has heard from Signor Guariglia, the Italian Ambassador to the Vatican, that "His Holiness's displeasure at the treatment of the Church in Germany has greatly increased of late. He feels he must now take a more critical attitude towards the disagreeable events taking place in Germany."[35] This in turn began to affect Italo-German relations. Signor Guariglia also handed von Bergen a list of closed religious establishments in Germany and of confiscated Church property, adding that such senseless conduct only gave the Anglo-Saxons an excellent occasion to present themselves as the defenders of religion. How painful it was, said Guariglia, for Italy as the great Catholic power to be hindered, owing to the conduct of her ally, from playing this traditional role as defender of the Faith.[36]

On the 21st October, 1942, Ribbentrop in a long personal telegram to von Bergen said that henceforth all differences with the Vatican were to be avoided at all costs. Measures were being taken to that end in Germany. The Vatican should be informed that there had been no confiscation of Church property since the 30th July, 1941, and that all

[34] Ibid.
[35] *A.A. Pol III Büro des Staatssekretärs*, Vol. 4, telegram, 12th October, 1942.
[36] Ibid.

anti-religious press propaganda had been forbidden. (It is perhaps no coincidence that when this conciliatory telegram was being written the battle of El Alamein had just begun.)[37]

The tide was turning, and the Vatican knew it. In his Christmas 1942 radio address to the world, the Pope was more forthright than he had ever been before. Although he still mentioned no country by name, it was clear that his condemnation of modern "Statolatry" was directed against the totalitarian systems; while his dictum that Nature had given the Family precedence over the State was the antithesis of the Nazi and Fascist doctrines. He also went out of his way to say that the servitude of the working classes was often worse under the modern almighty State than it was under the capitalist system. But the most important part of his long address concerned "the hundreds of thousands who, through no fault of their own, and solely because of their nation or race, have been condemned to death or progressive extinction". This was a clear enough reference to the Jews; but the Western Allies still considered it was not strong enough. Several governments, including the Belgian, British, Polish and Brazilian made a joint protest to the Vatican that the Pope should have stigmatised Germany by name for its persecution of the Jews. This grieved the Pope who believed he had met all possible demands for plain speaking.

But Heydrich's R.S.H.A. had no doubt about the Christmas address which it analysed most carefully on the 22nd January, 1943.

In a manner never known before [the report says] the Pope has repudiated the National Socialist New European Order. His radio allocution was a masterpiece of clerical falsification of the National Socialist *Weltanschauung*. It is true, the Pope does not refer to the National Socialists in Germany by name, but his speech is one long attack on everything we stand for ... Human personality he sees in entirely individual-liberal terms. The notion of personality emanating from a collective society he regards as an aberration. He is pleased, he says, that this approach (by us National Socialists) "is in ever increasing measure meeting growing opposition". God, he says, regards all peoples and races as worthy of the same consideration. Here he is clearly speaking on behalf of the Jews ... When he turns to economic matters, he refers to "new systems which are a labyrinth of false doctrines with unforeseeable results for human society". Here again he is referring to National Socialism; for he says that when the economy

[37] Ibid., Vol. 5.

and work are not dictated by supernatural religious principles, both work and workers are deprived of nobility... That this speech is directed exclusively against the New Order in Europe as seen in National Socialism is clear in the Papal statement that mankind owes a debt to "all who during the war have lost their Fatherland and who, although personally blameless have, simply on account of their nationality and origin, been killed or reduced to utter destitution". Here he is virtually accusing the German people of injustice towards the Jews, and makes himself the mouthpiece of the Jewish war criminals.[38]

This Christmas broadcast of 1942 was perhaps the most important made by the Pope during the war. So important did the *Osservatore Romano* consider it that the paper was still publishing interpretative articles on it in May 1943. Ribbentrop realised what it meant, for he instructed von Bergen on the 24th January, 1943 to seek an immediate audience with the Pope. "There are signs," he wrote, "that the Vatican is likely to renounce its traditional neutral attitude and take up a political position against Germany. You are to inform him that in that event Germany does not lack physical means of retaliation."[39]

To this von Bergen replied on the 26th January, 1943:

I spoke to His Holiness in the sense of your instructions. When I hinted that relations between Germany and the Papacy might be broken off, with all that that implies, His Holiness remained quite silent. Then, in the calmest manner possible, he said that he did not care what happened to himself, but that a struggle between Church and State could have only one outcome — the defeat of the State. I replied that I was of the contrary opinion. His Holiness was evidently not aware how strong was the feeling of Catholics in Germany over the unpatriotic behaviour of many of the Catholic clergy. An open battle could bring some very unpleasant surprises for the Church — and from such a struggle only the common foe, Bolshevism, would emerge victorious. I told the Pope therefore that the air should be cleared — in the first place, by ceasing the complaints by the Vatican, and by a more moderate line in the press, in particular in the *Osservatore Romano*, which day in day out pours out its poison against Germany — but never refers to Red Spain or the Popular Front in France.

[38] *A.A. Abteilung Inland*, pak. 17, Vol. 1, R.S.H.A. report, 22nd January, 1943.
[39] *A.A. Pol III Büro des Staatssekretärs*, Vol. 6, 24th January, 1943.

To this the Pope replied that the attitude of the *Osservatore Romano* could be explained quite simply — all the interest, all the cares and worries of the Vatican, were at the moment centred on Germany. "Pacelli," finished von Bergen, "is no more sensible to threats than we are. In event of an open break with us, he now calculates that some German Catholics will leave the Church — but he is firmly convinced that the majority will remain true to their Faith. And that the German Catholic clergy will screw up its courage, prepared for the greatest sacrifices."[40]

The Pope's encyclical *Mystici Corporis* of July 1943 was equally clear. In this he condemned the "legalised murder" of the deformed, the insane and the incurable, as a violation of natural and divine law. About attacks on Catholics on account of their faith, he said he considered such offences as directed against his own person. A further important indication of his changing attitudes towards Germany is revealed in a despatch from the British Ambassador in Madrid in October 1942. He reported that Señor Suner on a recent visit to Rome had told the Pope that the Germans could still win the war, and that the Vatican would do well to adapt its policies accordingly. To which the Pope replied, "If the Germans win, it will mean the greatest period of persecution that Christians have ever known."[41]

As the Allies gradually gained the upper hand in 1943, two problems troubled their relations with the Vatican: the declaration of Rome as an open city; and the internment of Italian clerics in Italian territories over-run by the Allies (the north African littoral, Syria, Abyssinia, etc.).

Concerning the first of these, the Vatican considered that Rome, on account of its religious shrines and art treasures, should be spared the rigours of war. It belonged, the Vatican argued, to all mankind, not to Italy alone. The *Osservatore Romano* recalled that in A.D. 544 Belisarius dissuaded Totila from destroying Rome by the plea that Rome belonged to the whole world, and that whoever destroyed it would be destroying not the city of another, but his own city. Understandably, civilised people the whole world over hoped that the war would not touch a city

[40] Ibid., 26th January, 1943. The Italian Socialist, Ignazio Silone, recognised that "In certain memorable Christmas messages the Pope has upheld the rights denied and violated by the totalitarian States with a force and nobility that make him the spokesman of the human race."

[41] F.O. 371/33412, Sir S. Hoare to Mr. Eden, 28th October, 1942.

which was more a common possession of humanity than the capital of a very recent national State. The British government said they hoped they would not have to bomb it; but they refused to enter into any binding agreement not to do so. It was an important centre of rail communications, an airport, and in the event of operations in southern Italy, Axis supplies must inevitably pass through it. Moreover it was the seat of an enemy government. In this connection, they recalled Mussolini's boastful remarks about the Italian part in the bombing of London in 1940. In the House of Commons the Prime Minister announced that, should such a step as the bombing of Rome become militarily and strategically necessary, his government reserved full liberty of action. And an air marshal said that the R.A.F. would not be influenced by "sentimental considerations".

These two statements shocked the Vatican deeply. The argument that Rome was the capital of a belligerent State was clearly regarded by the Pope as subordinate. In the fourth dimensional, timeless atmosphere of the Vatican, Rome was the Eternal City of Papal tradition, not the incidental capital of a united Italy, still less of a transitory Fascist State.

On the 27th August, 1941 Mgr. Tardini summoned Mr. Osborne and questioned him closely about the exact meaning of the words that the Allies "over Rome would not be influenced by sentimental considerations". Did this mean, he asked, that the British bombers would show no respect for art, civilisation and humanity? Mr. Osborne replied by referring to its military and strategical targets, and also to Mussolini's claims about the Italian bombing of London. The Pope, he said, had not condemned the destruction of Christian shrines in England — St. Paul's, Coventry, Canterbury.

This argument appeared to have little effect; for Mgr. Tardini comments bitterly in his "Notes" (27th August, 1941), "The mentality of the British Minister is always the same. He is English, and for him London is more than Rome. He is a Protestant, and for him London is the holy city, as Rome is for us. Indeed, Rome is for Protestants a real and true *signum contradictionis*."[42] Later his *sostituto*, Mgr. Montini, repeated the argument to Mr. Osborne of the special links the Pope had with Rome, of which he was also bishop. "A rather difficult interview," writes Mgr. Montini in his "Notes", "and on Mr. Osborne's part not very accommodating."[43]

The anomalies of the Italian Concordat regarding the Vatican State in

[42] *Actes et Documents du Saint Siège*, Vol. 5, No. 52.
[43] Ibid., 27th September, 1941.

the event of Italy going to war now became glaringly apparent. A British suggestion was made that the Papal city should be clearly illuminated at night so that Allied bombers attacking targets in Rome could avoid it. The Papal reply was, quite understandably, that this would immediately cause trouble with the Italian State, because the Vatican would then serve as a beacon lighting the way to the capital. The British government countered that this only provided clear proof that the Vatican was not independent, and must therefore be treated as enemy-occupied territory.[44] Deadlock ensued.

As long as the war kept away from Italy, these anomalies of the Concordat were not revealed. But when hostilities approached, first over the bombing of Rome, and secondly when the Allied front moved to the Italian peninsula itself, they became acute. As the Allies advanced they were being constantly begged by the Vatican to spare this ecclesiastical building or that, to regard this or that town as an "open city", on account of its sacred buildings; to refrain from requisitioning monasteries and nunneries for hospital purposes; even to take precautions against damaging the Vatican lorries careering about the countryside near the battle zone.

To complicate matters even further, the British government had received intelligence in early 1941 that the Fascists were training a special air squadron to bombard the Vatican City with captured British bombs, if the British bombed even the vicinity of Rome. Two British bombers which had been shot down in northern Italy had, they learned, been brought back to Rome where they were to be presented after the bombing as a *corpus delicti*, proof that the British did not hesitate to destroy the greatest sanctuary in the Catholic world. The British Foreign Secretary gave this information to the Prime Minister on the 30th January, 1941: "We are letting this story leak out in New York. It may well discredit Mussolini and show the lengths to which the Fascist regime is ready to go to vilify us. It will also serve as a discreet reminder that we have not abandoned the idea of bombing Rome."[45] In fact on the 5th November, 1943, one lone plane without markings did bomb the Vatican — four bombs which caused considerable damage to buildings, but mercifully hurt no one. Its identity was never established, and both sides naturally accused the other of "the barbarian attack on the centre of the Catholic Church".

The question of bombing Rome was also complicated by the

[44] F.O. 371/37548, memorandum by Mr. V. Cavendish-Bentinck.
[45] F.O. 371/29918, Mr. Eden to the Prime Minister, 30th January, 1941.

American position, which was quite different from that of Great Britain. The U.S.A. had nearly thirty million Catholics, and President Roosevelt did not wish to alienate them. On the other hand, if the Protestants of America, who constituted by far the largest number of the population, heard that military considerations, which might shorten the war, had been disregarded because of Catholic influence, Roosevelt would have difficulties of another kind. Mr. Eden was in America in the spring of 1943, and he commented, "Harry Hopkins said to me today in the presence of the President that there would be 'one hell of a row in the U.S.A if Rome were not bombed owing to Catholic pressure'." Finally, the U.S.A. came down in favour of the British view that, unless the most stringent conditions could be laid down, and enforced, regarding the demilitarisation of the city, we should not regard Rome as an open city.

By early 1943 the war was approaching Italy, and Allied preparations for a landing in Sicily were under way. The Pope knew this, and in January 1943 he told Mr. Tittmann, the American Chargé d'Affaires, that if Rome were attacked he would make a public protest, adding that he was certain of the effect this would have on Catholics throughout the world, and that his protest would be particularly harmful to the Allied cause. He also said he thought the bombing of Rome would turn the Italian people against the Allies and towards Communism. He also told Tittmann that he had urged the Italian government to transfer elsewhere all military objectives within the city (it appeared that some sort of evacuation had in fact started). Rome should therefore, he contended, be declared an open city.

The Allies were unable to ascertain how far this "demilitarisation" had proceeded, and in any case Mussolini and his government still appeared to be in the city in August 1943. They still therefore retained full liberty of action. Their policy was to be amply justified. In July 1943, just before the invasion of Sicily — and undoubtedly to give a further and perhaps final shove to the toppling position of Mussolini — the Allies bombed Rome for the first time. A powerful contingent of aircraft attacked the main goods yard in waves, destroying it and killing several hundred people. Unfortunately, the near-by church of San Lorenzo was also hit and partially destroyed. The Pope immediately visited the site and commiserated with the families of the dead, with tears in his eyes. So great was the crush that he could not get back into his car, and he had to walk through the crowd, jostled and petitioned on every side.

Nevertheless the bombing had an immediate strategical and political effect on the Fascist Grand Council, who now showed indecent haste in speeding Mussolini's departure. When he fell he was replaced by the Badoglio government which was installed on Allied territory. Rome was bombed again on the 14th August, 1943, whereupon the Badoglio government, from its seat in Bari, declared it an open city. But the Allies still refused to recognise this, because the Germans had now invaded the city and were in full military possession. Moreover the Allies considered that when the Germans had been expelled, the Badoglio government must have its seat in Rome (the prestige of the Badoglio government would be lowered if it were in a provincial city); and this precluded all possibility of its being declared an open city. During the period from August 1943 to May 1944 — the month when the Allies took Rome — they forebore to bomb Rome further, although the German army was in full possession of the city. In spite of Papal exhortations and threats about the sympathies of South American Catholics, and Italy going Communist if the Allies bombed Rome, the Allies behaved with considerable diplomatic skill. They kept their heads and refused to be trapped by the "open city" device; and yet they used their vast bombing power virtually only once, at precisely the right moment, contributing undoubtedly to the collapse of the Fascist government. Thanks to the humanity of the Allies — compared with what had happened in other European cities, Warsaw, Rotterdam, Belgrade, Coventry, London — Rome got off remarkably lightly. Yet in March 1945 the *Osservatore Romano* claimed that it was due entirely to the Pope's diplomatic action that Rome had been saved from total aerial destruction. He was *Defensor Civitatis*. This claim seems somewhat exaggerated. The city's salvation was due, not to the Pope's appeals to the belligerents, and still less to his admonitions, but to Marshal Kesselring's decision not to stand at Rome or, perhaps even more, to the rapidity of General Alexander's advance.

The other cause of tension between the Vatican and the Allies as the latter over-ran territories previously under Italian rule, in Abyssinia and the north African littoral, concerned the quantities of Italian clerics and ecclesiastical missions left behind. Briefly, the British regarded them as enemy aliens and quoted chapter and verse to show that many of them were even engaged in pro-Fascist propaganda, if not activities. The Vatican, on the other hand, maintained that the work of the missions was supernatural not mundane, spiritual not material. Cardinal Maglione, the Secretary of State, told Mr. Osborne that clerics lose their national feeling when they become churchmen, because their allegiance is then *only* to Pope and Church. Maglione added that he would not engage a cleric to work under him who did not satisfy this demand. Moreover, he contended, the head ecclesiastics such as Mgr. Testa in Beirut, Mgr. Barlassina in Jerusalem and Mgr. Castellani in Abyssinia, whom the British wished to expel for alleged pro-Italian activities, were not to be regarded as Italians at all, but as the Pope's personal representatives, and therefore citizens of the Vatican, a neutral State. Once again, the anomalies of the Italian Concordat were sharply revealed.

The British line was not necessarily of objection to any individual cleric (although they had specific evidence against some of them), but to the presence on British territory of *all* persons of enemy race, whether they had Vatican nationality or not; and that in each case the onus of proof was not on the British to show why they should be removed, but on the Vatican, who must persuade the Allies that, notwithstanding the cleric's Italian character, there was some particular reason why he should, as an exception, be allowed to continue to function.

As the Vatican repudiated this attitude completely, claiming that "mission activity cannot be subordinated to the vicissitudes of international politics", the British proceeded to specify individual cases. The most blatant was that of the Pope's personal representative in Addis Ababa, Mgr. Castellani, the Apostolic Delegate (who had arrived there, we have already seen, at the end of the Abyssinian war in 1936, a rabid Fascist who had been the Italian army bishop on Rhodes). The British Army occupied Addis Ababa in April 1941, and about a month later a search party which had been alerted found in the Papal Legation a quantity of small arms concealed in luggage, and a wireless transmitter of the latest Italian army type, operated by nine Italian ex-soldiers. They all had passes signed by Mgr. Castellani establishing their position in the Papal Legation. Mgr. Castellani, said the British, did not communicate their existence to the British military commander, although he must have been aware of the irregularity of such conduct. They also found a quantity of specie in various currencies, and some bullion, all Italian government property which had been transferred just before the British entry into Addis Ababa from the Banca d'Italia (from whom it would, of course, have been confiscated as enemy property) to the Papal Legation. When questioned about this, Mgr. Castellani admitted its existence in his safe, and explained it as a gift to be used for the relief of distressed Italians after the British occupation. The British also discovered that he was receiving sums of money from Italians in Addis Ababa for transfer to their relations in Italy through the wireless transmitter to the Vatican, a recipient at the Vatican then paying the

Italian in question. This was virtually transfer of capital from Ethiopia to an enemy country. In May 1941 arms and ammunition were found in the store-house and priests' quarters of the Capucin Mission at Direawa. And in October 1941 a quantity of arms, ammunition and hand grenades were found in the priests' rooms of the Apostolic Mission at Asba Tafari, and also behind the altar canopy of the church. Under Castellani, the British also found an Italian military chaplain organising an intelligence service to report on the political reliability and opinions of certain Italians. He was in possession of a Fascist party membership card describing him as a *squadrista* and *sciarpa littoria* (one of the highest ranks in the Fascist party).

In spite of all this, the British did not intern Mgr. Castellani at first because, as Apostolic Delegate, they saw that he enjoyed a vaguely defined degree of immunity. But after the latest discoveries, they requested the Vatican to withdraw Castellani to Italy. When this request was ignored, orders came from the highest quarters in England. The Foreign Secretary, Mr. Eden, commented, "We seem to have been very slow and lax in our dealings with this intriguing priest. Let us be rid of him. I really can't help Vatican feelings."[46] Mgr. Castellani was accordingly arrested by the British Army on the 29th November, 1942, and taken under escort to the coast at Direawa where he was repatriated to Italy. The Vatican protested hotly, but there was nothing they could do.

The situation was much the same in Palestine where the Archbishop Barlassina (whom we have also already met as a rabid Italian nationalist in the Holy Places troubles of the twenties) was still the Pope's representative and Patriarch of Jerusalem. Mr. O. Lyttleton, the British Minister in the Middle East, reported that there was definite evidence against him, and that the Vatican should be asked to replace him. In Lyttleton's words, "reinforced by substantial financial and property aid, the Roman Catholic Church here has been increasingly the medium for the dissemination of Fascist political propaganda and indulging in political activities inconsistent with its spiritual function".[47] Lyttleton also asked that Mgr. Jacopozzi in Alexandria should be replaced by a non-enemy archbishop.[48]

There were similar cases all over the Middle East. General Spears, the British Minister in Syria asked for the Italian Archbishop Testa to be

46 F.O.371/31595, 28th October, 1942.
47 F.O. 371/33414, 23rd January, 1942.
48 F.O. 371/26328, 6th February, 1942.

eplaced in Beirut as he was flouting censorship regulations; Spears
escribed him and his clerics as "disseminating propaganda, encouraging
spionage, sabotage and the escape of prisoners".[49] Spears recommended
he same expulsion for the General of the Jesuits at Beirut University,
'ather Bonnet Eymard, who was "victimising Jesuit Fathers associated
vith the Free French Movement". Similar accusations were made
gainst two Italian Fascist priests in Cyprus, Lamparelli and Alessio.

When the demands for the removal of these men were made to the
Vatican, they were again indignantly refused. To do such a thing, it
rgued, would create a dangerous precedent for the Japanese treatment of
nissionaries in the Philippines, Attempts were therefore made at the
Vatican to enlist American support against the British action. In 1943
Cardinal Spellman visited the Vatican, where he was persuaded that the
British attitude towards priests and missions in the Middle East was
rimarily Protestant or anti-Catholic in inspiration; and that the alleged
trategical and political considerations were only a façade.[50]

Notwithstanding this, the British again took action and expelled or
nterned all the Italian missions in the Middle East. The last round in this
itter struggle was a letter to the British authorities from Cardinal
Tisserant, Secretary of the Congregation of the Eastern Church and
ompetent authority for Ecclesiastical Affairs in Abyssinia. In this, he
tigmatised the British for "having obliterated the Catholic religion in
Abyssinia". Of the eleven mission stations there before the war, he said,
omplete with schools, dispensaries, hospitals, relief organisations, run by
orty-three missionary priests, none remained. There was no one to
ninister to the spiritual needs of the Italians in the prisoner-of-war
amps. Four hundred and fifty Italian priests, monks and nuns had been
nterned in Egypt and Palestine, and as many expelled.

Who was right in this unfortunate affair, which caused such bad blood
etween the Vatican and Great Britain for several years? There can be
ittle doubt that before the Second World War, the Fascist government
;ave free passages to all Italian missionaries bound for the Middle East,
vhether to Italian or foreign territory, such as Palestine and the Holy
Places. The number of mission stations was greatly increased thanks to
;overnment subsidy; and it was clear that in addition to their evangelical
unction, they were to be used by the government as instruments for
olitical penetration.

It does seem, however, from all the evidence available that, although

[49] F.O.371/30199.
[50] F.O. 371/37542, despatch from Mr. Osborne.

the Vatican was most jealous of the rights and prerogatives of its priests, and defended them strenuously, it was ignorant of some of their un-priestly activities. Had they known of them from their own sources, it is certain that they would have condemned them. To Mr. Osborne who, incarcerated in the Vatican, had the disagreeable task of dealing with all this, may be left the last word. To Mr. Eden on the 6th August, 1942 he wrote, "I am satisfied that any subversive appeals to the patriotic instincts of Italian ecclesiastics and missionaries are of local origin and are not tolerated, still less abetted by the Vatican authorities. Hence their sense of righteous indignation."[51]

Lastly, the Pope became annoyed with the Allies because, as he considered, they thwarted his charitable work. In April 1944 the Vatican submitted to the Allies an ambitious but somewhat impracticable scheme for sea transport of food supplies for starving Rome, notably flour, from north Italian ports by ships flying the Papal flag. The project became more and more ambitious and underwent kaleidoscopic variations concerning the ships to be purchased, the ports to be used for unloading and the roads over which the supplies would reach Rome. The Pope took the greatest interest in the project, but the Allies stated that it would "place severe restrictions on Allied operations in an area of military importance"; and they refused to countenance it.[52]

[51] F.O. 371/33414.
[52] F.O. 371/50084, Annual Report for 1944 from Sir D'Arcy Osborne, April 1944.

19

The Nazi Experimental Church

————

In the autumn of 1941 a curious German document came into the possession of the Allies, who used it for propaganda. On the 28th October, 1941, President Roosevelt broadcast to the American nation that it was a Nazi directive purporting to describe "the abolition of religion as we know it". It laid down thirty points for the creation of a "German National Church" which, after the German victory, would replace all traditional Churches; this Church would be based on an "entirely new religious conception related to National Socialism". A few days after the President's broadcast, a certain A. A. Berle Jnr. informed a group of Y.M.C.A. youth leaders that he too possessed this document. Neither the President nor Mr. Berle gave any precise details, but the thirty points were published by the American press and radio.

In Germany, the President's contention that the document emanated from Nazi sources was ridiculed, and Hitler himself referred to it mockingly in a speech on the 9th November, 1941 in Munich. The Vatican naturally showed considerable interest in intelligence from such an elevated source as Roosevelt, and the Germans were at some pains to dispel any credence the Papacy might lend to it. Von Bergen was instructed to inform the Secretary of State that the document in question *was* German; but that it dated from 1930 and was the handiwork of a man called Bildt of Stettin, who had been arrested in that year for disturbing a religious gathering by proclaiming these extraordinary views.[1] In 1938, added von Bergen, the Press Agency Havas had republished the document, and President Roosevelt had been naive enough to use it for propaganda.

That there was clearly some question about the authenticity of the document was indicated by its removal from the Allies' propaganda arsenal; no more was heard of it. The Vatican, too, now appeared doubtful, because the *Osservatore Romano* was on the point of publishing the document, when the editor received instructions from higher quarters to refrain. The Vatican archives possess today the proofs of an article on the "Thirty Points", with a note attached, "Not to be published."[2] It would appear therefore that Roosevelt and the State Department had been misled. And yet at about this time a document of a very similar nature, which was undoubtedly authentic, was sent by Cardinal Bertram of Breslau to the Pope. The President's information, if not accurate, was undoubtedly connected with events which were taking place. This document had been drawn up by Greiser, the Nazi Reichstathalter of the Warthegau, a part of occupied Poland, and it contained fourteen points regulating the religious situation in the *Gau*.

This again might not appear of any great importance, were it not that the Warthegau had a very special role to play in the Nazi New Order for Europe. It had been designated as the *Exerzitienplatz*, or "Experimental Ground", on which certain fundamental Nazi policies — to be applied after the German victory to the Greater Reich and its dependencies — were to be tested and tried. The map shows the remoteness of this part of Poland tucked in between Silesia and Pomerania, taking its name from Warthe, a tributary of the Oder.[3] Here, far from both the Western and the Russian spheres, the racial principles of the Nazi ideologist, Rosenberg, could be put into practice, tested, experimented upon, and modified as required, in a political vacuum. Such a method clearly

---

[1] *Actes et Documents du Saint Siège*, Vol. 3, p. 35.

[2] Ibid., p. 36.

[3] The Polish territory under German control was divided into two regions. The Polish provinces contiguous to the Reich, including the Wartegau, were simply annexed to Germany. The second region, with its capital in Warsaw, was known as the Gouvernement Général, being a kind of overflow or vague territory for Poles transported from the West, containing a "Jewish Reserve", and later the Jewish Extermination Centre.

appealed to the scientific side of the German mind — a kind of forcing ground or greenhouse for new ideological plants and hybrids which would, if all went well, later be mass-produced for the whole of Europe under the New German Order. The privileged position of Greiser, the governor or Reichstathalter, was in itself indicative; he could correspond directly with the Führer, and possessed local powers far exceeding those of other Gauleiters.

Three Catholic prelates, Canons Steuer, Paech and Father Breitinger O.F.M., wrote from Poznan to the Pope on the 28th September, 1941 that in the Wartegau "measures are being applied which conflict completely with those in the normal Reich legislation". The religious measures clearly indicated what was in the Nazi mind. It was significant that in the Wartegau the number of Catholic priests arrested and either shot or sent to concentration camps for "political offences" was considerably higher than in the rest of Poland. The *Actes et Documents du Saint Siège* state that by the end of 1941, of the 2000 priests active before the war in the area now called the Wartegau 700 were dead, and about the same number were in concentration camps.

Of the fourteen points in the document which came into the possession of Cardinal Bertram, the most important was that the Catholic Church in the Wartegau was to be deprived entirely of its juridical personality (as an institution recognised by law), being reduced to a simple association of *droit privé* known as "The National German Roman Catholic Church", which might have no relations with the outside world (i.e. with Rome). It was to have no laws, decrees or regulations of its own (Canonical); these would be stipulated by the government. An important, and very significant, point was that only adults could be members, and that their children could not form youth groups within the new Church. It could not possess property, nor could it undertake any charitable activity. Ministers of the new Church would have no special civic position, being regarded as ordinary citizens, and they would have to practise a civil occupation in addition to their priestly activities.[4] Lastly, but of equal significance for the Polish element, the minimum age for marriage was to be for men, twenty-eight; and for women, twenty-five. Greiser announced that the Wartegau was not a party to any agreement or concordat concluded with the Holy See — on the ground that the Polish Concordat could not apply here, as the Wartegau was not part of the Polish Gouvernement Général; nor, he said, did the Reich Concordat of 1933 extend to a *Gau* which had not existed as such in 1933. This

4 *Actes et Documents du Saint Siège*, Vol. 3, No. 207.

effectively precluded any visits by the Papal Nuncio in Berlin to report on conditions there. Thus, the whole area of this forcing ground or prototype State appeared to be hermetically sealed off from the outside world.[5]

It seems that these plans for the Wartegau were drawn up by the extreme anti-clerical elements in the Nazi party; and they wished to implement them immediately after the Polish campaign. But more cautious counsels prevailed. It was not until after the intoxicating victory of June 1940 in the West, that permission for full implementation was granted. Once started however, the measures went forward at such a pace that on the 2nd September, 1940 the Vicar-General of Gniezno, van Blericq, managed to convey a message to Orsenigo, the Nuncio in Berlin, asking for Papal intervention. He said that if nothing were done, within three months the Catholic Church in the Wartegau would have been completely eliminated. After consulting Rome, Orsenigo sent a letter of protest to the German Foreign Minister, Ribbentrop.[6] This was ignored, so he sent three more urgent protests. All being ignored, the Vatican then sent a series of notes to the Wilhelmstrasse protesting against the situation in the Wartegau. When no reply was received to any of these, the Vatican gradually began to realise that the affairs of the Wartegau were evidently outside the competence of the German Foreign Office (nor does the Nuncio appear to have been aware until now that they were reserved entirely to the party and its ideologists). Nevertheless, appeals from the clergy in the Wartegau continued to pour in to the Vatican through the only channel available, the Nunciature in Berlin. When Orsenigo suggested to the Vicar-General of Gniezno, van Blericq, that he should come himself to Berlin to speak to the Foreign Office or the Ministry for Ecclesiastical Affairs, van Blericq was refused permission by the German authorities to leave his diocese.[7] He was evidently already regarded as a German State Official, enjoying none of the rights of Canon Law stipulated in the German Concordat of 1933.

The demand by van Blericq for a Papal intervention in the Wartegau

---

[5] Thanks largely to the Nuncio in Berlin as intermediary, a regular courier service between the German episcopate and the Vatican was maintained until the last year of the war, enabling Pius XII to form a fairly accurate estimate of what was happening to the Church in Germany. But this concerned only the territories of the old Reich and Austria, for the bishops could obtain little information about the religious situation in the occupied territories.

[6] *Actes et Documents du Saint Siège*, Vol. 3, No. 301.

[7] Ibid., Nos. 200 and 235.

was not complied with; and on the 28th July, 1942 Father Breitinger, the (German) Apostolic Administrator of the Wartegau wrote to the Nuncio, "One now hears Polish Catholics asking if there can still be a God when such injustice is possible, or if the Pope who — they had so often been told when things went well — had their interests at heart, had forgotten them completely now that their life was so intolerable."[8] Polish children in the Wartegau were, he said, being taken from their parents and deported *en masse* to Germany; and mothers who tried to hold them back were murdered. When such crimes, which cried to Heaven for condemnation, were committed, the inexplicable silence of the Supreme Pontiff became a cause of spiritual ruin. The Apostolic Delegate foresaw that if the Allies won the war, "the Protestants of America with their money will find the field well prepared for conversions in Polish Catholic hearts oppressed by bitterness". Similar complaints reached the Vatican from M. Raczkiewicz, the President of the Polish government in exile, and from Mgr. Radonski, the Bishop of Wladislavie, also in exile. These men even went further and referred to "the Polish people deprived of everything, dying of hunger while the Pope remains silent, as if he no longer cares for his flock".[9] Cardinal Hlond, who was also in London, wrote to the Secretary of State, Maglione, in August 1941 that, from information received by the Polish government in London, the Pope was believed by the people of Poland not only to have abandoned them, but to be actively supporting the Axis Powers. He said that while the confidence of the people in their clergy (what remained of them) continually increased, their attachment to the Vatican diminished. And because the Pope did not speak up strongly enough, there was even a movement among younger Poles to break with Rome and create an autonomous Polish-Catholic Church. Even worse, with the recent signature of a pact between Russia and the Polish government in exile, the Poles believed that the Bolshevists would reconstitute a Polish State, while the Pope would continue to support the oppressive measures of Hitler and Mussolini.

To this Cardinal Maglione replied that the Pope had spoken up clearly enough in his encyclical *Summi Pontificatus* of October 1939 — but that under the German occupation this encyclical (whose dissemination in Germany, it will be remembered, had been forbidden by Heydrich of the R.S.H.A.) had not been allowed to reach the Polish people. Since then he had on three occasions expressly condemned occupying powers,[10]

[8] Ibid., No. 410.
[9] Ibid., No. 287.   [10] Presumably Germany and Russia.

warning that they would call down divine wrath on their own peoples if they continued to treat subject peoples without justice and humanity.[11] Moreover, continued Maglione, the Germans did everything in Poland to minimise the interest the Pope took in the country. The Vatican attempts, for instance, at sending help in the form of clothing, food and money to German-occupied Poland had been constantly rebuffed. All the Germans would allow were small parcels, such as olive oil for church rites, wine for Mass, books of theology and piety, raisins, jams and powdered milk for babies. The Vatican believed that this was being done deliberately to prove to the Poles that the Pope had abandoned them; for the Poles were evidently completely unaware that the Germans had prevented anything more substantial being sent from the Vatican. They were even publishing documents in Poland maintaining that the Pope supported "The New Order".

But Cardinal Maglione's strongest defence of the action — or lack of action — by the Vatican was to quote the opinion of the man who would have known more about the clerical situation in Poland than any other, Mgr. Sapieha, the Archbishop of Cracow. In February 1942, Mgr. Sapieha decided that the situation was so bad that he must describe it to the Pope. He did so in a letter which he handed to the Abbé Scavizzi, an almoner on the Italian hospital train, for delivery in Rome to the Vatican. In this he described the full horror of the Nazi oppression and the concentration camps, "deprived," he said, "of all human rights, delivered to the cruelty of men to whom any sentiment of humanity is unknown. We live in terror, continually in danger of losing everything if we attempt to escape, thrown in the camps from which few escape alive. Thousands upon thousands of our brothers are detained there without any form of trial, among them many priests both secular and regular." But no sooner had he given this letter to the Abbé Scavizzi than he thought better of it, and sent him a message before he left instructing him to destroy it immediately, "lest it should fall into the hands of the Germans, who will then shoot all the bishops and perhaps many others". The Abbé carried out these instructions, but not before reading the letter memorising as much as he could and conveying it to the Vatican on his return to Rome. This is curious behaviour in a man like Sapieha who, we have seen earlier, had a reputation of imperturbability—indicative therefore

[11] The first occasion was his Easter message of 1941; the second a message to the United States on the occasion of the Eucharistic Congress of St. Paul in Minnesota; the third at the Festival of St. Peter and St. Paul on the 29th June, 1941.

all the more of the appalling uncertainty prevailing in occupied Poland.[12]

Explaining further why the Vatican had to act with circumspection, Cardinal Maglione concluded his reply to Mgr. Radonski, "If you ask then why the documents sent by the Polish bishops have not been published in Rome, the reply is that the Pope has only followed the same course as that adopted by the Polish bishops themselves. They have stated that these documents were not published in their dioceses for fear if they were, their flock would become the victims of even worse persecutions."[13] He based this undoubtedly on another communication received at the Vatican from Archbishop Sapieha in October 1942: "We are alas unable to communicate publicly to the Faithful the contents of Your letters, because this would give rise to further persecutions. In any case, we are already suffering on account of our secret communications with the Holy See."[14]

Somewhat earlier, Mgr. Tardini had expressed much the same view:

In the present circumstances, a public condemnation by the Holy See would be exploited for political ends by one of the parties engaged in the conflict. Moreover, the German government would probably do two things. Firstly, it would increase the persecution of the Catholic Church in Poland; and secondly, it would prevent the Holy See from having any further contact with the Polish Episcopacy, so that it would not be able to carry out its charitable works which at the moment, if in a reduced form, is still possible.[15]

Nevertheless, a year later, on the 2nd June, 1943, at the Feast of Sant'Eugenio the Pope spoke up unequivocally on behalf of Poland in a speech to the Cardinals' College which was broadcast over the Vatican radio in Polish. Fifty thousand copies were also sent clandestinely for distribution in Poland and other countries inhabited by Polish exiles.

No one [said the Pope] familiar with the history of Christian Europe can ignore or forget the saints and heroes of Poland . . . nor how the

[12] Mgr. Sapieha had asked permission to resign in 1939 on account of age and ill health. But Pius XII persuaded him — in view of the uncertain and threatening international situation — to stay on in his post. Sapieha therefore remained throughout the war in Cracow, where he became the mouthpiece of the persecuted Church, bringing down on himself the wrath of the Gestapo.

[13] *Actes et Documents du Saint Siège*, Vol. 3, No. 460, 9th January, 1943.

[14] Ibid., 18th May, 1942.

[15] "Silenzi e parole di Pio XII per la Polonia durante la seconda guerre mondiale", *Civiltà Cattolica*, 5th May, 1962.

faithful people of that land have contributed throughout history to the development and conservation of Christian Europe. For this people so harshly tried, and others, who together have been forced to drink the bitter chalice of war today, may a new future dawn worthy of their legitimate aspirations and the depths of their sufferings, in a Europe based anew on Christian foundations.

The *Osservatore Romano* published this speech under the headline, "The sufferings of the Polish people on account of nationality or race. The melancholy grandeur and aspirations of the smaller nations."

Polish exiled leaders all over the world who had been complaining about the Pope's taciturnity immediately thanked him publicly. President Raczkiewicz wrote from London on the 26th July, 1943, "Deeply moved by the words Your Holiness has addressed to Poland . . . my heartfelt gratitude. The martyred Polish people will find in this declaration great comfort and encouragement to persevere." General Sikorski wrote from Beirut, "In the name of the Polish Armed Forces I wish to express to Your Holiness our profound gratitude for Your words . . . which will confirm all Poles in their resolution to continue the struggle against barbarian paganism." Most appreciative of all was the letter from Mgr. Sapieha himself, from Cracow.

We thank Your Holiness for this speech in which You spoke so warmly of our unhappy nation. Hitherto, we have had countless demonstrations of the paternal love of the Holy Father for our nation — but this tribute is of historic importance. The Polish people will never forget the noble and holy words — which will also serve as an effective counter to the poison of enemy propaganda against the Holy See. If we obtain permission to print the speech, we shall do all we can to give the words of Your Holiness the greatest possible publicity. I say this under reserve, because every printed word must obtain the permission of the Nazi Party, under pain of severe penalties.

This put an end to Polish complaints, and Cardinal Hlond wrote, "The Pope's words have placed before world opinion without ambiguity or doubt the sympathy of the Sovereign Pontiff for the cruel sufferings of the smaller nations."[16]

Regarding the Pope's personal reaction to the many criticisms about

[16] Ibid.

his "silence", Mr. Hugh Montgomery has a revealing comment when he presented his credentials at the Vatican on the 11th September, 1942.

I told His Holiness [he writes] that the Poles had hoped for some further expression of sympathy from the Holy See. At this a look of great concern came over His Holiness's face, and he said, "But I have already done so much!", and he referred particularly to his broadcast of the 13th May. He told me that this pronouncement had been suppressed in Germany — which showed that the Nazis appreciated what it meant. The Poles, he added, did not know what difficulties faced the Vatican. Other messages to them had, he said, been prevented from reaching their destination by the Germans. If he were to go into details and mention names, it would only harm the unfortunate victims.[17]

[17] F.O. 371/33414, letter from Mr. Montgomery, September 1942.

20

Pope, Bishop and Priest in the Axis States

WHEN A MODERN NATION GOES TO WAR THE WHOLE POPULATION is involved, and the Churches of that nation, one of whose principal functions is to provide spiritual help, are also totally involved. Whether the clergy of that nation consider the war just or unjust is incidental. Several million soldiers, the youth of the nation, who are not responsible for the war, are faced with the possibility of sudden death; and those who are devout demand the blessing of their spiritual pastors. It cannot be refused. When Nazi Germany went to war, many German Catholic clerics must have regarded the cause, if not as downright unjust, at least as controvertible. But this could not absolve them from their pastoral duties. To conscientious Catholic ecclesiastics the eternal welfare of individual souls is of greater moment than any political considerations; and the young men to whom they gave their blessing were about to risk their lives.

A number of books have been published since the war which, if only by implication, contend that the unjustness of the cause *did* absolve them from these duties, which they should not have undertaken. Mr. Gordon Zahn in *German Catholics and Hitler's Wars* cites the cases of many Catholic clerics in Germany who blessed the departing soldier and entreated him to do his duty for *Volk und Vaterland*. Mr. Gunther Levy in *The Catholic Church and the Third Reich* quotes the Fulda Pastoral Letter issued by all the German bishops a few days after the outbreak of war in September 1939: "In this decisive hour we exhort our Catholic soldiers to do their duty, full of the spirit of self-sacrifice. We call on all devout Catholics in civilian life to pray that God's Providence may bring the war to a victorious conclusion, with a peace beneficial for *Volk und Vaterland*."[1]

The statements and quotations of both these authors are fully authenticated, comprising a complete list of all these patriotic utterances by the German episcopate and clergy during the war. Mr. Zahn says that after his year's research in Germany after the war, he came to the conclusion from interviews with hundreds of people that "any Catholic who refused military service during the war would have received no support whatsoever from his spiritual leaders".

Undoubtedly, there were Catholic clerics like the military Bishop Rarkowski who were Nazis, demanding from Catholic soldiers unswerving loyalty to the Führer in all circumstances. Of the German dead in the short and unequal Polish campaign, Rarkowski said from the pulpit, "Their sacrifice for Germany's honour and future was not only beautiful and sublime in a human sense, but it was a holy death . . . Their sacrifice will be entered in the ledgers of God and preserved in the archives of eternity." And he described Hitler as, "the shining example of a true warrior, the first and most valiant soldier of the Greater German Reich".

One or two other German bishops, such as Bertram of Breslau, inclined to this view, even if they did not express it so flamboyantly, and sent official messages of congratulation on Hitler's birthday. (So annoyed was Mgr. Preysing, Bishop of Berlin, over this that he threatened to resign unless Bertram made it clear that the telegram of congratulation was personal and not connected with the episcopate.) Indeed by far the greatest number of Catholic prelates were, as before the war, hostile to the Nazi regime, their attitude summed up, as Ferdinand Strobel says in *Christlich Bewährung*, by the prayer, "We will fulfil our patriotic duty to Germany Beyond this, O Lord, deliver us from the Nazi regime." And the Nuncic Mgr. Orsenigo, reported in early 1940 that "a large part of the German clergy has adopted in private an attitude hostile to the war, hoping even for a German defeat".[2]

This last contention seems exaggerated. The Catholic clergy were undoubtedly patriotic, but it was a "German" and not a "Nazi

[1] *Gemeinsames Wort der deutschen Bishofe*, Martinius Blatt, No. 38, 17th September, 193
[2] *Actes et Documents du Saint Siège*, Vol. 2, p. 48.

patriotism. Bishop von Galen of Münster put it well at the beginning of the war: "We will do our duty out of love for our German Fatherland. Our soldiers will fight and die for Germany — but not for those men who bring shame upon the German name before God. Bravely we will fight against the foreign foe. But against the enemy in our midst, who strikes and tortures us, we cannot fight with weapons — only with our stubborn endurance." Von Galen was the most outspoken of the Catholic bishops, attacking many of the Nazi measures, such as euthanasia for the infirm or demented, openly from the pulpit. He denounced the "concentration camps to which Germans are sent without trial", the "public robbery of Church property", and he likened the resistance of Catholics to an anvil on which the Nazi hammer would finally break.

On the 13th July, 1941 — when the German military spring tide was in full flood — he said from the pulpit of St. Lambert's:

We must be prepared to see one convent after another requisitioned by the Gestapo; its inmates, our brothers and sisters, children of our own families and loyal compatriots, flung into the streets like harlots and outlaws, hounded out of the country like vermin . . . not one of us is safe, even if he is the most loyal and blameless citizen; not one of us can be certain that he will not one day be dragged from his home, robbed of his liberty, thrown into dungeons and concentration camps by the Gestapo. I am well aware that this can happen to me today, any day.

A week later, on the 20th July, 1941, he preached in even stronger terms from the Liebfraukirche Church in Münster. This was the famous "anvil speech" — "If you ask a blacksmith he will tell you that whatever he forges receives its shape not from the hammer but from the anvil. The anvil cannot hit back, nor does it need to; it only has to be hard, firm, resisting. If an anvil is sufficiently tough, firm and hard it will outlast and break the hammer." This superb piece of imagery was widely reported in the Allied press.

Again on the 3rd August, 1941 he castigated the euthanasia of mental patients as a violation of the Fifth Commandment. It was particularly galling for the Nazis that this sermon impressed their great war hero, the "ace" aviator, Colonel Werner Molders, so much that he wrote to his chief, Marshal Göring, asking if these accusations were true. When Hitler bestowed the diamond order of knighthood with oak-leaves and swords on Molders, the aviator brought the same question up to him. Both Hitler and Göring had to deny that the Nazis encouraged euthanasia. In reply to

Nazi complaints about these public pronouncements — of extraordinary courage in such a totalitarian State — Bormann wrote, "I agree, the death penalty would be appropriate for Galen. But in view of the war situation, it is unlikely that the Führer would consent to the carrying out of such a measure at the moment"; and Goebbels explained, "Simply to have Galen hanged would not be sufficient in this instance. If we hang him we can regard the population of Münster, and probably all Westphalia, as of no more use to us during the war. To postpone a measure however, is not to renounce it. When the war is won . . ."

Hitler also decided to take no action because he did not wish to make Catholic martyrs in war-time. There were thirty million Catholics in the Reich alone, many of them devout, many of them in his armies. In the *Tischgespräche*, he says that after the war Galen will be called to account for every word he had uttered, if he is not quick enough to find refuge in the Collegium Germanicum in Rome.[3] In Alfred Rosenberg's diaries discovered in 1948 is the laconic entry, "After the victorious conclusion of the war, Bishop von Galen to be shot."[4]

The methods for dealing with von Galen during the war were therefore laid down in a Reichskanzlei directive. "His derogatory words and actions are to be ignored. If they have to be reported in the press — then in the shortest space possible, and suitably selected. No mention is to be made of his personality. The line we must take is that the Catholic Church forms a unity, and the pronouncements of individual bishops are not recognised." In fact, after one of von Galen's sermons denouncing euthanasia, he was arrested. But so great was the public outcry that he was immediately released, and the population of Münster carried him back in triumph to his palace.

Mr. Levy has quoted from the patriotic letter of the Fulda bishops issued immediately after the outbreak of war. But by 1941, the tone of their Pastoral Letter is quite different. Signed by Cardinals Bertram, Faulhaber, Innitzer, Conrad and Sigismund and five bishops, it was read out from all the pulpits of the Reich on the 6th July, 1941. After protesting against the closing of churches, schools, monasteries and convents, it referred scathingly to "a book sold in hundreds of thousands of copies, which asks us to choose between Christ and the German people. With a flaming protest we refuse to make such a choice." This was of course Rosenberg's *Myth of the Twentieth Century*. It then implored parents to undertake the education

---

[3] *Hitlers Tischgespräche im Führerhauptquartier*, 1941–2 (Paul List Verlag, 1952) pp. 438–9.

[4] *Der Monat*, No. 10, 1949; also *Katholische Nachrichten Agentur*, No. 23, 1963.

of their children, ending with the words, "The harder it becomes regularly to celebrate God's worship in the churches, all the more must the Christian home become a small church on its own." Of this letter Heydrich of the R.S.H.A. wrote to Ribbentrop, "The Fulda bishops' message constitutes a direct attack on the German State. No reference whatsoever is made to our fight for the existence of the German people against Bolshevist Russia. Rather, the bishops exaggerate certain measures taken in the last years by the State to curb the excesses of the clergy . . . Here we see what a bitter and irreconcilable enemy we have in the Catholic Church."[5]

The authors Levy and Zahn contend that the German Catholic clergy did not condemn the Nazi atrocities sufficiently, partly out of cowardice and partly because they supported Hitler's war against Communist Russia. Like their Curial leaders in Rome, they undoubtedly hoped that Bolshevism would be destroyed; but this did not mean that they hoped Hitler would win the war. That they could not be accused of cowardice was revealed frequently enough during the war; but their courage was revealed only when their own interests and principles were under attack. In the case, for instance, of the persecution and extermination of the Jews, they made relatively few protests. Here their behaviour must be contrasted with that of the Catholic clergy in the occupied territories, France, Belgium, Holland, etc. (see below, Chapter 21). In those lands, to help the Jews became, whatever were individual feelings for or against Jewry, a patriotic act — to hide them in churches and convents, nourish them, give them money. There were, as succeeding chapters will reveal, hundreds of cases of this. But in Germany, apart from a few cases in Berlin — such as that of Mgr. Lichtenberg who condemned the persecution from his pulpit, and chose to share the fate of the Jews in a concentration camp — little concrete help was given by the Catholic clergy to the Jews. In his book, Mr. Levy quotes a group of German Catholic and Protestant theologians who investigated after the war, in 1950, and came to this conclusion, "It is true that among the German clergy there were some individual cases of those who helped the Jews, but the great majority when confronted with this unprecedented challenge were found shamefully wanting."[6]

To sum up — the anti-Nazi pronouncements of the German episcopate, by von Galen, Faulhaber, von Preysing, etc., all reveal great personal courage and protest against the restriction of the religious rights of *the*

---

[5] *A.A. Pol III Inland*, paks. 44 and 45, *Kirchliche Angelegenheiten*, pp. 0072 and 0073, letter from Heydrich, 7th October, 1941.

[6] *Thesen christlicher Lehrverkundigung im Hinblick auf umlaufender Irrtumer über das Gottesvolk des alten Bundes.*

Germans themselves. But these bishops appear not to have been aware of, or made reference to, the danger of National Socialism to humanity as a whole.

When Italy went to war in June 1940, her Catholic clergy acclaimed the declaration and blessed soldiers bound for the front, as they had in the Abyssinian war. As late as September 1942, well after the first Italian military reverses, the Archbishop of Bologna in a pastoral letter could still write, "Italian justice will triumph"; and he applauded "the heroic, self-sacrificing behaviour of our soldiers". When Russia came into the war, the Catholic paper *L'Italia* wrote, "Italians can be proud that the spiritual weapons of the Church, too, are ranged in the struggle against Bolshevism."[7] The extreme case of clerical nationalism was published in the *Regime Fascista* (15th March, 1942). The Rev. Ettore Civati, a military chaplain, wrote about the war: "England is anti-Catholic and anti-Roman, with the morals of a pirate; a country of vast possessions and rich bankers, where the poor miners are left to rot in the mines. Her army is composed of mercenaries of every colour and she has taught the Australians to pillage. England's motto is, 'First me, then my horse, then my dog, then everyone else'." Over this article, the British Minister was instructed to complain at the Vatican on the grounds of Article 43 of the Concordat by which ecclesiastics were forbidden to be members of political parties, or write in their press (i.e. the ultra-Fascist *Regime Fascista*). Mgr. Montini to whom the complaint was made was, Mr. Osborne said, "most embarrassed and duly mortified".[8] Shortly after, Civati was suspended from his sacerdotal duties by the Bishop of Como. Nevertheless, we see here once again the relative independence of the episcopate from the Vatican, particularly in time of war.

This nationalism in the early stages of the war was not confined to the Italian clergy in Italy. Reports came from many parts of the world, in particular from South America, that — in the words of Sir C. Orde from Santiago — "the loyalty of the Nuncio to Fascist Italy is stronger than his loyalty to the Pope".[9] In the Belgian Congo the Italian Apostolic Delegate, Mgr. Dellopiano, became so unpopular on account of his Axis sympathies that macaroni was thrown all over his palace steps.[10] While

[7] *A.A. Pol III Kirche Allgemein*, Heft 1, 1942–44, reports collected for R.S.H.A.

[8] F.O. 371/33414, report from Mr. Osborne.

[9] F.O. 371/25893, 25th March, 1941.

[10] F.O. 371/26328, report of 7th October, 1941. He was also said to have celebrated a special Mass when the Italians conquered Abyssinia.

from Caracas came the report that Mgr. Tosti, the acting Nuncio, was working very closely with the Axis delegation: "Indeed," wrote the British Minister, "he serves almost as an additional Italian diplomatic agent."[11] In England itself the British government had to request the recall of Mgr. Mozzoni, the Italian Secretary to the Apostolic Delegate, who was suspected of forwarding clandestine correspondence to Italy through the delegation bag to the Vatican.[12]

There were many examples of this kind after Italy entered the war — the Catholic hierarchy moved, it appeared, by a mixture of Italian patriotism and fear of Bolshevism. But by the end of 1942 signs appeared that the clergy, like the Italian people, were beginning to tire of a war which seemed to promise less and less for Italy. The Provost of Terni complained in the periodical *Regime Fascista* of "the attitude of certain Catholic priests which is now indifferent, even hostile, to the war". A priest in Brianza said from the pulpit, "We Catholics have no enemies. All men are our brothers in our universal Faith, including the English, the Americans, the French and the Russians." At this the Fascist fanatic, Farinacci, exploded, "How disgraceful that there should be such priests in Italy — while Catholics in other lands stand firmly behind their governments! In other countries Catholics are loyal Englishmen, loyal Frenchmen, loyal Canadians. In Italy however we appear to have our own brand of 'universal Catholic'."[13]

But nothing he could do or say stopped the mounting clerical opposition to the war. Don Orione of the Angelicum wrote in *Gerarchia* that Italy's ally, Germany, was no longer properly speaking a Christian nation. That he could write this in a paper whose editor was Vito Mussolini was significant. Von Bergen commented that its publication in a Mussolinian paper "shows Italian preoccupation with what is happening in Germany". He was referring as discreetly as possible to the persecution of the Jews.

"We hear," reported Heydrich's R.S.H.A. in November 1942, "that anti-German utterances by Italian priests during the Sunday sermons are becoming more frequent. Typical of these was one in Albano San Alessandro. He regretted, he said, having to give up his church bells to make armaments, and then said, 'And what is worse, the order comes not from our own Italian government, but from the

---

[11] F.O. 371/26312, despatch from Mr. Gainer, 19th June, 1941.
[12] F.O. 371/33430.
[13] *A.A. Pol III Kirche Allgemein*, Heft 1, 1942–4, reports collected for R.S.H.A.

rulers of Luther's fatherland. In Italy today are two Crosses,' he said 'that of Christ the King, and the Hakenkreuz.' "[14]

In September 1942, the *Regime Fascista* severely criticised the *Osservatore Romano* for its "politically minded Director and his four anti-Fascist colleagues. With their biased and ambiguous articles, they confuse the believer who loves our Italian Fatherland. It is regrettable that such men Italian Catholics all of them, should lend their ear to Anglo-Saxon propaganda . . ." Farinacci also referred to the "anti-Italian combination inside the Vatican, of Montini, della Torre, Gonella and the Anglo-Saxon Ambassadors". (Gonella wrote most of the articles in the *Osservatore Romano* before Italy's entry in the war.)[15] In the same paper, Farinacci wrote that, "In the Vatican today are the representatives of all the enemy nations — together with a pack of Jews and anti-Fascists of all colours, and the *Osservatore Romano* clique. How can anyone call this paper neutral? It pours out floods of ink and tears over Poles and Frenchmen — but will not spare a word for the churches bombed in Genoa by the English; nor about the sorely tried German Catholics and their churches in the Rhineland."[16]

Myron Taylor had just made his famous ride through Rome to the Vatican in a sealed car, which gave Farinacci a further opportunity for attacking the Vatican. After his visit to the Pope, Myron Taylor announced, or was said to have announced, "Only one or two more bombardments of Rome will be necessary to destroy what is left of Italian morale." Farinacci again exploded. "This Jewish messenger of Roosevelt! How could he have obtained that information? When he came through the city in a closed car, and spoke to no one! How — but through the Vatican! These defeatists! How much better it was in the last war when Benedict XV would have no diplomats from the belligerents living in the Vatican. Now, this Pope lets in all our enemies."[17]

After September 1943 and the fall of Fascism in Rome, Mussolini invoked the Concordat for continued recognition of his new Fascist State at Salò on Lake Garda. The Vatican replied that the Concordat had been made, not with the Fascist government, but with the Italian State; and that State under its legitimate Head, Victor Emmanuel III, was now at Bari.

[14] *A.A. Akten Repetorium*, p. 0026, Italy at war.

[15] F.O. 371/30174, *Regime Fascista*, 3rd June, 1941.

[16] When the Nuncio, Borgongini-Duca, protested to Count Ciano about the scurrilous attacks on the Papacy in the *Regime Fascista*, Ciano replied, "Do as I do. Don't read the *Regime Fascista*." *Actes et Documents du Saint Siège*, Vol. 5, p. 60.

[17] *A.A. Pol III Akten Repetorium*, p. 0026, reported article from *Regime Fascista*. On the 22nd October, 1942 *Osservatore Romano* denied that Mr. Taylor had made this statement.

This was a severe blow to Mussolini who had been hoping to regroup his military forces in the north. Now many of the more devout elements of the Italian army who would have joined him felt their duty lay with the Badoglio government.

Most of them could not cross the German lines and had to live in German-occupied Italy, where they were in danger of being shot as traitors. At first, a number found refuge in the Vatican. But this proved too compromising; and in February 1944, the Vatican instituted a special commission under Mgr. Moscatelli to conceal these Italian officers and men all over the city and the surrounding countryside. The work was done by five Jesuits who gave money to families who would conceal and feed them. The German R.S.H.A. knew about this, and reported that the funds came from the Vatican itself.[18] The R.S.H.A. also reported that at one point after the Italian armistice, there were as many as 180 Italian political refugees from the north who had been granted asylum in the Vatican (among them the composer Pietro Mascagni). That the Vatican was literally "Catholic" in its attitude towards the asylum it granted is revealed in the names of some of the men it protected — Togliatti, Nenni, Saragat — leading Communists and Socialists whom the Germans were pursuing. On Vatican instructions these enemies of religion were hidden in the basilica of St. John Lateran.

The Vatican's refusal to recognise Mussolini's Salò government was severely criticised by the leader of the neo-Fascist ecclesiastics in the north, the priest Don Calcagni. He and his colleagues, Don Cantelli and Don Scarpellini, even published their attacks on the Pope in the *Regime Fascista*. Don Calcagni wrote, "Let the Holy Father give a clear indication to doubting souls which road they should follow to save their country, whether they should stand by helplessly while it is destroyed." In another religious weekly, *Italia Cattolica*, with neo-Fascist tendencies, Don Calcagni wrote, "We cannot, like the Holy See, remain outside the *mêlée*; instead we Italian Catholics must do what the Pope ought to do." He further reproached the Vatican for being "pro-Jew", and for "taking more interest in the fate of New Zealanders than in that of the Italians, and for expending tears, protests and prayers for occupied Poland and Belgium, but none for downtrodden, divided Italy". He was very properly suspended *a divinis* by his bishop.[19]

Meanwhile, the neo-Fascist party in northern Italy distributed leaflets

---

[18] *A.A. Pol III Inland*, pak. 16, 1960–4, p. 17, despatch from N.S.D.A.P. Munich to S.S. Hauptsturmführer Kolrep, 22nd February, 1944.

[19] F.O. 371/44230, despatch from Mr. Osborne, 13th May, 1944.

exhorting the population "to revolt against the Church", as the cause of all their misfortunes. Posters attacked Cardinal Schuster of Milan (who in the time of the Abyssinian war had been known as the "Fascist Bishop"). The *Regime Fascista* on Good Friday 1944 wrote that the Vatican "now sides with Jews, Anglicans and Communists. When Church and State", it wrote, "lived harmoniously together in Italy, the country flourished and reached its apogee with the conquest of Abyssinia. After the Spanish war, however, things changed, and now the Church justifies all nations except Italy and Germany."[20] The paper even accused the Vatican of being responsible for the bombing of civilians.[21]

The Vatican's choice of Seredi as Prince Primate of Hungary had displeased the Nazis as early as 1927. During the Second World War his influence in Hungary, which had joined the Axis to fight Russian Communism, was considerable. His sermons and pastoral letters during the war are revealing — anti-German, yet couched in a language so elliptical that it was difficult for the Germans to make a specific objection. In his 1942 Lent Pastoral Letter he wrote, "The time has come when attempts are being made to force mankind to abandon God — in one place with the use of Neronian methods, by destruction and execution — in another, by the methods of Julian the Apostate, with silent oppression, the dispersal of the religious Orders and religious education in the schools, with the withdrawal of the conditions of existence from certain members of the community."[22] The last was a reference to the Jews, whose persecution was just beginning in Hungary. On New Year's Day 1943 in St. Stephen's Cathedral, the reference was clearer:

We Hungarians have sometimes been called a *Herrenvolk*. That is untrue, nor do we wish to be such a people. For this reason, we have always refused to recognise any other race as a *Herrenvolk*. There is no such thing on earth as a *Herrenvolk* — only those who serve God, and those who serve the Devil. No nation is inferior to another . . . Murder is murder, and he who, for political reasons, orders mass executions will not receive the rites and consolations of the Church. Nor will the

[20] F.O. 371/43944, report on occupied Italy from Resident Minister, Mr. H. Macmillan, 6th May, 1944.

[21] F.O. 371/43946, report from Mr. H. Macmillan, 25th July, 1944.

[22] *A.A. Pol III Akten Repetorium*, p. 0035, report from the German Legation, Budapest, 16th March, 1942.

Church grant the sacraments to those who, on ideological grounds, abduct human beings for forced labour.[23]

The German Foreign Office addressed a complaint to the Hungarian government, suggesting that the Prince Primate would do better in his sermons to emphasise the importance of a common front with Germany against Russian Communism. To which Horthy's government replied that, by the Constitution of Hungary, the Prince Primate was allowed complete freedom of speech.

At this time it was not known that Jews being transferred to "labour camps" in the East were in fact going to "extermination camps". But then in April 1944 an extraordinary event took place. Two Slovak Jews managed to escape from Auschwitz and reach Bratislava, where they gave an eye-witness account of the gas chambers and crematoria to the Papal representative in Slovakia.[24] Until now the Jews in Hungary had not been rounded up (largely due to the ingenious evasive methods employed by Admiral Horthy, in spite of continual pressure from the Nazis); but Vrba, one of the men, reported that the gas chambers in Auschwitz were being enlarged because, as the Nazi gaolers had boasted, "soon we shall have fat Hungarian sausages".

The Papal representative in Slovakia, Mgr. Burzio, immediately conveyed this appalling information to Rome; whereupon the Pope sent the following telegram to Admiral Horthy:

Supplications have been addressed to Us from different sources that We should exert all Our influence to shorten and mitigate the sufferings that have for so long been peacefully endured on account of their national or racial origin by a great number of unfortunate people belonging to this noble and chivalrous nation. In accordance with Our service of love, which embraces every human being, Our fatherly heart could not remain insensible to these urgent demands. For this reason We apply to your Serene Highness, appealing to your noble feelings, in the full trust that your Serene Highness will do everything in your power to save many unfortunate people from further pain and suffering.

The wording of the telegram may appear mild, even obscure, to those unacquainted with the language of diplomatic exchange. In the words of Robert A. Graham (to whom I am indebted for this account), "Some may

[23] Ibid., reported by R.S.H.A. Obersturmbannführer Mylius, 25th January, 1943.
[24] One of them, Rudolf Vrba, has related the event in his book *I Cannot Forgive*.

find significance, I know not what, in the fact that the Pope does not use the word 'Jew' in his message. Those who make complaints on this score betray their ignorance, or prejudice, or both."[25] In Budapest, Horthy and his government understood perfectly well what the Pope meant. On the 1st July, Horthy replied, "I have received the telegraphic message of Your Holiness with deepest understanding and gratitude. I beg Your Holiness to rest assured that I shall do everything in my power to enforce the claims of Christian and humane principles. May I beg that Your Holiness will not withdraw Your blessing from the Hungarian people in its hour of deepest affliction."

The Vatican had also informed other countries of the appalling information about the gas chambers received from its representative in Slovakia — thanks to which the Hungarian government was now subjected to a moral barrage of indignation from many neutral and enemy countries. Vrba attributes this to the action of the Vatican envoy in Slovakia, to whom he had told his story: "When I spoke to the Papal Nuncio in Svaty Jur [suburb of Bratislava] I had of course no idea of the international repercussions which would result from our meeting." These included telegrams to Horthy from the King of Sweden, the President of the International Red Cross; speeches on the subject by Archbishop Spellman, the Archbishop of Canterbury, Anthony Eden, Cordell Hull; intervention by the Turkish, Swiss and Spanish governments. Mr. Braham, author of *The Destruction of Hungarian Jewry* says that Horthy was prevailed upon by "international pressure including that of the Pope", to countermand the orders for Jewish deportations.[26] Mr. Anthony Eden also stated in the House of Commons in early July 1944 that the Pope had addressed a strong protest to the Hungarian government about the deportation of the Jews.

Unfortunately however when the Germans got wind of Horthy's intention of signing a separate peace with the Allies, they carried out "Operation Panzerfaust", by which a puppet regime under Szàlasi, the leader of the Arrow Cross and a loyal creature of the Third Reich, was installed. With the moderate Horthy deposed, the road was now open for the Nazis' "Jewish experts" who arrived in Budapest under Eichmann. The deportations now began in earnest.

The Pastoral Letter which involved Seredi in trouble with the Germans was undoubtedly inspired by the Pope's open telegram to him in October

[25] For a fuller account see Robert A. Graham, *Pope Pius XII and the Jews of Hungary in 1944*, the 1964 King Lecture delivered to the U.S. Catholic Historical Society.
[26] Op. cit., p. xxii.

1944 expressing sympathy with the Jews in their persecution.[27] Seredi wrote:

> The law cannot punish people who have not committed crimes, simply because other members of their race may have. Such victims of injustice have always been protected by the Church, and they always will be protected ... With infinite sorrow we learn of acts in this Christian Hungary which are in direct defiance of the laws of God ... We do not question that certain elements among our Jewry may have had a demoralising influence on Hungarian economic life, nor do we doubt that the Jewish question should be solved in a lawful, equitable manner. But we would forfeit our moral leadership and fail in our duty, if we did not demand that our countrymen should not be handled unjustly on account of their origin or religion. We therefore beseech the authorities that they, in full knowledge of their responsibility before God and History, will revoke these harmful measures.[28]

Seredi issued this Pastoral Letter when he had failed, as he said, to persuade the puppet regime to revoke the anti-Semitic laws; and he instructed the clergy to read it from the pulpit. But the regime must have had prior knowledge of its contents, for they acted promptly. Copies of the Letter which had not reached their destination, and were still in the post, were confiscated; and a government delegation including the Prime Minister suddenly descended on Seredi in his palace at Esztergom. What passed between the two sides at the meeting is not known. It can be surmised, for immediately afterwards Seredi cancelled despatch of copies of the Pastoral Letter which had not yet been sent out and he made an announcement on the radio that evening instructing the clergy who had received the Letter to regard it as purely personal, and not to read it out from the pulpit. His instructions did not reach them all, and it was read out in a number of churches.

The German documents do not say what influence was brought to bear on Seredi on this occasion. He had shown himself courageous enough in the past. At all events, if he was silenced for the moment, the Vatican was not. A public announcement to the Catholic Press Agency, Kipa, which was diffused all over the world, described the Pope's efforts on behalf of Hungarian Jewry:

[27] Ibid., p. 728.
[28] *A.A. Pol III Akten Repetorium*, p. 0031, Ungarn, 29th June, 1944.

The Holy See is deeply concerned, and will do all in its power to mitigate the pains and sufferings of those who are persecuted on account of their nationality or race. During last June [1944] the situation of Hungarian Jewry worsened, and measures even more stringent than those employed before were announced. On learning of this, the Holy See immediately employed all its influence to prevent the implementation of such inhuman decrees. Particular instructions were issued to the Hungarian episcopate to take the necessary steps. On the 25th July the Holy Father sent a personal telegram to the Regent requesting him to use all his influence to prevent further deportations. If as a result they were suspended, and the position of the Jews, until last week, somewhat improved it was in part due to this move of the Holy See. But now things had worsened again . . .

The "worsening" was Eichmann's notorious "Death March". As few trains were now available to take the Jews to the extermination camps, Eichmann and his colleagues decided to march the remaining Jews, some 20,000 from Budapest to the Theresienstadt camp for extermination. When the news of this reached Cardinal Seredi and the Papal Nuncio, Mgr. Rotta, they immediately organised relief vehicles to accompany the marching people, many of whom were old and infirm, or mothers carrying babies. The cars displayed the Papal insignia and contained food and medicine. Their commander carried with him several thousand blank Papal safe-conduct passes, signed by the Nuncio Mgr. Rotta, and a letter from him authorising the commander "to find and help on the roads and in the camps all persons of Jewish origin who enjoy the diplomatic protection of the Holy See." By distributing these passes, some 2000 Jews were rescued from the fate which overtook the remaining 18,000. During the next month the Nuncio, working with the Red Cross, distributed hundreds of these safe-conduct passes. To a Red Cross worker who objected that the issue of forged or blank documents violated the Geneva Convention, he replied, "My son, you need have no qualms of conscience, because rescuing innocent men and women is a virtue. Continue your work for the glory of God." During the last months before the end of the war, the Nuncio hid 200 Jews in his palaces and instructed all priests to do the same.

When Budapest was finally occupied by the Russian army, the Nunciature was looted. The Nuncio therefore appealed to the Russian military authorities, who immediately sent a guard. But after three days of ffective protection of the Nunciature, the guard himself looted the remises and left.[29]

The Japanese government had suggested establishing diplomatic elations with the Vatican as early as 1922, having realised during the First World War that "the Vatican is an excellent source of information". But his was prevented at the last moment by the growing power of the nationalist Shinto movement.

In July 1941, nearly six months before the Japanese attack at Pearl Harbor, Japan again suggested that diplomatic relations should be established with the Vatican. As the Shinto nationalists now ruled Japan, this suggestion must have been inspired by strategic considerations concerned with the immediate future. However, it is a precept of Vatican policy never to refuse the request of any State for representation, and negotiations were begun. They were still in progress when Japan attacked America in December 1941. Within a matter of hours, the mastery of the Pacific had changed hands; within two months Japan had over-run Malaya and the Philippines, Guam, Hong Kong, Borneo, Sumatra, Java and Singapore. Some eighteen million Catholic subjects had been added to the Empire of the Rising Sun, of which eleven million were in the Philippines, four million in Indo-China and Siam, and three million in China. The Japanese *Times*, a semi-official journal, announced that Japan would give full protection to Catholics wherever her armies had conquered, and that her relations with the Vatican must inevitably become "closer and more extensive as the constructive work in the Greater Asian Prosperity Sphere progresses".[30] Clearly for the Japanese, anxious to allay possible unrest among their new Catholic subjects, relations with the Vatican were important. They might be worth several divisions. On the 26th March, 1942, came the announcement that Japan and the Vatican had established diplomatic relations.

In normal times the Western Allies would have had no objection to this; but now, as it amounted to a recognition of the Japanese conquests, they were highly incensed. Mr. Osborne was instructed to protest:

His Holiness's acquiescence at this moment in the appointment of a Japanese Representative to the Holy See has caused a most unfavourable

[29] F.O. 371/50095, Telegram from Sir D'Arcy Osborne, 31st March, 1945.
[30] A.A. *Pol III Akten Repetorium*, p. 0027, Japan. See also the article by the Jesuit Father d'Elia in *Osservatore Romano*, 28th December, 1942.

impression on His Majesty's Government, who find it difficult to reconcile the decision with the frequent Vatican professions deploring the extension of the war. His Holiness's action is likely to be widely interpreted as condonation of Japan's treacherous and unprovoked action. His Majesty's Government are reluctantly forced to conclude that His Holiness has again deferred to pressure from the Governments of the Axis powers.[31]

To this the Secretary of State, Cardinal Maglione, replied that the question of diplomatic relations with Japan went back as far as 1922, and that it was only now that the Japanese Parliament had voted the credits. Now that Japan ruled over another eighteen million Catholics, it was all the more important to establish diplomatic relations, because greater help could thus be extended to them. If the Vatican had not responded to the Japanese initiative, the Catholic missions would have suffered. He also felt this put the Church in a better position to help Allied prisoners-of-war in Japanese hands. He denied that the Japanese representation was in any way due to Axis pressure, and asserted that the Vatican could not have rejected a proposal which offered such advantages for the spiritual interests of the Church. Vatican acceptance of the representative of any government in no way implied endorsement of that Government's policies.

The Vatican was now in full diplomatic contact with all the Axis Powers — but not with any of the Allies (Great Britain had a Minister at the Vatican, but there was no Nuncio in London; while the President's envoy was purely personal, and there was no regular diplomatic contact with Washington). The Americans also complained. In a long telegram to the Vatican, Mr. Sumner Welles asked if the Church was not aware of the atrocities committed by the Japanese against Christians and the Holy Shrines, especially in the Philippines? The news of diplomatic relations with Japan, he said, had made a most painful impression among American Catholics; while the American Protestants and Communists would find a new arm for their propaganda against the Catholic Church. He added that President Roosevelt had said, "Knowing Pius XII as I do, I find the news unbelievable."[32]

To this Cardinal Maglione replied that the decision of the Vatican was dictated entirely by the need to protect the interests of Catholics, and was not inspired by any political considerations. The Vatican could not refuse the request for diplomatic relations by any nation desiring them. Where-

[31] *Actes et Documents du Saint Siège*, Vol. 5, No. 261, 23rd February, 1942.
[32] Ibid., No. 276.

upon Mr. Tittmann, the American Chargé d'Affaires, asked Cardinal Maglione pertinently if the Vatican would accept a representative from the Soviet Union if that country proposed diplomatic relations. The Cardinal replied that religion was not persecuted in Japan as it was in Russia, and that "Anyway, those gentlemen haven't applied yet".

On the 9th May, 1942, the new Japanese Ambassador presented his letters of credence to Pius XII in the Great Throne Room of the Vatican. This caused further trouble, because the Americans objected that their man, Mr. Myron Taylor, had been received only in the *little* Throne Room. Cardinal Maglione explained that the Japanese envoy was the *official* representative of his country, and as such had been received with the protocol due to Ambassadors, whereas Mr. Taylor, being the personal representative of President Roosevelt, came into a different category.

The whole imbroglio is revealing and symbolic of Vatican diplomacy. The interest of Catholics come before all others, including the rightness or wrongness of national causes. The last word may be left to the Germans who had, for the first time, found themselves in the wings, as it were, of the war, from where they observed the whole incident with much satisfaction. "There is," reports the R.S.H.A. to Heydrich, "a very strong anti-Christian feeling among the victorious Japanese, who regard Christianity as aiming at the destruction of the old Asiatic culture. They know that Catholicism must be exterminated if a truly New Order is to arise in Asia."

The phrase "Catholicism must be exterminated if a truly New Order is to arise" should be noted. The R.S.H.A. reports in the Bonn and Koblenz archives are most revealing of the attitude adopted by the Nazi leaders towards the Catholic Church. Again and again in secret memos by Himmler and his chief lieutenant, Heydrich, we come upon the word *ausrotten* (exterminate) in connection with the Catholic Church. In a round-robin to his subordinates Heydrich writes, "We should not forget that in the long run the Pope in Rome is a greater enemy of National Socialism than Churchill or Roosevelt."[33] He warns them, however, against adopting the crude methods of openly atheistic Nazi leaders like Martin Bormann who have a simple solution for dealing with recalcitrant Bishops — shoot the lot. Because the struggle will be long, says Himmler, it will require more subtle methods.

At first sight, it may seem curious that he here echoes the words used twenty years earlier by the Soviet Foreign Minister, Chicherin, in his famous interview with Mgr. d'Herbigny (p. 135): "Rome's methods are

[33] *A.A. Pol III Informationsberichte über die politischen Kirchen.* May/June 1943.

more effective in the long run than guns or armies. The result of the struggle (with Rome), my friend, is uncertain. What *is* certain is that it will be long." Curious — because the Communist and Nazi leaders surely regarded one another as antipodes? Yet, here, as in many other instances since 1945, they clearly had much more in common than they were aware of themselves.

21

Pope, Bishop and Priest
in the Occupied States

———

WELL BEFORE THE SECOND WORLD WAR, THE OLD ANTAGONISMS
between the French Third Republic and the Vatican were diminishing.
The missionary work of the Church among the French working classes,
the social welfare activities of such men as Cardinals Verdier and Liénart,
had done much to free the Church from political and class associations. A
passive antagonism still remained, it is true, sufficient to prevent any
conciliatory legislation; but the defeat of 1940 seemed to renew the
religious spirit of the French. In the words of M. Pange, "The war has
allowed religious sentiment to manifest itself in France with a force
which would have been unthinkable to our anti-clericals thirty-five years
ago." The descendants of these anti-clericals, the governments of men
like Daladier and Reynaud, had been careful not to interfere with
the Catholic Church again. Indeed, when necessity demanded, these
Socialists and Free-thinkers even invoked its aid. In May 1940, when the
German armies were crashing through the eastern defences, they came in
a body solemnly to the Sacré Coeur to crave divine protection for the
nation. Ironically, the prayer they sent up that day, the 19th May, 1940,
was "*Venez saints de France! Chassez l'ennemi qui essaie de blesser à mort*

cette nation qui est au Christ, et qui veut rester au Christ!" M. André Demaison in the *Petit Journal* (24th December, 1940) described them as "having tried at the last hour to renew the cult of Nôtre Dame. Shamelessly, with their teeth chattering, all these Free-thinkers assembled before Sainte Geneviève." But this sudden religious fervour was of no avail. On the 18th June, the Third Republic collapsed and Marshal Pétain, a devout and, it was thought, a practising Catholic, assumed command of what remained of France.

In the first months of his rule, his government introduced a number of reforms most welcome to a Church which had suffered so greatly under the Third Republic. In the words of the *Revue des Deux Mondes* (15th September, 1940), he introduced "a political and social programme which was clearly inspired by the twentieth-century Papal encyclicals". He revoked the laws of 1904 forbidding priests from teaching in schools — an action acclaimed by Paul Claudel as "*le premier coup porte aux lois infâmes.*" Religious instruction was made compulsory in public schools; and soon thirty per cent of the younger children were attending Catholic elementary schools. The Grande Chartreuse was restored to the Carthusian Order, and certain property rights were guaranteed to monastic Orders and religious societies. Laws were passed against abortion and alcoholism; and divorce was made more difficult. He satisfied the Maurras Action Française group by outlawing the Freemasons, to whom Maurras had long attributed all French disasters. In return, the Action Française sought to rally its former Catholic support behind the Marshal. Having been violently anti-German at the time of the condemnation of the Action Française, Maurras now favoured National Socialism as a political doctrine for France. The truer a Frenchman remained to the Catholic Church, he said, the better a National Socialist he would be.

In the early days, all this could only be hailed by the French bishops and clergy. "Pétain is France and France is Pétain," said Cardinal Gerlier, the Primate of France, and added, "In one of the most tragic hours of our history, Providence has given France a leader around whom we can be proud to gather. Marshal! You gave yourself to France. And now France has replied by giving herself to you. We pray God to bless you and bestow wisdom on your Ministers." France had obtained, it seemed, in the person of the Marshal, a Catholic Head of State imbued with Catholic Conservative ideas, who would lend his ear to the spokesmen of the Church. "For the first time in half a century," wrote the *Union Catholique*, "we see a Head of State who enters the church as a believer and practising Catholic, not simply as a politician with his nose in the air who, as occasion demands, has to make an *acte de presence*."

This was not quite accurate. Pétain was not the devout and practising Catholic of his votaries' image. In 1920 he had married a divorced woman, Alphonsine Hardon, and although in 1929 he could have "regularised" the marriage in church, he did not bother to do so. (He did it after he became Head of State, secretly.) Before the war he had attended Mass only on official occasions, and he did not communicate. His general attitude towards the Catholic religion then was, to say the least of it, *insouciant*. When someone had criticised the quantity of religious services in the Catholic Church, he replied, "A good Mass never did anyone any harm. You follow it, or you don't follow it. I'd rather listen to it any day than the sermons of those Dominican youngsters." And to a group of visiting Musselman dignitaries in Vichy in 1941, he said, "The main thing is to have a religion, and a good one. It doesn't matter which." His attitude towards the Catholic Church was to a certain extent Maurrassian. It was a fine organisation. He took a number of Action Française adherents into his government.

France is a Catholic country in which the majority profess to being Catholic, paying lip service to the Faith without practising it. Most of the population recognise that in some strange way the Catholic Church is one of the pillars of French civilisation. The defeat of 1940 made many Frenchmen who had been sceptical about religion turn to it again; and the churches in the early Vichy days were full. Pétain and his followers managed somehow to convey the notion that France had sinned in the lotus years of the twenties and the thirties, and that the defeat in 1940 was condign, even divine, retribution. For this depravity they adduced a number of curious reasons — contraception and the low birth-rate, gambling, the immoral writings of Marcel Proust and André Gide, Pernod, bathing-shorts, permanent waves ... More heinous however than all these decadent habits was France's dereliction of religious practice and belief. The great General Weygand even said that France had been beaten because, "for half a century her governments had expelled religion from the schools". In the Pétain era, pilgrimages were regularly undertaken to Lourdes, Fatima, Nôtre Dame de Boulogne — "*Nôtre Dame des Douleurs, priez pour la France qui a péché.*" A popular contemporary brochure described "322 different saints to pray to, according to the nature of the request". In this atmosphere of self-castigation, the aged

Marshal's cry of *"Travail! Famille! Patrie!"* seemed to sound a new and healthier note. In a speech on the 26th August, 1940 he said, "France will again cultivate the virtues which made her great. She will reinstate the essential elements of Christian morality which form the basis of our civilisation. The spirit of enjoyment has destroyed what the spirit of sacrifices erected. I invite you to a moral rebirth."

The bishops and clergy naturally approved of this. A Marseillais prelate, Mgr. Delas, compared the seven stars which shone at the Nativity with the seven stars piqué on the Marshal's sleeve — "another brilliant constellation which also points the way ahead". The poet Valéry-Larbaud compared Pétain resurrecting France with Christ resurrecting Lazarus; and a religious post-card showed two adjacent medallions, one bearing the effigy of Christ, the other of Pétain. When Paul Claudel's play *L'Annonce faite à Marie* was performed in Vichy, the dramatist wrote an ode to the Marshal:

France, écoute ce vieil homme qui sur toi se penche et qui te parle comme un père,
Fille de Saint Louis, écoute-le et dis, 'En as-tu assez maintenant de la politique?
Ecoute cette voix raisonable sur toi qui propose et qui explique cette proposition comme de l'huile, et cette vérité comme de l'or.[1]

As Ambassador in Spain, Pétain had seen how religion could help a regime, and he took a number of clerics into his government. It was said in Vichy that he liked having bishops as much as generals at his table; and the German Ambassador in Paris, Abetz, reported that "Pétain is surrounded by too many clerics". Pétain even attempted in 1941 to entice the Archbishop of Paris, Cardinal Suhard, into his Conseil National, which would have involved the prelate in politics. Suhard admired Pétain, but he felt this would be a supererogation, and he excused himself. The most fervent Pétainiste among the French bishops was the aged Cardinal Baudrillart, the Rector of the Paris Catholic University, who had been in Spain where his eyes had been opened, he said, by the civil war. He saw a Communist behind every tree, and feared the revival of the Commune. For this reason he exhorted Frenchmen to join the Légion des Volontaires Français which was fighting beside the Germans in Russia, and which he

---

[1] This tendency to equate successful temporal rulers with sacred symbols is not without precedent in France. In the Church of St. Louis, Vichy, is a stained-glass window showing St. Louis and beside him St. Napoleon, St. Hortensia and, of all people, St. Eugenia (Napoleon III's Queen, Eugenie).

described as "the crusaders of the twentieth century". He even said he was sure the Pope would approve of them — a statement which was solemnly repudiated by the Vatican. Old and senile, he died in 1942, still nursing his illusions.[2]

Although on the broadest lines the Papacy supported Marshal Pétain, it refused to open negotiations for a concordat with him until it was certain that his government was firmly established. As the war continued and he came under increasing pressure from the Germans, the possibility of a concordat therefore diminished. The first phase of good relations between Church and State may be said to have lasted approximately until the visit of the Primate of France, Cardinal Gerlier of Lyons, to Rome in January 1941. There he must have received certain instructions from the Pope for, after his return to France, the Church's policy of accommodation with Pétain was gradually modified into what may be termed "conditional support". As Vichy's capacity to resist German demands grew weaker (notably for the return of Laval to the government), so the Church in France began to assert its independence of Vichy.

In 1940 Cardinal Gerlier had, we have seen, enthusiastically greeted the advent of the Pétain regime, and on several occasions had associated himself with Pétain's Ex-Service-Men's organisation, La Légion Française des combattants, once blessing the Légion's flag in his own cathedral of Lyons. But he had never endorsed the Montoire policy of collaboration with Germany, and had always drawn a distinction between Pétain and Laval. Now after his visit to Rome, he revealed a growing intention to keep the Church from becoming too closely associated with the regime. In the words of Jacques Rochelle, Gerlier now regarded Pétain not as France ("Pétain is France and France is Pétain"), but as "the lesser of two evils" — the greater being Laval.[3] Unlike his aged contemporary Cardinal Baudrillart, he was not deceived by the Nazi "anti-Bolshevik crusade", and refused to allow Mass to be said for the prominent French anti-Bolshevik legionary, Sabiani, who had died at the Russian front. His own Lyons diocese had always been a centre of resistance,[4] and he soon came to be regarded by the German-controlled Paris press as the leader of the French opposition to collaboration. His official title as first churchman of

---

[2] *Actes et Documents du Saint Siège*, Vol. 5, No. 160. It was considered that the absence at his funeral of any high Nazi official was a mark of Hitler's disapproval of the Vatican repudiation.

[3] *The New York Times*, 20th July, 1942.

[4] It was the home of the "Left Catholic" anti-collaboration papers, *Esprit* and *Temps Nouveau*.

France was "Primat des Gaulles", but the Paris press dubbed him "Primat des Gaullistes". He insisted on maintaining in the unoccupied zone all the Catholic Youth organisations such as the Jeunesse Ouvrière Chrétienne (Jocistes), which was banned by the Germans in occupied France. For this he was congratulated in a personal letter from the Pope.[5] His praise of the Catholic organ La Croix, for its independent attitude, made him still more obnoxious to the Germans, and his protest against the deportation of the Jews was read from all the pulpits of his diocese and soon, in spite of Laval's censorship, broadcast throughout France.

On the 10th September, 1942 Laval had stated publicly that he intended to "cleanse France of its foreign Jewry", and he ordered 20,000 Jews to be assembled for deportation in the German-occupied territory in the East, and therefore to certain extinction. The R.S.H.A. reported, "A split is occurring in France between Church and State as a result of Laval's anti-Semitic measures. The Primate of France has ordered Catholics to prevent the deportation of Jews, particularly children. The Jesuits who have hidden several hundred Jewish children have refused to give them up, and have been arrested. A number of pastoral letters, in particular those of the Archbishop of Toulouse, Saliège, express strong protests against Laval's measures."[6]

This split had been evident before in occupied France, where the Germans had suppressed all organs of Catholic Action, invaded and searched monasteries and convents, surrounded the Archevéché of Cardinal Suhard in the rue Barbet de Jouy and locked him up for three days on the ground of "Judeo-Masonic activities" — behaving, in short, as they did in their own land. The reason they gave for these perquisitions was the bishops' alleged complicity with German émigrés; but it appears to have been the Cardinal's correspondence with the Vatican which was of the greatest interest to them. In the unoccupied zone this had not happened, and the split between Church and State appeared only after the ascendancy of Laval. The French bishops, of both zones, made this protest to Vichy:

The mass arrest of the Jews last week and the ill-treatment to which they were subjected, particularly in the Paris Vélodrome d'Hiver, has deeply shocked us. There were scenes of unspeakable horror when the deported parents were separated from their children. Our Christian conscience cries out in horror. In the name of humanity and Christian

[5] Semaine Religieuse of Lyons, 27th February, 1942.
[6] A.A. Pol III, Heft 1, 1942–4.

principles we demand the inalienable rights of all individuals. From the depths of our hearts we pray Catholics to express their sympathy for the immense injury to so many Jewish mothers and children. We implore you, M. le Maréchal, to see that the laws of Justice and Right are not debased in this way.

In the unoccupied zone the Archbishop of Toulouse, Saliège, ordered an appeal to be read from the pulpits in his diocese emphasising Christian ethics: "That men, women and children can be rounded up like a herd of cattle, that members of the same family can be separated from one another and transported to unknown destinations — to live through this horror, is that what is reserved for us today? In the concentration camps of None and Recebedon disgraceful scenes have taken place. Jews are men too! Jewesses are women too! They too belong to the human race, they are our brothers and sisters. Let no Christian ever forget this!" He finished by insisting that from time immemorial the French had always respected the right of the human being whatever his race, adding, "Chivalrous and great-hearted France, Thou art not responsible for this insult to Justice." The Primate of France, Cardinal Gerlier, said that the ways of Church and State in France had now parted, and that he was ready to lead the French people through "the bitter days that lay ahead until the end of the war". The Catholic Church would no longer bless soldiers of the Légion des Volontaires Français, nor read a Mass for those who died there.

The Vatican supported these statements. On the 14th September, 1942, Mr. Osborne reported that the Pope had informed him that the Vichy Nuncio, Mgr. Valeri, had been instructed to protest against the persecution of the Jews in France. He had been told to inform Marshal Pétain that the deportations were a gross violation of the religious beliefs the Marshal had professed when he took office. The Pope himself then made a formal protest to Pétain, and suggested that all convents and monasteries should become places of asylum for Jews. Regarding the role of the French clergy, Mgr. Valeri, again acting on Vatican instructions, said the Pope's denunciation of these brutalities must be supported by the clergy, according to their Christian duty. In regard to collaboration with Germany, he said that since the German clergy, *with the approval of the Vatican*, were now in open opposition to the pagan Nazi regime, it would be unthinkable for the French clergy to advocate collaboration. The unfortunate Pétain, who had now lost control and was being bombarded on both sides for his inadequacy, could do very little. He told Mgr. Valeri that the

Germans were now accusing him of "tacking, to deceive them", whereas he was in fact, "not navigating at all, but simply floating".[7] (*Je ne navigue pas, je fais la planche*.) His Christian State was now also coming under attack from the French Catholic intellectuals. Jacques Maritain denounced it as "a clerical or decoratively Christian State masking totalitarianism". And in his book *À travers le desastre*, Maritain refers to the "political exploitation in Vichy of religious appearances".

The Vatican radio spoke against Laval's anti-Semitic measures — to which he replied that he would not tolerate interference from the Vatican.[8] To a group of foreign journalists in Vichy he said, "No one can deter me in my determination to deal with the Jewish question. The bishops may protest, but we are masters in our own house. Their domain is religion, mine is government." *Le Petit Parisien*, a paper that supported him, wrote on the 12th September, 1942, "The French clergy never tire of protesting against the deportations of the Jews; but they never protest against the English and American air attacks on the French civilian population. With their protests they are organising a conspiracy against the government."

The period of conciliation and compromise between Church and State in France was over. By supporting the Germans' racial measures against the Jews, Laval had awoken a strange form of French patriotism. It is some tribute to the humane traditions of France that the breach between Church and State in Vichy — both of which appeared to have so much to offer one another — should have occurred over the persecution of the Jews. There was to be no second Dreyfus Case in France.

In other countries occupied by Nazi Germany much the same problems arose for the Catholic Church. And the Church responded to them in the same way as in France, at first with a degree of co-operation and then, as the tenets of the Faith were increasingly flouted by the Nazis, with open opposition. In Belgium, a strong tradition of Catholic resistance to German occupation dated since the First World War, in which the Primate, Cardinal Mercier, had been a national hero. He had spoken regularly from the pulpit against the Germans, and had even at one point brought on himself the anathema of the Kaiser. On another occasion the Germans arrested and imprisoned him. His ceremonious funeral in 1927, which was attended by all the Heads of State of the ex-Entente Powers, was regarded by Germany as an unnecess-

---

[7] *Actes et Documents du Saint Siège*, Vol. 5, p. 58.   [8] Ibid.

ry demonstration of anti-German feeling long after the war was over. In the first stages of the new German occupation of 1940, such opposition appeared less likely. The Primate, Cardinal van Roey, was a more onciliatory man than Mercier. He was also on good terms with King eopold who, unlike his father King Albert, had remained in Belgium and ccepted the German occupation in 1940. Both men, King and Primate, lso condemned the Allied bombings of German installations in Belgium, nd disapproved of the "Free Belgian" government in England. Initially, 1e Catholic Church seems to have got on reasonably well with the iermans. It was significant that while the Germans immediately took over 1e Liberal and Free-thinking University of Brussels, they were careful not) interfere with the Catholic University of Louvain. The British Foreign)ffice also commented, "It is perhaps more than a mere coincidence that 1e determined men of the Belgian Parliament who came over here on the ill of France to support the British are Free-thinkers and Socialists."[9]

But it was not long before Cardinal van Roey found himself forced to ondemn certain German actions which violated the tenets of the Church. n the New Year 1942, the German Reich's Commissioner for Belgium .ecreed that, to increase war production, coal miners must work on undays and on days hitherto devoted to Church festivals. The Archbishop of Mecheln protested in a Pastoral Letter which was read from he pulpits and circulated all over the country. In his Pastoral Letter of April 1944 in connection with Pius XII's encyclical *Mystici Corporis Christi*, Cardinal van Roey denounced the Nazi racial theories now being practised in Belgium. Race and blood, he said, play a very small and unimportant part in the differences between human beings. He also protested to General Falkenhayn, the German C-in-C, that if Belgian workers continued to be deported to labour camps in Germany, the restoration of ood relations between the two countries after the war would become mpossible. To this he received the very German reply that countries vhich refused to co-operate in Germany's New Order after the war vould be erased from the map of Europe. In return Germany condemned 'the many anti-German utterances by Catholic priests in churches and chools, and the anti-German demonstrations tacitly permitted by the Church at what would appear to be normal Church festivals and 1olidays".[10] They complained that a section of the Belgian clergy had

---

[9] F.O. 371/26342, minute by Mr. Aveling, 10th February, 1941.

[10] *A.A. Pol III Akten Repetorium, Abteilung Inland*, IIg p. 0020, Belgian despatch rom Dienstelle des Auswärtigen Amts, Brussels, *Schwierikeiten mit der katholischen Kirche n Belgien*, 18th July, 1942.

refused to take part in the burial services of Rexists (Belgian Nazis), or in commemoration services for members of the Walloon and Flemish Legion killed fighting on the Russian front.

Nevertheless it appears that, in spite of the far more hostile attitude of the Third Reich towards the Church, the situation was less tense than during the First World War. The Catholic Church in Belgium had more trouble with their home-grown Fascists, the Rexists, than with the Germans. These Rexists took their name from *Christus Rex*, and purported originally to be a young Christian movement; but they were severely condemned by Cardinal van Roey for "translating what was a Catholic movement into a political party with totalitarian leanings".[11] To this, their paper *Le Pays Réel* retaliated by attacking the Church: "Certain priests are much more concerned on Sunday mornings with the proclamations of Mr. Churchill than with the gospel of the day. These unbridled sermons, these continual meddlings in politics, these insults to Hitler and Germany, this use of religious freedom for provocative ends, this atmosphere of rebellion fostered by so many priests and monks, is absolutely intolerable."

The leader of the Rexists, Degrelle, was a fanatical National Socialist and also, curiously, a member of a very devout family who was accustomed to communicating regularly at Mass. On the 25th July, 1943, he presented himself after the service at the communion rail in the church of St. Charles in Bouillon, and knelt with the other worshippers. The priest, Father Ponselet, distributed the Host to the communicants but ignored Degrelle and ostentatiously passed him by. According to the R.S.H.A. report,[12] Degrelle said loudly, "I require you to give me the sacrament"; to which the priest replied, "I refuse to do so because you are wearing that uniform". (His bishop, the Bishop of Namur, had decreed that the sacraments might not be administered to Belgians wearing the Rexist S.S. uniform.) Degrelle then stood up and ordered Father Ponselet to clear the communion table and leave the church. Ignoring these orders, the priest turned and walked back towards the sacristy, followed by Degrelle hurling insults at him. Degrelle then turned and ordered four Rexists who had been standing at the back of the church to arrest Father Ponselet. This was done and the priest was escorted to the near-by house of Degrelle's parents, where he was incarcerated in the cellar.

Meanwhile, the German authorities had learned of what had happened

---

[11] *Sunday Times*, 2nd February, 1941.

[12] *A.A. Pol III Akten Repetorium, Abteilung Inland*, IIg, p. 0020, report by R.S.H.A., 10th November, 1943.

om the enraged members of the congregation. The Germans, too, were
noyed that the whole incident should have been connected with
egrelle's S.S. uniform, and they ordered Father Ponselet to be im-
ediately released. But this did not close the incident. Two days later, on
e 27th July, 1943, Degrelle's father went as usual after the service to the
mmunion rail in the same church, St. Charles. As he knelt at the rail, he
as approached by Father Ponselet who told him quietly to leave the
urch and to return the next day at 10 a.m. to appear before a church
ibunal. This as a devout churchman he did, to be presented by Father
onselet and four other priests with a document which he was required to
gn dissociating himself entirely from his son's behaviour. If he refused to
gn, they said, he would in future be deprived of the sacraments. He
gned.

A month later, on the 22nd August, 1943, in the Cathedral of Namur,
egrelle was publicly excommunicated, the sentence being also pro-
ounced in St. Charles, Bouillon. The R.S.H.A. report states that Degrelle
ied once again to persuade the Germans to arrest Father Ponselet; but
ey refused on the ground that he, Degrelle, "had provoked the incident,
d such an arrest would further incense the population who are on the
de of Ponselet". If the incident is faithfully reported by the R.S.H.A. —
d as the report was for official consumption there is no reason to doubt
— it is an unusual example of Nazi moderation when confronted with a
solute priest.

As the war continued, the Catholic clergy of both Belgium and Holland
oke up ever more forcefully against Nazi measures, particularly against
e forced labour to which their countrymen were transported in
ermany. Although only one third of the population of Holland is
atholic, their bishops were among the most courageous in their stand.
n the 19th April, 1942, they agreed with the Dutch Protestants in a joint
eclaration to be read from all the pulpits in the country. It advised the
outh of Holland, who were being encouraged to enlist in National
ocialist labour organisations, not to do so unless financial reasons
endered it imperative, and even then only after discussing the matter with
priest. But the most downright and courageous of all their declarations
as the Utrecht Pastoral Letter of the 12th May, 1943, read from all the
atholic pulpits, in which direct mention is made of the Jewish
eportations:

Beloved Brothers in Christ! The trials to which our land is subjected
become harder to bear. For nearly three years our people have been

daily presented, by the use of every possible form of persuasion, with
conception of life which is the negation of everything that Christianit
stands for. In every domain, National Socialism seeks to extend i
influence, to assume leadership in all branches of life. Although it h
acquired a powerful position, the resolute opposition of most of ou
people remains unbroken. This is for us a great comfort, a source c
confidence in the future. If our people remain true to their Faith, to the
Father in Heaven, in spite of all oppression and promises of materi;
advantage, our people will never become National Socialists . . . [The
came the passage about the Jews.] Deportation on such a scale has neve
been seen before in the Christian era. To find a parallel we must go bac
to the Babylon captivity, when God's Chosen People were led in
exile, and when the prophet Jeremiah could do no more than lamen
"On the heights is heard a plaintive tongue, a cry of lament — Rachel i
tears for her lost children." This deportation, my Brethren, is not only
calamity, it is an injustice that cries to Heaven . . .[13]

It may seem curious that the Reich Commissioner for Holland at
tributed the attitude of the Dutch bishops largely to the example of th
German Bishop von Galen in Münster; but that city is very close to th
Dutch frontier which marches for almost all its length with Germany. H
refers in a despatch to "the stubborn opposition of the Catholic clergy i
Holland, which is undoubtedly strengthened by the attitude adopted b
certain German bishops, in particular by von Galen of Münster".[14] Vo
Galen's statement of the 13th July, 1941 about the measures taken by th
Gestapo against the Jesuits has, continues the Reich Commissioner, bee
very widely reported in a Dutch translation. He then adds that as in th
Reich itself, where the "highest authority" (Hitler?) had ordered tha
conflicts of this kind with the Church are to be avoided until after th
war, he has decreed that no further measures are to be taken which migb
unnecessarily exacerbate Catholic feeling, or complicate an already tens
situation. Once again, as in Belgium, the invisible but considerable powe
of the Vatican is clearly revealed.

[13] *Ecumenical Press and News Report*, No. 22, July 1943.
[14] *A.A. Pol III Akten Repetorium*, Niederlande, despatch entitled *"Hirtenbrief de
Niederl. Bischofe"* from Reichskommissar, 22nd September, 1941.

22

Anton Pavelitch, a Catholic Dictator

ON THE 10TH APRIL, 1941 WHEN HITLER DISMANTLED THE Yugoslav State, he enriched the European vocabulary with a new word, "Poglavnic", the Serbo-Croat for "Leader". Germany had its Führer, Italy its Duce, and the new Croatian State, modelled on Fascist lines, was to have its Poglavnic. A rabid Croatian nationalist whose real name was Anton Pavelitch, this man had been expelled from Yugoslavia in the twenties for his anti-democratic activities, and Mussolini had given him asylum in Italy. As early as 1921, he had founded the Croatian Fascist Party, the Oustachi (Upright), whose avowed aim was the overthrow of the triunate Yugoslav State which had been created in 1919 by the treaty of St. Germain. He contended that in this hybrid State his own country, Croatia, had been given a position which was much inferior to that of Serbia, seat of the monarchy, which enjoyed all the fruits of the union.

Hitler and Mussolini could only approve of such a man, who announced that he would spread Fascism not only in his own land but throughout the Balkans. In the thirties, Mussolini gave him every facility for preparing his Oustachi, in training camps at Bovino, the Aolian isles, as well as the use of Radio Bari for transmitting his propaganda across

the Adriatic. His Oustachi were fanatical racialists, as obsessed wi
exterminating Serbs as were the Nazis with exterminating Jews; but
the inter-war years their activities had to remain clandestine, extendi
no further than assassination (King Alexander in Marseilles in 193.
waiting for the great day. It came in April 1941.

Although modelled on the Führer and the Duce, the Poglavnic differ
from those Dictators in one very important respect — he was a devo
and practising Catholic. That this may have been not unconnected wi
the fact that the Croats are Catholics and the Serbs Orthodox, does n
detract from his sincere and regular devotions.[1] When he became He
of State, he immediately wrote to the Pope expressing filial loyalty -
"When Divine Providence entrusted me with the reins of governmei
my first resolve was that the Croatian people should remain faithful
their glorious past, to the Holy Apostle Peter and his successors, that o
country, penetrated with the words of the Holy Gospel, should becon
the realm of God. It is for this grandiose task that I humbly ask Yo
Holiness to grant me Your support." He surrounded himself wi
Catholic priests as counsellors, and one of them was in charge of h
children's education. He had a personal confessor and, like any Valois
Habsburg, a private chapel in his palace.

The Vatican regarded the Poglavnic and his new State with mixe
feelings. If it disapproved of the nationalism and racialism, it could on
applaud the Catholicism with which the Poglavnic infused his follower
To find the same degree of religious fanatacism, one would have to g
back to the sixteenth-century wars of religion or, perhaps more appro
priately in this case, to the auto-da-fé of the Spanish inquisition. Mor
over, the Vatican could not forget the unfavourable position which th
Catholic Church had occupied under the triunate monarchy. Few Croa
had been able to attain high position in the army, diplomatic service c
the administration, unless they changed their religion or married
woman of the Orthodox faith.[2] The Orthodox Church received a
annual state subsidy of forty-six million dinars; the Catholic Churcl
which was larger, thirty-two million. The long-drawn-out negotiatior

[1] In Yugoslavia, nationality and religion have always been closely related. A mai
when asked what is his religion, will reply with what appears to him perfect logic, "I a
a Serb."

[2] Of 127 officials in the Ministry of the Interior, 113 were Orthodox Serb; of 137 i
the Ministry of Justice, 116 were Orthodox Serb; of 117 generals in the army, 115 wei
Orthodox Serb. (Figures in 1939). Figures quoted by Rogositch in La Situation
l'Eglise Catholique en Yugoslavie.

r a concordat in the twenties had been continually bedevilled by
rthodox politicians. But under the Poglavnic's regime all this was rectified.
he activity of the Freemason Lodges was suspended. The stipends of
atholic priests were increased, as were the funds for the upkeep of
ligious buildings. One statute of the new Constitution gave particular
tisfaction to the Vatican: "The centre of gravity or base of the State, and
e moral force of our people, must be intimately related to the regularity
f its religious and family life," while the government solemnly
ondemned "Atheism, Blasphemy, Intemperance, Immorality and
fendacity". It was not surprising, therefore, that the Archbishop of
agreb, Mgr. Louis Stepinac, welcomed the new State, and gave a dinner
or the Poglavnic and the other Oustachi leaders when they returned from
aly. On the 28th April, 1941, the Archbishop published a Pastoral Letter
viting the Catholic clergy to follow the Poglavnic, and support the new
tate not only because it was Croat but "as representative of the Holy
atholic Church. It is easy here," he said, "to discern the hand of God.
Vhat has happened is an ideal long cherished and desired." He asked them
o pray for the Poglavnic, so that God might grant him the necessary
isdom to accomplish his high mission; and he ordered a *Te Deum* to be
ung in all the churches in the presence of the new authorities. In a personal
tter to the Poglavnic he wrote, "Poglavnic! We come before you as the
gitimate representative of God's Church in this independent Croatia, to
reet you with our heart's best wishes as the Head of State, assuring you of
ur loyal and sincere collaboration, in the hope that our country will now
njoy a happier future."

The Poglavnic had only been in power a month when he requested an
udience of the Holy Father. This placed the Vatican in a somewhat
mbarrassing position, because his reception would be exploited as recog-
ition by the Vatican of the new State; and, as the Secretary of State
nnounced, "The Holy See will not depart from its principle of neutrality
nd impartiality by recognition of changed frontiers and State divisions
uring hostilities; this must wait until the end of the war." On the other
and, the Poglavnic was a good Catholic and to refuse him an audience
night damage the interests of Catholics. It was finally decided that he
hould be received, but in a purely private capacity, alone and unaccom-
anied by his suite, and not as Head of State. (The same private audience
vas accorded to the Duke of Spoleto, who had been proposed by the
ascists as the future King of Croatia.) He was received on the 18th May,
941 by the Pope who told him that any question of recognising his new
tate must await the peace treaty. Naturally, the Royal Yugoslav

Government in exile complained bitterly that "Anton Pavelitch, a mercen ary for many years in the pay of foreign governments condemned to deat *in absentia* by the French courts for the murder of King Alexander i Marseilles, should be received at all at the Vatican". And Mr. Eden, th British Foreign Secretary, complained to the Apostolic Delegate, Mg Godfrey, "I am much disturbed by this reception, and cannot accept th Vatican's description of M. Pavelitch as a statesman. In my view, he is regicide. It is incredible that His Holiness should receive such a man."[3] M Osborne accordingly conveyed the complaint and was received by th Pope himself, who said that Pavelitch was a much maligned man, and ha really had nothing to do with the murder of King Alexander.

The 1941 Croatia was almost double the size of the old, containing large population of Orthodox Serbs, over two million in a population c seven million. It soon became clear what was the attitude of the Oustacl government towards these unfortunate people, ominously expressed b the Minister of Education, Budak, on the 8th June, 1941. "As for th so-called Serbs living here," he said, "they are not Serbs at all, bu creatures brought here from the East by the Turks, who used them a vassals and slaves. They have remained united only because they belong t the Orthodox Church, and for that reason alone we have been unable t assimilate them. So they had better learn now what is our rule. Either the incline before our religion, or they get out." On the 19th June, 1941 to th *Catholic Action* his words were even more ominous: "The Orthodox Serb have entered these parts as guests. It is high time they left. I know tha many of them do not wish to leave. In that case, they must accept ou religion . . . They had better learn that there are only two religions her the Catholic and the Moslem."[4]

He soon proved that these were not empty words. Reporting on th events of the next three years, the German Legation in Zagreb sent thi sinister despatch to Berlin: "At the time of the foundation of the Grea Croatian State in 1941 the country contained over two million Orthodo Serbs. As a result of measures taken during the war by the Oustachi sometimes in co-operation with Catholic priests, in particular th Franciscans, the figure has been reduced to about 300,000. To avoic persecution, the Orthodox have often transferred in droves t Catholicism."[5] These terrible words are echoed by an independent investi

---

[3] F.O. 371/30174, meeting between Mr. Eden and Mgr. Godfrey, 23rd May, 1941 Also letter from Mr. Osborne to Mr. Nicols, 13th June, 1941.

[4] Of other denominations there were half a million Musselmans, the relatively insignificant 70,000 Pravoslavs, and 45,000 Jews.   [5] *A.A.*

;ator, Carlo Falconi, who since the war has visited Communist ʏugoslavia where he has had access to contemporary Foreign Office locuments. According to him, in these three years the Oustachi carried ɔut one of the most fearful pogroms of Orthodox known to history.[6] A arge part of his book is taken up with these atrocities, often with ιair-raising details. For instance, on the 28th April, 1942 in the middle of he night, hundreds of Oustachi surrounded a number of villages inhabited ɔy Serbs, and rounded up some 250, including the Orthodox priest, Bozin, ιnd the teacher, Ivankovitch. These unfortunate people were escorted into he fields where, having been made to dig a trench, they were trussed by he Oustachi and buried alive. At Vakovar on the Danube (again according to Falconi), the Oustachi slit the throats of some 180 Serbs and threw :heir corpses into the river. At Otocac they arrested 330 Serbs, including :he Orthodox priest and ex-M.P. Dobrosavljevitch, and his son. The 330 were despatched in a ditch with hatchets and axes, the boy being hewn to pieces in front of his father, who was made to recite the Orthodox prayers during the holocaust. After this his hair and beard were pulled off and his eyes put out. He was then despatched with a hatchet. Mgr. Platov of Banja Luka, aged eighty-four, was shod with horse-shoes and then made to walk. When he fainted, his beard was pulled off and a fire was lit on his chest. The most sacrilegious spectacle of all, says Falconi, took place at Glina on the 14th May, 1941 where hundreds of Serbs were assembled in their church for what they were told would be a religious service, to celebrate the passing of the new Constitution. In the church they found everything prepared, as if for a Mass. The Oustachi leader asked who among them had a certificate of conversion to Catholicism. There were two, who were immediately permitted to leave the church. The doors were then barred and the massacre began. The church, says Falconi, was transformed into a vast slaughter-house from which no one escaped. It is understandable that an avalanche of conversions to Catholicism quickly took place.

Estimates of the slaughter in the four years of war are given by the *Encyclopedia Treccani* as 700,000, that is ten per cent of the population. The *Encyclopaedia Britannica* avoids figures, but says, "the massacre of Serbs during the Second World War was surpassed in savage violence only by the massive extermination of the Polish Jews." Later, in 1952, Edward

---

[6] Carlo Falconi, *Le Silence de Pie XII* (Editions du Rocher, 1965). The fact that Signor Falconi did not speak Serbo-Croat and that the Yugoslav Communist officials would have made their own selection of the documents he consulted invalidates some of the anti-Catholic conclusions drawn by this author.

Kardelji, the Yugoslav Foreign Minister, said before Parliament that "Oustachi bands in the Croatian State destroyed or fired 290 Orthodox churches, killed 128 Greek Orthodox priests, and hundreds of thousand of devout Orthodox, men, women and children." According to Signor Falconi, the Catholic clergy not only did not condemn these atrocitie publicly, but as in the case of Mgr. Ivan Saric of Sarajevo, wrote odes in honour of the Poglavnic, "the adored guide", and in the Catholic weekly magazine approved of "revolutionary measures in the service of Truth, Justice and Honour", declaring that "it is stupid to suppose tha the disciples of Christ should think the struggle against Evil can be conducted wearing kid gloves". Signor Falconi also asserts that Franciscan priests accompanied these murderous bands, encouraging them in their atrocities. The explanation, he says, is that the Franciscans had had for centuries a reputation in Croatia for resisting the Turks, and that "this activity was easily transferred to resisting the Orthodox". One Franciscan, Bozilar Bralo, he describes dancing round the corpses in his soutane after the massacre at Alipasin-Most. He names seven others who massacred the Orthodox and fired their houses.

Here he is supported by Brigadier Maclean who telegraphed from Belgrade in 1945, "I can bear out the fanatically pro-Oustachi attitude of the Franciscans in Bosnia. Tito recently told me that on grounds of military necessity and internal security it would be necessary for him to take drastic action against these particular Franciscans, although he was strongly opposed to any form of religious persecution."[7] Another reliable source — and this time from an ardently Catholic quarter, Captain Evelyn Waugh of the 37th Military Mission — confirms all this. "For some time," he writes, "the Croat Franciscans had caused misgivings in Rome by their independence and narrow patriotism. They were mainly recruited from the least cultured part of the population, and there is abundant evidence that several wholly unworthy men were attracted to the Franciscan Order by the security and comparative ease which it offered. Many of these youths were sent to Italy for training. Their novitiate was in the neighbourhood of Pavelitch's H.Q. at Siena where Oustachi agents made contact with them and imbued them with Pavelitchs' ideas. They in turn, on returning to their country, passed on his ideas to the pupils in their schools. Sarajevo is credibly described as having been a centre of Franciscan Oustachism." Waugh adds however that the number who took the oath (to Pavelitch) and joined the party was negligible. Of the excesses he reports, "A ruffian in Oustachi

[7] F.O. 371/48910, Brigadier Maclean to Sir O. Sargent, 9th February, 1945.

niform bearing the name of Majstorovic who was practising great uelties on the prisoners at the notorious Jasenovic concentration camp as identified as the former friar, Father Filipovic. At the same camp other priest, Father Brkljacic was serving as an Oustachi officer. Father ujanovic took office as Prefect of Gospic where he is credibly reported have taken a hand in the massacre of Orthodox peasants."[8]

The stories of the massacres of Serbs as a whole are too well authen-cated to be questioned. An Italian general, Mario Roatta, who served in roatia writes in his memoirs, *Cento Milioni di Baionette*, of "the exter-ination on a vast scale of Orthodox Serbs and Jews (there were few of ne latter), tens and thousands, including old men, women and children. ens of thousands of others were allowed to die of privation in the oncentration camps." What may be questioned is the allegation that ranciscan priests, men of God, took part in these atrocities. Clearly the resent Communist government in Yugoslavia would place every docu-nent in the hands of Signor Falconi which revealed the Catholic Church the worst possible light. But Falconi goes on to quote the most reliable urce of all, the French Cardinal Tisserant, who endorses these fearful ccusations. He quotes from an interview Cardinal Tisserant had with r. Rusinovic, the Oustachi representative in Rome during the war. ccording to the latter, Tisserant said to him:

If you knew what returning Italians tell me about Croatia, you would be appalled. According to them murder, arson, acts of banditry and pillage of the Serbs are the order of the day. I don't know how true this is, but one thing I do know is that certain Franciscans, for example Father Simic of Knin, have taken part in attacks on the Orthodox population and destroyed the Orthodox church in Banja Luka. I know from a sure source that the Franciscans have behaved outrageously in Bosnia-Herzegovina. Educated, cultivated, civilised men do not do such things — even less priests . . . I know the Italians do not love the Croats and therefore say things about you which may not be true — but the case of Simic I know well. You should punish people who are guilty of such crimes.

t should be noted that Cardinal Tisserant's conversation was with an)ustachi official, who may well have reported it *ad usum delphini*. Not ntil the Vatican releases its own documents on the subject of the

---

[8] Ibid., Captain Evelyn Waugh to Brigadier Maclean, 30th March, 1945.

Franciscans can the truth of these allegations be properly challenged substantiated.

There is plenty of evidence however in other diplomatic files, notab the German (the *Auswärtiges Amt* archives in Bonn), to form an accura assessment of the part played by the Catholic clergy and particular during this fearful period of Croatian history by Archbishop Stepina We have seen how the Archbishop welcomed the Poglavnic and tl Oustachis in 1941; and clearly a Church, one of whose avowed functio is to proselytise, would not discourage the peaceful conversion Orthodox Slavs. Moreover, Stepinac shared the Vatican's fear Communism. In a letter to the Vatican on the 18th May, 1943, l referred to "the terrible destiny which would overtake the Croati Catholics were Bolshevism to occupy the Balkan peninsula and tl Danubian basin ... The development of Catholicism here is close linked with the Croatian State [i.e. the Poglavnic's] and its health is tl health of that State."[9] In early 1942, he spent twelve days in Rome, which the Oustachi representative there Dr. Rusinovic wrote, "At tl Vatican, it appears that he spoke most favourably of the Poglavni saying he had never been surer of the destiny of the Croatian people tha at the present."

Everything, in short, would point to the Archbishop's continue support of the Poglavnic's State. Yet the German Security Departmer (R.S.H.A.) who were exceptionally well informed in a country whic the German Army was virtually occupying, evidently thought otherwis In May 1943 the R.S.H.A. representative in Zagreb, in a secret report Reichsführer Heinrich Himmler, stated:

The Croatian government recently sent Dr. Cecelja, a Catholic prie whom they regard as completely reliable, to Archbishop Stepinac act as middleman between the Church and themselves. Dr. Cecelja w instructed to inform the Archbishop that they were far from satisfie with his attitude towards the new Croatian State. Not only did l never have a good word to say for the devout Catholicism of tl Oustachi, but he was known to criticise the government in privat and now increasingly in open gatherings. To this the Archbisho replied that the Church had its own laws of God. Dr. Cecelja could te

[9] The *Osservatore Romano* of the 11th October, 1946 doubts the authenticity of th letter which was quoted by the prosecution in Archbishop Stepinac's trial at the hands the Communists after the war. The Vatican journal says no trace of it has been found the Vatican.

his government that the Church would always condemn measures which terrorised the public. The sole responsibility, said the Archbishop, for the growing and dangerous Communist partisan movement, for instance, would be laid at the door of the government who were acting too severely, even unlawfully, against Orthodox Serbs, Jews and gypsies, imitating the methods of the Germans [sic]. These people were being terrorised into taking to the woods and mountains and joining the resistance movements.

t appears that at this point Dr. Cecelja attempted to minimise the ffect of the government measures against the Serbs, whereupon the Archbishop Stepinac became "very excited", saying he refused to vithdraw one word of what he had said. On the contrary, he hreatened to use these words in the pulpit. He would not yield. The Justachi were now practising the methods of the National Socialists, o that their regime could be regarded as hostile to the Church as that f the German Nazis.[10]

Another German report, this time from the Legation in Zagreb (i.e. rom the diplomats, as distinct from Himmler's man) says much the ame. It speaks of "the personal intervention of the Archbishop in avour of the Orthodox Serbs and Jews", and of "a personal note of he 6th March, 1943 by Archbishop Stepinac to the government in which he wrote 'by these methods you are helping to create the Communist partisan movement. As a result of unlawful measures, you have caused a number of despairing people to join the partisans.' " It adds that "in a sermon on the 21st June, 1942, Archbishop Stepinac even went as far as to criticise severely the book by the Minister of Education, Milo Budak, *Revolutionary Blood*. Against 'the eulogy of Hate' the Archbishop opposed the Christian concept of brotherly love. And in another sermon on the 28th March, 1943, he condemned the Poglavnic's doctrine of a new mankind created and based on racial lines."[11] Then publicly on the 31st October, 1943 on the occasion of the Festival of Christ the King he said in a sermon, "The Catholic Church cannot admit that a race or a nation, simply because it is larger or stronger, can use violence against another which is smaller or weaker. We cannot admit that innocent people should be massacred simply because a soldier has been killed, perhaps in an ambush, even if it is claimed that he is a member of a superior race. A system which

[10] *A.A. Pol III Akten Repetorium*, p. 0027, *Beziehungen zu Kroatien*, 1942–3.
[11] Ibid. The signature is indecipherable.

consists in shooting hundreds of hostages for a crime whose author ha not been apprehended is a pagan system. It has never borne good fruits, nor will it ever do so."[12] This sermon was read out by the priests from the pulpits the following Sunday and thirty-three of them were arrested by the Germans.[13]

Another report from the same sequence of German Foreign Office documents refers to Archbishop Stepinac and the Jewish question in Croatia.[14] As there were only 75,000 Jews in the country this was, compared with the problem of the Orthodox Serbs, of less importance to the Oustachi racialists. Nevertheless in imitation of their German masters, in March 1943 they ordered all Jews to report to the police authorities for transfer to camps in Poland. Archbishop Stepinac at least must have regarded it in this light, for he immediately complained about it in an official letter to the Poglavnic, supporting this in the pulpit the following Sunday with the words, "No civil power or political system has the right to persecute a person on account of his racial origins. We Catholics protest against such measures, and we will combat them." These courageous words had their effect and, as the German reports with some irritation, a few days later the police order was rescinded. But worse than this — from a German point of view — the Archbishop had a Jew named Professor Milan Schwarz working for him. The R.S.H.A. reported from Zagreb on the 20th May, 1943 that this man "endangers the work of our mission" and that he is to be deported to Auschwitz where he will be interrogated on his relations with the Archbishop.[15] In these reports of the Archbishop's misdemeanours the German adds, this time with a note of glee, that the Archbishop also criticises their Italian allies — but for their cowardice not their atrocities. Archbishop Stepinac told Dr. Cecelja that the Italian troops were so frightened of the Yugoslav partisans that they hardly dared venture into the open. In the Archbishop's own birthplace, Hveta Jana, near Zagreb, large, well-armed Italian forces when confronted by a few hundred partisans had barricaded themselves in a well-fortified place from which, instead of sallying forth and chasing the partisans away, they had fired volley after volley of heavy artillery

[12] *Osservatore Romano*, 12th February, 1960.

[13] *A.A. Pol III Akten Repetorium*, p. 0027, *Beziehungen zu Kroatien*. According to this, the next day the London radio gave the figure as eighty-three arrested, and the day after Cairo gave it as 183.

[14] *A.A. Pol III Informationsberichte über die politischen Kirche*, May/June 1943, *Oek. pr. und Nachrichtendienst*, No. 22, 1943.

[15] *A.A. Pol III Akten Repetorium*, p. 0027, *Beziehungen zu Kroatien*, 20th May, 1943.

shells at them, missing them entirely and destroying the local Catholic church, of which he was particularly fond.[16]

Captain Evelyn Waugh says that in June 1941 Stepinac led a delegation to Pavelitch to protest against the persecution of the Jews, and that many of his clergy wore a yellow star in the streets to ridicule Pavelitch's attempt to ape the bigger Dictators. In his long report, Captain Waugh adds that in 1944 Stepinac issued a condemnation of acts of cruelty committed *by both sides*.

In short, Archbishop Stepinac had become no longer a supporter of the Oustachi regime, as he had been in 1941. How can these episcopal tergiversations be explained? Quite simply, it would appear, because he had become aware of the methods used for the conversion of the Orthodox Serbs, of what he described euphemistically in a Pastoral Letter as "exterior constraints". In this Letter he wrote, "Entry into the Catholic Church is welcomed only when the candidate has given proof of his honest and sincere desire to embrace the Faith, *convinced of its truth as well as of its necessity for saving souls* [author's italics]. Entry cannot be achieved through exterior constraints." Cardinal Stepinac was certainly no Oustachi, thanks less to lack of nationalism or patriotism with which as a Croat he was well endowed, than to his disapproval of their methods and their racialism borrowed from the Nazis. It was not long before the Poglavnic, who was determined either to convert all the Orthodox Serbs or exterminate them, began to apply in Rome for Stepinac's removal or replacement. It appears from Don Masucca, the secretary of the Papal Legate in Zagreb, that the Poglavnic requested Stepinac's replacement three times between 1943 and 1945.

That the Vatican should refuse these requests from the man who had started his career as Head of State with their almost unqualified approval is a sign that the Pope and his secretaries were also learning of the atrocities taking place in the name of proselytisation in Croatia. Signor Falconi, in his well-documented book, significantly entitled *Le Silence de Pie XII*, asks why then did not the Holy Father condemn the Oustachi for such inhumanity? The question is certainly pertinent. In this case the Vatican could hardly argue, as in the case of the atrocities committed in Poland, that it had insufficient sources of information at such a distance for confirming rumours. Croatia borders Italy by land and sea, and communications between the two countries during the war were untrammelled. The relations between the two Dictators, Mussolini and Pavelitch, were the closest, and the flow of Italian officers, officials and

[16] Ibid., R.S.H.A. report of May 1943.

army padres as well as the Vatican's own emissaries moving between the two countries, was continuous. Several of the clergy were members of the Croatian Parliament, and the Church had access to government information. The Papal Legate Marcone was always free to travel where he liked, and he must have heard of, if not seen with his own eyes, some of the atrocities.

That the Vatican knew what was happening is proved by the statements of Don Cherubin Segnic, sent to the Vatican as the Poglavnic's "Ambassador Extraordinary". In his journal he writes that when he saw Mgr. Montini (then Under-Secretary of State, today Pope Paul VI) to transmit the Poglavnic's respects, "Mgr. Montini showed exceptional interest and curiosity about events in Croatia. He listened most intently and critically. And I realised that calumnies about our State had reached the Vatican — and that I must try to dissipate them." Another Croatian representative, Dr. Rusinovic, had an interview on the 4th March, 1942 with Mgr. Montini, who now appeared really perturbed. "But what is happening in Croatia?" asked Montini. "Why is so much being said about it? Can it be possible that crimes of such a nature are being committed? Is it really true that prisoners are so maltreated? . . . You cannot imagine how many protestations we are receiving about what is happening in Croatia. About the reprisals taken by the Oustachi against innocent people." His information, Mgr. Montini said, came from reliable sources that the Poglavnic was "the instigator of a strategy of extermination". Rusinovic immediately denied all these rumours, arguing that neutral journalists had visited the concentration camps and declared that the prisoners were humanely treated, in good hygienic conditions, with adequate food etc. Montini, he says, admitted that he had listened to these rumours "with considerable reserve", and that he was glad to be able to discuss matters with a Croatian Catholic.

After the Liberation of Yugoslavia in 1945 and the expulsion of the Germans, a new problem arose for the Catholic Church, that of persecution by the triumphant Communist partisans. Their government under Tito had been officially recognised by Great Britain and America. In spite of Tito's remark to Brigadier Maclean that he was "strongly opposed as ever to any form of religious persecution", he had a good deal of difficulty in controlling the atheist extremists among his followers.

Captain Evelyn Waugh of the 37th Military Mission in Yugoslavia submitted a detailed report on the 30th March, 1945 in which he said that Catholic priests were being executed without trial as part of a deliberate

Communist policy of extermination of the Church in Yugoslavia. He quotes dozens of individual cases with names and horrifying details of the executions — and this of priests who were in no way connected with the Ustachi and who had led blameless lives during the war. The importance of Captain Waugh's evidence is that he later went to Rome where he had an audience of the Pope. He had been instructed by the F.O. that as a British officer bound by the Official Secrets Act he risked court-martial if he divulged information acquired in the course of his duties.[17] But he undoubtedly imparted the information included in his official despatch to high Catholic dignitaries, almost certainly to the Pope himself. For the memorandum which Cardinal Tisserant handed to Sir D'Arcy Osborne on the 11th May, 1945 bore unmistakeable traces of the Waugh report. In it the Vatican contended — just as Waugh had — that the British government, which had virtually "created" Tito, was under a moral obligation to prevent and condemn the enormities committed by the Tito partisans against Catholic priests in Yugoslavia. "Even," said Cardinal Tisserant to Osborne, "if certain Catholic ecclesiastics did play a political role during the war, this is not sufficient reason for slaughtering the whole lot." And he included in the memorandum most gruesome details and eye-witness accounts of the massacres, very similar to those described by Captain Waugh.

Captain Waugh appears also to have conveyed the information in his report to his Catholic friends in England, for on the 30th May, 1945 Captain McEwen M.P. got up in the House and asked the Foreign Secretary if he was aware of the "atrocities" committed by Tito's partisans against Catholic priests. On this episode Mr. G. L. M. Dermott of the Foreign Office comments, "There can be little doubt from the way in which the question in the House was framed that it arises out of Captain Evelyn Waugh's report. We have refused to accept Captain Waugh's conclusions, and H.M.'s Ambassador in Belgrade has pointed out to what extent they are biased."[18] In the House Mr. Eden replied therefore to Captain McEwen that he would not accept the implication that H.M.'s government were in any way responsible for the internal administration of Yugoslavia, which was the responsibility of the Yugoslav government alone.

[17] F.O. 371/48910. On the 24th March Sir O. Sargent forbids Captain Waugh to use it "as propaganda against the government's policy . . . Not only must it not be published, but he should be told that if he shows it to persons outside the Foreign Office he does so without our consent and at his own risk."

[18] F.O. 371/48911, 29th May, 1945.

This was virtually the end of the Waugh affair, because the British authorities declared that to indict him on a military secrets charge would draw too much attention to the alleged misdeeds of a government they wished to support. At the Foreign Office Mr. Addis comments, "Mr Waugh has obtained his information from Catholic priests in Croatia. I don't think we can accept his figures as in any way reliable. When permission to publish his report was refused Captain Waugh became petulant, and he said that if he could not do this presumably we could not prevent him from talking to his Catholic friends. Personally, I think it would be futile to try to prevent him from doing this."

The British government had been convinced that Captain Waugh's report was biased and exaggerated, through the British Ambassador in Belgrade, Mr. Stevenson, who made this damning comment on the report, "The Catholic clergy of Dubrovnik provided the source of a large part of the information contained in Captain Waugh's report. The evidence produced by them was translated for Captain Waugh by Mr Carey, the Assistant Press Secretary at this Embassy, who points out that significant passages in their evidence have been omitted [in the Waugh report]."

The whole episode is proof of the strong support given to Marshal Tito by the British Government, disinclined to hear a word against him and his Communist regime, because it was resisting Hitler. Yet events in the Communist "satellite" countries since 1945 — the arrests and persecution of priests, still not abated today — would seem to confirm that Captain Evelyn Waugh's diagnosis of Communist persecution of the Church in the new "satellite" states was broadly correct.

23

Pius XII and the Jews

JULES ISAAC IN HIS *The Teaching of Contempt: the Christian Roots of Anti-Semitism* contends that the Christian conception of the Diaspora is "sheer fiction". For over a thousand years Christians have been taught, in the words of St. Augustine, that "the Jews who rejected Him and slew Him were accordingly dispersed over the face of the whole earth". This, says Isaac, is untrue. According to him, the Diaspora began 500 years before our era, "extending over many centuries before and after the birth of Christ, but principally before". There were three Diasporas he says: the first when the Jews were expelled from the Kingdom of Judah by Nebuchadnezzar, to settle principally in Babylon and Egypt, but also in other parts of the vast Persian Empire. A second Diaspora came with the conquests of Alexander and the Hellenisation of the Orient. The third Diaspora began with the founding of the Roman Empire (Pompey took Jerusalem in 63 B.C.). There was, Mr. Isaac maintains, no definite dispersion but "a progressive impoverishment of Palestinian Judaism; it was worn away progressively like Balzac's *Peau de Chagrin*".

Nevertheless the view had been generally accepted among Christians that the Diaspora is sufficient evidence of the guilt and divine punishment of the Jews for the crime of Deicide. No theory, says Mr. Isaac, has had a more baneful effect on the Jewish minorities living in Christian countries than this contention that their race committed Deicide. "The view may no longer be accepted by the best modern biblical scholars, but it has had overwhelming acceptance throughout the Christian world down to our own times." The Gospels present the Roman, Pontius Pilate, as an honest man anxious to find Jesus innocent and save his life, who yields in spite of himself before the furious pressure of the Jews — not only of the Jewish leaders but of the people themselves intent on bringing about the crucifixion of Jesus, one of their own people. St. Mark 11:18 has "and the scribes and the chief priests heard it and sought how they might destroy him; for they feared him, because all the people was astonished at his doctrine". Mr. Isaac questions this, for the whole country was under the Romans and crucifixion was a Roman form of execution (the Jewish one was stoning, as in the case of Stephen). Isaac quotes the philosopher Philo of Alexander to show that Pontius Pilate was not the honest man of the Gospels but a bloody tyrant who would instantly execute a dissident like Jesus Christ. "Luke the Evangelist also mentions a massacre of Galileans ordered by Pilate (13:1). The Romans, not the Jews, killed Christ."

For over 1500 years the early Fathers of the Church, Tertullian, Origen, Justin Martyr, have influenced and inflamed Christian passion on this subject. Origen wrote, "and therefore the blood of Jesus falls not only on the Jews of that time, but on all generations of Jews up to the end of the world". In view of this consistent "teaching of contempt", there is no particular reason why the Catholic Church should have any sympathy, except on the purest humanitarian grounds, for the race which said, "What was good in Christ's teaching was not new, and what was new was not good", and regarded him as a second-rate prophet. The Middle Ages offer plenty of examples of rooted Catholic hatred of the Jews. As far back as the twelfth century Church councils enacted that Jews should wear the Yellow Star and that they might not mix with Christians. As late as 1555 Pope Paul IV's anti-Semitic Bull founded the ghettos in Italy, and enacted that no Jew might own a house. It forbade them to employ Christian domestic servants, and the only commerce they could practise was in the rag and bone and the scrap-iron trades and usury. They could not use the courtesy title *Signor*. "Is it so astonishing then," says Jules Isaac, "that there should emerge out of German Catholicism the cruellest, most relentless advocates of Nazi racism — a Himmler, an Eichmann, a Hitler, a Heydrich. These men have only taken and carried to its logical conclusion a tradition which, since the

Middle Ages, has been well established throughout the Christian world."

It is a long and gloomy story, and had not matters improved greatly in the last three hundred years, one might well despair of humanity. The encouraging fact however is that by the second decade of the twentieth century the curse of active anti-Semitism seemed to have been lifted from Western Europe; and the Catholic Church had completely repudiated it. It is significant that Pope Pius XI could say on the 20th September, 1938 to a group of pilgrims, "Mark well that in the Catholic Mass, Abraham is our Patriarch and forefather. Anti-Semitism is incompatible with the lofty thought which that fact expresses. It is a movement with which we Christians can have nothing to do. No, no, I say to you it is impossible for a Christian to take part in anti-Semitism. It is inadmissible. Through Christ and in Christ we are the spiritual progeny of Abraham. Spiritually, we are all Semites."[1]

Nevertheless, when considering Catholic–Jewish relations during the Second World War, it is well to remember, as Mr. Isaac says, the long and inimical past. Some people like Gunther Levy, author of *The Catholic Church and the Third Reich*, contend that this past was far from dead, and that the Catholic Church was not against "a moderate anti-Semitic policy, if kept within humane limits". Levy says that when Hitler came to power and began developing his racial theories, there was little clerical objection, provided "he did not use methods inconsistent with ethical precepts and natural rights".[2] Levy concludes, "A Church which considers that a *moderate* form of anti-Semitism is justified, and objects only to immoral extremes is surely poorly prepared to act effectively against the Nazi doctrine of Hate."

Against him — before trying to examine this matter dispassionately — we must counter another Jewish writer, Pinchas E. Lapide, who was the Israeli Consul in Italy for some years. In his book *The Last Three Popes and the Jews* he contends that "the Catholic Church saved more Jewish lives during the war than all the other Churches, religious institutions and rescue organisations put together. Its record," he says, "stands in startling contrast to the achievements of the International Red Cross and the Western Democracies . . . the Holy See, the Nuncios and the entire Catholic Church saved some 400,000 Jews from certain death." Mr. Lapide relates that when he was received after the war by John XXIII

[1] *A.A. Pol III Judenfrage — Stellungnahme des heiligen Stuhls*, despatch from von Bergen, 20th September, 1938.

[2] Archbishop Grober, "Race", *Handbuch der religiosen Gegenwartsfragen.*

and he congratulated him on what he had done for the Jews when, as Mgr. Roncalli, he was Apostolic Delegate in Turkey, "the Pope interrupted me several times to remind me that on each occasion he had acted only on the precise orders of Pius XII."[3]

From his own experience during the war, Mr. Lapide describes how when he arrived in Calabria with his Palestinian unit after the Allied invasion of 1943, he found a camp of some 500 Jewish refugees from Czechoslovakia. They told him hair-raising stories of their escape from Bratislava to the Black Sea and the Aegean, where they were recaptured by the Italians. They were about to be handed over to the Germans, and certain transport to Poland, when the Pope intervened with the Italian government. The result was that they were fed, clad and supervised by the Papal Aid organisation, which also set up a school for their children. These Jews later wrote to the Pope thanking him for saving them from "almost certain death". "Your Holiness has not only sent us large and generous gifts on the 22nd May, 1941 and the 27th May, 1943, but has also shown your lively and fatherly interest in our physical, spiritual and moral well-being. (Signed) J. Hermann. Dr. Max Percle. October 1944." Mr. Lapide says that he has seen similar letters from three other Jewish camp delegations representing 1600 people who arrived in Rome during the winter of 1944.

Another prominent writer, Mr. Maurice Edelman M.P., President of the Anglo-Jewish Association, who had a private audience with Pius XII after the war, declared to the London Council of the Association that the intervention of the Pope was responsible during the war for saving tens of thousands of Jewish lives. Then there is the expert on Vatican affairs, Mr. Bernard Wall, who in his *Report on the Vatican* tells how the Pope helped young Polish Jews to escape to the U.S.A. with Vatican credentials; and also of "an Irish Monsignore who during the war got in and out of the Vatican premises in disguise, and ran a veritable Scarlet Pimpernel organisation on behalf of the hunted and persecuted Jews in Rome". On the 22nd June, 1943, the Cardinal Secretary of State told Mr. Osborne that they had just received a telegram of the warmest thanks from a Jewish organisation in Jerusalem for their help to the Jews.[4]

In private, the Pope undoubtedly did an immense amount for the Jews. He instructed the churches, monasteries and convents to raise the limit of the number of guests normally taken in, so that as many Jews as possible

---

[3] Mr. Lapide adds that Mrs. Golda Meir (now Prime Minister of Israel) cordially thanked Pius XII "whose voice has been raised so often in favour of the Jews".

[4] F.O. 371/24363, despatch from Mr. Osborne.

could find asylum. As there were 155 of these establishments in Rome, nearly all extra-territorial property of the Vatican — access to which was therefore forbidden to the Italian police — this was a dispensation of considerable value to the Jews. During the German occupation of Rome, they sheltered some 5000 Jews, and several dozen found refuge in the Vatican itself.[5] In gratitude for this, the American Jewish Welfare Board wrote to Pope Pius XII on the 21st July, 1944, "We are deeply moved by this remarkable display of Christian love, the protection afforded to Italian Jews by the Catholic Church and the Vatican during the German occupation of Italy — particularly as the risks incurred by those who gave shelter were immense." It is therefore, I think, established beyond all doubt that the humane work of the Pope in helping suffering European Jewry during the Second World War, not only by large donations[6] but by hiding them from their persecutors, was in the finest charitable traditions of the Catholic Church. Criticism of Pius XII for his conduct during the war arises from quite different grounds.

On the 1st September, 1939, Poland was invaded, the country which had already been selected by the Nazis for their *Endlösung*, or "Final Solution" — the extermination of the Jewish race in Europe. The Nazis had good reasons for choosing Poland. The situation of the proposed death camps in the far east of this eastern country would provide excellent security. The Jewish population of Poland was the largest in Europe, about three million, and Polish anti-Semitism was almost as virulent as in Germany itself. The Poles, alone of the nations which Germany over-ran during the war and subjected to the racial laws, were relatively indifferent to the fate of their Jewish compatriots. It was not, however, till 1942 that the *Endlösung* was in full swing, in the camps of Auschwitz, Maidenek and Treblinka; and it took some months before the first information about what was happening began to filter back to

[5] For a list of monasteries, etc. which sheltered Jews see Renzo di Felice, *Storia degli Ebrei sotto il Fascismo*. The *Palestine Post* of 22nd January, 1946 reports that at Assisi in the monastery founded by St. Francis a synagogue for the concealed Jews was installed in the basement: "While Catholics worshipped overhead, they knew that underneath the Jewish victims of the Nazis were also praying."

[6] On the 26th September, 1943 the Gestapo ordered the Jewish community in Rome to produce fifty-five kilograms of gold within thirty-six hours; failing this, 300 hostages would be taken. As this amount could not be raised so quickly, the Chief Rabbi approached the Vatican, which contributed immediately fifteen kilograms towards the sum.

the West, principally through German soldiers on leave from the Russian front.* It is in connection with this that the Pope has been severely criticised. He should, his critics say, have pronounced publicly against the Nazi crime of genocide, condemning it before the whole world. His principal accuser is Mr. Gunter Levy, a German Jew who left Germany in 1939 for Palestine and, later, the U.S.A. In his scholarly and well-documented *The Catholic Church and the Third Reich*, Levy contends that by the end of 1942 the Vatican must have had "basic knowledge" of the gassings and exterminations in Eastern Poland. For this basic knowledge he lists three important sources: Dr. Joseph Müller, an officer in Canaris's *Abwehr*, who was appalled by what he learned at work, and who was "a close friend of Cardinal Faulhaber"; Dr. Hans Globke, a Catholic and senior official at the Innenministerium dealing with racial questions; and finally, the S.S. officer Gerstein, an expert on cyanide gas who joined the S.S. deliberately, knowing he would be sent to Auschwitz where he could find out the truth about the rumours brought home by the soldiers. Information from all these quarters, says Levy, must somehow have filtered back to Rome by the end of 1942. Moreover in November 1942 Mr. Myron Taylor was informed at the Vatican that, while they were without specific proof, they believed that the stories about the massacre of Jews in Eastern Europe to be "largely if not completely true".[7] Why then did not Pius XII, custodian of the world's ethical and moral values, publicly castigate "the greatest crime in history"? Why, others have asked, did he not excommunicate Hitler? The principal reason for taking either of these steps would have been, of course, to force the Nazi leaders, under pressure of Catholic opinion in Germany and the world, to abandon, or at least relax, the persecution of the Jews.

Excommunication, history has shown, is a Papal weapon which has to be used with considerable care. On certain occasions it has been effective, and it brought Henry IV to Canossa. But that was in the Age of Faith. Its effect on Elizabeth I of England was disastrous for the Catholic Church. It brought about the final secession of the Anglican Church, the execution of hundreds of English Catholics, and the English heretics' domination of the world's sea routes, hitherto controlled by the Catholic Powers. Moreover, most English Catholics remained loyal to their temporal ruler. It was equally ineffective against Napoleon, who had brought the Pope to France, where the humiliated Pontiff was made to witness his self-coronation. Nor did the excommuni-

---

*The information was conveyed to the British government by the Polish government in London.

[7] F.O. 371/30922, despatch from Lord Halifax, 19th November, 1942.

cation have any effect on Napoleon's *Grande Armée* whose soldiers cheerfully accompanied their Emperor to Jena, Wagram, Friedland . . .

Its effect on Hitler was predictable by anyone who had close contact with him in his private life. In the *Lagebesprechungen* is an entry for the 9th September, 1943 when the German troops occupied Rome, and there was question of what to do with the Allied diplomats who had taken refuge in the Vatican — "That doesn't matter. I'll go into the Vatican when I like. Do you think the Vatican worries me? We'll grab it. Yes, the whole diplomatic bunch is there. I couldn't care less. That bunch in there, we'll drag them out, the whole swinish pack of them. What does it matter? We can apologise afterwards, that's nothing to worry about . . ."[8] And in the *Table Talk* he says, "After the war we'll have no more attempts by the Church interfering in matters of State . . . After the war, there'll be no more Concordats. The time is coming when I'll settle my account with the Pope."

An interview the Nuncio, Mgr. Orsenigo, had about this time with Hitler to bring up the Jewish question is further proof that the Führer, never a shining example of self-control, was now subject to fits of frenzy and brain-storms:

As instructed I went to Berchtesgaden, and was received by Hitler [writes Orsenigo]. The moment I raised the question of the Jews, the correct atmosphere of the exchange of views became quite different. Hitler jumped up and went to the window, where he began drumming on the pane with his finger-tips. You can imagine how uncomfortable was my position — having to continue the discussion with his back! Nevertheless, I went on until I had had my say. Whereupon Hitler turned on me as abruptly as he had swung away, and marched to a table on which was a glass of water. He picked it up, and with a motion of disdain flung it to the ground. Confronted with this brand of diplomatic intercourse, I considered my mission as over.[9]

We now know that Hitler planned at one point to kidnap the Pope and imprison him in the Wartberg in Upper Saxony.[10] "For some days,"

[8] Helmut Heiber, ed., *Hitlers Lagebesprechungen* (Deutsche Verlag-Austalt, Stuttgart, 1962), p. 329. This is also confirmed by Alan Bullock in his *Hitler — A Study in Tyranny.*

[9] Declaration by Mgr. Orsenigo to Professor Eduardo Senatra a few days after the interview with Hitler. Reported in *Petrus Blatt*, the Berlin diocesan paper, 7th April, 1963, and quoted from the *Documentation Catholique* of the 18th August, 1963.

[10] *Oggi*, 19th September, 1963; also, more reliable, the German diplomat, von Kessel, "Der Papst und die Juden", *Die Welt*, 6th April, 1962.

says Alan Bullock in his *Hitler — A Study in Tyranny*, "he played with the idea of an immediate coup against the Vatican." Albert von Kessel, the German Botschaftsrat at the Quirinal goes further.

Between September 1943 and June 1944 he considered kidnapping the Pope and taking him to Germany. We had definite information that had the Pope resisted, he would have been shot while trying to escape. Our Ambassador at the Vatican, von Weizsäcker, had to do battle on two fronts. On the one hand, he had to persuade the Pope not to say anything too extreme, which might have fatal consequences. At the same time, he had to convince Hitler, by ingeniously phrased despatches, that the Pope was not too ill-disposed towards Germany, and that Catholic gestures in favour of the Jews were insignificant, and not to be taken seriously. [Von Kessel finishes] We knew that a violent protest by the Pope against the persecution of the Jews would have certainly put the Pope in great personal danger, and it would not have saved the life of a single Jew. Like a trapped beast, Hitler would have reacted to any provocation with extreme violence. Hitler, kept at bay by the Allies, and their Unconditional Surrender demand, was like a beast of prey pursued by hunters, capable of any hysterical excess or crime.[11]

It is enough to cite the fearful case of the Fosse Ardeatine. Because some German soldiers were killed by a street bomb in Rome in 1944, Hitler ordered all the houses in the area to be flattened, and every human being, men, women and children, living there to be shot. Some 350 perished.

What effect would excommunication then have had on such a man in 1943? The lessons learnt from other upstart modern Dictators indicate that Hitler would not have behaved as Henry IV did at Canossa.

Some time before this the Church had had a sharp lesson of what Hitler could do if the Church made an *ex cathedra* condemnation of Nazi activities. In Holland were a large number of baptised Jews, a greater percentage than anywhere else in Europe. Whereas by the end of 1942, all the other Dutch Jews were being rounded up and shipped off to Poland, these baptised Jews had not been touched by the Nazi occupying

[11] Cf. above Chapter Nine, "The German Concordat". When negotiating the German Concordat Cardinal Pacelli wanted a clause protecting baptised Jews inserted but the Nazi government would give no more than a verbal promise that they would regard baptised Jews as Christians.

forces, presumably because they were, nominally, Christian.[12] In July 1942, the Catholic Church together with the Reformed Church of Holland protested in a telegram to the German Reichskommissar against the deportation of Dutch Jews, and threatened to make the protest public if the deportations were not discontinued. The German authorities replied that if the Churches would remain silent in this matter, they would continue to make a special exception of the baptised Jews, who would continue to be regarded as Christians. The Reformed Church agreed to this and let the matter drop. But the Catholic Archbishop of Utrecht refused and issued a Pastoral Letter sharply condemning the Nazi persecution of the Jews. Whereupon the Germans arrested all the baptised Catholic Jews and deported them to the death camps in the East.[13] (Among them the philosopher Edith Stein who died there in a gas chamber.) The baptised Protestant Jews on the other hand were not touched.

The Pope himself clearly realised the futility of excommunication. Don Pizzo Scavizzi reports him as saying at the time, "I have often considered excommunication, to castigate in the eyes of the entire world the fearful crime of genocide. But after much praying and many tears, I realise that my condemnation would not only fail to help the Jews, it might even worsen their situation ... No doubt a protest would have gained me the praise and respect of the civilised world, but it would have submitted the poor Jews to an even worse persecution."[14] The praise and respect of the civilised world? The acclaim of decent men like Levy, Friedlander and Hochhuth? But would his action have been effective?

This leads to the more difficult question of why Pius XII did not speak out publicly, branding the Nazis for the fearful happenings in Eastern Europe.[15] Those who criticise him contend that a Papal condemnation of Germany referring specifically to the "Extermination of the Jews", announced over the Vatican radio, and repeated in a thousand pulpits throughout the world, would have had a far greater effect than the

[12] A.A. Büro des Staatssekretärs, 1942.
[13] Max Beloff, ed., On the Track of Tyranny (London, 1960), chapter entitled "Jews and Non-Jews in Nazi-occupied Holland". Also Gunter Levy, Die katholische Kirche und das dritte Reich (Piper, 1965), p. 333.
[14] La Parrochia, April 1964.
[15] In January 1942 at the Wannsee Conference in Berlin, the Nazis decided on the Endlösung or "Final Solution" of the Jewish problem, namely the extermination of all Jews in the territories under their control. This, it was estimated, would involve the destruction of some eleven million human beings.

repeated descriptions by the Allies of the *Endlösung* which were regarded in many neutral, and even Allied, countries as propaganda. Moreover contend these critics, many Jews who had been reassured by the German authorities that they were merely being transported elsewhere for work would have known the truth, and instead of presenting themselve meekly for the journey to the unknown destination, would have gon into hiding.

In the summer of 1942, Mr. Myron Taylor handed Cardinal Maglion a memorandum from the Jewish representative in Palestine, containing precise information about the mass extermination in occupied Poland and the deportations to death camps from Germany, Belgium, Holland France, Slovakia, etc. Taylor asked "whether the Holy Father had any suggestions to make how the power of civilised public opinion could b practically used to prevent this barbarous behaviour".[16] On the 10th October, 1942, the Vatican replied that it could not at the moment b sure that the reports about these extreme measures taken by the German against the Jews in Poland "correspond to the truth".[17]

This seems very difficult to countenance. Admittedly, in the First World War, the Allies had shown themselves masters of propaganda besmirching the Germans with such success (German soldiers cutting of the hands and arms of Belgian girls, etc.), that many people, even in England, thought the Ministry of Information (as our propaganda ma-chine was euphemistically called in the Second World War) was over-playing its hand with its tales of Jewish extermination. Such things could not happen in the twentieth century. The Germans were a civilised people, even if they were temporarily ruled by gangsters.

Nevertheless, even if the Vatican refused to accept wholly the reports of foreign powers about the extermination camps, on the ground that they contained a large element of propaganda, it had surely reliable sources of information of its own. The French Catholic clergy, for instance, spoke up loudly against the persecution of the Jews, and their protestation reached the ears of the Vatican. When the Jews were being rounded up under the second Laval Ministry, the French bishops, we have seen, made a formal protest to the government of Vichy. Nor could the protest of the Archbishop of Westminster, Cardinal Hinsley, have been lost on the Vatican. On the 8th July, 1942 he spoke on the B.B.C. of the crimes committed by the Germans in Poland, of "700,000 Jews massacred since the beginning of the war. Their innocent blood cries out

[16] U.S. Diplomatic Papers, 1942, III, p. 776.
[17] Ibid., Tittmann's account of the reply by the Vatican.

to the heavens for vengeance. And we have plenty of evidence, including copies of German documents describing the extermination."[18]

In his *private* messages to Heads of States in connection with the persecution of the Jews, Pius XII certainly "spoke up". What could be more forthright than his message to the Slovak government on the 7th April, 1943?

> The Holy See has always entertained the firm hope that the Slovak government, interpreting also the sentiments of its own people, Catholic almost entirely, would never proceed with the forcible removal of persons belonging to the Jewish race. It is therefore with great pain that the Holy See has learned of the continued transfers of such a nature from the territory of the Republic. This pain is aggravated further now that it appears, from various reports, that the Slovak government intends to proceed with the total removal of the Jewish residents of Slovakia, not even sparing women and children. The Holy See would fail in its Divine Mandate if it did not deplore these measures, which gravely damage man in his natural right, merely for the reason that these people belong to a certain race. The pain of the Holy See is even more acute, considering that such measures are carried out among a people of great Catholic traditions, by a government which declares it is their follower and custodian.

A year later at the height of the Hungarian–Jewish deportations the Pope cabled to Admiral Horthy, as we have seen (25th June, 1944), "to use all possible influence to cease the pains and torments which innumerable persons must undergo for the sole reason of their nationality or their race".

But this still does not answer the question of why the Pope did not condemn *ex cathedra* the author or fount of the Jewish atrocities, Adolf Hitler in person, without whom Laval, Salazci, Farinacci and the smaller anti-Semite fry would have been powerless. The answer is given by Mr. Tittmann, the American Chargé d'Affaires at the Vatican, who reported to the State Department in September 1942 that he had learned from Vatican officials that the Pope would not condemn the *Endlösung* openly, because he did not·wish to make the situation of Catholics worse in Germany and the occupied territories.

Moreover, reported Tittmann, the Pope had said he could not condemn the Nazis *by name* unless he also condemned the atrocities committed by

[18] J. Nobécourt, *Le Vicaire et l'Histoire.*

the Russians — and this, His Holiness presumed, would be displeasing to Russia's Western Allies. Before condemning he would also have to send his own investigation team on the spot to confirm what was alleged by one or other of the belligerents — and this in war-time would be impossible.[19]

One particular letter to a German bishop by the Pope reveals both that the Pope was well aware of the Jewish deportations, and why at the same time he would not condemn the Nazis specifically. It is dated 30th April, 1943 to Bishop von Preysing of Berlin, the German bishop closest to the Pope, with whom he had formed a friendship when, as Mgr. Pacelli, he was Nuncio in Berlin in the late twenties. It is probably the most important of the ninety-three Papal communications to German bishops in the Second World War.

"It was for us," he wrote,[20] "a great consolation to learn that Catholics, in particular those of your Berlin diocese, have shown such charity towards the sufferings of the Jews. We express our paternal gratitude and profound sympathy for Mgr. Lichtenberg who asked to share the lot of the Jews in the concentration camps, and who spoke up against their persecution in the pulpit."[21] The Pope then made a significant point:

As far as episcopal declarations are concerned, We leave to local bishops the responsibility of deciding what to publish from Our communications. The danger of reprisals and pressures — as well perhaps of other measures due to the length and psychology of the war — counsel reserve. In spite of good reasons for Our open intervention, there are others equally good for avoiding greater evils by not interfering. Our experience in 1942, when We allowed the free publication of certain Pontifical documents addressed to the Faithful justifies this attitude.[22]

In Our Christmas message, We said a word concerning the Jews in the territories under German control. The reference was short, but it was well understood. It is superfluous to say that Our love and paternal

---

[19] U.S. State Department, F.R.U.S., Diplomatic papers 11912 and 740, 00116. European War, 1939. Quoted by G. O. Kent, "Pius XII and Germany", *American Historical Review*, No. 70 (1964).

[20] *Actes et Documents du Saint Siège*, Vol. 2, No. 105. Also quoted in P. Rassinier, *L'Operation "Vicaire"* (Table Ronde, 1965).

[21] Mgr. Lichtenberg was sentenced to two years' imprisonment for this and he died in Dachau.

[22] The Dutch bishops' declaration on behalf of the Jews, already referred to, which resulted in the baptised Jews being sent to Auschwitz.

solicitude for all non-Aryan Catholics, children of the Church like all others, are greater today when their exterior existence is collapsing, and they know such moral distress. Unhappily in the present state of affairs, We can bring them no help other than Our prayers.

"No other help than Our prayers." In the opening pages of this book a reference was made to the very successful play by the German dramatist, Rolf Hochhuth, *The Representative*, in which this passive attitude of the Pope is condemned. The play has been translated into some twenty languages, and staged in most countries of the civilised world. Its blank verse has been compared with that of Schiller's *Don Carlos*, and millions of people have been influenced by it. Their opinion of Pius XII is that of Herr Hochhuth. So many books have been written about it, for and against Herr Hochhuth's thesis, that further comment here may seem superfluous. The sole reason for adding to the discussion is that the material treated here — the German and British Foreign Office archives, which are essential for any historical research on the period — have not been consulted by Herr Hochhuth.

Not only has Papal diplomacy between 1922 and 1945 been examined here through these sources, but also the character and personality of Eugenio Pacelli. For the first, the essential humanitarian character of Vatican policy at all times has been clearly demonstrated. For the second, the reader may well ask himself in the light of these documents if Pius XII could have behaved as he did when he first appears in the fourth act of Herr Hochhuth's play. He comes on to the stage talking excitedly about the stocks and shares in which the Vatican has invested, and which are being affected adversely by the Allied bombing of Italy. He is filled he says *"mit brennender Sorge"* (the choice of the phrase appears deliberate) about the bombing of "Our factories", and adds that the Germans have been "more friendly than the destroyers of San Lorenzo" [the Allies]. He also talks of selling some of the Vatican stocks and shares to "influential men around Roosevelt", because this may limit the bombing of Rome. When Gerstein's emissary erupts into the room, and informs him of the extermination camps in Poland, the Pope shows no interest whatsoever — and this at the very moment when in the Trastevere, under the Pope's own window as it were, the S.S. is rounding up the Jews of Rome for shipment to Poland. About his indifference to the fate of the Jews, Hochhuth concludes in an article about his play, "Perhaps never before in history have so many people paid with their lives for the passivity of one single politician."

The play is based primarily on information provided by a historical character, Kurt Gerstein who, being a chemist familiar with cyanide gas deliberately insinuates himself into the S.S. in order to work in Auschwitz and see with his own eyes if the fearful tales he has heard of the gassing are true. Having seen that they are, he attempts to transmit them through the Nuncio in Berlin, Mgr. Orsenigo, to the Pope. In the play, Herr Hochhuth puts this reply to Gerstein's revelations into the mouth of Mgr. Orsenigo, "But mein Herr, anything I learn here of this kind is in a private capacity. I am not allowed to take this into account. When I came here in 1939, I was instructed in my official capacity to avoid most carefully anything which might cause conflict of any kind between the Holy See and the German government. I should not even be talking to you. Please, you must go! God bless you, and God help those to whom you refer. I will pray for these victims."[23]

We have seen from the German documents that Mgr. Orsenigo, when Germany was triumphing in France in 1940, appeared markedly pro-German ("I hope your armies enter Paris through Versailles", etc.), and he was certainly instructed by Pius XII when he took up his post in 1939 to avoid any friction with the National Socialist State. It is reasonable therefore to suppose that he might have made some such reply to Gerstein. But that is not the point. If he saw Gerstein at all it was only fleetingly. The long interview depicted in Herr Hochhuth's play never took place. When Gerstein was in French captivity after the war, he stated that he had tried to see the Nuncio in Berlin in 1943. In his own words, "I attempted to report these things to the Nuncio in Berlin. There I was asked if I was a soldier. When I said I was not, then all further conversation was refused and I was asked to leave."[24]

Clearly, the Nuncio's staff were most suspicious of a man in S.S. uniform offering evidence about S.S. atrocities. They asked him if he was a soldier because, had he been one, he might conceivably have been involved in the Army plot against Hitler. When he said he was not, they must have supposed that the S.S. was trying to involve the Nuncio in a plot against the regime. Gerstein then adds, "I reported all I had seen in the camps to hundreds of persons, among them the Sindicus [Corporation lawyer] of the Catholic bishop, Dr. Winter, with the request that it should be passed on to the Vatican." As the whole play is based upon Gerstein and the long interview with Mgr. Orsenigo in Berlin, it is clear that Herr Hochhuth has allowed his imagination very

[23] Act 1, scene 1, p. 26 in the Rowohlt edition.
[24] *Vierteljahrshefte für Zeitgeschichte*, I, Jahrgang, 1953, p. 192.

ree play. As for the Pope himself, this portrait of a callous, money-
ninded, cynical and selfish man is contradicted by everything in the
German and British Foreign Office documents.

Some months after the play was first staged in Germany, the Society
or Jewish–Christian collaboration protested to the German Chancellor,
Adenauer, against its continuation, describing it as "historically erron-
ous". The German Protestant Church, too, in the person of the
Archbishop of Berlin, Dr. Dibelius, stated that the play did "a disservice
o Germany and the world", because of its baseless calumniation. He
onsidered that in the matter of the Jews, Pius XII had acted with
"mature consideration", following the dictates of his conscience, at-
empting above all to help *single* individuals — because to rescue groups
luring the war was impossible. Dr. Dibelius added that in an interview
e had with Pius XII, he had found him very different from the character
lepicted in *The Representative*.[25] Another Protestant, the Bishop of
Oldenburg, Dr. Jacobi, wrote in an open letter that if Pius XII had
:nown of — or had had indicated to him by such eminent bishops as
'aulhaber and von Galen — more effective means of helping the Jews, he
vould undoubtedly have done so.

In fact, when the notorious arrests of the Jews in Rome took place, the
'ope acted most promptly. He instructed Mgr. Hudal, the Rector of
,anta Maria dell'Anima, to complain officially to the German military
ommander, General Stahel. Simultaneously, according to Mr. Osborne,
'the Cardinal Secretary of State summoned the German Ambassador to
vhom he protested against the arrest of the Jews. The latter took
mmediate action, with the result that a large number were released . . . I
nquired at the Vatican," continues Mr. Osborne, "if I might report this
o you, and was told that I might do so, but strictly for your infor-
nation, and on no account for publicity, since any publication of
nformation would probably lead to renewed persecution."[26]

We may legitimately ask what were Herr Hochhuth's sources. They
ppear to have been the text of a lecture given by Cardinal Tardini in
959; two articles by Father Leiber, one on the death of Pius XII, the
ther on the Jews in Rome;[27] and the biography of Pius XII by Dr.
Galeazzi-Lisi, published in French in Paris (because no Italian publisher
vould touch it). Then there were "the confidences made to Hochhuth

[25] "Bishop Dibelius zum Stellvertreter", *Berliner Sonntagsblatt*, 7th April, 1963.

[26] F.O. 371/37255, report from Mr. Osborne, 31st October, 1943.

[27] R. Leiber S.J., "Pie XII e gli Ebrei di Roma", *Civiltà Cattolica*, 1961, I,
p. 449–58.

during a journey to Rome by a member of the Curia who had no
wished his name to be revealed, being pledged to secrecy until his death"
Not very convincing.

The last word about the play may be left to the present Pope Paul V
when, as Cardinal Montini, he wrote a letter to *The Tablet* in June 1963
Had Pius XII done, he writes, what Hochhuth castigates him for no
doing, "his actions would have led to such reprisals and devastations tha
Hochhuth himself — the war being over, and he now possessed of a
better historical, political and moral judgment — would have been able
to write another play, far more realistic and interesting than the one he
has in fact so cleverly, and also so ineptly, put together. What is the gain
to art and culture when the theatre lends itself to injustice of this sort?"[28]

[28] *The Tablet*, 29th June, 1963. This letter was received in London an hour after the
author had become Pope Paul VI.

Conclusion

AT THE BEGINNING OF THIS BOOK, A CRITICAL EVALUATION OF the Vatican by an unknown Protestant clergyman, Dr. Henry Townsend, was quoted, because it summed up the opinion of many people throughout the world. He said that "between 1919 and 1945 the policy of the Vatican in four European countries has given one severe blow after another to the Christian religion". He supported this charge with a number of examples taken from "the Fascist States", Italy, Germany and Spain, illustrating how the Vatican had either failed to condemn their enormities, or had actually connived at them. In the light of the documents consulted here, particularly the German, how justified is his charge?

In this book we have seen what precisely is the political goal of the Vatican. The goal is not as Hitler and Rosenberg contended — "While always talking about love and humanity, the Vatican is in fact interested in only one thing, Power — Power over men's souls, and hence over their lives." They, and many with them, see the Catholic Church as concerned essentially with material gains. They recall Leo X's, "Since God has given us the Papacy, let us enjoy it", and the pragmatic behaviour of Alexander VI. In our own times, Herr Hochhuth in his play *The Representative* reveals Pius XII very much in the same light.

The charge against Pius XII has already been disposed of. And th pragmatic Renaissance Popes were exceptions; for every Alexander V there were a hundred good and pious Popes, whose names no on bothers to recall. No, the goals of the Vatican are not those of a la State; they are transcendental not immanent. Its aim is to "save souls which includes the making of converts regardless of race or nationalit The care of souls, liberty to celebrate Mass and administer th Sacraments, above all to impart religious education to the young — th is what the Church aspires to — in short, to prepare man for after-lif To obtain the best conditions for achieving this in the various natic States, of whatever political colour, is its aim. If the Vatican believ that a Republic is more amenable than a Monarchy for this apostol activity, it will support the Republic (Spain in 1931). If it believes th this apostolic activity can be furthered by a concordat, it will concluc one, as it did even with a State like Nazi Germany. If it believed th this activity could be furthered in Russia by a concordat with th Communist State, it would conclude one tomorrow. Bearing in min this goal of Papal policy, we can make some reply to the accusations.

The Vatican is accused of "supporting Fascism, and giving its blessin to the Italian campaign in Abyssinia". We have seen to what extent th Vatican "supported Fascism" — only in as far as it believed the apostoli activity could be promoted better under a stable government and a all-powerful ruler than it could during political party strife of th "Liberal" party, which had lasted in Italy from 1870 to 1922. It did nc follow from this, however, that the Vatican approved of Fasci ideology; on the contrary, Pius XII condemned it. As for "giving i blessing to the Italian campaign in Abyssinia", this is untrue; th Vatican was careful not to pronounce during the war. However th Italian bishops did, in favour of the war; and many people sti doubtless believe that an episcopal pronouncement must reflect th views of the Vatican. But, as we have seen a number of times in th study, the Vatican, although in theory the most absolutist of State often has less control over its hierarchy than the most constitutiona monarch has over his Ministers.

The Vatican is also accused of having "provoked a large part of th Spanish civil war". This accusation has been refuted in the chapter "Th Papacy and the Spanish Imbroglio". From 1931 for five years th Vatican did all it could to support the new Republican government because it saw it had more popular support than had the effet Monarchy. Incidentally, the popular notion that the Vatican alway

pports reactionary monarchies is also disposed of several times
tween 1922 and 1945.

The remaining charges concerning Nazi Germany and the Jews have
en extensively answered in the latter chapters of this book. In brief,
hile detesting Nazism, the Vatican considered for many years, as did
ost of the Western world, that it was a lesser evil than Communism.
r in the Fascist States some degree of apostolic activity was permitted.
. Soviet Russia it was prohibited.

There is no doubt however that mistakes were made by the Vatican in
he Age of the Dictators". Pius XI's belief that a series of concordats
ith the Dictators would promote the Church's apostolic activity more
fectively than would Catholic political parties appears to have been, on
e whole, mistaken. He evidently assumed that Hitler, with his accession
▸ power, would become more moderate and respect the provisions of a
ncordat, as monarchs had in the past. But, as Mr. Chamberlain also
scovered, it is useless to make agreements with gangsters.

Less an error of policy than one of domestic organisation was the
most exclusively "Italianate" nature of the Sacred College. During the
)39–45 war, twenty-seven of the forty-six Cardinals were Italian; and
ineteen out of the twenty in the Curia were Italian. The establishment
f this preponderance dates from the Council of Constance and there
ave been no non-Italian Popes since 1523.[1] The men who composed the
uria during these centuries were almost all of Italian speech — but they
ere of different State allegiance. They would not have described
emselves as "Italian" — but as Venetian, Florentine, Roman,
Jeapolitan, etc. Even after the unification of Italy, they were far from
eing ardent Italian patriots; indeed most of them regarded the new State
nd the usurping House of Savoy with hostility. But with the advent of
fussolini and militant Fascism, the Italians, all of them, became men of
ne nation. Although the Catholic Church claimed to be international,
e members of the Curia, the Papal court and the Papal diplomatic
rvice were now nearly all men of one nation — in the same way that
e dignitaries of the Anglican Church or the Church of France are men
f one nation. And it is hard for Italians, as for men of other nations, to
aintain complete impartiality. It is significant too, as Mr. F. W. Deakin
eports in *The Brutal Friendship*, that Mussolini told Himmler when the
tter was on a visit to Rome in 1942, "The Pope will not make things too
ifficult for me. He is after all an Italian at heart."

During the 1939–45 war the Vatican, although nominally sovereign,

[1] Of the 260 Popes in the Church's history, over 200 have been Italian.

became completely dependent on the Italian State which could at an
moment cut off its essential supplies, food, water and electricity. S
dependent was it in June 1940 when Italy entered the war that tl
freedom of the Vatican press (*Osservatore Romano*) was curtailed owing
Italian pressure; while the comings and goings of foreign diploma
accredited to the Vatican, as also their correspondence, was subjected
severe and galling restrictions by the Italian government.

What can be done about this? Pius XII appears to have been aware
the anomaly, which was discussed at the reforming Vatican II Council i
1964. No definite decisions have yet been taken. But it would seem th
the following reforms are necessary. Firstly, the Lateran treaty will ha
to be replaced by a new one in which the Vatican State will receive a
international, as distinct from an Italian, guarantee of its independence an
inviolability. Under such a statute, the Papal territory would be enlarge
to enable the Vatican City to possess its own electricity plant, telephon
system, water supply, bakery, etc., as well as quarters for the Cardina
resident in Rome and the diplomatic corps accredited to the Vatican. Th
Papal State should also include an airport and a seaport at or near Osti
with a corridor — or at least a private road or railway accessible to th
outside world — connecting it with the Vatican. This too would b
guaranteed internationally.

Regarding the Curia and the Congregations, approximately one thir
of the Cardinals resident in Rome should be foreigners. The Papal diplo
matic service should also possess a number of prelates of non-Italia
origin to send to countries with which Italy might be at war, thereb
avoiding such controvertible situations as arose with the British i
Abyssinia and Egypt during the Second World War. Lastly, cogen
reasons have been advanced why the Papacy should no longer be a
Italian preserve. As early as 1924 Mr. Colin Coote wrote, "Speaking as a
outsider, I should say that nothing would so much contribute to the reviva
of the international prestige of the Papacy as the institution of a rule tha
the Pope should be chosen from each of the great nations in turn, and no
merely from the Catholic nations."[2]

This leads to the final questions — how well is the Papal diplomati
service equipped to carry out its policies? Potentially, as far as its source
of information are concerned, probably better than any other State in th
world. Political as well as ecclesiastical news of all kinds pours into th
Vatican through its Nuncios, bishops, priests and missionaries from a
over the world. Moreover, whereas the diplomat of the lay State come

[2] In *Italian Town and Country Life* (p. 141) by Colin R. Coote.

to contact with only a limited section of the population — the upper nd official classes — the Catholic priests and missionaries move among eople of all classes, and can report to their bishops every variation of ublic opinion. Against this, however, must be contrasted the Secretariat f State, as the Papal Foreign Office is called. It is widely, if not niversally, believed that it is a hive of political activity, even intrigue, affed by men of unusual ability who plan far into the future. Whatever aay have been the case in the past, it is clear from this study of Papal iplomacy between 1922 and 1945 that such a notion is erroneous.)uring this period, the Vatican possessed a Secretariat of State of a most ntediluvian model. Almost every lay State possesses a Ministry for oreign Affairs with a large staff divided into political and technical epartments. At the Vatican, however, this consists today of the Cardinal nd three Under-Secretaries who deal with all the correspondence and :e the innumerable visitors, clerical and lay, thronging the waiting-)oms. In this, they are assisted by twelve juniors who deal with routine aatters, and who are normally not authorised even to interview iplomats on simple questions such as the allocation of admission tickets) Papal functions. The total strength of the Secretariat, including rchivists and typists, is barely that of two political departments in the 'ritish Foreign Office. The information which comes into the Vatican aay be unrivalled in quantity and quality, but it cannot be properly igested and handled by four men working almost unaided.

Several examples of this were seen between the two world wars. In the)ntroversy over the Holy Places in Palestine, the Vatican appears to ave had no proper notion of how a Mandate worked. In the Maltese ispute with Great Britain, it never really understood the position of ord Strickland as Prime Minister of a British self-governing colony. In 1exico and Spain, it too readily attributed everything to the noxious ifluence and action of Communism. While in the case of Russia itself, it ever used all the information available. It followed the development of :ommunism in that country with great care, even establishing a special ontifical Commission for Russia under the distinguished Jesuit, Mgr. 'Herbigny. Yet it became so obsessed with the anti-religious nature of :ommunism as to have no balanced view of it politically. Fear of Russia ppears to have blinded Pius XI and his Secretaries of State, Gasparri and acelli, to certain Socialist movements in the world which they too :adily labelled "Red" and "Communist". These movements may have een inspired by very different motives — simply overdue re-adjustments a the social system or political development in certain countries such as

Mexico. This fact appears to have been recognised by 1964 in the Vatica
II Council; and a less rigid attitude towards Communism is now likely
be adopted.

These reforms are necessary at a time like the present when, in commc
with other Christian bodies, the Catholic Church has to a large exte
lost her hold on the working classes, especially in the big industri
centres, with a view to stemming the tide of unbelief and winning ba
those who have been led astray by the apostles of hell — paganism ar
atheistic Communism. Whatever may be thought of the relative merits
the Catholic Church and the various national and "free" Churches, it mu
be admitted that the size and doctrinal unity of the former body alo
suffice to make it a far more potent factor for the world's good or ev
than any of the smaller and less disciplined Christian bodies. Nor w
many Christians be found to deny that the influence of Catholicism is c
the whole an influence for good. In spite of certain shortcomings ar
blemishes, it is an institution of such unique value that without it t
civilised world would be immeasurably poorer.

Bibliography

Actes et Documents du Saint Siège relatifs à la Seconde Guerre Mondiale: (ed. Libreria Editrice Vaticana)
   Vol. 1, *Le Saint Siège et la guerre en Europe (mars 1939–août 1940).*
   Vol. 2, *Lettres de Pie XII aux Évêques Allemands,* 1967.
   Vol. 3, *Le Saint Siège et la situation religeuse en Pologne et dans les Pays Baltes,* 1967.
   Vol. 4, *Le Saint Siège et la guerre en Europe (juin 1940–juin 1941),* 1967.
   Vol. 5, *Le Saint Siège et la guerre mondiale (juillet 1941–octobre 1942),* 1969.
Acton, Lord, *The Rise and Fall of the Mexican Empire.*
Adolph, W., *Unveröftlichte Bormann-Akten über den Kirchenkampf,* Wichmann Jahrbuch, 1954; *Verfälschte Geschichte. Antwort an Rolf Hochhuth,* Norus Verlag, Berlin, 1963; *Hirtenamt und Hitlerdiktatur,* Berlin, 1965.
Albrecht, *Der Notenwechsel zwischen dem heiligen Stuhl und der deutschen Regierung,* Matthias Grunewald, Mainz, 1965.
Alexander, E., *Church and Society in Germany.*
Altmeyer, K-A. *Katholische Presse unter N-S Dikatur. Die Katholischen Zeitungen und Zeitschriften Deutschlands in den Jahren 1933–1945,* Berlin, 1962.
Aperçu sur l'Oeuvre du Bureau d'Information, Vatican 1939-46, *Humanities at Work during the War,* Tip. Pol. Vatican.
Arendt, H., *Origins of Totalitarianism.*
Barbier, J., *Monseigneur Tchou,* Centurion, Paris, 1955.
Barlas, C., *John XXIII and his Attitude towards the Jews,* Davar, Tel Aviv, 1959.

Barres, M., *La grande pitié des Églises de France.*

Beales, A. C. F., *The Catholic Church*, Penguin, London, 1941. *The Catholic Church and International Order*, Penguin, London, 1941.

Beals, C., *Mexico — an Interpretation*, Hubsch, New York.

Beau de Loménie, E., *L'Église et l'État*, Fayard, Paris, 1957.

Bechy, *The Holy See and Italy.*

Beck, J., *Dernier Rapport, Politique Polonaise, 1926–1939*, Edition de l Baconnière, Neuchatel, 1951.

Bello, N., *The Vatican Empire*, Trident Press, New York, 1968.

Belloc, H., *Survivals and Arrivals*, Sheed and Ward, London, 1929.

Beloff, M., ed., *On the Track of Tyranny*, London, 1960; "Jews and Non-Jews i Nazi-occupied Holland".

Bender, O., *Der gerade Weg und der National-Sozialismus*, Phil. Dis., Munich 1954.

Bernhart, J., *Der Vatikan als Weltmacht*, Paul List, Munich.

Bierbaum, M., *Nicht Lob, nicht Furcht. Das Leben des Kardinals von Galen*, Verla₁ Regensberg, Münster, 1957.

Binchy, D. A., *Church and State in Modern Italy, 1870–1931.*

Blakiston, N., *The Roman Question. Extracts from Despatches by Odo Russell fro₁ Rome 1858-1870*, Chapman and Hall, London, 1962.

Blanshard, P., *Communism, Democracy and Catholic Power*, Cape, London, 1952.

Boissevain, J., *Saints and Fireworks. Religion and Politics in Rural Malta*, Athlon Press, London, 1965.

Borkenau, F., *Austria and After*, Faber, London, 1938; *The Spanish Cockpi* Faber, London, 1937.

Braham, R. L., *The Destruction of Hungarian Jewry*, Pro Arte, New York, 1963

Brenan, Gerald, *The Spanish Labyrinth*, Cambridge University Press, 1950.

British Blue Book, *Correspondence with the Holy See relative to Maltese Affair* *January 1929–May 1930*, Command paper 3585.

Broussaleux, S., *La persécution religieuse en U.R.S.S.*, Bonne Presse, Limog₍ 1943.

Buchheim, H., *Glaubenskrise im dritten Reich*, Stuttgart, 1953.

Bull, G., *Vatican Politics*, Oxford University Press, New York, 1966.

Bullock, A., *Hitler — A Study in Tyranny*, Odhams, London, 1952.

Bureau d'Information allié, *Cent millions de martyrs catholiques*, 1932.

Cardinale, I., *Pontifical Diplomacy*, Graz, 1959.

Carreras, L., *Grandeur chrétienne de l'Espagne*, Sorlot, Paris, 1936.

Casini, *Mensonges et Silences sur Pie XII*, ed. Regan, Monte Carlo.

Castellan, G., *L'Allemagne de Weimar*, Armand Colin, 1969.

Catholic Truth Society, *The Pope and the People. Extracts from Letters of Four Pope*

Cereti, *Diario*, Università Cattolica, Milan, 1931.

Chambre, H., *Christianisme et Communisme*, Fayard, Paris, 1959.

Charles-Roux, F., *Huit ans au Vatican*, Flammarion, 1949.

Churchill, W. S., *The World Crisis, The Second World War*, Cassell, London, 1960.

Cianfarra, C. M., *The Vatican and the Kremlin*, Dutton, New York, 1950; *The War and the Vatican*, Burns and Oates, London, 1945.

Ciano, G., *Diario*, Milano Roma, 1946; *L'Europa verso la Catastrofe*, Milan, 1949.

Civiltà Cattolica, Jesuit Review.

Clonmore, Lord, *Pope Pius XI and World Peace*, Robert Hale, London, 1937.

Conrad, W., *Der Kampf um die Kanzeln*, Topelmann, Berlin, 1957.

Coote, Colin R., *Italian Town and Country Life*, Methuen, London, 1925.

Cronin, A. J., *The Keys of the Kingdom*, Gollancz, London, 1943.

Curvers, A., *Pie XII, le Pape outragé*, Laffont, 1964.

Dansette, A., *Histoire religieuse de la France contemporaine*, Flammarion, 1965; *Destin du Catholicisme Français*, Flammarion, 1957.

Dauphin-Meunier, A., *L'Église et les structures économiques du Monde*, Fayard, Paris, 1957.

Daulnaie, J., *Ils ont dispersé l'éritage, 1789–1962*, Cedre, Paris, 1963.

Deakin, F. W., *The Brutal Friendship*, Harper and Row, 1963.

Delmasure, A., *Les Catholiques et la politique*, Colombe, Paris, 1960.

Desclausais, J., *Catholicisme et Franc-Maconnerie*, Revue Internationale, 1938. Sociétés secretes.

Deurlein, E., *Der deutsche Katholizismus*, 1933.

Deutsch, H. C., *The Conspiracy against Hitler in the Twilight War*, O.U.P., London, 1968.

Diamant, A., *Austrian Catholics and the First Republic*, Princeton, 1960.

Documents on British Foreign Policy, 1919–1939, edited by E. L. Woodward and R. Butler, H. M. Stationery Office, London, 1947.

Documents on German Foreign Policy, 1918–1945, Series D, Vols. IV and VII, Washington, 1951 and 1954.

Documents on German Foreign Policy, 1918–1956, Editor-in-chief: Paul R. Sweet, U.S.A., The Hon. Margaret Lambert, Gt. Britain. H. M. Stationery Office, London, 1957.

Documents Diplomatici Italiani, La Libreria dello Stato, 1952–3.

Dollard des Ormeaux, *Sang des Martyrs*, Fides, Paris, 1952.

Dragon, A., *Au Mexique rouge*, Spes, Paris, 1937.

Duclos, P., *Le Vatican et la seconde guerre mondiale*, Pedone, 1955.

Duquesne, J., *Les Catholiques français sous l'occupation*, Grasset, 1966.

Eden, A., *Facing the Dictators*, Cassell, London, 1962.

Études (magazine of French Jesuits): articles by the Comte d'Harcourt on the anti-Christian character of the Nazi movement. (1) "Catholisme, Hitlerisme et Bolchevisme", 20th January, 1937; (2) "Après l'Encyclique", 5th May, 1937; (3) "L'Offensive Hitlérienne contre l'Église", 20th June, 1937.

Eugene, O., *Petite histoire des missions franciscans*, Franciscans, Paris, 1942.

Faber, R., *Der Vatican*, Goldmann Verlag, Munich, 1968.

Falconi, C., *I Papi del Ventesimo Secolo*, Feltrinelli, 1967; *Le Silence de Pie XI* Editions du Rocher, Monaco, 1965.

Felice, R. di, *Storia degli Ebrei sotto il Fascismo*, Torino, 1962.

Ferrari, F. L., *L'Azione Cattolica e il Regno*, Florence, 1957.

Fest, J. C., *The Face of the Third Reich*, Weidenfeld, London, 1970.

Fitzgibbon, C., *The Shirt of Nessus*, London, 1956.

Fontaine, N., *Saint Siège, Action Française et Catholicisme intégral*, Lib. Univ Gamber, Paris, 1928.

Foreign Relations of the United States, U.S. Government Printing Office Washington, 1955.

Flische, A. and Martin, V., *Histoire de l'Église*.

François-Poncet, A., *Au Palais Farnese. Souvenirs d'une Ambassade*.

Frank, F., *An Outsider in the Vatican*.

Frank, H., *Im Angesicht des Galgens*.

Friedlander, S., *Pius XII and the Third Reich*. Knopf, New York, 1966.

Fuchs, L., *Les Catholiques Américains avant et après Kennedy*, Alsatia, Paris, 1969.

Furman, Lieut-Col., *Be not fearful*, Roy Publishers, New York, 1959.

Galeazzi-Lisi, R., *Dans l'Ombre et dans la Lumière de Pie XII*, Flammarion, 196(

Galter, A., *Le Livre rouge de l'église persécutée en U.S.S.R.*, Fleurus, Paris, 1957

Gannon, R., S. J., *The Cardinal Spellman Story*, Doubleday, New York, 1962

Garrone, Mgr., *L'Action catholique*, Fayard, Paris, 1958.

Gasparri, *Il Protettorato Cattolico della Francia nell' Oriente e nell'estrem Orienete — studio storico di un prelato Romano*, Ed. Vatican, 1904.

Gay, F., *Dans les flammes et dans le sang*, Blondet, Paris, 1936.

Gerdemann, W. and Winfried, H., *Christenkreuz und Hakenkreuz*, Kat. Ta Verlag, Köln, 1931.

Germino, D. L., *The Italian Fascist Party*, University of Minnesota Pre Minneapolis, 1959.

Giobbio, Mgr., *Lektionen über Diplomatie*.

Giordani, I., *Vita contra Morte — La Santa Sede per le vittime della seconda guerr mondiale*, Mondadori, 1956.

Giovanetti, A., *Roma Città Aperta*, Milano, 1962; *L'Action du Vatican pour la pai* Fleurus, Paris, 1963; *Der Vatikan und der Krieg*, Köln, 1962.

Gisevius, H. B., *Bis zum bitteren Ende*.

Goebbels, J., *Tagebuch*, Otto Hess, Berlin, 1962.

Gonella, *The Papacy and World Peace*, Hollis and Carter, 1945.

Graham, R. A., *Pope Pius XII and the Jews in Hungary in 1944*, The 1964 Kin Lecture delivered to the U.S. Catholic Historical Society at Marymoun College, New York; *Vatican Diplomacy*, Princeton University Pres Princeton, 1959; "Spie naziste attorno al Vaticano durante la seconda guerr mondiale", *Civiltà Cattolica*, 3rd January, 1970.

Greene, G., *The Power and the Glory*, Heinemann, London, 1940.

Grunberger, R., *The Twelve Year Reich. A Social History of Nazi Germany, 1933–1945*, Holt, Rinehart and Winston, New York, 1971.

Grunewald, M., *Der Notenwechsel zwischen dem heiligen Stuhl und der Regierung*, Mainz, 1956.

Grüning, E., *Mexico and its Heritage*, Stanley Paul, 1928.

Guennon, *Les Missions d'hier et aujourd'hui*, St. Paul, Paris, 1962.

Guignebert, C., *Le probleme religieux dans la France d'aujourd'hui*, Garnier, 1922.

Gurian, W., *Der Kampf um die Kirche im dritten Reich*, Lucerne, 1936.

Guest, J., *Broken Images*.

Gwynn, D., *The Action Française Condemnation*, Burns and Oates, London, 1928; *The Vatican and the War in Europe*.

Halecki, O., *Pius XII*, Weidenfeld, London, 1953.

Hales, E. E. V., *The Catholic Church in the Modern World*, Eyre and Spottiswoode, London, 1958.

Harrigan, W. M., "Pius XII's effort to effect a detente in German–Vatican relations 1939–1940", *Catholic Historical Review*, Vol. 49, No. 2 (July 1963), pp. 173–91.

Haslip, Joan, *Imperial Adventurer, Emperor Maximilian of Mexico and his Empress*, Weidenfeld, London, 1971.

Hausner, G., *Speech of Public Prosecutor at Eichmann Trial*, Jerusalem 1961.

Heer, F., *Der Glaube Adolf Hitlers*, Bechtle Verlag, 1968.

Heiber, H., ed., *Hitlers Lagebesprechungen*, Deutsche Verlag-Austalt, Stuttgart, 1962.

Herberichs, G., *Théorie de la paix selon Pie XII*, Pedone, 1964.

d'Herbigny, M., S.J., *La guerre anti-religieuse en Russie soviétique*, Bussière, Paris, 1930.

Hilberg, R., *The Destruction of the European Jews*, Quadrangle Books, Chicago, 1961.

Hochhuth, *Der Stellvertreter*, Rowohlt, Hamburg, 1963.

Hochland, *German Catholic Review*. Article by Dr. E. W. Böckenförde, 1961.

Hoffmann, K., *Schlaglichter*, Freiburg, 1947.

Hory-Broszat, V., *Der kroatische Ustoscha-Staat*.

Hourdin, G., *La Presse Catholique*, Fayard, Paris, 1957.

Howard, E. P., *Il Partito Popolare Italiano*, Florence, 1957.

Hudal, Bishop, *Nietszche und die moderne Welt; Der Vatikan und die modernen Staaten*.

Hughes, P., *Pope Pius XI*, Sheed and Ward, New York, 1937.

Huxley, A., *Beyond the Mexique Bay*, Albatross, 1947.

Ignotus, *Stato Fascista, Chiesa e Scuola*, Libreria del Littorio.

Isaac, J., *The Teaching of Contempt*, Holt, Rinehart and Winston, New York, 1964.

Jean-Nesmy, *Pour ou Contre "Le Vicaire"*, Desdée de Brouwer, Paris.

Joffroy, P., *A Spy for God*, Collins, London, 1971.

Junker, D., *Die deutsche Zentrumspartei und Hitler*, Klett, Stuttgart, 1969.

Kallay, N., *Hungarian Premier*, O.U.P., London, 1954.

Keesing's Contemporary Archives, British Columbia House, London.

Kelly, F. C., *Blood Drenched Altars*.

Kent, G. O., *A catalogue of files and microfilms of the German Foreign Ministry 1920–1945*. Compiled for the Hoover Institution, Stamford University California, 1962; "Pius XII and Germany. Some aspects of German–Vatican relations, 1933–1943", *American Historical Review*, Vol. 70, 1964, pp. 59–78 "The Archives of the German Foreign Ministry at Whaddon Hall", *The American Archivist*, January 1961, pp. 43–54.

Kerdreux, M. de, *Dans l'intimité d'un grand pape, Pie XI*, Salvator, Paris, 1963.

Kern, *Le communisme contre Dieu*, C.E.A., Paris, 1935; *Prissonier du Guepou, La Cause*, Paris, 1935.

Kloidt, F., *Verräter oder Martyrer*, Patmos, Dusseldorf, 1962.

Konstantin, Prince of Bavaria, *Papst Pius XII*, Kindler, Munich, 1959.

Kordt, E., *Nicht aus den Akten 1928–1945*, Stuttgart, 1950; *Wahn und Wirklichkeit*, Stuttgart, 1948.

Laferla, A, V., *The Story of Man in Malta*, Aquilina, Malta, 1958.

Lama, F. Ritter von, *Papst und Kurie in ihrer Politik nach dem Weltkrieg* Illerissen, Bayern, 1925.

Langer, W. L., *The Undeclared War, 1940–41*, New York, 1953.

Lapide, P. E., *The Last Three Popes and the Jews*, Souvenir Press, 1967.

Leclercq, J., *Le Chrétien devant l'argent*, Fayard, Paris, 1957.

Ledre, C., *Une leçon tragique. Les crimes du Front Populaire en Espagne*, Lyon.

Ledit, J., *Archbishop Cieplak*, Palm, Montreal, 1963.

Lehrl, J., *Bildungskrafte im Katholicismus der Welt*, Herder, Freiburg-im-Breisgau, 1936.

Leiber, R., "Pius XII", *Stimmen der Zeit*, No. 165, 1958 and No. 167, 1960.

Lenz, J. M., *Christus in Dachau*, Libri Cattolici, Vienna, 1957.

Leo XIII, (letter) *Humanum genus* on Freemasonry, 1884.

Levai, J., *L'Église ne s'est pas tue*, Editions du Seuil, Paris, 1966; *The Black Book on the Martyrdom of Hungarian Jewry*, Central European Times Publishing Co., 1948.

Levy, G., *Die katholische Kirche und das dritte Reich*, Piper, 1965.

Lias, G., *Religious Persecution*, H. M. Stationery Office, London, 1942.

Loewel, R., *A la recherche de Torquemada*, Denoel, Paris, 1938.

Loewenich, W., *Die Geschichte der Kirche*, Siebenstern, Munich, 1948.

Maistre, J. de, *Du Pape*.

Malley, F., *L'Inquiétante Amérique Latine*, Cerf, Paris, 1962.

Manuel, F. E., *The Politics of Modern Spain*. McGraw-Hill, New York, 1938.

Marc-Bonnet, H., *La Papauté Contemporaine*, Presses Universitaires de France, 1951.

Marchand, R., *L'Effort democratique du Mexique*, Dreyfus, Paris, 1938.

Marshall, C. C., *The Roman Catholic Church in the Modern State*, Faith Press, London, 1931.

Martini, A., "Appelli alla Santa Sede dalla Polonia durante la Seconda Guerra Mondiale", *Civiltà Cattolica*, No. 2683, 7th April, 1962; "Il Cardinale Faulhaber e l'Enciclica 'Mit brennender Sorge' ", *Archivum Historiae Pontificiae*, 2 (1964), pp. 303-20; "Pio XII e Hitler", *Civiltà Cattolica*, 1965, I, pp. 342-54; "Silenzi e parole di Pio XII per la Polonia", *Civiltà Cattolica*, 1962, II, pp. 237-49.

McCullagh, F., *The Bolshevik Persecution of Christianity*, Murray, London, 1924.

Meldungen aus dem Reich, Auswahl der geheimen Lagebetichte der S.S. 1939-1944, Luchterhaud Verlag, 1969.

Micheles, V. A., "The Lateran Accord", *Foreign Policy Information Service*, Vol. 5, 10th July, 1929.

Monsterleet, J., *Les martyrs de Chine parlent (1937-1952)*, Amiot, Paris.

Montagne, H. de la, *Histoire de L'Action Française*.

Monzie, A. de, *Mgr. d'Herbigny — Visite en Russie*.

Muller, H., ed., *Katholische Kirche und Nationalsocialismus*, D.T.V., Munich, 1965.

Mussolini, B., *Gli Accordi del Laterano*, Libreria del Littorio, Rome, 1929; *The Cardinal's Daughter*.

Mussolini, M., *Date a Cesare*, Libreria del Littorio.

Nasliau, J., *Les memoirs de Vienne*, Mechithariste, 1955.

Negro, S., *L'Ordinamento della Chiesa Cattolica*.

Nobécourt, J., *Le Vicaire et l'Histoire*, Editions du Seuil, Paris, 1964.

Oliviera, A. R., *Politics, Economics and Men of Modern Spain*, Gollancz, London, 1946.

Omrcanin, I., *La Martyrologie Croate, 1940-51*, Guillemot, Paris, 1962.

Orlando, *I miei rapporti di governo colla Santa Sede*, Garganti.

Ormesson, W. de, *Pie XII tel que je l'ai connu*, Pedone, Paris, 1968.

Pacelli, F. (Pius XII), *Diario della Conciliazione*, Libreria Editrice Vaticana, 1959.

Padellaro, N., *Portrait of Pius XII*, New York, 1957.

Papen, F. von, *Der Wahrheit eine Gasse*, Paul List Verlag, Munich, 1952.

Pallenberg, C., *Vatican Finances*.

Paris, E., *Genocide in Satellite Croatia. 1941-45*, American Institute of Balkan Affairs, Chicago; *The Vatican against Europe*.

Patti Lateranesi, Convenzioni ed accordi successivi fra il Vaticano e L'Italia, Tipografia Poliglotta Vaticana.

Patry, R., *La religion dans l'Allemagne d'aujourd'hui*, Payot, 1926.

Payne, S. G., *The Spanish Revolution*, Weidenfeld, London, 1970.

Pernot, M., *Le Saint Siège, l'église catholique et la politique mondiale*, Colin, 1924.

Petrusblatt. Katholisches Kirchenblatt für das Bistum Berlin, 1946.

Peyrefitte, R., *Les Clefs de Saint-Pierre*.

Picker, H., ed., *Hitlers Tischgespräche*, Paul List Verlag, Munich, 1952.

Pilliers, P. de, *La Franc-Maçonnerie et Leon XIII son calomniateur*, Le Saunier, 1887.

Pius XI, *The Pope and Catholic Action* (addresses), Catholic Truth Society, London, 1930.

Pius XII, *Guide for Living*. *Selected Addresses and Letters*, Evans, 1958; *Lettres aux Evêques Allemands*, Vatican Library, 1966; *Wartime Correspondence with President Roosevelt*, Macmillan.

Poliakov, L., *Le IIIe Reich et les Juifs*, Gallimard, Paris, 1959; "The Vatican and the Jewish Question", *Commentary*, November, 1950.

Prescott, W. H., *The Conquest of Mexico*.

Purdy, W., *The Church on the Move*.

Questione Maltese. Feb. '29–Giugno '30, Tipografia Poliglotta Vaticana, 1930.

Raab, H., *Kirche und Staat*, D.T.V., 1966.

Randall, Sir A., *Vatican Assignment*, Heinemann, London, 1956; "A British Agent at the Vatican", *Dublin Review*, Spring 1959; "German Catholics and National Socialism", *Dublin Review*, Spring 1965; "The Tragic Dilemma of Pius XII", *Dublin Review*, Summer 1962; "Pius XII's Stormy Path", *Dublin Review*, Autumn 1966; "The Pacelli 'Diary'", *Dublin Review*, Summer 1959; "The Holy See and Diplomacy", *The Tablet*, April 9th and 16th, 1966.

Ranke, *History of the Popes*.

Rassinier, P., *Le Drame des Juifs Européens. L'Operation "Vicaire"*, Table Ronde, Paris, 1965.

Ratti, A. (Pius XI), *Le Lettere di Varsovia*.

Rémond, R., Les Catholiques, les Communistes et les Crises, *'29–'39*, Colin, 1960.

Remy, *Pourpre des Martyrs*, Fayard, Paris, 1953.

Renouvin (doyen de l'Imprimerie nationale), *Documents diplomatiques français publiés par La Commission de Publication des Documents relatifs aux origines de la guerre de 1939*.

Roatta, M., *Cento Milioni di Baionette. L'esercito italiano in guerra, 1940-44*, Milan, 1946.

Robinson, R.A.H., *The Origins of Franco's Spain*, David and Charles, Newton Abbot, 1970.

Robles, G., *Spain in Chains*.

Rosa, G. de, *Storia del Movimento cattolico in Italia*, Bari, 1966.

Rosenberg, A., *Der Mythus des 20. Jahrhunderts; Politisches Tagebuch*.

Ross, E. C., *The Social Revolution in Mexico*.

Rossini, G., *Il movimento cattolico nel periodo fascista*, Cinque Lune, Rome, 1966.

Roth, H., *Katholische Jugend in der Nazi Zeit. Daten und Documenten*, Altenberg, Dusseldorf, 1959.

Rotkirchen, L., *The Destruction of Slovak Jewry*, Yud Vashem, Jerusalem, 1960.

Salleron, *Les Catholiques et le Capitalisme*, La Palatine, Paris, 1951.

Salvatorelli, L., *Die Politik des heiligen Stuhls nach dem Krieg*.

;alvemini, *Il Partito Popolare e la Questione Romana.*

;ant'Elia, A. M. di, *Instantanés inédits des quatre derniers Papes*, Aubanel, Avignon, 1958.

.chnabel, F., *Die katholische Kirche in Deutschland*, Herder, Freiburg-im-Breisgau, 1965.

;chnuschnigg, K. von, *Kreimal Österreich.*

;chwaiger, G., *Geschichte der Papste im 20 Jahrhunderts*, D.T.V., Munich, 1968.

;hirach, B. von, *Ich glaubte an Hitler.*

;torrs, Sir R., *Orientations*, Nicolson and Watson, 1937.

;traelen, H. van, *Où va le Japon?*, Castermann, 1960.

;trobel, F., *Christliche Bewährung*, Verlag Walter, Switzerland, 1946.

;turzo, L., *Popolarismo e Fascismo. Saggi e testimonianze*, Civitas, Rome, 1960.

;truve, N., *Les Chrétiens en U.S.S.R.*, Éditions du Seuil, Paris, 1963.

;uffert, G., *Les Catholiques et la Gauche*, Maspero, Paris, 1960.

Tardini, D., *Memories of Pius XII*, Newman Press, Maryland, 1961.

Tcharykov, N. V., "The Roman Question", *Contemporary Review*, March, 1930.

Teeling, W., *The Pope in Politics.*

Thomas, H., *The Spanish Civil War*, Eyre and Spottiswoode, London, 1961.

Tisserant, E., *L'Église militante*, Bloud, Paris, 1950.

Torre, G. della, *Azione Cattolica e Fascismo. Conflitto del 1931*, 1945.

Toscano, ed., *Atti Diplomatici Italiani*

Trevor-Roper, H., *The Rise of Christian Europe*, Thames and Hudson, London, 1965.

Troeltsch, E., *The Social Teaching of the Christian Churches*, Allan and Unwin, London, 1950.

Trimarchi, G., *La formazione del pensiero meridionalista di Luigi Sturzo*, Morcelliana, Brescia, 1965.

Valeri, N., *Da Giolitti a Mussolini*, Parenti, 1956.

Vancourt, R., *Pensée Moderne et Philosophie Chrétienne*, Fayard, Paris, 1957.

Vatican White Paper, *Esposizione Documentata della Questione Maltese. Febbraio 1929–Guigno 1930*, Tipografia Poliglotto Vaticana, 1930.

Vierteljahrshefte für Zeitgeschichte, 1, Jahrgang, 1953, p. 177 (for Gerstein incident), Deutsche Verlag Anstalt, Stuttgart, 1953.

Vogelsang, T., *Die nationalistische Zeit*, Ullstein, Frankfurt am Main, 1967.

Wall, B., *Report on the Vatican*, Weidenfeld, London, 1956.

Waugh, E., *Robbery under Law*, Chapman and Hall, London, 1939.

Weber, E., ed., *Dollfuss an Österreich*, Reinhold, Vienna, 1935.

Weizsäcker, E. von, *Errinerungen*, Paul List Verlag, Munich, 1950.

West, M. L., *The Shoes of the Fisherman*, Morrow, New York, 1963.

Wheeler-Bennet, J. W., *The Nemesis of Power*, London, 1952.

Wilhelm II, *Memoirs* (Pacelli's visit 29th June, 1917).

Woodward, L., *British Foreign Policy in the Second World War*, H. M. Stationery Office, London, 1962.

Wulf, J., *Martin Bormann — Hitler's Schatten*, Guterslob, 1962.

Wynen, A., *Die Päpstliche Diplomatie*, Freiburg/Mr., 1922.

Zahn, G., *German Catholics and Hitler's Wars*, Sheed and Ward, New York, 1962; *In Solitary Witness. The Life and Death of Franz Jägerstätter*, Holt Rinehart and Winston, New York, 1964.

Zipfel, F., *Kirchenkampf in Deutschland*, de Gruyter, Berlin, 1965.

Zolli, E., *Before the Dawn*, Sheed and Ward, New York, 1954.

Zurcher, F., *Croisade contre le Christianisme*, Rieder, Paris, 1939.

Index

Index

INVENTORY 1983

LIBRARY
FLORISSANT VALLEY COMMUNITY COLLEGE
ST. LOUIS, MO.

JAN 1 2 1978